INNOVATIONS IN DIE DESIGN

Karl A. Keyes
Editor

Published by:
Society of Manufacturing Engineers
Marketing Services Department
One SME Drive
P.O. Box 930
Dearborn, Michigan 48128

INNOVATIONS IN DIE DESIGN

Library of Congress Catalog Card Number 81-84032

International Standard Book Number: 0-87263-073-0

Manufactured in the United States of America

SME wishes to express its acknowledgement and appreciation to the following publications for supplying the various articles reprinted within the contents of this book.

American Feintool, Inc.
11280 Cornell Park Drive
Cincinnati, Ohio 45242

Automated Tapping Systems
Highway 35
Keyport, New Jersey 07735

Institution of Engineers, Australia
11 National Circuit
Barton, A.C.T.
Australia

Manufacturing Engineering
Society of Manufacturing Engineers
One SME Drive
P.O. Box 930
Dearborn, Michigan 48128

Production Engineering Co.
Box 215
Elmhurst, Illinois 60126

Schmid Corporation of America
7006 S. State Road
Goodrich, Michigan 48438

Sheet Metal Industries
Queensway House
2 Queensway
Redhill
Surrey RH1 1QS
England

Tooling & Production
Huebner Publications, Inc.
5821 Harper Road
Solon, Ohio 44139

Torin Corporation
Kennedy Drive
Torrington, Connecticut 06790

Grateful Acknowledgement Is Also Expressed To:

George Dibble
Small Parts, Inc.
600 Humphrey Street
Logansport, Indiana 46947

Sam Gruber
J.V. Manufacturing Co., Inc.
Box 350
Burtner Road
Natrona Heights, Pennsylvania 15065

Arnold Miedema and Edwin Stouten
Capitol Engineering Co.
1375 Monroe Ave., N.W.
Grand Rapids, Michigan 49505

John S. Weber
Chromalloy American Corporation
Sintercast Division
165 Western Hwy.
West Nyack, New York 10994

PREFACE

A good die designer like any professional mechanic needs to have a working knowledge of all kinds of dies and some understandng of the special design considerations unique to each type. For the most part, books on the subject of die design pertain mostly, if not exclusively, to power press dies. With this thought in mind, this volume will present a collection of articles on tooling for slide machines and fineblanking presses. It is recognized that the major difference between die types relate to the machining in which it is used. However, basic design fundamentals such as alignment, stock control, shock control, slug control, wear control and load balancing remains the same for all dies.

The enclosed reference material on die design was not intended to be used as basic text. This volume contains a collection of the tried and proven design applications which merit being preserved for the seasoned die designer.

The material in this volume represents some of the innovative design efforts of several well-known individuals such as Federico Strausser and John Weber. Some material such as "Hints for Die Designers" by Arnold Miedema and Edwin Stouten of Capitol Engineering Co. is being presented for the first time. In addition, articles that are considered 'classics' are presented as a review of the established methods for proper die design.

Chapter One, "Practical Design Concepts", begins with a look into the future with computers used in die design. Additional articles discuss the proper use of cams, lifters and pushers in dies. Interesting applications such as a tapping unit engineered to go directly in the die set are explored. This potentially successful method for tapping at a rate equal to the press stroke represents many painstaking hours devoted to perfecting the timing required.

"Power Press Dies" is the theme of Chapter Two. An outline of the necessary design steps combined with example strip layouts provides insight into the many variations possible within the definition of a progressive die. Besides the normal blanking and forming operations, much time is given to the development of progressive draw dies. Material covering design considerations for transfer, lamination and carbide dies round out the chapter.

In Chapter Three, fineblanking dies and their unique design requirements are discussed. Systematic design procedures which start with piece part evaluation and proceed to the strip layout and design requirements are examined. A review of die building techniques enable the designer to best understand the basic fundamentals associated with a productive design. All of the various types of fineblanking dies are presented including the sliding punch, fixed punch in single station compounds or multi-station progressive made either as a complete die or as permanent components.

Insight into the mystique surrounding four-slides, multi-slide and verti-slide machines is covered in Chapter Four entitled "Dies for Single Purpose Machines". The average designer knows very little about this type of extremely versatile tooling. Not only are these machines versatile, but the unusual can be accomplished with a material utilization factor similar only to transfer type power press dies.

I wish to express my gratitude to each of the authors and to the publications which were very generous in supplying the material you will find on the pages of this volume. They include: *American Feintool, Inc., Automated Tapping Systems, The Institution of Engineers/Australia, Manufacturing Engineering, Production Engineering Co., Schmid Corporation of America, Sheet Metal Industries, Tooling & Production* and the *Torin Corporation.* My appreciation is also extended to *George Dibble* at Small Parts, Inc., *Sam Gruber* at J.V. Manufacturing Co., Inc., *Arnold Miedema* and *Edwin Stouten* at Capitol Engineering Co., and *John Weber* at Chromalloy American Corporation.

A special thanks to Bob King and Judy Stranahan of the SME Marketing Services Department for their help in preparing this book.

Karl A. Keyes
Vice President
International Fineblanking Corp.
Editor

SME

The informative volumes of the Manufacturing Update Series are part of the Society of Manufacturing Engineers' effort to keep its Members better informed on the latest trends and developments in engineering.

With 60,000 members, SME provides a common ground for engineers and managers to share ideas, information and accomplishments.

An overwhelming mass of available information requires engineers to be concerned about keeping up-to-date, in other words, continuing education. SME Members can take advantage of numerous opportunities, in addition to the books of the Manufacturing Update Series, to fulfill their continuing educational goals. These opportunities include:

- Chapter programs through the over 200 chapters which provide SME Members with a foundation for involvement and participation.

- Educational programs including seminars, clinics, programmed learning courses and videotapes.

- Conferences and expositions which enable engineers to see, compare, and consider the newest manufacturing equipment and technology.

- Publications including Manufacturing Engineering, the SME Newsletter, Technical Digest and a wide variety of books including the Tool and Manufacturing Engineers Handbook.

- SME's Manufacturing Engineering Certification Institute formally recognizes manufacturing engineers and technologists for their technical expertise and knowledge acquired through years of experience.

In addition, the Society works continuously with the American National Standards Institute, the International Standards Organization and other organizations to establish the highest possible standards in the field.

SME Members have discovered that their membership broadens their knowledge throughout their career.

In a very real sense, it makes SME the leader in disseminating and publishing technical information for the manufacturing engineer.

TABLE OF CONTENTS

CHAPTERS

1 PRACTICAL DESIGN CONCEPTS

TABLE OF CONTENTS (Cont.)

2 POWER PRESS DIES

TABLE OF CONTENTS (Cont.)

3 FINEBLANKING DIES

TABLE OF CONTENTS (Cont.)

CHAPTER 1

PRACTICAL DESIGN CONCEPTS

Presented at SME's Manufacturing Management 1981 Update Seminar, April 1981

CAD/CAM for Die-Making Industry

by Hajimu Kishi
Fujitsu FANUC Ltd.

INTRODUCTION

In the 1970's, the trend in advanced mass production technology was away from cutting machinery and towards die-based pressing and moulding. The 1980's will continue to see the advancement of this trend, and die manufacturing technology is expected to develop at a rapid pace.

Today, leading industries such as automobiles and electrical goods use dies to manufacture a majority of basic components. The highest level of technology is required for accurate and efficient die making, so that a wide range of manufactured goods can be produced economically.

Therefore, it can be said that the development of die technology is critical to support modern industries. Further, the automation of methods for designing and making dies has great importance for the continued development of industrial societies. However, the die manufacturing field has many problems to overcome, including maximized cost-performance, quick delivery of finished dies, as well as increased labor costs and lack of skilled personnel.

AN OVERVIEW OF DIE-MAKING INDUSTRY

Dies are used in a variety of industries including pressing, forging, casting, rubber, glass, ceramics and plastics. Manufactured goods using die cast parts range from airplanes to toasters, and from automobiles to toys.

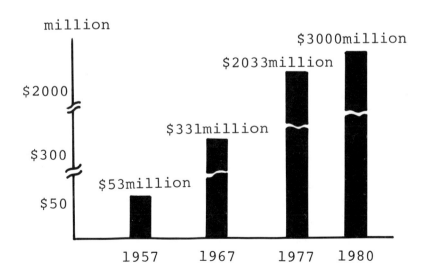

Figure 1   Amount of die products

The die productions in Japan have become equal in value to total production of machine tools. In 1957, US$53 million worth of dies were produced. By 1967 the figure rose to $331 million, in 1976 it was $1.634 billion, in 1977 it rose steeply to $2.032 billion. At last, in 1980 production was at the $3 billion level that was equal to the whole amounts of machine tool productions. (Figure 1)

Figures for 1976 in Japan reveal another interesting fact. Out of 7409 companies involved in die making, 93.7% had 20 or less employees, and 84% had less than 9 workers. Only 0.4% had staffs numbering over 100 (see Figure 2). This situation is probably also true in the U.S. and Europe.

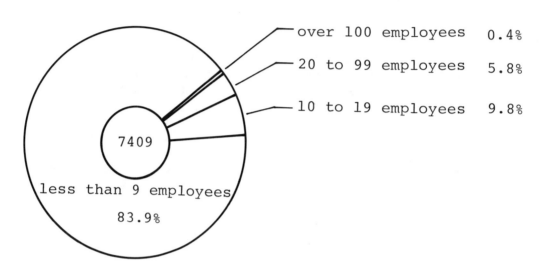

Figure 2   Die making industries by scale

The fact that such a vital industry such as die making employs such a small number of people makes it quite a unique phenomenon. This is probably due to a number of factors.

(1) One die can produce a large quantity of products
     and need not be replaced very often.
(2) Dies are individually produced.
(3) Each die is made to order.

The die making process is illustrated in Figure 3. Costs can be generally divided into 18% for materials and 82% for labor, management and operating costs. Thus die costs are mostly based on overhead. If we estimate overhead at about 80% with labor expenses at about 63%, then the personnel cost runs about 80% x 63% = 50%. Thus, if personnel expenses increase 10% in a year, the cost of the die must increase by 5%.

The high cost of overhead, in addition to customer demands for lower price and quick delivery, make the automation of the die making industry an important priority, especially for forming specified shapes.

With the above situation, the die industry has recently attracted the interest of the computer technology. There is a large amount of research and development activity focusing on computer-aided design (CAD) and computer-aided manufacuring (CAM) using geometric modeling techniques.

Drawing of
Dies

Die Material

Rough Cutting

Finish
Cutting

Polishing

Accomplished
Dies

Figure 3   Die making process

However, these expensive CAD and CAM systems are not readily adaptable to the economic needs of the die making industry composed of small-scale job shops. For this reason, NC machine tools which can be upgraded gradually, and small-scale automatic "device" which prepare NC tapes can fit into the industry without requiring major changes in the present industrial and economic structure.

DIE SCULPTURED SURFACES AND NC MACHINES

Die shaping can be divided into two general types: 2-dimensional shapes and 3-dimensional shapes. The 2-dimensional and 3-dimensional shapes characterized by planes, spheres, cones or cylinders, etc. can be easily processed by the automatic programming technique with the desk-top device. NC milling machines and wire-cut electric discharge machines can be used for these arithmetic shapes.

For un-arithmetic 3-dimensional shapes such as smooth surface, there are many cases dominated by the designer's sense. This is an obstacle for spread of NC machine tools. The modeling of smooth surface shapes can be automated with what is called "sculptured surface software" systems (see Figure 4), used largely by the automotive industry. In this technique, key points in the shape as specified by x, y and z coordinate values and other coordinates are interpolated automatically to form a smooth surface. Although the large automobile manufacturers have developed these sculptured surface software systems to a high degree, the costs are quite prohibitive for die makers, and this technique is useful mainly for automobile body.

expression method	shape example	software
1) arithmetic expression plane sphere sylinder cone etc.	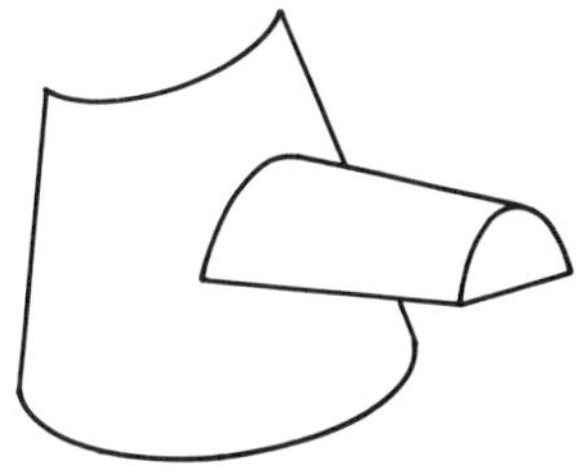	FAPT DIE-I APT ADAPT etc.
2) sectional shape data	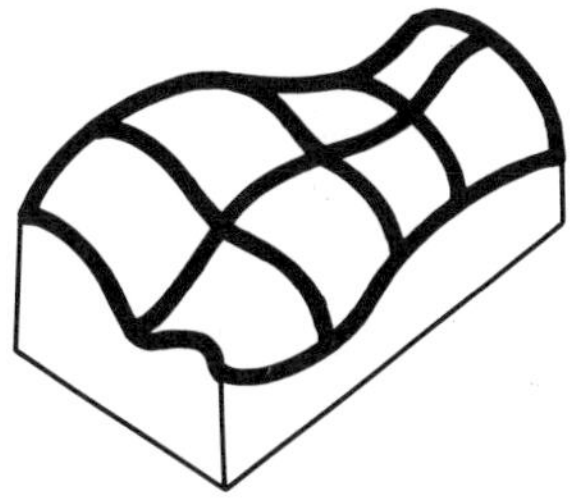	FAPT DIE-II
3) point coordinates	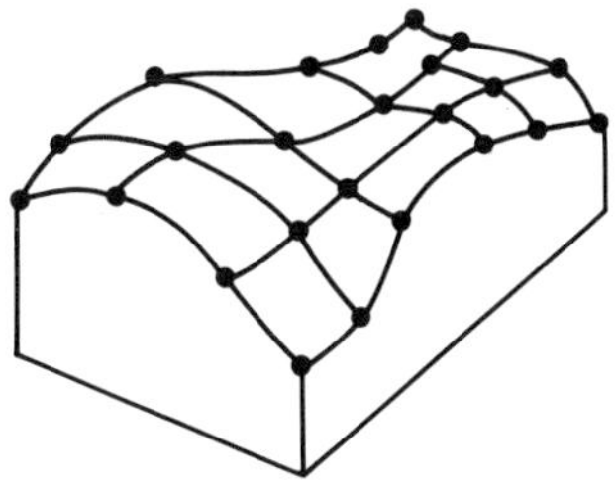	FMILL

Figure 4   Software for 3-dimensional shaping

Typically the die makers receive specifications from the industry in the form of sectional diagrams for a 3-dimension sculptured surface. With these specifications, die makers are expected to form the intermediate section and the finished shape so that it is functional or pleasing to the eye.

It is at this point in the die making process that the use of NC machine tools and the new software technique generating sculptured surface can play an important role. Given this background for the die making industry, it is necessary to adapt a higher level NC system by developing a low-priced, automatic, desk-top NC tape preparation device for machining die sculptured surfaces generated from only the die sectional diagram specified in the design sheet. Therefore, the industry demands a new method of die sculptured surface generation, which can perform high speed processing using a small-scale hardware device.

CLASSIFICATION AND DEFINITION OF DIE SCULPTURED SURFACES

The die sculptured surfaces are defined by a combination of two kinds of section curves. One is called "basic curve" and the other is called "drive curve". The basic curve is a shape element which governs the motion of a drive curve. The drive curve is a shape element which moves in reference to the basic curve. Both curves are defined by line segments, circles, range-of-points curves, and combinations of them. The drive curve is moved along the basic curve to define the contoured die shape. When there are one basic curve and one drive curve, for example, the sculptured surface is as Figure 5 according to whether the condition in which the drive curve moves is parallel, radiate, or normal (see Figure 5). Some shapes may have the relation that is perpendicular or connection. (Figure 6)

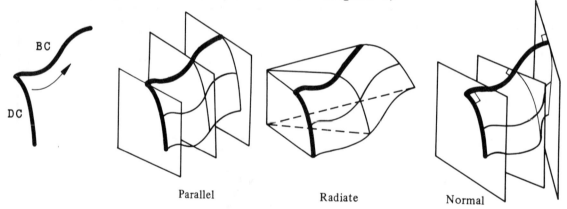

Figure 5   Sculptured surface generated by the same input data

By using these properties, die sculptured surfaces defined from sectional diagrams can be classified by a 3-digit numbering scheme as shown in Figure 7 and 8. Surface geneating method characterized numerically in Figure 8 are illustrated in Figure 9.

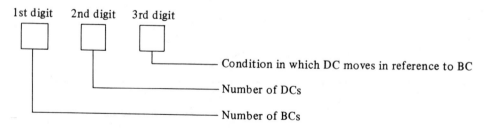

The condition of the drive curve is parallel, radiate, normal, perpendicular, or connection.

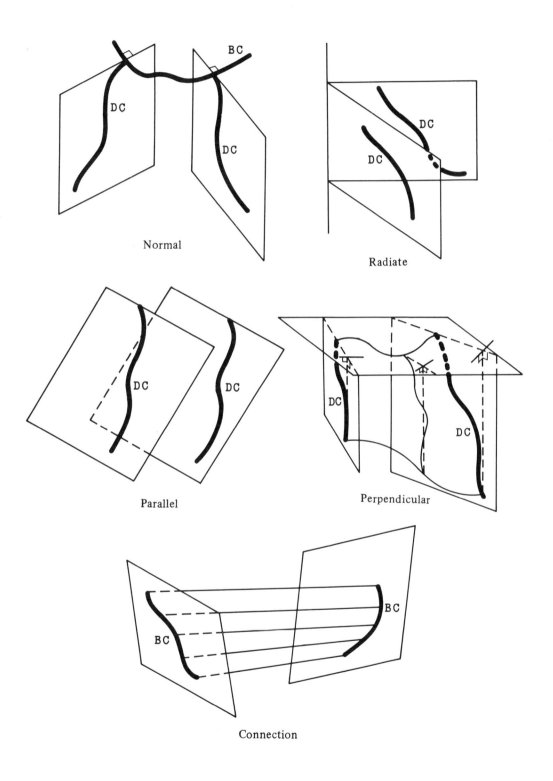

Figure 6   The condition of drive curve

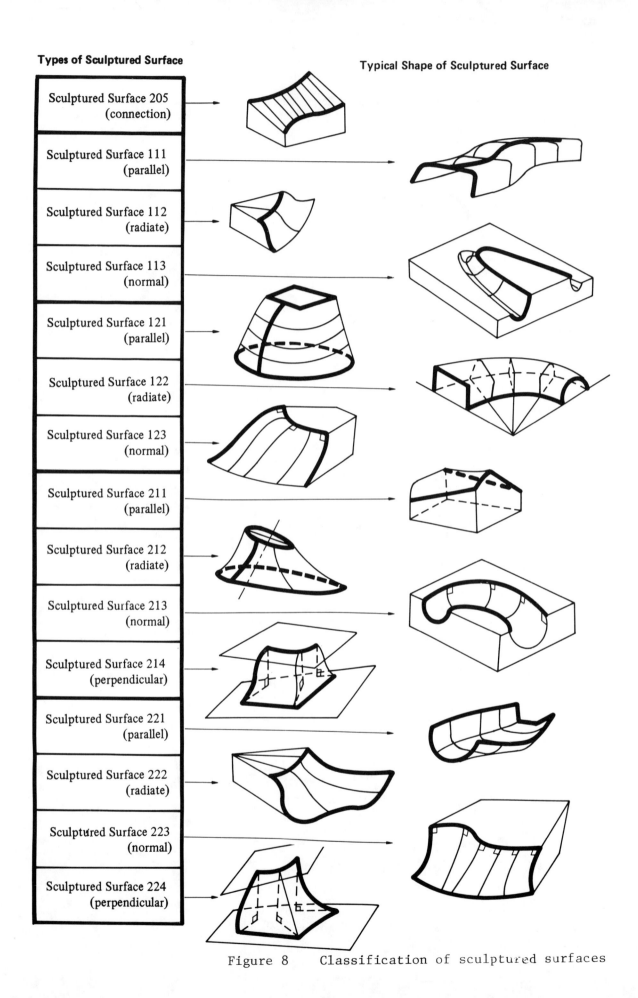

Types of Sculptured Surface	Typical Shape of Sculptured Surface
Sculptured Surface 205 (connection)	
Sculptured Surface 111 (parallel)	
Sculptured Surface 112 (radiate)	
Sculptured Surface 113 (normal)	
Sculptured Surface 121 (parallel)	
Sculptured Surface 122 (radiate)	
Sculptured Surface 123 (normal)	
Sculptured Surface 211 (parallel)	
Sculptured Surface 212 (radiate)	
Sculptured Surface 213 (normal)	
Sculptured Surface 214 (perpendicular)	
Sculptured Surface 221 (parallel)	
Sculptured Surface 222 (radiate)	
Sculptured Surface 223 (normal)	
Sculptured Surface 224 (perpendicular)	

Figure 8   Classification of sculptured surfaces

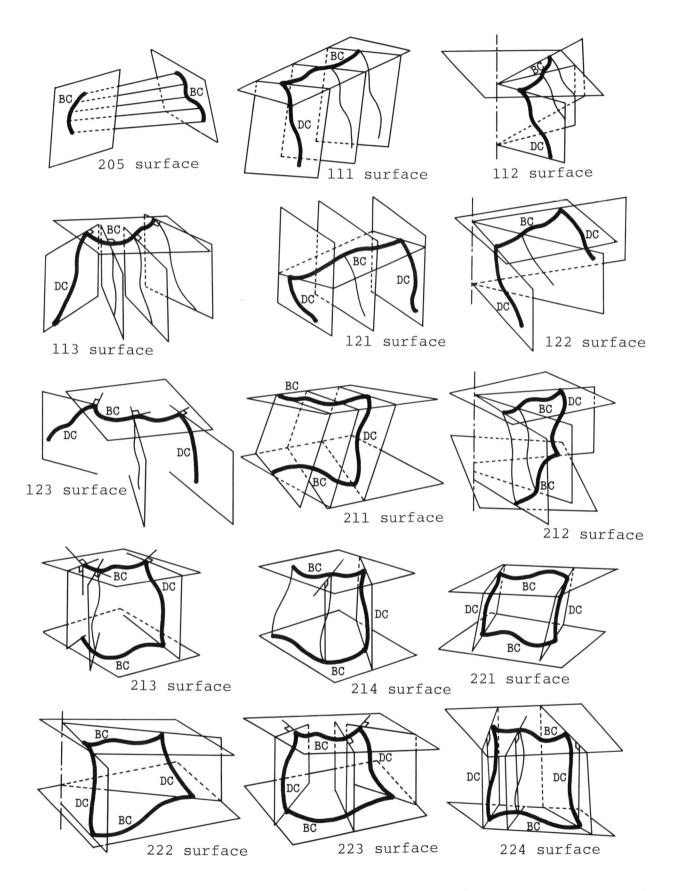

Figure 9   Generation of sculptured surface

205 surface

111 surface

112 surface

113 surface

121 surface

122 surface

123 surface

211 surface

212 surface

213 surface

214 surface

221 surface

222 surface

223 surface

224 surface

1st digit (number of BCs)	2nd digit (number of DCs)	3rd digit (condition of DC)	Remarks	Name of sculptured surface
2	0	5	Connection	Sculptured Surface 205
1	1	1	Parallel	Sculptured Surface 111
		2	Radiate	Sculptured Surface 112
		3	Normal	Sculptured Surface 113
1	2	1	Parallel	Sculptured Surface 121
		2	Radiate	Sculptured Surface 122
		3	Normal	Sculptured Surface 123
2	1	1	Parallel	Sculptured Surface 211
		2	Radiate	Sculptured Surface 212
		3	Normal	Sculptured Surface 213
		4	Perpendicular	Sculptured Surface 214
2	2	1	Parallel	Sculptured Surface 221
		2	Radiate	Sculptured Surface 222
		3	Normal	Sculptured Surface 223
		4	Perpendicular	Sculptured Surface 224

Figure 7   3-digit representation of sculptured surfaces

CYLINDRICAL SCULPTURED SURFACES

The idea of shape definition presented above can also be applied to rotating bodies such as propellers, screws, fan blades, etc. As shown in Figure 10, such shapes can be characterized by sectional curves on cylinders. In the figure, two cylinder radii determine drive curves 1 and 2. The basic curve is fixed, and as the drive curve moves along the basic curve, the drive curve shape changes from 1 to 2. Figure 11 shows the classification by the number of basic and drive curves required to define the cylindrical sculptured surface.

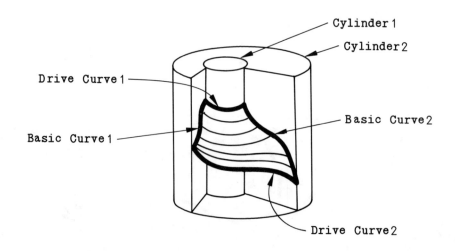

Figure 10   Cylindrical die sculptured surface

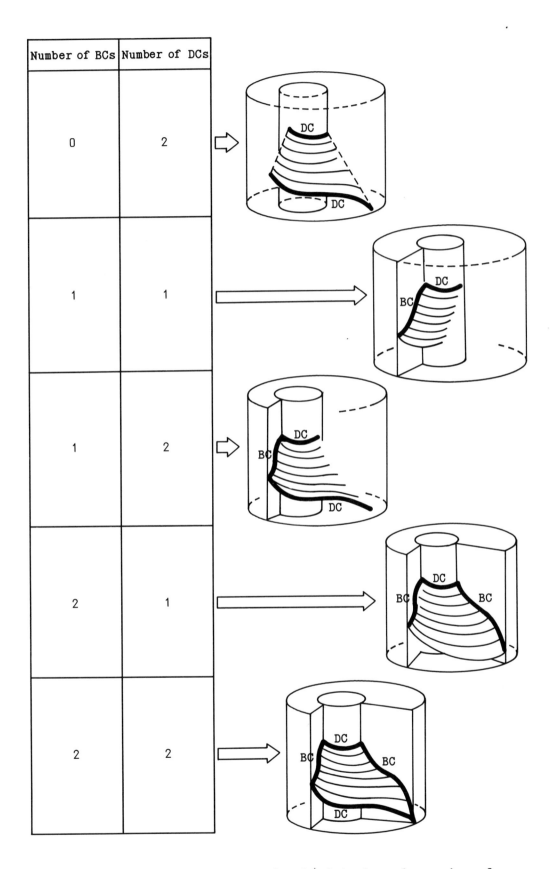

Number of BCs	Number of DCs
0	2
1	1
1	2
2	1
2	2

Figure 11   Classification of cylindrical sculptured surface

DESKTOP APPLICATION

The idea presented in the preceding two sections has been applied to the FAPT DIE-II software which is designed for the desk-top type NC tape preparation system with graphic display, "FANUC SYSTEM P-MODEL D". (Figure 12)

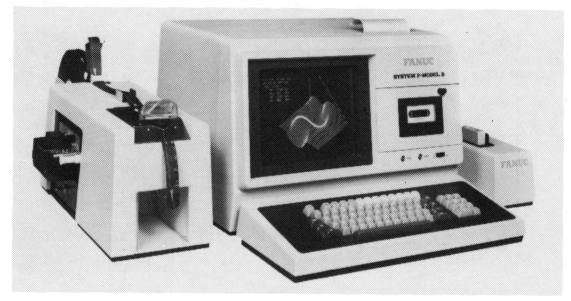

Figure 12   Desk-top NC tape preparation system with graphics display
"FANUC SYSTEM P-MODEL D"

FAPT DIE-II is designed to be easy to operate, so that sculptured surface can be generated and edited with the support of a sophisticated graphics programming system. Other functions available for die making applications include:

(1) Gradiation and drawing machining
(2) Cutting direction selection
(3) Tool offset in 3 dimensions
(4) Work area specification
(5) NC tape generation for raw materials, rough cutting and finishing

Figure 13 shows some examples of die sculptured surface generation with the FANUC SYSTEM P-MODEL D which is called system P-D. The thick lines represent sectional drawing input, and the plotted surfaces which are generated automatically can also be in the figure.

FANUC SYSTEM P-MODEL D

The system P-D is especially designed for automatic NC programming applications. It is a desk-top device with graphics display functions. It uses the FAPT language, which was also developed especially for NC programming applications.

The System P-D enables the movement of cutter to be calculated automatically from input FAPT partprogram, and displayed graphically so that details of the cutter path can be confirmed visually on the graphic display CRT. The FAPT DIE-II software is one of a complete line of support softwares for all types of NC machining. (Figure 14)

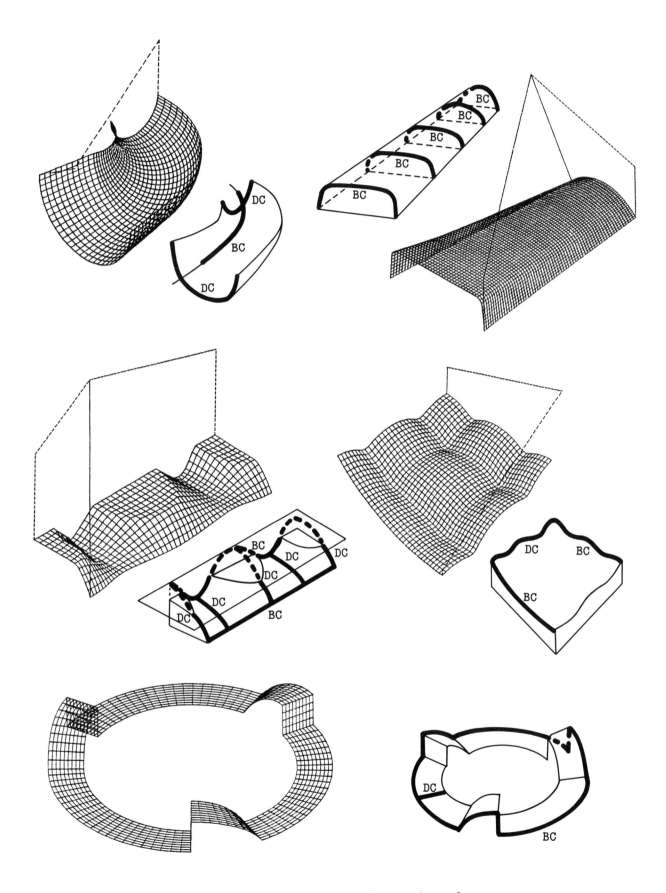

Figure 13   Example of die sculptured surface

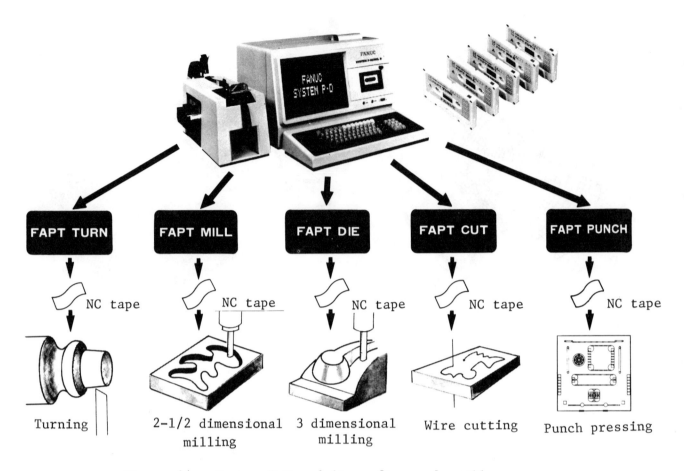

Figure 14   System P-D and its software for all purpose

Software for the System P-D has been stored on convenient magnetic tape cassettes.

1)   FAPT TURN ... Automatic programming system for turning

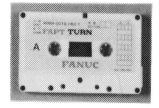

FAPT TURN permits area machining in the spindle (Z-axis) facing (X-axis) directions. Finishing area compensation, tool nose radius compensation and clearance compensation can all be carried out for the machining area, and thread cutting and grooving can also be specified.

2)   FAPT MILL ... Automatic programming system 2 1/2-axis milling and drilling

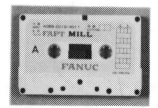

FAPT MILL is an automatic programming system for handling milling and drilling tasks ranging from positioning to contouring. In addition to processing 2 1/2-dimensional shapes, it can also perform machining shape and tool movement copy functions, as well as curve fitting and patterning.

3) FAPT DIE .... Automatic programming system for machining dies

For 3-dimensional machining dies. In two types: FAPT DIE-I and FAPT DIE-II

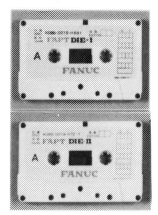

FAPT DIE-I is an automatic programming system enabling simultaneous machining of 3-dimensional shapes, including oblique planes, cylinders, cones, spheres and free combinations thereof.

With FAPT DIE-II, NC tape can be prepared to permit simultaneous 3-dimensional machining of sculptured surfaces. An assortment of library cassettes are available to match surface type and needs.

4) FAPT CUT .... Automatic programming system for wire-cut electric discharge machines.

In two types: FAPT CUT-I and FAPT CUT-II

FAPT CUT-I is an automatic programming system in which FAPT programming language has been enhanced by a wire-cut EDM function, for simple programming of ellipses, Archimedean curves, etc.

FAPT CUT-II represents an upgraded version of FAPT CUT-I which includes an involute gear function. NC tape for involute gear applications can be prepared easily using such data as module and gear number, pressure angle, etc.

5) FAPT PUNCH .. Automatic programming system for turret punch presses

In two types: FAPT PUNCH-I and FAPT PUNCH-II

FAPT PUNCH-I permits graphic display of NC tape data, thereby enabling premachining confirmation and tape editing and correction as needed.

FAPT PUNCH-II is an automatic programming system for turret punch presses which is designed to carry out complex coordinate value computations and to permit punch operations via nibbling command. Automatic pitch value calculation is also possible.

6) FAPT EDITOR .... NC tape editing system

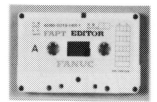

FAPT EDITOR is a system created for carrying out editing and correction of FAPT language and other NC tape data derived from paper tape readers, keyboards, magnetic cassette tapes and other I/O devices. It can also be applied to manual tape preparation.

7) FAPT TRACER .... Manual NC tape preparation and checking system

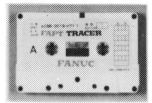

With FAPT TRACER, the cutter path in lathe, milling and drilling operations is automatically converted to graphic display. Graphic display appears automatically upon completed input of each block of NC tape data, thereby permitting NC tape preparation simultaneous with visual confirmation. Machining time can also be calculated.

8) FAPT TEACHER ... FAPT self-learning system

FAPT TEACHER is a visual training system for self-study of FAPT programming language. Using FAPT MILL and FAPT DIE as learning and practice courses, FAPT TEACHER includes full explanatory and graphic display as well as actual learning via the conversational mode. Both English and Japanese language versions are available.

9) FAPT DOCTOR .... Diagnostic system

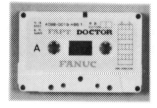

FAPT DOCTOR is a diagnostic system designed for early detection of failure sources. It can also be used for operational confirmation purpose during system installation.

CONCLUSION

Computer hardware and software technologies are advancing at a rapid pace. Capabilities thought to be impossible with current technology are likely to be commercially available sooner than we expect. It is thus quite important that the most advanced systems today are flexible to tomorrow improvements.

For example, over 200 DNC (Direct Numerical Control) systems were installed in the U.S. and Japan, and are now operating smoothly. However, DNC sales have virtually halted because the systems are not adaptable to new requirements. At the manufacturing site emphasis must be placed on flexibility. The developing industry require the Flexible Manufacturing System. (see Figure 15)

Figure 15   Cell of the flexible manufacturing system

Engineers must avoid conceptualizing only from the data processing point-of-view. It is imperative that the designs of production technology be based on real conditions in the factory and in the marketplace.

The die making industry is an excellent example of this kind of impractical engineering. Large-scale CAD and CAM systems simply do not meet the practical and economic realities of the industry composed of the smallest scale job shops. The low cost and easy-to-use desk-top device with high-performance capabilities such as the FANUC SYSTEM P-MODEL D will remove the obstacle for the automatic die making. Isn't this exactly what the industry requires? Isn't this the real "CAD/CAM System For Die Making Industry"?

Balance Loading of Blank Pressures

by Sam Gruber
J.V. Manufacturing Co., Inc.
and
Karl A. Keyes
International Fineblanking Corp.

There are six die principles that must be considered when designing perforating on blanking operation into any die. Proper use of these princibles; alignment, stock, slug, shock and wear control, and balance loading, will assure maximum productivity with a minimum amount of maintenance down time. Balance loading is the least understood of the principle and yet it can make the difference between a trouble-free, long-running die and an unpredictable mediocre one.

Using the following formula will simplify the steps required to determine the center of load.

Formula for Finding Center Line of Blanking Pressure

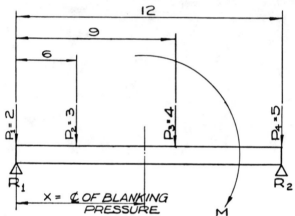

P = PERIMETER
R = REACTION
M = MOMENT

M ABOUT R_1 = $P_2 \times 6 + P_3 \times 9 + P_4 \times 12 - R_2 \times 12 = 0$

$R_2 \times 12 = P_2 \times 6 + P_3 \times 9 + P_4 \times 12$

$R_2 = \dfrac{18 + 36 + 60}{12} = \dfrac{114}{12} = 9.5$

$R_1 = P_1 + P_2 + P_3 + P_4 - R_2 = 4.5$

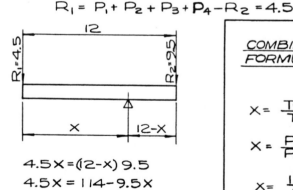

$4.5 X = (12-X) 9.5$

$4.5 X = 114 - 9.5 X$

$14 X = 114$

$X = \dfrac{114}{14} = 8.143$

COMBINING THE TWO FORMULAE

$X = \dfrac{\text{TOTAL M}}{\text{TOTAL P}}$

$X = \dfrac{P_2 \times 6 + P_3 \times 9 + P_4 \times 12}{P_1 + P_2 + P_3 + P_4}$

$X = \dfrac{114}{14} = 8.143$

**Drawing courtesy of Sam Gruber, J.V. Manufacturing Co., Inc.**

Presented at SME's Metal Stamping Conference, September 1977, copyright courtesy of Production Engineering Co., Elmhurst, Illinois

The Productivity Aspects of Die Design

by Corwin J. Bray
Production Engineering Co.

Productivity is synonomous with profit; and the greatest opportunity to lower cost comes through better methods. A very complex process begins when we take a piece part drawing, convert it into a set of mechanical tool drawings, have the tool built, put the tool into production, and hopefully, make a profit from an estimate that was made previously. For some companies, this seems to be extremely easy. For other companies, it is extremely difficult.

Consider the cost ramifications of the stamping operation, and the various facets involved, such as labor, materials, facilities, equipment, and tools. What are investments today as compared to, say, five years ago, or think about today's costs as compared to what they will be five years hence. Are any of today's jobs potential runners for the next five years? Let's carefully analyze what our position will be five years from now when we are attempting to run that same stamping for nearly the same cost. Will we compete? Will we retain the business? These are questions that relate to productivity and consequently, to the methods of die design and engineering used within the operation.

Think about the stamping when it comes in the door for cost estimating. There are normal routine considerations to be made, but is the stamping really evaluated? Most times, an engineer designing a mechanical part for a particular product only understands his product needs. Consideration is seldom given to the problems he may be designing into that particular piece part. We should not try to change their designs or their concepts, but it is our obligation to inform designers when they have gone to extremes. This assistance will also promote stamping sales. The problems that we see at a glance could require hours of study on the part of a non-stamping oriented design engineer.

A plus or minus .001 tolerance on a form, an extruded hole, or on a lanced leg, may cost the customer thousands of extra dollars. Most certainly, it is going to cost many headaches. Very possibly, the same dimension could just as well be plus or minus .005.

How about materials? Can we help the customer there? Does he need to use cold rolled special killed steel? Perhaps, because of experiences and problems he has had in the past, he has standardized. Between $1,200 and $1,500 per year extra may be spent, just to specify a special killed steel, when commercial quality would do just as well. We can identify these things quickly by utilizing our internal expertise.

The quality-related characteristics of the stamping depend upon many different things. Particularly, the capability that we have within our organization. Of course, we don't all stamp the same quality parts. We most certainly stamp them to conform to the piece part drawing, and consequently, we satisfy the quality control of our customer. But the quality of parts that one stamper makes, as compared to that of another, will vary with the type of product dealt with. A stamper running bumper brackets from 3/16" hot rolled steel certainly has quality problems, as does the stamper running .008 thick nickel silver to make integrated circuitry lead frames. However, the part quality and their equipment are going to be considerably different. The approaches to their stamping problems are radically different. Therefore stamping quality is related back to our own people. Other factors to consider are: what are we accustomed to running? How have we been trained? What type of stamping equipment do we have? What type of tools do we have? And lastly, what are our overall facilities? All these questions relate to the evaluation that must be made before even taking on a new stamping.

	LABOR	MATERIAL	FACILITIES	EQUIPMENT	TOOLS
5 YEARS AGO 1975	TOOLMAKER 8.00 TOOLDESIGNER 8.00 OPERATOR 5.00	CRCQ .16#	17.50 SQ. FT.	20.00/HR.	20.00 PER HR.
TODAY 1980	TOOLMAKER 11.50 TOOLDESIGNER 12.50 OPERATOR 6.50	CRCQ .42#	20.00 SQ. FT.	25.00/HR.	25.00 PER HR.
5 YEARS HENCE 1985	TOOLMAKER 17.50 TOOLDESIGNER 19.00 OPERATOR 10.00	CRCQ .70#	31.00 SQ. FT.	38.00/HR.	38.00 PER HR.

Figure 1

Tool design analysis starts with the piece part drawing which we have already discussed in some detail. How do we lay out the strip? What is the best method to run that particular part? Let's assume that we are going to run a progressive die. With today's hardware and software that is available to the tooling industry, we have a tremendous opporutnity to capitalize on the technology that has been developed from processes such as numerical control and computerization. Tool designs can now be made by computer and computer controlled plotters that will actually draw up the design and detail each section. That is the business of some specialty tool design companies. But the productivity aspect of tool design still has to be designed into the die. It must be programmed even on a computer. Now, through the use of computers, a layout of the developed blank can be made, fed into the computer, and printed out with the most economical progression and the best angularity to minimize scrap loss. To optimize the bending lines of a formed leg to give it maximum strength, merely ask the computer to give another five degrees bias on the progression angle, and it can replot the entire strip layout. An entirely new strip layout with the proepr adjustments for progression and all the die section locations can be achieved. Utilizing optimum strip layout may save five to ten percent in material. On a medium sized part, this saving could easily represent eight to ten thousand dollars per year. Even though productivity ideas may not be generated by the computer, it can free our designers to apply their expertise to that end. This approach could also save hours and hours of manual layout. Computerized die design is available today!

ELIMINATING PRESS STOPPAGES

Press stoppages must be eliminated. Every time that line is shut down, it costs money. We do not produce on time, our custmomers are upset, and most of all, we are not making a profit. The press stoppage requires the attention of the operator, supervisory people, die setup men, staff engineers, tool makers, and tool room supervisors. Very easily, as many as five or six people may be involved with the press stoppage. We have all seen it happen just because of a so-called ordinary press stoppage. Why did we get this stoppage? Let's examine some of the basics. . .The things we should think about, but do we? No matter how hard we work to improve productivity, only by using intelligence, imagination, and probably a little more capital, are we going to resolve the majority of press line stoppage problems.

We want our tool designers to be productivity conscious. But we have the same tool designers that we have had for the last ten years. Are we going to fire all tool designers and hire all new ones with all new ideas? It must be an attitude change throughout the entire organization. Be willing to look at the other side of the coin. Attention must be given to ideas that have not been considered before. Perhaps we have tried ideas and failed. A lot of new thinking must be drawn out of our tool designers. Maybe it is going to require getting them off the beaten track and taking a fresh approach to figure out new ideas and concepts. Above all, everyone throughout the organization must be willing to support and implement new programs.

Tool designers must know sectioning, thickness for perforator plates, punch length, and all the normal die standards. These are the basics, but let us consider the subtle areas that are always there.

HOW TO IMPROVE DIE SET-UP

A major area that always seems to create a lot of problems and can be reconciled by the tool design people is die set-up. In most cases, tool designers do not even consider die set-up. It is just a matter of sliding the die onto the bolster plate, grabbing a couple of straps and bolts, and clamping the upper show. Some other clamps and bolts lock it to the bolster plate. Now it is all set to go. It is not realized that many times this in itself, has caused the press stoppage. Walk into the shop tomorrow morning and check every set-up. How well is it located? How well is it clamped into the press? How well is it aligned for material flow? At least one half of the tools will be inaccurately set. Is it the fault of the die setter? At the time of tool design, these considerations should be made to improve the die setter's job. Die set-ups could be faster with less press stoppage with proper tool design.

Locate the tool with a centerline keyway in the bolster plate and a sliding key at each end of the die. The sliding key can be retracted upward after the alignment and clamping is completed. During maintenance in the tool room, sliding keys will not cause unbalance at the base of the die. This is a very easy way of locating the tool on the centerline of the press and on the centerline of the feed. It also gives feed to die perpendicularity needed to insure smooth flow of the material through the stock guidance of the die.

Location can also be made with shot pins. And again, these are things the tool designer could put into the tool when it is being built. Jig boring a pattern of holes in the bolster plate, which are compatible to the family of dies run in the press, permits a fast accurate set-up. This will achieve centerline alignment, perpendicularity to the feed, and right to left location balance for off-center tonnage loading.

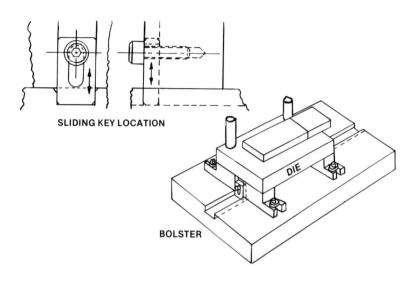

SLIDING KEY LOCATION
& U-SLOT CLAMPING

Figure 2

Commercial, hardened bushings, and shot pins can be used to avert wear over the long term.

Backstop locators are probably least popular due to the variation of die sizes. It is unusual to have similar size die shoes to utilize backstop locators. Die location, whether it comes through keyways, shot pinning, or backstops should be done by the die designer at the outset.

Clamping is another subject. It is easy in some cases to grab a set of clamps and find a few blocks of cold rolled steel, seven nice slugs, stack them all up, and make a nice clamp block assembly. That is not the way it should be approached. Commercially, there are many clamps available that do an excellent job. Preferably, have the tool builder put the holes directly through the die shoe. With tee slot and U-notches in the edge of the die show, bolt through the shoe into the tee nut. Tee slotted bolster plates and rams offer very efficient clamping of tools. Clamping blocks or building blocks are not required with tee slots. The same can be applied to the upper half of the die shoe. This is probably the best method to use. There are other ways that are well applied. One would be die clamps that insert into holes directly drilled into the edge of the die show. Predetermined location of holes above the lower face, or below the upper face of the shoe, are required. These clamps require no blocking or shimming because the dimensions from the shoe face to the hole centerlines are standardized to suit the commercial clamp. There are other types of commercial clamps available, but they require clamping blocks. Clamps with clamp blocks require more set-up time and normally are prone to being lost. For this reason, I would emphasize the use of a pre-engineered type of clamping system.

A few years ago a hydraulic clamping system was devised and designed to accommodate the average tool within the average stamping facility. The concept utilized a positive-locking hydraulic clamp system, gibbed upper and lower die adapter plates, backstops, and a roller platform die cart. By merely selecting adapter plates large enough for the family of tools to be used in a press, all dies are drilled and tapped to accept the common adapter. This provides common die location, easy die handling, and fast, positive clamping. Combined with the powered shut height adjustment and digital read-out, die setting could be accomplished in a very short time. This system applied to a 60 ton OBI press and a family of twenty dies would cost approximately ten to twelve thousand dollars. Averaging two die changes per day, the entire system would be justified on a one-year payback.

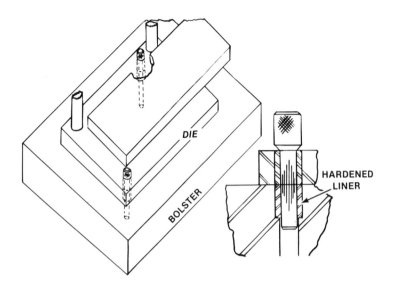

SHOT PIN LOCATION

Figure 3

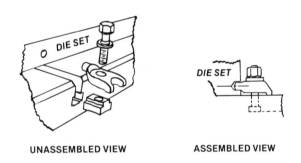

UNASSEMBLED VIEW   ASSEMBLED VIEW

DIE SET CLAMP

Figure 4

IMPROVED STOCK THREADING

A great deal of die damage occurs at the start of a new coil, or at the tail end of and old coil. We must provide the operator with a pre-trimming station, or appropriate staging stops in the die. On the newer equipment with extremely accurate feeds, after the first hit is made, the strip can walk through without any problem. This will override the need for having manual die stops. But what about that leading edge that leaves a one-quarter moon section on the die? These sections cannot be removed with a bridge or solid stripper on the tool. Blowing loose sections out of the tool probably will not work. Why not make a pre-trim station for the tool. An arbor press fixture with a pre-trim die seems to be the most popular method. These design considerations do not cost a great deal of money and they will eliminate press stoppages.

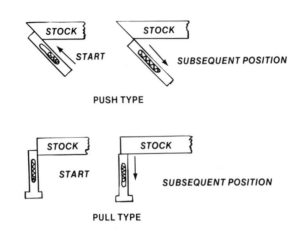

PRIMARY STOPS

Figure 5

With less accurate feeds, one must design in primary and secondary strip stops. The number of secondary stops depends upon the die layout, but one too few can cause major miss-hits in the tool. Analyze the tool to determine exactly what is needed.

French stops are very effective when hand feeding coil stock. However, they are the "nemeses" of today's modern roll feeds. The theory of use to the designer is great, but in actual practice they end up destroying new, accurate feeds. The reason lies in the fact that die setters rarely take the trouble to back off the feed once it hits home on the French stop. The result is slipping rolls, broken gears, and worn out clutches. Consequently, dies are broken because of badly mangled, inaccurate feeds. All this because of an innocent French stop. The real classic case comes when one utilizes a French stop, a solid stripper, and a form in the die. The result is a strip locked in the tool. It cannot be removed forward or reverse. This really gives the die setter something to do with his spare time. Elimination of French stops also saves material. A five to seven percent reduction in material usage can be achieved on a 2 1/2" x 3" x .06" thick piece-part. Converted to dollars, this would represent five hundred to one thousand dollars per year savings, based upon a quantity of one hundred thousand to two hundred thousand parts. Multiply this sum by a dozen parts and it represents a tidy little savings to put into the profit column. To the die setter and press operator, French stops, damaged equipment, and downtime are anonyms.

PART AND SCRAP EJECTION

This is the area that separates the men from the boys in die design. Whenever possible, blank the part through or cut off the part. Do not use blow offs, shedders, or knock outs. If the part will tolerate blank-through ejection, it is far superior to any other method. Once this is designed into the tool, it is fixed. Now the tool is capable of running at much higher speeds. The press speed is not limited by the piece-part ejection from the die. The same thing is true with scrap. When possible, always push the scrap through. Do not leave the little whiskers, the little skeleton sections, or the little slug on top of the die. This only creates grief and downtime. The law of gravity guarantees that everything is free and clear. Other methods of getting that piece-

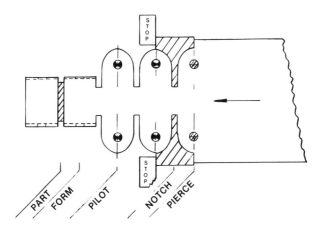

FRENCH STOP (DOUBLE)

Figure 6

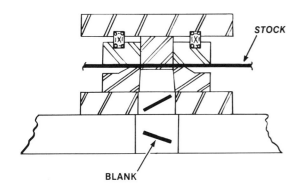

DROP-THRU BLANKING DIE

Figure 7

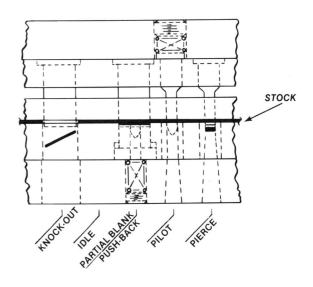

PUSH-BACK DIE

Figure 8

part to scrap out the tool does not need to be engineered or set up. The part or scrap is clear to fail directly into conveyors, or into containers, to be carried away.

Many times parts must be extremely flat, and a blank through die can cause dishing. When this is the case, consider a pushback die and a knockout station. This gives the ability to punch out flat parts, push them back into the scrap skeleton, advance the progression, and simply knock them out of the strip through the bottom. Again, we are striving to eliminate auxiliary methods for ejection. When a new die is being constructed, the additional cost of a pushback station may be in the area of an additional ten percent of the total die cost. Shearing the die one time due to non-ejection can easily pay for this additional investment.

A compound die station is normally used to obtain flat parts. Slow press speed is a resulting problem. A push-back die station will permit the press to run three or four times as fast. Again, considering productivity added profits, we would typically spend one thousand dollars more on the die to gain two thousand five hundred dollars, based on one million parts per year. Net savings would be one thousand five hundred dollars, not including the major factor of reduced tool repair.

The alternate methods for ejection are cyclic air blow-off, mechanical shedders, or knockouts. How well can we apply knowckouts? The press closes and punches out the piece part. The upstroke of the press is wasted because ejection can be accomplished only at the top of the stroke. When the part is finally ejected, the race is on. Now, during the down stroke, the part must move faster than the press ram in order to eject clear, prior to die closure. Failure to clear in time results in a double in the die. Press speeds are normally reduced to prevent this very occurrence.

If ejection must be mechanical, use a cam style knockout. It permits ejection early during press upstroke and allows seventy to eighty percent more time to clear the die. This extra ejection time will permit the press to be run fifty to one hundred percent faster.

BETTER STOCK GUIDING

Extra attention must be given to the flow of material in the tool. When press speeds are high or feed lengths are long, consider the effects of stock guiding.

Coil materials that have a low ratio of thickness to width tend to present major problems because of camber. High ratios present columnar strength problems and must be pulled through the guide. These conditions, coupled with slitting burr, utilizing raw strip edges, and coil curvature, create a situation requiring exact decisions by the die designer. A part prone to camber, but necessitating the use of a raw edge, would be a prime candidate for centering cam actuated stock guides. This allows for adverse flow conditions, yet permits the use of raw strip edge. Level flow of the strip is always essential, especially in high speed presses. The die designer can improve the set-up man's job by standardizing on a flow line hieght. Too many times height misadjustments of feed to stock guide flow line result in friction, creating faulty feeds. Every effort should be made to design flow heights to a standard.

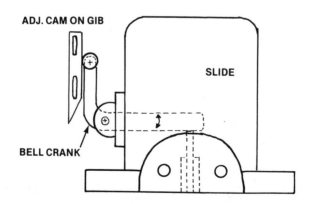

CAM TYPE KNOCK-OUT
(SLIDE SHOWN AT TOP)

Figure 9

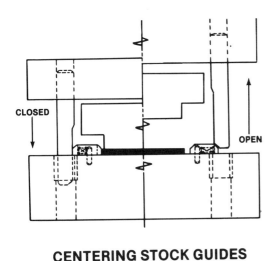

**CENTERING STOCK GUIDES
DOUBLE CAM ACTUATED**

Figure 10

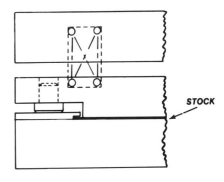

**SPRING STRIPPER
W/BALANCE PADS**

Figure 11

DIE STRIPPER FUNCTIONS

Solid strippers are economical. They fall into the class "You get what you pay for."
They do not control materials during punch penetration and withdrawal. Therefore, with
the strip floating, there will be an excessive amount of broken perforators, pilots,
and distorted material. It will also limit access into the tool for clean-up and periodic visual inspection. Solid strippers can be well utilized to guide punches. This
seems to be the most appropriate application outside of initial cost.

Spring strippers give you the best of everything in controlling the strip, but they are
expensive. The initial cost will be saved many times over through less die breakage and
downtime. One area of caution is stripper balance. Do not permit cocking when starting
a new strip. This is especially important with materials 1/16" thick and greater.
Cocking will be prevented with the use of balancing pads. These pads should be of
equal thickness to the material.

PREVENTING PILOT BREAKAGE

Pilot breakage can be more of a problem than punch breakage. Materials with a low thickness to pilot diameter ratio will present more pilot breakage problems. If they are
press fit stationary pilots, they must penetrate the material when a misfeed occurs.
How many misfeeds they can withstand depends upon the pilot diameter and length. Rest
assured that the first time will cause some damage. Frail pilots must be supported
with guides to prevent deflection.

Spring loaded pilots will prevent material penetration in most cases. No pilot penetration; no breakage. Many designers say accuracy will be lost if slip fit clearances are
used. Honestly, how many jobs are really that critical? Spend a few dollars on spring
loaded pilots and keep those presses running.

CURES FOR SLUG RETENTION

Books could be written about slug retention. When a slug pulls, do we set the die deeper to drive the slug on through? Do we put shear on the punch, notch the punch, dull
the punch, put ejector pins in the punch, notch the die, or angle the die? Let's examine
material stress equalization. Consider the coiled stock that is being fed through the
press. There are stresses in that coil due to rolling, slitting, and rewinding. As
we start gutting, perforating, notching, lancing, forming, and drawing, we are setting

up more stress in the material. For example, let us consider a part from fifteen thousandths thick phos bronze alloy that has 1/8" diameter holes. Punch out the slugs and they pop right back up. The strip jams, causes a misfeed, and shears the tool. Now we have a one hundred dollar regrind job, excluding lost press time. Why does it happen? Could it be resolved? Precision stock straighteners are available. They operate in the realm between conventional stock straighteners, which simply remove coil set, and the roller leveler, which can remove residual stress in most material. A precision stock straightener flex rolls the stock enough to equalize the stress across the strip. Those 1/8" diameter slugs no longer pop out of the die bushing. Why? Because the stock is flat and the stress is equal over the entire area of the slug. Therefore, when grinding the tool, we save money. Special shapes and angles need not be maintained to prevent slug pulling. Less punch and die will be ground away because penetration is shallower. And this is possible only if we prevent slug pulling.

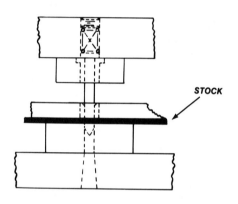

SPRING LOADED PILOT

Figure 12

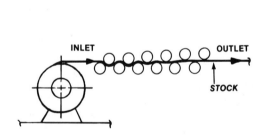

FLEX ROLLING

Figure 13

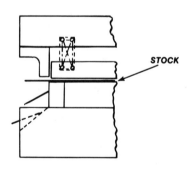

**DIE MOUNTED
SCRAP CHOPPER**

Figure 14

Today's carbide lamination dies are worth at least two hundred dollars per one thousandths inch or die life. Now we can fathom the extreme importance minimizing die grinding.

CHOOSING SCRAP CHOPPERS

The best scrap chopper is the die mounted type. The main reason is maintenance. Grinding the die grinds the scrap chopper and it is easily times with the tool. All other scrap choppers rarely are maintained. They usually run until they form the material instead of chopping it. Then and only then, does someone look at its cutting condition. Most scrap choppers are also inaccurately timed.

They may be cutting or pulling when the feed is released for piloting. Net results are misfeeds, broken pilots, and sheared discs.

FACTS ABOUT DIE LUBRICATION

A recirculating die lubrication system is highly desirable on most operations. It applies proper amounts on either side of the strip, conserves lubricant, provides better overall housekeeping and can be installed between the feed and the die. The location is important because if mounted before the feed, the rolls or gripper jaws could iron off most of the lubricant. This could also cause the feed to slip and feed inaccurately.

Should designers consider die lubrication? Designing pockets in the tool that could become filled with die lubricants will cause hydraulic action, thus marking or even distorting the piece part. What lubricant should be used in the tool? The press operator normally has this decision delegated to him. If running a carbide die, a sulphur base lubricant should never be used. This would cause the carbide binders to erode, and the tool will fall prematurely. Lubricant specifications should be part of the of the routing process. Many times a tool will make beautiful samples. Then in the production press, after fifty pieces, it is galled. The part is welded to the draw punch. Everything is designed properly. But what has happened? Correct lubrication specifications were not established at the outset. Processings and operating people must be advised as to the importance of proper lubrication selection.

DIE MALFUNCTION DETECTION

Damage to tools or presses can be prevented by electronic die sensing. Consider the piece part that you have not been able to blank through. Design in a sensor to check feed advance, stock buckle, end of material, misfeed pilot, and high strippers.

If a misfeed pilot is used, it is easy to install a commercial limit switch and achieve misfeed detection by actuating the press stop circuit. In order to detect a misfeed with a pilot, the press and die must be almost closed.

Unless the press is extremely slow, or has an oversized brake with a fast reaction time, a miss-hit is inevitable. This probably will shear the tool, or at least make the location pilot punch through the strip. During a normal run, there may be several misfeeds. Multiply the times a misfeed occurs by the number of times the pilots punch through the stock and there will most certainly be a broken or bent location pilot. This will cause serious damage to the tool. Misfeed pilots must be extra long to provide ample press stop time. This extra length will dictate the feed cycle. Therefore, the feed cycle will be limited by the extraction and entrance of the misfeed pilot.

A more logical approach would be to sense the end of the strip for feed advance. The feed cycle can then be timed early to enhance ejection or stop time. Consult a reputable press room equipment supplier for particulars, as this requires intimate knowledge of die design and malfunction detection.

Checking for stock buckle between the feed and the die is another method to eliminate pilot probes. Most failures to advance the stock accurately comes from slugs pulling, or poor material conditions. Either case would cause the feed to buckle the strip when resistance occurs in the tool. Again, we can utilize our feed cycle to our advantage and permit more stopping time.

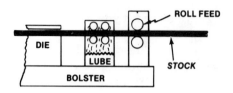

**RECIRCULATING
STRIP LUBRICATOR**

Figure 15

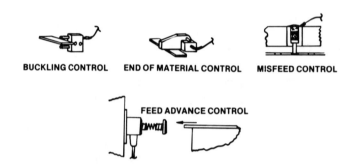

BUCKLING CONTROL   END OF MATERIAL CONTROL   MISFEED CONTROL

FEED ADVANCE CONTROL

**ELECTRONIC SENSORS FOR
DIE MALFUNCTION DETECTION**

Figure 16

The cost of one miss-hit cannot be precisely defined. Outwardly, the operator may see little or no change in die performance. But quite possibly the number of hits will be reduced between regrinds. A die that should run one hundred thousand hits now only gets eight thousand hits before excessive burr appears. The one miss-hit at the beginning has been forgotten, but it is the true reason for getting 20 percent less from the die.

These figures are representative of cost involved with only one miss-hit. The product of the total cost for miss-hits would stagger the mind if it could be accurately determined.

Do, by all means, take advantage of the electronic sensing equipment that is available today. And do it in the tool design stages. Do not make the tool room retrofit those tools. It is much easier for the tool designer to do it on paper than later, when working with hardened tool steel.

Once the basic die design is completed with the appropriate considerations for productivity, the tool builder must be selected. The state-of-the-art in the tool builders' industry is changing radically. A tool builder must stay abreast with the latest developments of wire E.D.M., numerically controlled machines, duplicating equipment, and computerization of machine tools. To the leaders in the tool building industry, the byword now is numerical control. This is going to be a way of life. The most recent, most revolutionary new approach is the wire E.D.M. Within five years, anyone running or building dies will be required to use this method. It will be a must to remain in a competitive position.

We have talked about new tools. What about the existing tools? Can we upgrade what we now have to utilize some of these new concepts or new ideas? It very well may be economical to do so. One viewpoint would be extending of die life. In some cases a very minor change is required to accomplish this. We may double, triple, or quadruple, the life of a die simply by making a minor modification at the cutoff end of the tool. Let the piece part fall free and clear, instead of trying to blow it out of the tool. If there are fewer stoppages, it indicates there are fewer miss-hits, sheared and broken dies.

At the time of tool construction, the cost to go one station longer will be approximately 10 percent more on the average. Due to part configuration and processing, the cost to retrofit in this productivity feature on existing dies will range form 10 percent of the initial cost to complete replacement of the die. Generally speaking, dies are not designed with extra room nor are they conveniently compatible to retrofitting ideas. For this reason, much serious consideration must be given to the tool design job at hand, in order to achieve optimum productivity features.

Equipment selection and configuration is crucial to productivity of tooling. Standardize, where possible, in the areas that will enhance die setting. You will gain greater flexibility in machine utilization. A few examples would be: (1) Pre-engineered bolsters and rams. This permits easier die mounting and alignment. (2) Pre-engineered electrics. This provides extra contacts for use of cyclic air, die malfunction and pre-determined part counters. (3) Powerized machine adjustments. Included would be speed controls, shut height setting, and feed length setting. (4) Unitized control points. This includes installing manifolded air outlets, eye level rotary limit switches, and auxiliary hand tool outlets.

On existing equipment, the application of new techniques and methods by retrofitting can be accomplished in most cases. Utilize outside expertise to obtain new ideas. The latest state-of-the-art can be obtained from competent metal stamping suppliers. Infusion of new outside thought, in most cases, can be very productive in itself.

The implementation of new ideas that will enhance productivity is not extremely simple. It involves a system to report press stoppage. Once the report is made, the reason for stoppage must be identified, and corrective action taken. For this reason, the entire organization must take part in any effort to upgrade and improve productivity.

The execution of all the detailed items we have discussed now becomes paramount. Operational procedures must be passed down to the line supervisors and operators. Without aids and guidelines, productivity improvements will be of little value.

Every feature of the press, tool, feed, coil support equipment, safety devices, material handling, and automation devices must be right. Any shortcuts, at this point, will cause a weak link in the program, resulting in operational inability to conform to the new standards.

Our final task to achieve the "productivity aspects of die design" lies within the heart of the company. People must make the job happen.

Management's firm stand to attain more productivity is mandatory. Management must give direction and guidance to the overall approach. Establishment of communications, up and down the organizational ladder is essential. Dedication to properly trained personnel, at all levels, is imperative. Limitations of personnel and overall facilities should be recognized and placed into proper perspective. Manufacturing management at all levels must also learn the economics of productivity. The portion of burden costs applicable to inadequate tool design and execution must be isolated. This total figure will then become the "bogie" or goal towards which to work. Because management's major role is devoted to the P and L statement, they are the ones who must put the final stamp of approval on the entire productivity program. Information must be converted to motivation.

Staff personnel must be willing to consider new ideas and diligently work toward their success. Personal upgrading, through additional schooling, may be needed. When the communication lines are established, they are to be used, not abused. Information put into these channels must be precise and accurate. Training is an everyday occurrence for staff and line. They must constantly talk to outside sources and evaluate new information. This filtered and adapted information can then be used to improve their never-ending program toward achieving more "productivity." Failure to carry on continuing training at all levels will result in the eventual collapse of the productivity program.

Line personnel are the end of the organizational sequence. They must put into operation all programs and improvements that management and staff have implemented. Line attitudes must constantly be reviewed to insure that they are able to carry out new assignments. The real load is on them to produce efficiently, and to do it according to the new procedure.

Communication and training is a daily requirement to make old habits disappear and new productive habits routine.

Productivity aspects of die design are rarely attained for three major reasons: (1) Management fails to recognize the economics of productivity. (2) Staff fails to dedicate their time and efforts toward the implementation of productivity. (3) Line personnel fail to run presses at specified rates because making parts to print is more compelling than achieving operational efficiency.

"Optimum productivity" has never been achieved. This would be utopia and it will never happen. A better and more profitable venture is always just around the corner. Some companies can produce rings around their competition. Why? Because, the best organizations invariably do these things.

No stamping organization could go far wrong by taking a good look at its operations in terms of the factors discussed here or by challenging its suppliers to come up with new ideas.

SCRAPBOOK
Helpful Hints for the Die Designer
by Arnold Miedema
and
Edwin Stouten
Capitol Engineering Co.

For years, die designers have been searching for proven solutions to unique design problems. Arnold Miedema has been a collector of just such solutions, concerning everything from cam piercing and scoring for accurate forms to a complete list of miscellaneous ideas.

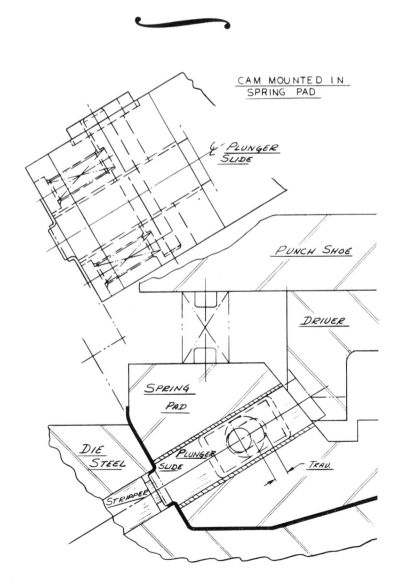

CAM MOUNTED IN SPRING PAD

PLUNGER SLIDE

PUNCH SHOE

DRIVER

SPRING PAD

DIE STEEL

PLUNGER SLIDE

TRAV.

STRIPPER

DIRECTION OF FEED

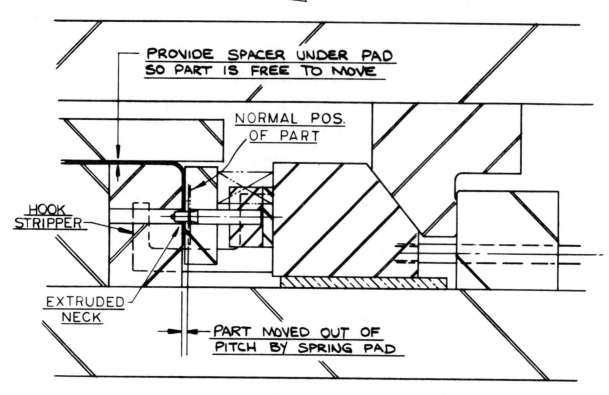

PROVIDE SPACER UNDER PAD
SO PART IS FREE TO MOVE

NORMAL POS.
OF PART

HOOK
STRIPPER

EXTRUDED
NECK

PART MOVED OUT OF
PITCH BY SPRING PAD

A PART MAY BE PUSHED "OUT OF POSITION" TO ACHIEVE
A HORIZONTAL FLANGE OR AN EXTRUDED NECK

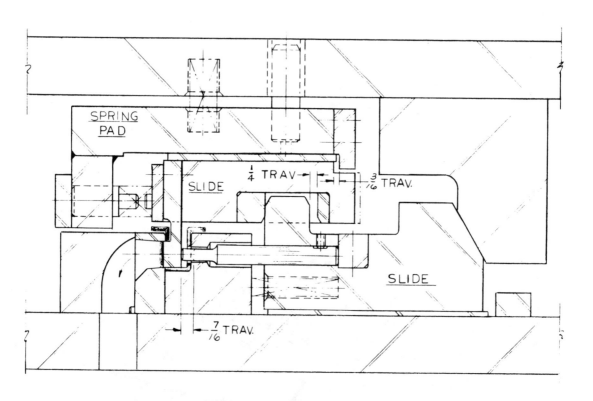

SPRING
PAD

SLIDE

$\frac{1}{4}$ TRAV.

$\frac{3}{16}$ TRAV.

SLIDE

$\frac{7}{16}$ TRAV.

PIERCING A HOLE TANGENT WITH THE INSIDE
SURFACE OF A PART $\frac{5}{8}$" WIDE

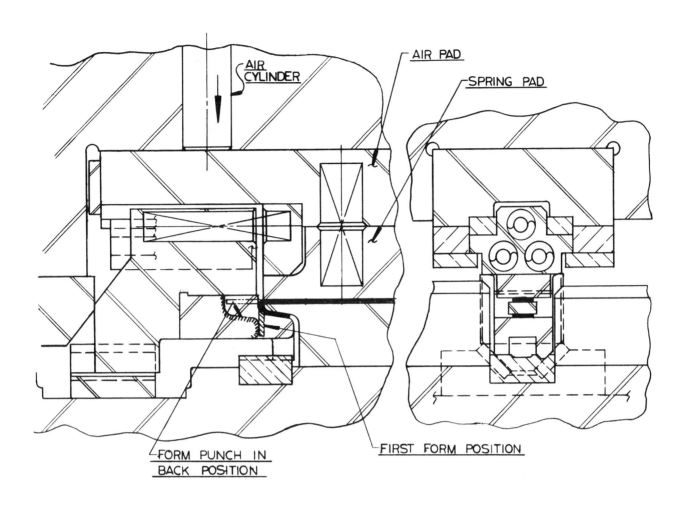

AIR
CYLINDER

AIR PAD

SPRING PAD

FORM PUNCH IN
BACK POSITION

FIRST FORM POSITION

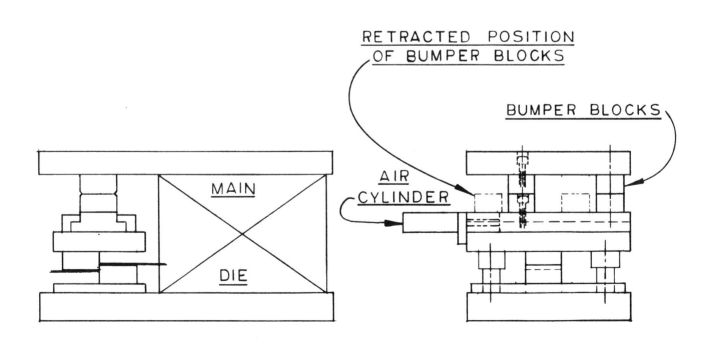

RETRACTED POSITION
OF BUMPER BLOCKS

BUMPER BLOCKS

AIR
CYLINDER

MAIN

DIE

GAG CUT-OFF DIE

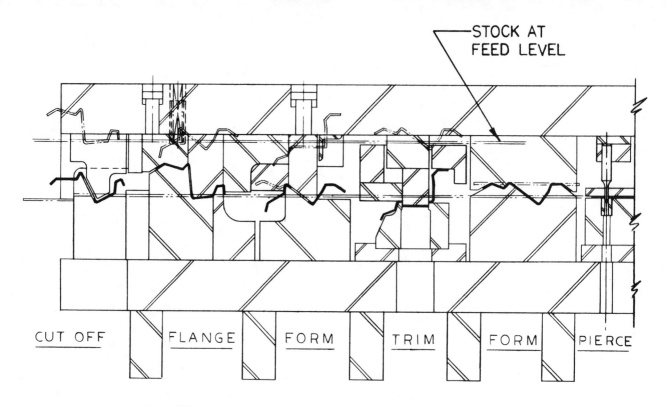

STOCK AT FEED LEVEL

CUT OFF   FLANGE   FORM   TRIM   FORM   PIERCE

ILLUSTRATION OF PARTS TIPPED IN WEB

FLOATING MANDREL

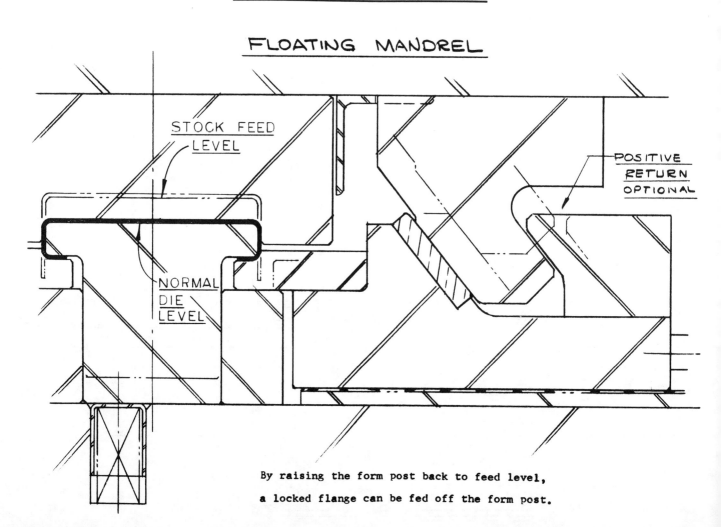

STOCK FEED LEVEL

NORMAL DIE LEVEL

POSITIVE RETURN OPTIONAL

By raising the form post back to feed level,
a locked flange can be fed off the form post.

36

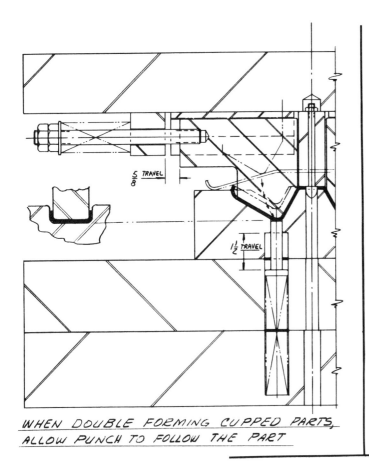

$\frac{5}{8}$ TRAVEL

$1\frac{1}{2}$ TRAVEL

WHEN DOUBLE FORMING CUPPED PARTS,
ALLOW PUNCH TO FOLLOW THE PART

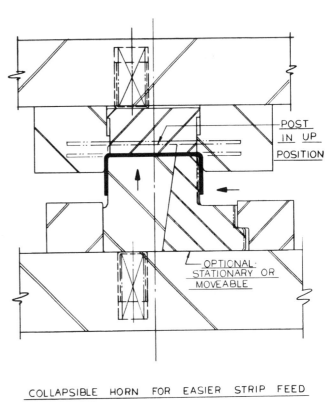

POST
IN UP
POSITION

OPTIONAL
STATIONARY OR
MOVEABLE

COLLAPSIBLE HORN FOR EASIER STRIP FEED

COIN CORNER TO CONTROL HOLE ALIGNMENT

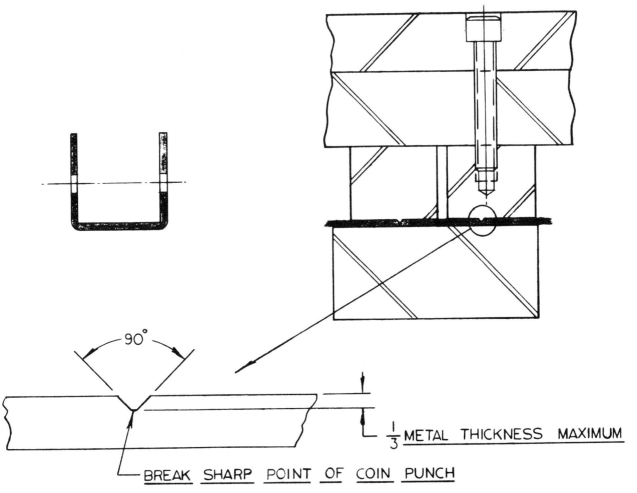

90°

$\frac{1}{3}$ METAL THICKNESS MAXIMUM

BREAK SHARP POINT OF COIN PUNCH

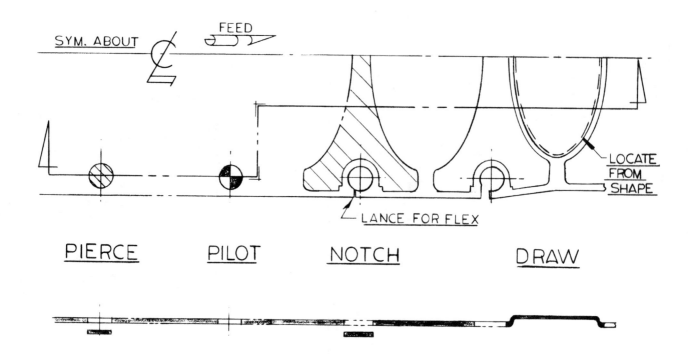

PIERCE   PILOT   NOTCH   DRAW

SYM. ABOUT

FEED

LANCE FOR FLEX

LOCATE FROM SHAPE

LANCE TO GIVE FLEX WEB

DO NOT PUT SET UP BLOCK
NEXT TO GUIDE PIN

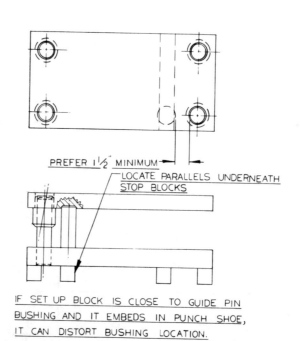

PREFER 1½" MINIMUM

LOCATE PARALLELS UNDERNEATH
STOP BLOCKS

IF SET UP BLOCK IS CLOSE TO GUIDE PIN
BUSHING AND IT EMBEDS IN PUNCH SHOE,
IT CAN DISTORT BUSHING LOCATION.

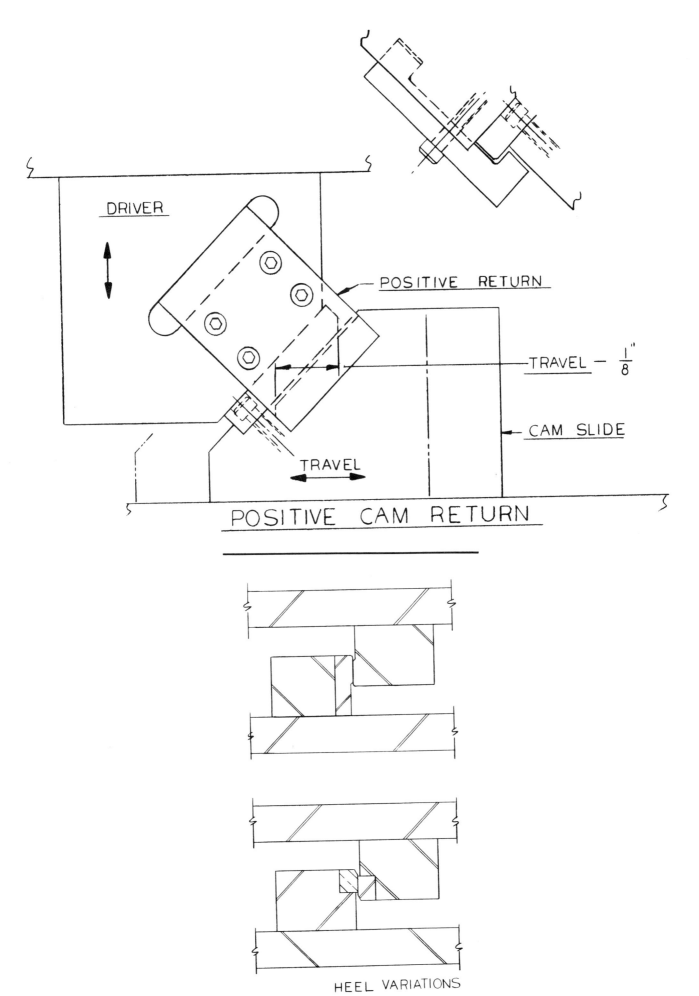

DRIVER

POSITIVE RETURN

TRAVEL — $\frac{1}{8}$"

CAM SLIDE

TRAVEL

POSITIVE CAM RETURN

HEEL VARIATIONS

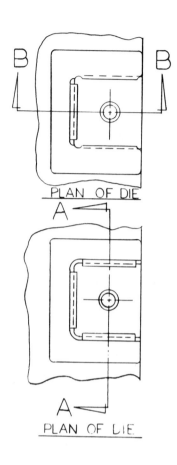

PLAN OF DIE

PLAN OF DIE

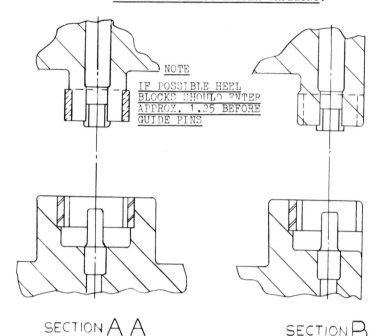

NOTE

IF POSSIBLE HEEL
BLOCKS SHOULD ENTER
APPROX. 1.25 BEFORE
GUIDE PINS

SECTION A A

IF DOUBLE WEAR PLATES ARE USED
(1) SHOULD BE HDN. STL., THE
OTHER #21 AMPCO BRONZE OR EQUIV.

SECTION B B

IF A SINGLE WEAR PLATE IS
SPECIFIED USE BRONZE WITH
FLAME HDN. DUCTILE OR HDN.
STEEL WITH SEMI STEEL
CASTINGS.

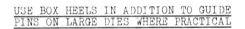

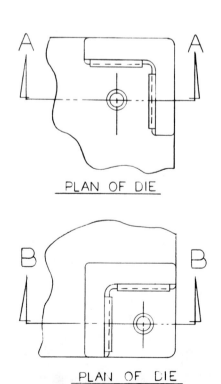

PLAN OF DIE

PLAN OF DIE

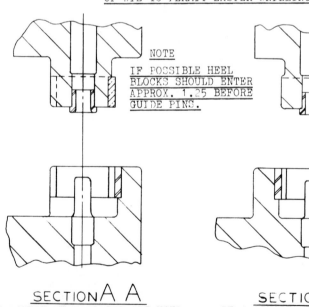

NOTE

IF POSSIBLE HEEL
BLOCKS SHOULD ENTER
APPROX. 1.25 BEFORE
GUIDE PINS.

SECTION A A

IF DOUBLE WEAR PLATES ARE USED
(1) SHOULD BE HDN. STL., THE
OTHER #21 AMPCO BRONZE OR EQUIV.

SECTION BB

IF A SINGLE WEAR PLATE IS
SPECIFIED USE BRONZE WITH
FLAME HDN. DUCTILE OR HDN.
STEEL WITH SEMI STEEL.

MISCELLANEOUS IDEAS

· Put a bead in the strip carrier if the material is thin or narrow.

· Put a radius on the inside corners of tool steel wherever permissible to prevent cracking.

· Put a C.R.S. sleeve around pierce punches which are mounted in hardened blocks, to permit moving the location, if required.

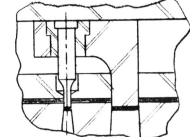

· Examine the conditions which exist as the die is opening during the press up stroke.

· Add a tab to balance a one-sided forming condition if the part is unstable. It can be cut off in a later station.

· Put the area of a part with difficult development to the outside of strip so that the die pitch is not affected.

· Provide inserts in form steels to permit easy adjustment of critical part surfaces.

· Provide an idle station for difficult parts to allow for additional operations, if required.

· Put a limit switch or detector on the <u>end</u> of the die to indicate a buckle or jam up in the feed.

· Put overload protectors on diagonal corners of the die to monitor a double metal thickness.

· To eliminate excessive pad travel, use a series of bends to achieve a long curved surface.

- Try to use a dowel length that is 4 times its diameter. This permits a large inventory of a single length for each diameter and a small inventory of other length.
- To achieve high production in a low speed press, run 2 or more parts at a time.
- Use a multiple stepped extruding punch to get a longer neck.
- Provide air vents in pinch trim steels.

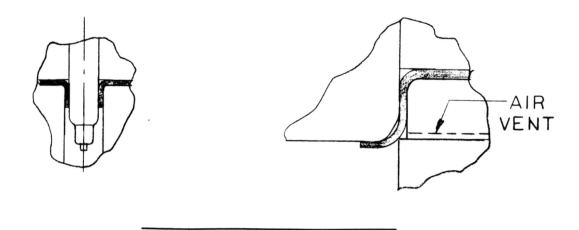

Reprinted with permission from Tooling & Production, April 1974

Tooling tricks for pressworking

by Federico Strasser
Santiago, Chile, S.A.

Press tooling is limited only by the imagination of the man who designs it. Here one contributor explains his solutions to a group of pressworking problems.

Double-acting piercing die

The stamping in **Figure 1** is a typical case of grills or other kinds of parts where a series of closely located ventilating slots must be pierced. In most such cases the closeness of the slots represents a serious problem because, if the distance between two adjacent slots is less than twice the stock thickness, there is a high risk for the die plate. For such cases a special second operation has been devised where the slots are pierced in two steps (half of them at each press hit; first the even ones, then the odd ones). In such a way the distance between two nearby die plate slots is increased considerably, so that die life becomes satisfactory.

The die, **Figure 2**, operates in the following way. A slide with an opening-nest for the blank is pulled out completely. A blank with the four small round holes already punched in it is put in the slide-nest. The slide is pushed into the die until it reaches stop No. 1. Now the press is tripped and one row of slots is pierced. At the same time stop No. 1 is made inactive. When the ram ascends, the slide can be pushed further into the die to stop No. 2 which is a simple, stationary dowel pin, located at the right distance from the cutting edges. Now, the press is tripped again, and the second row of slots is pierced between the slots of the first batch. The slide is pulled out and the finished stamping is removed from the nest.

The secret of the success of this die lies in the working principle of stop No. 1. This is a spring-loaded, headed plunger, with a small bullet-nosed tip on the bottom. The nose is pushed against a horizontal round rod. In the rest position (slide outside the press) the rod pushes the plunger-stop upward, so its top end protrudes above the die plate surface. The rod is held in this position by means of a spring-loaded detent near the entry side of the die. When the slide is pulled out after the piercing of the second row of slots it lifts the detent-plunger so the rod spring pushes the rod back into the initial position. (For clarity's sake, the freeing detail of the detent-plunger is omitted from **Figure 2**.)

The die in question can be very easily arranged to comply with OSHA requirements. Since it works in such a way that there is no need for the operator to put his hands into the danger zone (both for feeding and for part removal), the tool may be used with a completely surrounding protective guard which prevents reaching into the danger zone of the die.

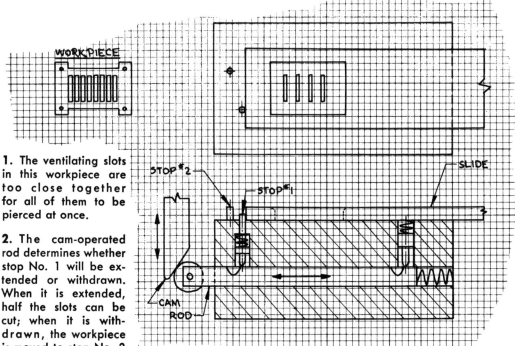

1. The ventilating slots in this workpiece are too close together for all of them to be pierced at once.

2. The cam-operated rod determines whether stop No. 1 will be extended or withdrawn. When it is extended, half the slots can be cut; when it is withdrawn, the workpiece is moved to stop No. 2 and the others are cut.

Dinking dies

A dinking die is a cutting die used without a matrix. The ones in question are steel-rule dies that work in combination with some nonmetallic board (wood, cardboard, plastic, etc.). In high production runs the boards have to be replaced frequently because they become damaged by the cutting edges of the dies. There is a solution for this trouble.

Mount a heavy sheet-metal plate on a set of correctly calibrated springs, like a small bolster plate, **Figure 3**. Only empirical tryouts can give the right spring strength. Start the tryouts by calculating the approximate cutting

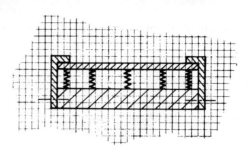

3. The spring-loaded plate "gives" when the die descends, thus escapes damage.

forces involved and select the springs so that the whole set is a little stronger than the calculated cutting forces. Use this spring-loaded plate in place of the board.

Advantages of this solution: uniform, clean, safe cutting action, without danger of damaging the cutting edges of the dies; no need for board replacement.

Punching a bent stamping

The bracket illustrated in the accompanying sketch must be pierced after forming if the hole is to be round and within tolerance limits, **Figure 4**. Besides, the piercing operation must be performed from inside out, because an attempt to do it from outside would certainly produce a cracked die plate. The die designed for this use is built and operates in the following way.

There are no stationary parts; every tool member is movable. There is a guided slide which carries many tool components, **Figure 5**. The punch is supported by a correct backing plate and held in a punch plate. There is also a spring-loaded, movable stripper with an attached internal spring-loaded pad, **Figure 6**. The stripper is aligned and held by four stripper bolts; the stripping action is insured by four compression springs. To load the tool, the slide is pulled out completely, a blank is slipped into the slot in the stripper, and the pad clamps the blank against the punch body. Then, the slide is pushed into the die and the press is tripped.

The top part of the die descends and a plunger enters into the corresponding hole in the punch plate and the slide, making sure that the latter is correctly aligned with the top part of the die. Then the die plate, which is mounted in the top part of the tool, contacts the blank and pushes it and the stripper down against the stationary punch. In this way the piercing operation takes place. When the press ram ascends, the stamping is stripped

4. This workpiece must be bent before it is punched because hole distortion is not permitted.

5. When the die plate assembly descends, it depresses the stripper and forces the workpiece down onto the punch.

6. The stripper has a spring-loaded pad which holds the work in position.

from the punch in the usual way; the slide is pulled out and the finished stamping is removed by hand. The piercing slugs are removed through an escape slot in the die holder and a closed flexible chute is attached to the same.

OSHA requirements are complied with because there is no need for the operator to reach into the die, either for loading or for part removal. Consequently, the die can be protected with a completely surrounding guard. ∎

Reprinted with permission from Tooling & Production, December 1978

Belleville springs in die design

by R Schafer
Tool Engineer
E C Styberg Engineering Co, Inc
Racine, WI

Pressworking of sheet metal often requires spring-loaded blank holders or strippers. These strippers are used in many dies, including compound, progressive, piercing, forming and blanking types.

The force behind the stripper pad is often a collection of die springs produced especially for this purpose. These springs are manufactured to supply medium pressure, medium heavy pressure, heavy pressure and extra-heavy pressure to the pressure pad or stripper.

But there are places where ordinary springs aren't strong enough. For example, when cutting thick or high-strength materials, you may need extra heavy pressure on the stock to prevent rollover. The same can be true for very small cross sections between successive holes. Or possibly the limited space in a die set will not allow placement of enough springs for the stripping pressure required.

In these cases the die designer or metal stamper may choose to use Belleville springs. In some cases it is the only practical pressure source that will meet these requirements.

A Belleville spring is a radially straight conical disc having a rectangular cross section, **Figure 1**.

Loads are applied uniformly around the inner and outer circumference and result in elastic deflection. The respective values of load and deflection are the characteristic of the disc spring. The spring rate corresponding to a single disc may be changed as desired by combining a number of discs in a stack. The following types of stacks are possible, **Figure 2**: A single disc, **Figure 2a**. Two discs stacked in parallel (double load at same deflection), **Figure 2b**. A spring stack with three single springs stacked in series (triple deflection), **Figure 2c**. A spring stack with three sets in series of parallel pairs (double the load and triple the deflection), **Figure 2d**. Springs can be stacked in parallel to meet the required load and stacked in series of parallel stacks to meet deflection requirements.

Application

For an example of the springs in use, consider a 2.36″ OD x 1.201″ ID x 0.1378″-thick spring, shown underlined in the table with **Figure 1**. By deflecting this spring to 75 percent of its free height, we get 4120 lb of force. Now, if we put two springs in parallel, we will get 8240 lb. We normally deflect these springs from 15 to 75 percent of their free height to build a little safety factor in the design. Deflection for 15 percent of 0.0591″ (from the table) is 0.0089″,

| For ordering use mm size | | | Size | | | | | | Force P in lb, deflection f in inch | | | | | | | |
| mm | | | inch | | | | inch | | f=0.25 h | | f=0.50 h | | f=0.75 h | | f=h | |
Da	Di	s	Da	Di	s	h	t	h/s	P	f	P	f	P	f	P	f
56	28.5	1.5	2.20	1.122	.0591	.0787	.1378	1.33	345	.0198	531	.0393	611	.0591	638	.0787
56	28.5	2	2.20	1.122	.0787	.0630	.1417	.800	434	.0157	758	.0314	1014	.0471	1224	.0630
56	28.5	3	2.20	1.122	.1181	.0512	.1693	.433	941	.0128	1795	.0256	2590	.0384	3350	.0512
60	20.5	2	2.36	.807	.0787	.0827	.1614	1.050	529	.0206	869	.0412	1080	.0618	1228	.0827
60	20.5	2.5	2.36	.807	.0984	.0709	.1693	.720	690	.0177	1232	.0354	1672	.0531	2060	.0709
60	20.5	3	2.36	.807	.1181	.0670	.1850	.57	1000	.0168	1851	.0335	2602	.0502	3303	.0670
60	25.5	2.5	2.36	1.004	.0984	.0748	.1732	.760	785	.0187	1380	.0374	1860	.0561	2270	.0748
60	25.5	3	2.36	1.004	.1181	.0651	.1832	.550	1019	.0162	1889	.0324	2670	.0486	3395	.0651
60	30.5	2.5	2.36	1.201	.0984	.0709	.1693	.72	775	.0177	1381	.0355	1875	.0531	2312	.0709
60	30.5	3	2.36	1.201	.1181	.0669	.1850	.567	1158	.0167	2140	.0334	3010	.0501	3814	.0669
60	30.5	3.5	2.36	1.201	.1378	.0591	.1969	.428	1495	.0147	2850	.0294	4120	.0441	5335	.0591
63	31	1.8	2.48	1.22	.0709	.0945	.1654	1.33	543	.0236	842	.0472	974	.0709	1026	.0945
63	31	2.5	2.48	1.22	.0984	.0680	.1673	.700	666	.0172	1195	.0344	1630	.0516	2020	.0689
63	31	3	2.48	1.22	.1181	.0709	.1890	.60	1099	.0177	2011	.0355	2818	.0531	3557	.0709
63	31	3.5	2.48	1.22	.1378	.0551	.1929	.400	1223	.0137	2350	.0274	3420	.0411	4430	.0551
70	25.5	2	2.76	1.004	.0787	.0984	.1771	1.250	540	.0246	850	.0492	1000	.0738	1070	.0984
70	30.5	2.5	2.76	1.201	.0984	.0945	.1929	.960	840	.0236	1420	.0472	1810	.0708	2100	.0945
70	30.5	3	2.76	1.201	.1181	.0827	.2008	.700	1050	.0206	1880	.0412	2570	.0618	3180	.0827
70	35.5	3	2.76	1.398	.1181	.0827	.2008	.700	1130	.0206	2025	.0412	2760	.0618	3420	.0827
70	35.5	4	2.76	1.398	.1575	.0709	.2279	.450	2970	.0177	3740	.0354	5380	.0531	6950	.0709
70	40.5	4	2.76	1.595	.1575	.0630	.2204	.400	1890	.0157	3620	.0315	5250	.0422	6830	.0630
70	40.5	5	2.76	1.595	.1968	.0472	.2441	.240	2600	.0118	5110	.0236	7570	.0354	10000	.0472

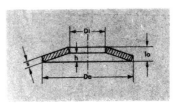

1. *Example of a typical Belleville spring. The table shows a portion of the listing of Schnorr Disc Springs.*

and 75 percent is 0.0443". The difference between these figures is 0.0354" deflection per spring stack. By stacking as many parallel series as required, we can obtain the required deflection.

Belleville springs can be a good pressure source and can be relatively trouble-free if a few suggestions are followed. A typical spring stack is shown in **Figure 3**. Again, we will use the standard 2.36" OD x 1.201" ID x 0.1378" thick x 0.059" free height Belleville spring. By using a 15 percent preload and two springs in parallel, we get a thickness of 0.326".

As explained earlier, we use 15 percent to 75 percent deflection or 0.0354" per spring. By using seven stacks in series we get a total deflection of 0.2478" and 8240 lb pressure per stack.

Belleville springs are made from hardened steel, so the guides and surfaces they are flexed against must also be hard. It is also desirable to contain the stack of springs in one package to elim-

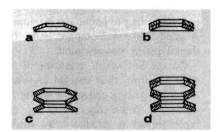

2. *Types of disc stacks. More springs provide extra force or deflection. The Styberg firm makes springs to order if standard springs are not the right size.*

inate a real mess of springs to stack and locate every time the die is taken apart for sharpening or repair.

We take standard 1-3/16"-dia round stock, cut it to length and tap both ends. This bar can be CRS carburized hardened or hardened tool steel. This is bolted to the stripper plate (as shown in **Figure 3**). We use a 1/8"-thick hardened

washer on the bottom of the stack for wear.

On the top of the stack, we use a thicker washer approximately equal to the thickness of the die life in the die. This is done to provide a hardened surface for the springs to flex against. Since the height of the stack is predetermined and does not have a great deal of latitude, we should keep it pretty consistent throughout the life of the die. Therefore, this thick washer on top of the stack is ground thinner, equal to the amount taken off the punches each and every time the die is sharpened.

We bolt a cap on the stack so that, when the stripper is removed for punch sharpening, the entire unit comes off as one package. The stripper is still controlled by the shoulder bolts the same as when any die spring is used. ■

3. *Disc springs are stacked on a steel core bolted to a stripper plate.*

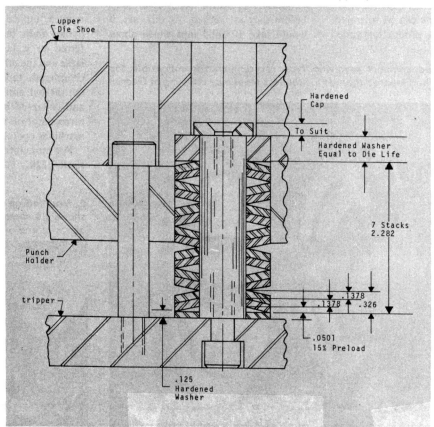

Reprinted with permission from Tooling & Production, January 1972

Stripper bolt restated

There has been some confusion about the Kwik-Strip bolts developed by Dove Die and Stamping Co., and sold by Jergens Inc. Here's a recap of the new stripper bolt's advantages.

As shown in the drawing, the bolts are easy to install and remove. Body drill through the punch holder (1/32" over bolt dia), drill a ¼" hole adjacent to depth slightly below counterbore depth, and then counterbore to desired depth. The only extra operation is drilling the ¼" hole, and this is now made easier by a spotting jig.

The result is easier removal of stripper plates without removing the die. The Kwik-Strip can serve anywhere a standard stripper bolt is specified, according to the manufacturer, and it drastically reduces press downtime for replacement of punches etc. Stripper plate comes out simply by removing socket-head cap screws that attach the plate to the bolts. They can eliminate up to 5 hr of setup time needed to remove and replace dies.

According to Dove spokesmen, it is indeed possible to remove plates safely without removing the die from the press or the punch holder from the press ram. The sketch shows a stripper as it would appear in a plain piercing die (upper half of drawing), and how the bolt is used in a compound die (lower part of drawing).

One man disassembles and removes the stripper using a hex key fitted to a ratchet wrench. He loosens all four lower screws evenly as on the bench, until all spring pressure is relieved. (A properly designed die set allows the bolt to be longer than the throw of the spring.)

To keep springs in their pockets, insert a thin strip of soft rubber between the coils near the end of the spring, extending about ½" on each side beyond the diameter of the spring. The rubber folds against the side walls as you push the spring into its pocket, holding it in place without affecting its operation.

On larger plates, one man loosens all six screws and removes all but two diagonally opposite corner screws. He places wood blocks under the stripper and calls in a helper to lower the plate to the blocks. They slide the plate out from the die on the blocks.

Practical Die Design With Steel-Bonded Titanium Carbide

By John S. Weber
Chromalloy American Corp.

As every Manufacturer aims for longer lasting and better performing dies, also higher quality parts, a great deal depends on two important matters: the proper design of the die and the kind of tooling material used for the die.

Whether it is a progressive, draw, transfer, lamination, powder metal, extrusion or multi-slide die, the best performing die will always be the one designed by the practical men with toolroom and pressroom experience.

It is well known that the cost of each die has to be estimated and has to fit into a "financial budget", therefore corner and cost-cutting is very customary. In many cases the above mentioned "savings" led to scraping of poor or non-performing dies, where stations have been eliminated, too much work crowded into one operation, insufficient flexibility in a design, in case of unexpected problems with variations of metal hardness or metal thickness.

A very popular slogan still persists: "Not enough time to build a good performing die, but plenty of time for debugging or rebuilding it".

It is the purpose of this paper to avoid most of the above mentioned shortcomings and designing good performing, trouble-free dies, also the use of better performing, longer lasting tooling materials to increase die-life on cut edges, draw radii, forms on bending dies also wear and tear on other tool and die components. Steel bonded titanium carbides are proven, better performing tooling materials.

STEEL-BONDED TITANIUM CARBIDES

Steel-bonded titanium carbides are powder metal products of sintered ferrous alloys, which contain a high percentage of titanium carbides. The composite metallurgical structure consists of very hard particles of titanium carbide embedded in a heat-treatable matrix or binder. When the matrix is in the annealed or soft state, the composite can be machined; but once hardened by conventional heat treatment, it is extremely hard and wear resistant. The round and oval shapes, (86-90 RC) hard, slippery titanium carbides provide the wear resistance and also have favorable friction characteristics. The titanium carbide grains used in the steel-bonded carbides have a hardness of 3200 Vickers, which is considerably higher than the hardness of the individual tungsten carbide grains. (2400 Vickers).

48

Comparison of Micro-structure
between Titanium Carbide and WC

Figure 1. In steel-bonded titanium carbides, rounded and smooth titanium carbide particles, about .0002-.0003 in size,
are embedded in an alloy steel matrix.
In the heat treatment, only the matrix
goes through the hardening transition,
while the hardness of titanium particles
are unaffected.

Titanium Carbide
Grade CM, 1000 X

Figure 1

Tungsten Carbide
12% Co-WC 88%,
1500X

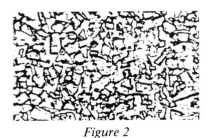

Figure 2

Figure 2. In the tungsten carbides (WC),
sharp-edge, angular tungsten carbide particles are embedded in a cobalt binding
agent. The hardness of the WC composite
depends on the percentage of tungsten carbide and cobalt; and once sintered, this
hardness cannot be changed.

PROCESSING OF STEEL-BONDED TITANIUM CARBIDE

Machining by Chip Removal:

Annealed titanium carbide, as it comes to the industry at a 40-43 Rc hardness, is
easily machined with conventional tool-room equipment and has the advantage that it
can be machined with highspeed steel cutting tools. WC cutting tools can also be
used, though this is not a "must", regardless of the high hardness of the titanium
carbide particles. It is necessary to follow certain procedures which differ somewhat
from those employed on alloy steels (Figure 3).

```
STEEL-BONDED TITANIUM CARBIDE MACHINING RULES

1.  USE SLOW SPEED--30 sfm MAX- (10. M/MIN.)
2.  TOOL MUST BE DRY - USE NO COOLANT OR LUBRICANT
3.  TAKE HEAVY CUT - .003 IN. MIN. DEPTH- (.012 M/M)
```

Figure 3

Grinding of Steel-bonded Titanium Carbide

In contrast to WC, which requires diamond grinding wheels for effective stock removal
and finishing, steel-bonded titanium carbides are ground with aluminum oxide wheels.
While identical types of wheels are employed for both conditions, annealed and hard,
the stock removal rate in the annealed state is much greater and wheel wear is substantially lower than grinding hard steel-bonded titanium carbide.

The performance of aluminum oxide wheels can be increased by crushing diagonal slots into the face of the wheel, using a hack-saw on slow strokes. Less wheel wear and a cooler grinding process are the results, also no heat checks will occur in grinding hard metal.

Intricate shaped components, forming, bending tools or form-rolls can be ground by the use of a dressing attachment such as a "Diaform" fixture. A 10:1 scale templet of the desired contour is placed on this attachment, which can be mounted on the end of any conventional surface grinder table. With a dressed aluminum oxide wheel by plunge grinding into annealed carbide blanks, components can be fabricated at the rate of making steel tools. Due to high stability of steel-bonded titanium carbide in heat treatment, most tools can be finished soft and subsequently hardened.

CONVENTIONAL EDM - MACHINING STEEL-BONDED TITANIUM CARBIDE

In the EDM process, machinable carbides have the advantage that forms, contours, and holes can be pre-machined by sawing, milling, or drilling close to finished size, leaving very little metal to be removed by EDM-machining; consequently, speeding up the toolmaking process machinable carbides lends itself well to the use of graphite based-copper impregnated electrode materials, which are easy to grind, do not wear out from-shaped or regular wheels, and have excellent wear ability in the EDM process.

Titanium carbide should be EDM machined in the annealed condition, taking advantage of its high stability in heat treatment, size change is .0002 per inch. Another reason to EDM machine titanium carbide while soft is, the avoidance of a martensitic, re-solidified, brittle layer on the surface of the tool. While the temperature for EDM machining metal varies from about 6000°F to 8500°F, depending on the setting of the EDM machine and the metal to be machined, the process can be called "burning out metal".

After finish EDM machining of the annealed steel-bonded carbide tool, martensitic re-solidified layer will be present. However, as the tool is being heat-treated from 1950-1975°F, this thin layer will be fully annealed; and in the quenching process, it will be hardened to the same degree as the base material, resulting in a uniform structure. When EDM machining hardened carbide- CM or tool steel, the high tempera-ture involved will gradually transfer deep into the structure of the tool, annealing the binder, while the presence of dielextric fluid (for cooling and flushing purposes also for better conductivity) will produce a quenching action on the surface of the tool resulting in a fractured, martensitic, resolidified layer.

WIRE EDM MACHINING FERRO-TIC® CM

The most modern and efficient way of metal processing, is the fabrication of components by the Wire EDM technique. In contrast to conventional EDM machining, where the pre-formed or shaped electrode is plunged into the metal, and the cavity takes the shape of the electrode, in Wire EDM machining, solid hardened metal can be cut with a travel-ing thin wire which is guided from a pattern or tape by a electronic computer system. The contact area of the thin wire generates less heat to remove metal, consequently a brittle hard layer of re-solidified metal is hardly present. On smaller sections an additional tempering is not necessary. Very accurate tool components with tolerances of ± .0002 can be easily fabricated, no afterwork is needed. Type of wire used for EDM machining is a .004-.009 soft copper wire, produced and distributed by Electro-tools Inc., Broadview, Il.

Basically all wire EDM machines work by a similar system and are alike. According to a fairly large user of FERRO-TIC is nearly as fast as that for hardened D-2 tool steel and twice as fast as for cutting tungsten carbide. On die sections, to cut thick metals, the OD of the wire can be matched to the corresponding die clearance and both components, the punch and die insert can be made in the same set up, having the advantage of uniform die clearance all around the cutting edges. (Figure 4).

Wire EDM Machine
FERRO-TIC Components
Figure 4

This very efficient way of making die components by the Wire EDM process finds more and more acceptance and lends itself best to fabricate FERRO-TIC tools.

HEAT TREATMENT OF STEEL BONDED TITANIUM CARBIDE TOOLS AND DIE COMPONENTS

Hardening of titanium carbide CM tools and components is accomplished by heating them to 1975°F, in a vacuum furnace and then quenching with nitrogen or other inert gas. Tic-carbide grade CM must be tempered at 975°F, for one hour, air cooled to room temperature, retempered at 950°F, and air cooled again. Hardness: 66-68 Rc. depending on the application.

Finished tools could be hardened in a protective atmosphere to prevent decarburization, soaked at 1950-1975°F, then oil quenched. A .003 thick foil of stainless steel can be used for protection, also to minimize the quenching thermal shock. One should make an air-tight bag or container out of it, double crimp the edges to seal in the components. Quench in oil while in the bag. Do not remove the component from the bag during quenching. Temper at 975°F, for one hour, retemper at 950°F as above.

DESIGN CONSIDERATIONS

Several important facts favor the choice of sectionalized designs for punches, die inserts, and other tooling components. For one, less of the costly, high wear resistant material needs to be used. For another, the reduced fabrication and high precision tolerance can by achieved with relatively small sections; and heat treatment is far simpler. In addition to these time and cost-saving factors, one should consider that small die sections, when properly press-fitted into the die plate cavities, are subject to lower stresses than could be in solid die plates. (Figure 5).

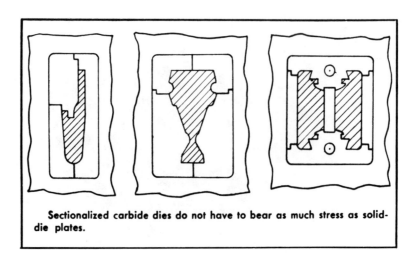

Sectionalized carbide dies do not have to bear as much stress as solid-die plates.

Figure 5

Designing Stamping Dies

Stamping, forming, and draw die work make up the majority of applications for steel-bonded carbide in the metal-working field. The need for rigid, precision 4-post die sets has been pointed out. Hardened and precision ground bushing and pins are preferred over ball bearing stamping plants, solid TIC guide bushings and pins are on trial for applications where up to one million hits are made in a 24 hour period, on a very short stroke. Many titanium carbide equipped progressive dies provide the same material for pilots and pilot bushings. By far the most important aspects of optimized die design with steel-bonded carbides are stripper design, sectionalizing of punches and dies, punch-to-die-clearance, and reliable methods for slug elimination.

Stripper Design

In order to achieve optimum performance in punching or stamping work, it is imperative to use spring-loaded pressure pads. Figure 6 shows a typical die design for a blanking operation which incorporates a well designed pressure pad; in this case, the panel constitutes the desired product, and the slug is scrapped. A modified design where the pressure pad is built into the die cavity is, of course, indicated when the panel is scrap, and the blanked-through part is the finished product. Why do we put such emphasis on the spring-loaded pressure pad in preference to the customary, less-expensive, positive stripper? In answer to this question, it is best to examine the forces acting on the tools and the metal during the punching action, and to account for the influence of stripper design on metal deformation.

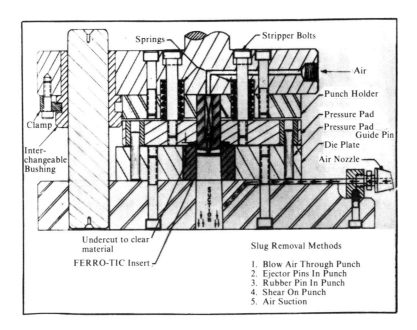

Typical Die Design
Figure 6

Punching with a Positive Stripper

This is more pronounced when a large gap is provided under the positive stripper in excess of stock thickness. Yet, if one tries to reduce the gap in order to minimize the deformation, minor variations of stock thickness may cause jamming of the feed. The softer the punched metal, the more deformation is likely to take place. (Figure 7-a).

The problems associated with positive strippers become even more apparent when one examines the conditions existing at the initiation of the cut. Stress concentrations are apparent both at the sharp corners of the punch and the die, as indicated by arrows. These stresses increase as the punch-to-die clearance decreases. (Figure 7-b).

When the break-through occurs, the stresses are released, resulting into plastic deformation, which causes a contraction of the panel around the punch. Now, the panel grips the punch tightly on a circumferential region above the cutting edge, resulting in erosion and wear during withdrawal. (Figure 7-c).

Punching with a Spring-Loaded Pressure Pad

In contrast to the above, a different stress pattern comes into existence when deformation and bulging of the panel is prevented by the hold down pressure of a well designed, sturdy, pressure pad. (Figure 7-d).

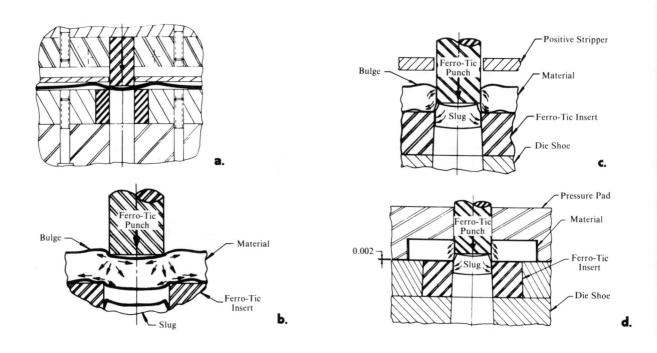

Figure 7

Here, roll-over of the metal across the cutting edges is reduced and lower stresses result in the punched panel; this lessens plastic deformation, contraction and wear during punch withdrawal. Thus, the added die construction cost of about 15% for the spring-loaded pressure pad is well justified in most cases, since it yields flat panels, reduced wear and trouble-free operations.

Die Design vs. Die Performance

In addition to punch and die wear, other factors of die performance are influenced by the choice of stripper design, and punch-to-die clearance. (See Figure 7-a through 7-d).

It is interesting to note that the most desirable combination consists of a pressure pad in connection with a 7-10% clearance of metal thickness per side between punch and die. In this case, only the slug pulling characteristic is below par, and must be corrected by adequate auxiliary design, such as ejector pins built into the punches, shear on the punches, or a suitable vacuum suction system. These aids for overcoming slug pulling are shown in Figure 6.

DESIGN CONSIDERATION FOR DRAW DIES

Similar to conventional carbides, the physical properties of steel-bonded carbides are characterized by a high compressive strength and relatively low tensile strength with negligible elongation. This imposes the need for supporting the carbide draw rings in such a way that high precompressive stresses are set up. Actually, the initial compressive stress should be equal or greater than the hoop stress generated in the draw ring as a result of the drawing action. A good method for precompressing draw inserts is illustrated in Figure 8.

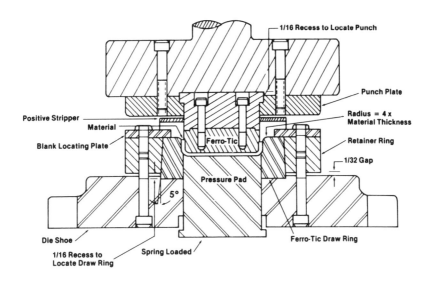

Conventional FERRO-TIC Draw Die
(For Shallow Draws)
Figure 8

Note, how a 5° taper on the outside diameter of the carbide draw ring is nested securely in a correspondingly tapered pocket of a high strength retainer ring; thus, all
radial draw forces resulting in hoop stresses are absorbed by the retainer ring.

Note also, the excellent alignment provided by rabbits on punch base and draw ring
providing concentricity for precision draws: dowels and other alignment devices
are thus eliminated, resulting in lower die cost.

Due to heat generation during the draw action for all draw dies and inserts, also
draw punches, Grade CM is recommended. CM grade is heat resistant up to 1,000°F
without annealing or loss of strength or hardness.

One should also consider in re-working or servicing of CM dies, do to the above mentioned facts, there is less chance of heat-checking or annealing the die components.

Compound Blanking and Draw Dies

Greater skill and experience are needed for designing successful compound blanking
and draw dies. This type of compound die is becoming more popular for many long-
run jobs, since the production of a finished cup in a single stroke sharply reduces
labor and equipment cost.

A typical compound blanking and draw die (Figure 9) shows a proven design for steel-
bonded carbide components in the draw plug, and the compounded cutting edge with the
internal draw radius. The latter, is the critical component since its design is determined by the depth of the draw. The shallower the draw, the thinner the cross
section of the draw ring. As a general rule, the heavier the gage of the drawn cup,
the deeper a draw is necessary in order to reduce the hoop stresses in the unsupported
draw ring to safe limits. For the best possible anti-galling properties, a working
surface is polished to expose the hard titanium carbide grains in slight relief above
the matrix background; and these alone have actual contact with the worked-on metals.

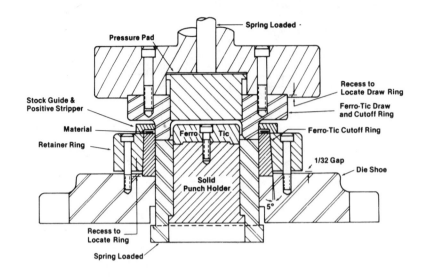

Compound FERRO-TIC Blanking and Draw Die
Figure 9

Double-Step Deep Drawing

A very uncommon way to make shells in one stroke is the double step draw die shown in Figure 10. The design of the building of such a die is more complex than a conventional die, but it saves in a long run on additional operations and also produces a higher quality part. Such dies are in operation to manufacture aerosol cans, beer and beverage cans and also similar containers in the cosmetic and chemical field.

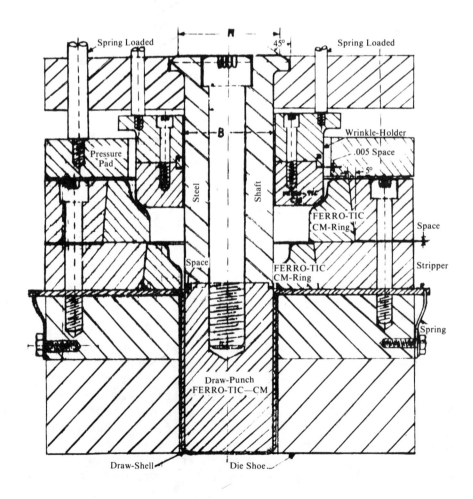

Double-Step Deep Draw Die
Figure 10

This die consists out of 2 draw-rings backed-up by 2 semi-hard retainers to absorb the hoop-stresses. The assembling and functioning of these rings must be studied carefully to prevent them from breaking in production. The upper retainer ring with a 5° taper exerts pressure on to the upper FERRO-TIC draw-ring which rests on top of the lower retainer ring, with his 5 taper exerting pressure on to the lower FERRO-TIC draw-ring. Using this system all working rings are under constant pressure during the drawing action.

Note also a pressure pad with synchronized timing to the wrinkle-holder. This way a smooth flow of metal is assured, resulting in a wrinkle-free shell.

Perforating-Extruding-Burnishing

As pointed out during the introduction about the aim to fabricate components the most economical way, possibly a multi operation in one stroke of the press. In recent years a very efficient method has been developed. To combine 3 operations in one stroke to make high quality extrusion is shown in Figure 11. It is well known that heavy gage metals can be perforated without a die or bushing in the die-plate. A perforator made out of steel bonded titanium carbide combined with an extrusion radius that ends in a cylinderic area about 3/32" long, then undercut to accomodate a radius beyond the straight part.

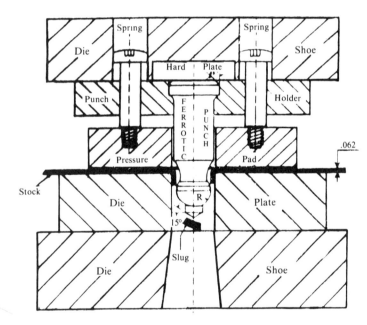

Perforating—Extruding and Burnishing Die
Figure 11

In operation the pressure pad in holding down the metal, while the 15° taper on the tip of the perforator starts penetrating the metal as the extrusion action starts the slug will fall off. Do to the excellent gliding properties of the titanium carbide a uniform flow of the metal takes place, resulting in a smooth and even extrusion. Pushing the punch below the undercut to let the extrusion settle and contract slightly, on the upstock the radius on the undercut will burnish the extrusion, producing a very precise hole.

Fabricating formed or bent metal parts with titanium carbide tool components have the advantage of better flow of metal over bending radii due to the built-in lubricity in titanium. No scoring or galling of the working surface on the punch or insert will occur. Due to the very high compressive strength of titanium, on thick metals it will perform particularly well. Because titanium has greater elasticity than WC highly stressed bending or forming tools will deflect and transmit the load to the back-up members to a greater degree and will avoid breakage. When designing, forming, or bending tools with carbide, one should take into consideration the avoidance of shoulders or heads on punches for ease of fabrication and less cost of carbide; but more important is the avoidance of stress concentrating on corners, on such components. Pressfit or clamp bending or forming punches into a semi-hard punch holder and secure them from pulling out with a screw from the top or a heel. If heads or shoulders on forming or bending punches are unavoidable, a 45° chamfer should be put on top of the shoulder to prevent overhang and deflection of the shoulder, and more evenly distribute the stresses. (Figure 12 - D-1 = D-2).

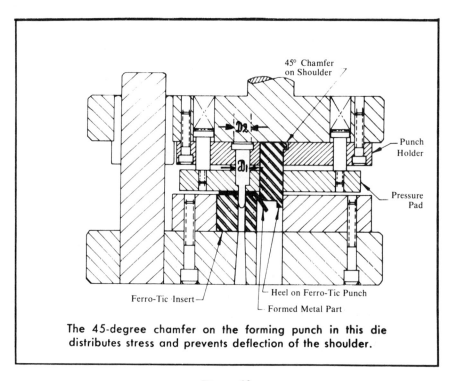

The 45-degree chamfer on the forming punch in this die distributes stress and prevents deflection of the shoulder.

Figure 12

Equally important is to put a heel on the tip of the bending punch for support or back-up before the forming or bending action occurs. In many multiple bending or forming stage dies, such as hinge dies, forming and bending punches and inserts can be tried while the titanium carbide is still annealed. After achieving the proper form or shape, the components are hardened for high performance.

Conclusion

General purpose, steel-bonded carbides are metallurgically suited for cutting, forming and draw work. There are about twelve other grades of FERRO-TIC available, each one with its own chemical composition and physical properties that are unobtainable with either tool steels or conventional carbides. They can be heat, corrosion, erosion, as well as wear resistant.

The Major Tooling Grades are FERRO-TIC "CM" and FERRO-TIC "C"

A very wide field of applications can be covered with FERRO-TIC "CM" due to its higher temper resistance and excellent compressive strength. Cutting, forming, bending tools, draw dies, and hotworking applications are some proven examples. It is replacing the original FERRO-TIC "C" in many of these uses. FERRO-TIC "C" is now mainly recommended for applications such as gages, wear plates, boring bars, grinding spindles, etc.

Good design, fabrication and heat treatment are necessary to obtain high performance with FERRO-TIC dies. These include spring-loaded pressure pads, adequate punch-to-die clearance, sectionalized punch and die inserts, effective slug elimination, and the use of rigid precision die sets. Building on the vast experience available with conventional tool steel dies, these special considerations are necessary in order to achieve with FERRO-TIC the typical 10:1 improvement.

There are many applications in plastics fabrication where Grade CM or other FERRO-TIC Grades are used that might be more corrosion or heat resistant.

FERRO-TIC has been used successfully for extrusion feed screws and for nozzles, for sprue bushings, pressure chambers and pistons. Special grades resist chloride attack and others are used for chopper blades, polyethylene extrusion dies and punches and dies for circuit boards or plastic credit cards. Stainless grades are now used as expander nozzles and for rolls in producing textured fibers.

The FERRO-TIC steel-bonded carbides have proven ability to resist the most severe erosion and provide long life for any component part that gets involved in the volume production of plastics or plastic parts. It is readily available in many stock sizes and can easily be fabricated into the most complex parts.

Reprinted from Manufacturing Engineering, June 1976

Selecting Die Materials for Sheet Metal

Important factors to be considered in selecting materials for blanking, drawing, trimming, flanging, and hemming dies

VICTOR A. KORTESOJA, *Chief Metallurgist*
Metal Stamping Div., Ford Motor Co.

MANY FACTORS affect the choice of die materials for blanking, forming, and trimming sheet metal in the production of automotive components. Two general factors that have been, and sometimes still are, used in choosing die materials are called "production volume" and "political" factors. Of the two, production volume — both hourly and yearly — is most important.

Production Requirements. Hourly production rates at Ford Motor Co. range from 400 to 900 stampings. The materials selected for draw dies must be able to meet these production rates with a minimum of downtime resulting from metal pickup and consequent scoring of the parts.

Formerly, the total production volume (overall life) expected from a draw die was considered only in making certain inner car parts such as wheel housings, since the design of such parts are not changed each model year. The one exception to this is all dies for trucks, where die material choices are made for a five-year use requirement. Now, however, as the frequency of car model changes is decreasing and the required life for die usage is increasing, material choices are becoming more critical for all outer panel draw dies.

There are many materials that can be used for each type of die. Consideration of the service and maintenance requirements, however, can result in an optimum choice for each application. Some of the materials being used by Ford for various dies are listed in TABLE 1.

Metal pickup on the dies and subsequent galling of production parts is the result of frictional heat developed between the die and workpiece. Pickup can be eliminated by a combination of proper choice of a die material that will not soften under the frictional heat encountered, and/or the application of a good drawing lubricant.

Political Considerations. So-called "political influences" in material selection come from diemakers, die repairmen, and production management. Diemakers want materials that are easy to machine and finish. When mistakes are made, they want a material that can be readily welded. Engineering design changes that require die modifications during construction, or even after the dies have been placed in production, are all too frequent. Additional changes are made to most dies during tryout.

It is impossible to choose die materials that will satisfy all factions. Production management all too often favors easy and quick repairability, forgetting that dies made from such materials will not usually produce 400 to 900 parts per hour week after week. Total productivity should be the most important consideration in die material selection.

Blanking Dies. Cutting edges of blanking dies are subject to impact loads. As the thickness and strength of the steels being blanked increase, these loads increase and chipping of the cutting edges is a common problem, especially on corners and projections. As a result, toughness and fatigue resistance are both desirable characteristics for blanking die steels. Depth of hardening must also be considered since the number of cutting edge sharpenings possible is controlled by the depth of usable hardness.

"Hot" or "cold" blank development of automotive blanking dies can affect the choice of die steel. With hot development, the blank contour is developed before the die is made, and less weldable die steels may be used if desired. With cold development, blank contours are estimated, and the blanking dies built accordingly. This results in the need for welding and grinding the blanking steels to obtain the needed final contours, which limits the choice of die steels to easily welded grades.

At Ford's Metal Stamping Div., production steel up to 0.061-inch (1.55-mm) thick is considered thin gage material. Until recently, Type W110 water hardening tool steel was most commonly used for blanking and trimming such steels because it was easily welded and readily available. After extensive testing on numerous dies, a change has been made to SAE 1060 steel, furnace heated and time quenched to a hardness of R_c 58-60. Reasons for this change included a deeper hardened case that permits more regrinds, and greater toughness for the cutting edges, while maintaining the same weldability as W110 tool steel.

SAE 160 is also used for dies to blank steels up to 0.090-inch (2.29-mm) thick. For blanking thicker steels, as well as high-strength low-alloy (HSLA) steels, S7 shock resisting tool steel is used. Type S7 tool steel has performed exceptionally well in blanking HSLA steels used in automotive bumper reinforcements, *Figure 1*, with about one-half million parts being blanked between grinds.

Draw Dies. The most widely used die material for drawing automotive body components from sheet steel is a chromium-molybdenum alloyed cast iron. As-cast Brinell hardness of these dies is maintained between 201 and 235 for good machinability. Also, the combined carbon is controlled to a

◄ *1. BLANKING bumper reinforcement from HSLA steel on a 2000-ton press.*

minimum of 0.75%, and a pearlitic matrix structure is specified. The result of these controls is a minimum flame hardening response of R$_C$ 60.

After a good panel has been drawn on such a die, reverse surfaces in the lower die, the draw edge and bead groove area, and the blankholder rings should be flame hardened. Character lines on the punch should also be hardened. Tests conducted on a fender draw punch using full hardening coverage resulted in a 50% reduction in slug marking.

Although properly flame hardened alloy iron works well for most draw dies, inserts of high carbon, high chromium tool steels such as Types D2, D5, or D7 are often used on deep draws and/or when thicker metal is being formed. For example, inserts made of both Types D2 and D5 are used in draw dies for forming body pillars and bumpers, and they help to prevent metal pickup and scoring.

Trim Dies. Automotive trim dies are usually composite sections, with the cutting portions made of tool steels and the bases from a low carbon steel such as SAE 1020. Weldability of the tool steel cutting portion is an important factor in material selection because the trim lines on drawn parts are developed after the dies are assembled, necessitating considerable welding and grinding. Many trim dies are placed in service with completely welded edges. Proper choice of the welding electrodes used on the cutting edges is also important because the edges must have a good combination of toughness and wear resistance.

Type W110 water hardening tool steel has long been used for the cutting edges of automotive sheet metal trim dies. Recently, however, a change has been made at Ford to SAE 1060 heat treated, water-oil quenched, and tempered to a hardness of R$_C$ 58-60. This change was made to provide a deeper hardened case, double the toughness, equal weldability, and lower cost. On composite trim dies for bumpers, cutting edges of Types S1 and S5 shock resisting tool steels are used because they offer higher toughness and minimize edge chipping.

Flanging Dies. At one time, flanging dies were the most troublesome at Ford's Stamping Div. Type W110 tool steel was being used exclusively for such dies, and considerable metal pickup and scoring problems were interrupting production. Investigations usually showed that the die steels were soft, caused by the die makers grinding off the hardened case during die tryout. In one case, 1/16 inch (1.6 mm) was ground from the working surface of the flanging steel, effectively removing the usable hardened case.

These problems have now been minimized by using three different tool steels for flanging (wiping) dies. Type O6 oil hardening, cold work tool steel is used for 0.023 to 0.075-inch (0.58 to 1.91-mm) thick steel parts with straight flanges up to 1-inch (25.4-mm) wide, *Figure 2.* Type D7 tool steel is used for parts in the same material thickness range, but having curved flanges, flanges over 1-inch (25.4-mm) wide, or folds occurring at the ends of character lines. For flanging steel parts having a thickness over 0.075 inch (1.71 mm), as well as those made from HSLA steels, Type T15 tungsten type high-speed tool steel is used for the dies.

Type T15 tool steel is not a favorite with diemakers, but its high heat and wear resistance provides optimum results for flanging providing breakage does not occur. In a closely controlled test, the three tool steels being used for flanging dies gave the results shown in TABLE 2. All the die steels were at optimum hardness at the beginning of

2. FLANGING die is made from Type O6 oil hardening, cold work tool steel.

the test, and the results correlate closely with the resistance of each material to softening under the frictional heat developed during flanging.

Hemming Dies. Automobile hoods, deck lids, and doors consist of an outer and inner panel that are hemmed and spot-welded together at the edges. The process consists of first flanging the edges of the outer panels inward 90 degrees, placing the inner panels in position, bending the flanges 45 degrees, and then finish hemming by flattening the flanges against the edges of the inner panels.

Both the 45-degree and finish hemming dies are subject to wear, and the finish die is also subjected to some impact. While wear resistance is an important factor in material selection, the need for frequent changes and adjustments of the die steels has made easy weldability more important. Types A2 and D2 tool steels were tried for these dies, but W110 is now being used with no production problems. ∎

TABLE 1. DIE MATERIALS USED FOR VARIOUS APPLICATIONS

Application	Part Produced	Die Material	Die Hardness R$_c$
Blanking Die Steels	Up to 0.090-inch (2.29-mm) thick.	SAE 1060.	58-60
	Over 0.090-inch (2.29-mm) thick, and all HSLA steels.	Type S7 tool steel.	58-60
Draw Dies	For most parts.	Chromium-molybdenum alloy cast iron.	60 (Flame hardened)
	Deeper drawn parts, and/or thicker metal.	Same cast iron with Types D2, D5, or D7 tool steel inserts.	60-65
Trim Dies	All parts except bumpers.	Composite sections: SAE 1020 base and SAE 1060 cutting edges.	58-60
	Bumpers.	Same base with Types S1 and S5 tool steel cutting edges.	55-60
Flanging Dies	From 0.023 to 0.075-inch (0.58 to 1.91-mm) thick, with straight flanges up to 1-inch (25.4-mm) wide.	Type O6 tool steel.	59-60
	Parts with same thickness range, but with curved flanges, flanges over 1-inch (25.4-mm) wide, or folds at ends of character lines.	Type D7 tool steel.	64-66
	All parts over 0.075-inch (1.71-mm) thick, and those made from HSLA steels.	Type T15 tool steel.	64-66
Hemming Dies	All parts.	Type W110 tool steel.	60-63

TABLE 2. TEST RESULTS WITH VARIOUS TOOL STEELS USED FOR FLANGING DIES

Tool Steel Used For Flanging Die, Type	Number of Parts Flanged Before Metal Pickup
W110	9-55
O6	69
D2	75
D7	140
T15	510-1560

Reprinted with permission from Tooling & Production, June 1972

1. Custom-formulated urethane die in giant Pacific straightside press forms top for Coleman jugs.

Urethane draws, forms, rolls

WELL KNOWN for its line of gasoline lanterns, the Coleman Co. of Wichita, Kansas, also makes many other products for the sportsman and camper: stoves, heaters, water jugs, tents, trailers—even sleeping bags and cooking fuels.

Variety in sizes, colors and models adds to the scope of product proliferation, and it's not a surprise that tooling is particularly important to cutting production costs. The company's engineers continuously search for methods to increase tool life and improve the flexibility of a tool—while maintaining high standards.

Use of custom-formulated urethane frequently enables Coleman to achieve these goals at nominal cost and downtime. The urethane, called ElastaCast and made by Acushnet Co., is formulated to precise hardness and elongation and has high resistance to abrasion and cuts.

One forming job using the material involves water jugs (Figure 1). These must come from the line in one-, two-,

and three-gallon sizes, and a 500-ton Hydropress press uses flat stock, CR 22 gage steel, to form the tops. A urethane male punch works against a steel die, and controlled pressure from the press avoids wrinkling of the sheet and secures fine convolutions. Changes in the thickness of the flat sheet are accommodated automatically by the urethane punch. Some jugs use up to 0.035″ sheet.

Figure 2 shows a design advantage resulting from the use of the elastomeric forming punch for tapered configurations. Pressure transmitted by the draw press causes the urethane to fill the steel female die. Consequently, tapered or dished shapes, such as jug tops, can be formed without wrinkling, and the thickness of the formed part can be held uniform throughout. Runs of 100,000 pieces per urethane punch are routine.

Design flexibility of a different nature is achieved when forming shrouds for catalytic heaters and hoods for a small camp stove using the urethane.

Here, the elastomer is in the form of a roll coating about 1½″ thick. Coleman tool engineers designed the two-roll forming machine (Figure 3). One roll is adjustable in compression, forcing the sheet against the urethane coating on the second roll. It displaces urethane in proportion to the compression, and the metal rolls into circular form with diameter dependent on the compression. The setup makes shrouds and hoods from 4″ to 14″ dia.

Still another plastic application is in forming thin copper-colored anodized aluminum trim used around the door of a portable cooler. One piece is 5 ft long, bent to fit around three sides of the cooler door. The second piece, about 2½ ft long, snaps into place along the fourth side.

A 100-ton press forms the highly finished trim to a slightly negative taper. Engineers put a slightly softer urethane core in the tooling pad and added a relatively thin urethane wear pad to get the necessary detail and to avoid marring the finish. ■

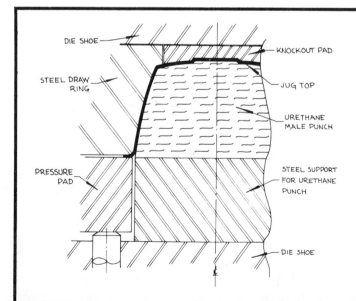

2. Die-design details. One setup handles several material thicknesses.

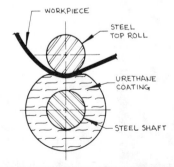

3. Roll former with 1½″ thick roll coating. Adjusted pressure between rolls determines the final workpiece diameter.

Reprinted from Sheet Metal Industries, July 1977

COPPER TECHNOLOGY

Aluminium bronze in forming dies

by L Ashton (Ampco Metal Ltd)

The advantages claimed for the use of aluminium bronze as a material from which, for example, press tools are manufactured, include the production of components with a superior surface finish and in materials which, in many cases, are 'difficult' to deep draw in steel dies. Typically, galling can be eliminated when drawing stainless steel. A further claimed advantage is the reduction of finishing costs achieved. The tool material has some limitations which are given in the article.

Today, as never before, there is a demand on manufacturing industry for finished articles or composite parts formed from a variety of sheet metals. Properly controlled and using the best possible die materials, manufacturers are able to reduce costs and achieve increased production combined with a better product. With the expansion and development of this vital stamping industry it has become increasingly important for very careful consideration to be given to the use of the correct die materials fully to achieve the advantages of formed and drawn parts.

To achieve the ultimate in production efficiency die materials should:

Have low coefficient of friction – for smoother draws and high heat transfer.

Not cause galling, scratching or pick-

Ampco 25 punch and die for the production of stainless steel caps. Note the maintenance of superior surface finish after the manufacture of 120 000 components with these tools.

up – to reduce polishing and other finishing operations.

Prevent pinching or tearing – thus reducing blank scrap.

Be non-magnetic so as not to attract metal particles which cause galling and scratching.

Not require heat treatment, in order to

These items of aluminium kitchenware were pressed in Ampco dies. The superior finish obtained on the pressings greatly reduced the amount of polishing required.

L'emploi du bronze d'aluminium dans les matrices d'emboutissage. L. H. Ashton

Aluminiumbronze in Presswerkzeugen von L. H.A shton

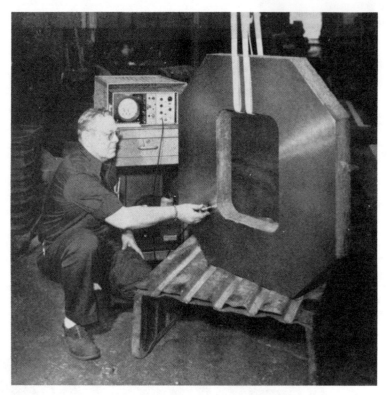

Ultrasonic checking of a cast Ampco 25 die plate for the production of stainless steel sinks.

eliminate extra machining due to warping.

Have the maximum possible life – for less frequent dressings.

Ampco Metal Ltd produce a patented copper-based alloy which, it is claimed, fully meets these important criteria; this alloy is part of a specialized range called Ampco Diebronzes, *viz*, Ampco 25. This alloy has proved outstanding in this field, being a hard aluminium bronze which is produced by a proprietary alloying process to obtain a claimed to be, unique metal structure. It meets all the above requirements, but is particularly outstanding in its ability to eliminate galling of the steel blank on the dies. As a result it is not uncommon for buffing and finishing costs to be reduced from between 50 per cent and 75 per cent.

The basic principle involved is that Ampco 25 is a hard, strong, wear-resistant bearing metal with qualities enabling the sliding action of a dissimilar metal over its surface to cause less friction and wear. Galling, scratching, loading and pinching are eliminated, leading to longer runs without redressing. Die life is increased and down time is minimized. The composition range and mechanical properties are shown in Table 1.

The characteristics mentioned above are critically important when forming or drawing stainless steel. Ampco 25 dies are used for tools working this material and for pickled steel, zinc, silver, lead, Inconel and Monel metal. The Ampco alloy is also used for the forming, bending and reduction of tubes in these metals.

Industries using Ampco 25 dies
Stainless-steel beer-barrel manufacturers utilize Ampco 25 because of the importance of eliminating all scratching and pickup and some prominent stainless-steel cooking-utensil manufacturers report that their products require only a fraction of normal finishing operations when made on Ampco 25 dies.

There is a long list of items which have been successfully manufactured in dies of this material, for example:

Automotive hub caps.
Headlights
Trims
Home-appliance parts

Dairy containers
Window frames
Sinks
Switch boxes

In general, the alloy finds most frequent application in the production of parts where the surface must be free from scratches, and where seizure would cause inadequate die life.

Its use is not recommended for drawing copper, brass, bronze, or unpickled steel, nor will it serve for forging, blanking and pinch draw dies.

Available forms
Ampco 25 can be sand cast close to size from simple wood patterns, or rings can be centrifugally cast for round shapes. It is also available, from stock, in bar up to 15in diameter in many extruded rectangular sizes, and as centrifugally cast die rings.

For short runs and for large components, where a solid bronze die would be uneconomical, the radius of a cast-iron or mild-steel die can be weld-overlaid with Ampcotrode 300 welding rod, which corresponds fully to Ampco 25 bronze. This eliminates galling and scratching of drawn material at the point of greatest deformation.

Accidental damage to an Ampco 25 solid die can be repair welded using Ampcotrode 300 rods.

Die design
Actual die design can only be covered in a general way due to the many factors involved, such as type of press, *ie* hydraulic, mechanical, fast or slow acting, ram pressures, hold-down pressures, shallow or deep draw, gauge of material, ultimate finish required, finish of raw stock, whether a combined blanking and forming operation, lubricant used, and quantity of finished pressings required.

With these factors in mind, dies can be

Bottom die of an Ampco bronze die set for the production of mild steel suspension components.

constructed by inserting rings or narrow strips in retainers of cast iron or mild steel so that the drawn metal is worked over an Ampco 25 surface. However, large-volume producers are using full rings or rectangular blocks slightly larger than the blank, for long-run jobs. This eliminates all possibility of scratching the blank on the die side. They are also making pressure pads from Ampco 25, which eliminates difficulty in mounting, as both pieces are cast thick enough to be self-supporting. This precludes the need for a retainer involving extra weight and machining to produce a complete die.

Segmental dies have the advantage of apparent lower initial cost, but ultimately the cost is generally higher, due to creasing at insert joints in the draw radius. It is also generally necessary to have a fairly large radius, which tends to make pressure-pad pressures high. Due to differences in the coefficient of friction between Ampco 25 and steel (or cast iron), unequal restraining pressures are put on the blank during the forming operation. This also holds true if the pressure pad is steel and the die Ampco, as different forces are at work on opposite faces of the blank. The steel pressure pad also has a tendency to pick up and scratch the inside of the drawn piece.

If the inside of a part requires a fine finish, the punch nose should be Ampco faced. This can be done with a solid plug, a ring, bar inserts, or by overlaying with 300Ampcotrode welding rod.

In some cases draw beads are being used on deep draws of rectangular shapes.

By milling slots in the die and inserting wear strips with 180deg radius and milling matching female slots in the pressure pad, compound working of the blank results in straight sides, elimination of wrinkling at the corners and lower pressure-pad pressures. These beads can be adjusted by removing metal from the bottom of the wear strip to lower them or by shimming to raise them. A bead of weldrod overlaid on the die has also served the same purpose.

The advantage of solid Ampco 25 self-supporting dies are many. Generally a smaller radius can be used, which eliminates bellying of straight drawn pieces. A smaller blank size can be used, thus more pieces from a sheet or smaller stock sheets can be used. Also, due to the small radius the draw can be taken closer to the edge of the blank, thus cutting down on trim loss. Pressure pad pressures can be decreased in some cases to the point of running jobs on lighter presses.

These factors give most fabricators lower costs far and away exceeding the savings that they originally thought might

be made by using a less expensive die.

Running with AMPCO 25 dies.
Blanking dies or shears should be kept in tip top condition so that blanks have no burrs or turned edges.

A new die or redressed die should be run-in slowly before operating at production speeds. At least the first twenty-five blanks should be formed with a thick lime water coating, after this using regular lubricant. This work hardens the radius, which increases life of the die and intervals of redressing.

Conclusion
The use of Ampco 25 as a die material produces parts with a superior surface finish, and in materials which are notoriously difficult to deep draw in steel dies. The increased cost of the copper-alloy die is very quickly recouped by the considerable lowering of finishing and polishing costs. The ease of repair of damaged dies, and the refurbishing of badly worn dies, is yet another favourable factor when considering die materials in relation to their costs.

Ampco 25 mechanical properties.

Alloy	Ultimate in Compression psi	Brinell (3000kg)	Rockwell (by conversion)	Thermal Conductivity BTU* hr/sq ft/ft/fF
AMPCO 25 sand cast	220,000	364	38C	26
centrifugally cast	225,000	375	39C	26
extruded	225,000	375	39C	26

*Tool steels have a median of 17 BTU hr/sq ft/ft/fF

Coefficient of friction: Under lubricated conditions, the nominal coefficient of friction between Ampco 25 alloy and stainless steel is 0.08. Under the same conditions, the coefficient of friction between tool steel and stainless is 0.11.

Automated Tapping System for Pressworking Dies
by William R. Pfister
Automated Tapping Systems

SINGLE OPERATION TAPPING

The A.T.S. method of tapping is achieved by combining stamping and tapping into a single operation. This eliminates the high costs of machines used in secondary operations, the labor involved, specialized tooling for individual parts, and extra handling.

This method utilizes the motion of the press to provide a power source for the unit, thus eliminating any outside motor. The tap is mechanically timed by the motion of the press, which prevents tap breakage and produces consistent, high quality threads.

The tapping head is the result of extensive research and development through on the job applications. It has proved to be the most economical means to tap stamped parts. The tapping head has been tested with many tapped parts of different configurations and has run quantities in the millions. This experience has produced a quality, efficient, accurate, and cost-saving method of tapping.

DESIGN FEATURES INCLUDE:

Removable lead screw assembly enables operator to change taps outside of die.

Twist-lock design of lead screw assembly used for maximum efficiency in quick change of tap.

Downward thrust safety device prevents tap breakage.

Lead screw tapping to produce better threads, reduce tap breakage, increase tap life, and reduce spoiled parts.

Simple, compact design enables more than one unit to be mounted for multiple tapped parts.

Only minutes are required to change from one die to another, making it practical for short and long run tapping.

SPECIFICATIONS

Operational Speed is recommended up to 60 strokes/minute.

Standard Length of Stroke is 3 and 4 inches.

Optional Strokes available up to 8 inch stroke.

Tap sizes come in two working ranges, from 4-40 to 10-24
and 8-32 to 3/8-16

Tapping Heads for special requirements are available.

METHOD OF APPLICATION

The tapping head is mounted in progression on the die set. The unit is self-contained receiving no outside motor. Any type of power can be used where an up and down motion is produced.

Tapping Head Action In Die Set (Side View)

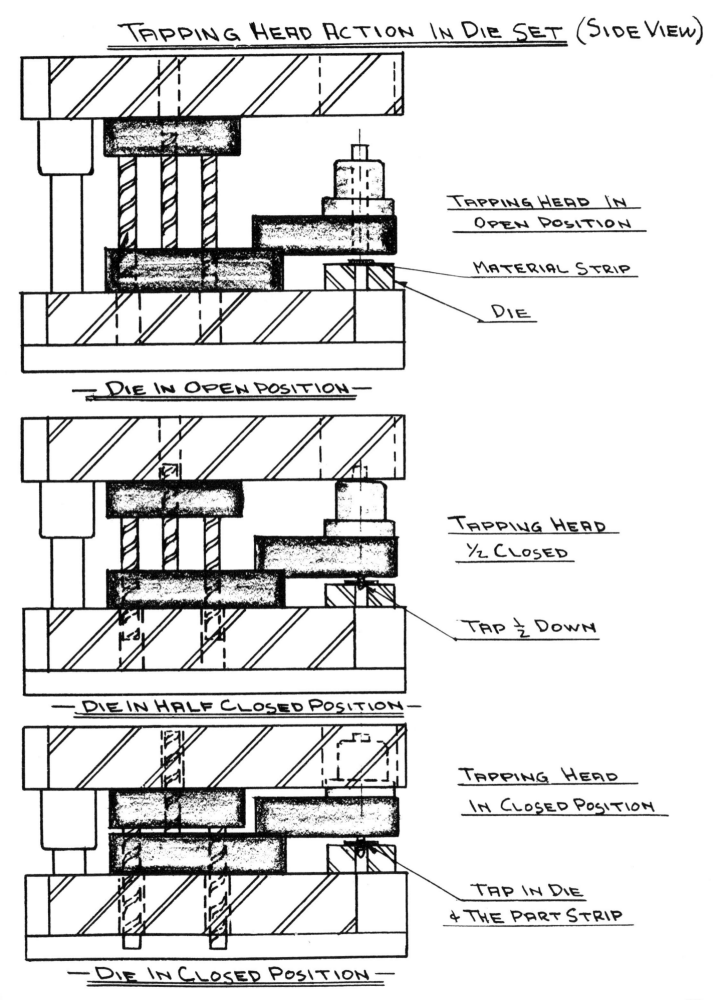

Tapping Head In Open Position

Material Strip

Die

— Die In Open Position —

Tapping Head ½ Closed

Tap ½ Down

— Die In Half Closed Position —

Tapping Head In Closed Position

Tap In Die & The Part Strip

— Die In Closed Position —

CHAPTER 2

POWER PRESS DIES

Progressive Die Design

by Arnold Miedema
and
Edwin Stouten
Capitol Engineering Co.

A progressive die performs a series of fundamental sheet metal operations at two or more stations during each press stroke in order to develop a work piece as the strip stock moves through the die. Each working station performs one or more distinct die operations, but the strip must move from the first through each succeeding station to produce a complete part. In order to move the parts through the die, they are tied together with carriers. The following types of carriers will be illustrated with pictures.

Solid Carrier
All required work can be done to the part without preliminary trimming. The part is cut off or blanked in the final operation.

Center Carrier
The periphery of the part is trimmed, leaving only a narrow tie near the middle of the part. This permits work to be done all around the part. A wide center carrier permits trimming only at the sides of the part.

Lance and Carry at Center
The strip is lanced between parts, leaving a narrow area near the center to carry the parts. This eliminates scrap material between parts.

Side Carriers
The carriers are attached to the sides of the part so that work can be done to the center of the part.
Variations include:
a.   Irregular trim in center
b.   Center lance to eliminate scrap
c.   Dogbone cutout for draw

One Side Carrier
The part is carried all the way, or part of the way, with the carrier on one side only. This permits work on three sides of the part.

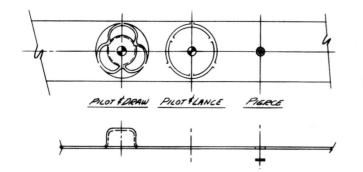

Solid Carrier

PILOT & DRAW   PILOT & LANCE   PIERCE

Solid Carrier

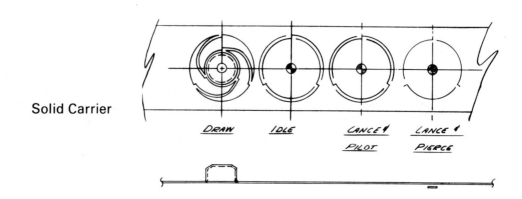

DRAW   IDLE   LANCE & PILOT   LANCE & PIERCE

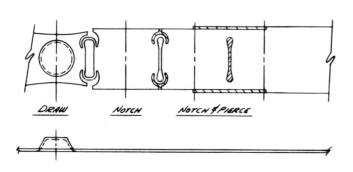

Center Carrier

DRAW   NOTCH   NOTCH & PIERCE

Center Carrier

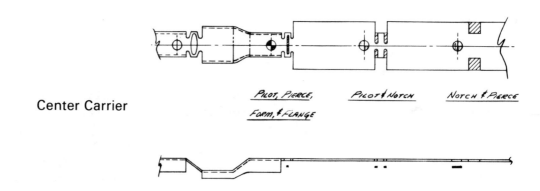

PILOT, PIERCE, FORM, & FLANGE   PILOT & NOTCH   NOTCH & PIERCE

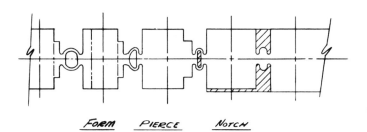

Center Carrier

FORM   PIERCE   NOTCH

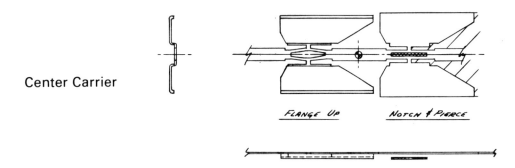

Center Carrier

FLANGE UP   NOTCH & PIERCE

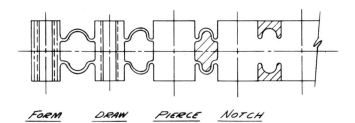

Center Carrier

FORM   DRAW   PIERCE   NOTCH

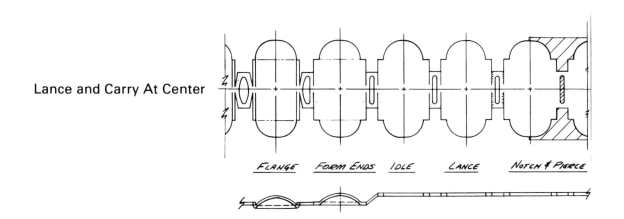

Lance and Carry At Center

FLANGE   FORM ENDS   IDLE   LANCE   NOTCH & PIERCE

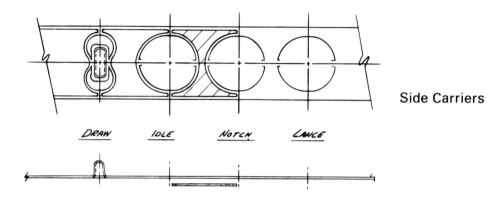

Side Carriers

DRAW   IDLE   NOTCH   LANCE

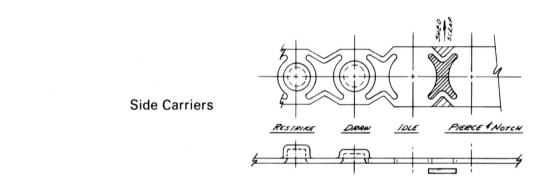

Side Carriers

RESTRIKE   DRAW   IDLE   PIERCE & NOTCH

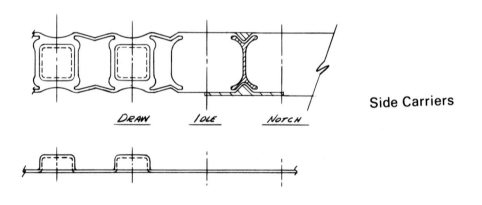

Side Carriers

DRAW   IDLE   NOTCH

One Side Carrier

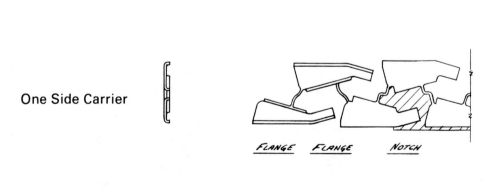

FLANGE   FLANGE   NOTCH

PROGRESSIVE DIE DESIGN PROCEDURE

Step 1. Analyze The Part
         a. What is the material and thickness
         b. What hole dimensions are critical – size and location
         c. What surfaces are critical
         d. What forms are required
         e. Where can carriers be attached
         f. Is direction of material grain important

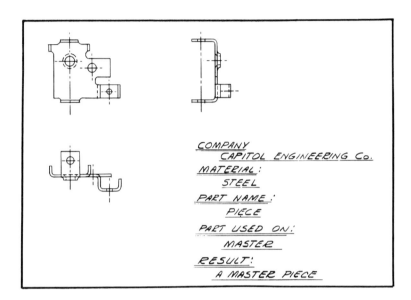

Step 2. Analyze The Tooling Required
         a. What production is required per month, year, total
         b. What presses are available. Bolster area, shut height, feed
             height, strokes per minute, air cushion, etc.
         c. What safety conditions must be met

Step 3. Make Dummy Drawings – A part dummy drawing shows the finished part
         and all positions in which the part will be formed in order to
         achieve the final form.
         a. Tips for dummy drawings:
             1. Show complete part
             2. Show all positions necessary to form part in plan and
                 elevation views
             3. Show over-bend positions if they are critical
             4. Show all necessary views to achieve clarity
             5. Show work lines and set up lines
             6. Provide vertical and horizontal center lines for measuring
                 when assembling the strip layout
             7. Show the strip carriers, if known, before strip layout is
                 assembled
             8. Trace dummy from part print, if part print is dimensionally
                 accurate (less time and less errors)
             9. Use design aids:
                 a. Wax for sample parts and carriers
                 b. Rubber skins
                 c. Plastic skins
                 d. Models
             10. Check accuracy

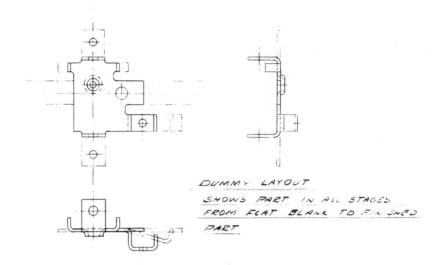

DUMMY LAYOUT
SHOWS PART IN ALL STAGES
FROM FLAT BLANK TO FINISHED
PART

Step 4. Make Strip Layout – a strip layout for a progressive die is a series of part dummy drawings marked up to indicate the die operation to be performed in each station of the die.
   a. How to construct a strip layout:
      1. Determine the proper progression for the part
      2. Tape on a drawing board a series of prints of the plan view of the part in die position using the horizontal center line for alignment.
      3. Apply clear tape over prints in order to hold prints together after removal from the drawing board.
      4. Mark <u>all</u> die operations on each station that will be performed in the die. (Use red color pencil for cutting operations and green or blue for forming operations.)
      5. Mark operations directly on prints or use overlay sheet for preliminary layout, but mark directly on the prints for final layout to prevent something being missed during die design.

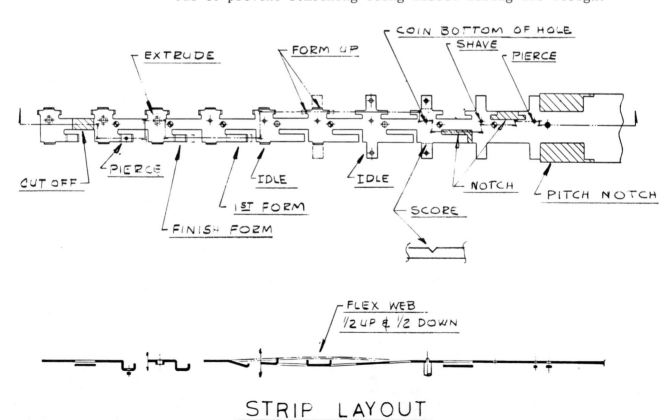

STRIP LAYOUT

Step 5. Discuss Proposed Process with another person for approval

Check List When Analyzing The Preliminary Strip Layout

1. What stations can be eliminated by combining with another station?

2. Are good die steel conditions maintained?

3. Does movement of part between stations require a stretch web?

4. Are idle stations provided to permit "breating" of strip, if stretch web is not feasible?

5. Provide for pitch notch(s), if possible, to maintain proper progression.

6. Avoid sight stop for first hit, if possible.

7. If possible, pierce in first station and pilot in second station to establish pitch control.

8. Provide adequate pilots for all subsequent stations.

9. Is there room for stock lifters to permit free flow of strip during feed?

10. Are close tolerance holes pierced after forming to eliminate development of hole location?

11. Use an overlay sheet to run a simulated strip through the die to check each operation and to spot any loose pieces of scrap which might be left on the die.

Step 6. Draw Plan Views by <u>tracing</u> proper part positions for each station from the strip layout

Step 7. Draw Plan of Punch over the plan of die to permit tracing as much as possible and to reduce scaling errors

Step 8. Make Views and Notes to communicate properly to the die maker (Remember: to <u>Assume</u> is to <u>Blunder</u>)

Step 9. Problem Areas to Watch
              Part lifters
              Part gages
              Part control — pilots, etc.
              Pad travels
              Scrap ejection
              Part ejection
              Poor die steel conditions
              Will the die fit the press
              Will the die fit production requirements

Step 10. Receive preliminary Design Approval

Step 11. Finish Design Layout

Step 12. Detail As Required

REMEMBER TO APPLY THE "K I S S" PRINCIPLE:

  Keep It Simple, Stupid.

GAGING THE STRIP

Use an adjustable gage on one side of strip for stock coming into the die
to allow for variation in coil width.

Put cap on running gages to prevent strip from lifting out of gages during
feed. The cap also will pull the strip off the pilots.

Provide adequate strip gaging so that pilots can enter strip.

Pierce and notch for feeding first station. (Not always possible)

Pilot in second station to establish progression.

Pilot in every working station, if possible and if necessary

Can use pilot for electrical detector for misfeed.

With long upper pad travel, a pilot on lower steels may be stronger, or
mount in the pad.

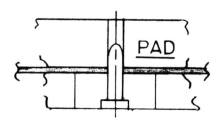
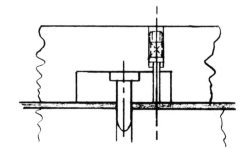

Use blade pilot if a good hole is not available.

Avoid sight stop for first hit, if possible.

PITCH NOTCHES

Try to notch for feed and pierce pilot holes in the first station.

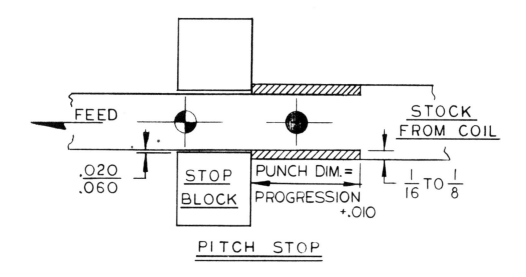

PITCH STOP

If possible locate pitch notch so that the leading edge of new strip will not have half pierces or half hits.

Notch approximately .010 more than progression and let the pilots pull the strip back to correct position.

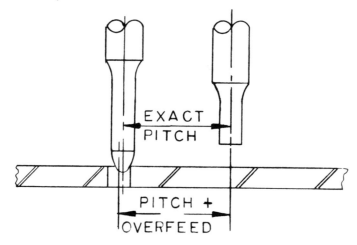

IF PUNCH CORNER BREAK DOWN PREVENTS FULL FEED TO THE STOP, PROVIDE STEP IN PITCH NOTCH

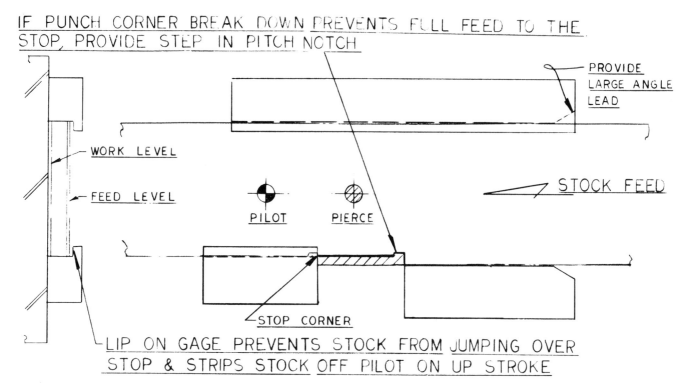

LIP ON GAGE PREVENTS STOCK FROM JUMPING OVER STOP & STRIPS STOCK OFF PILOT ON UP STROKE

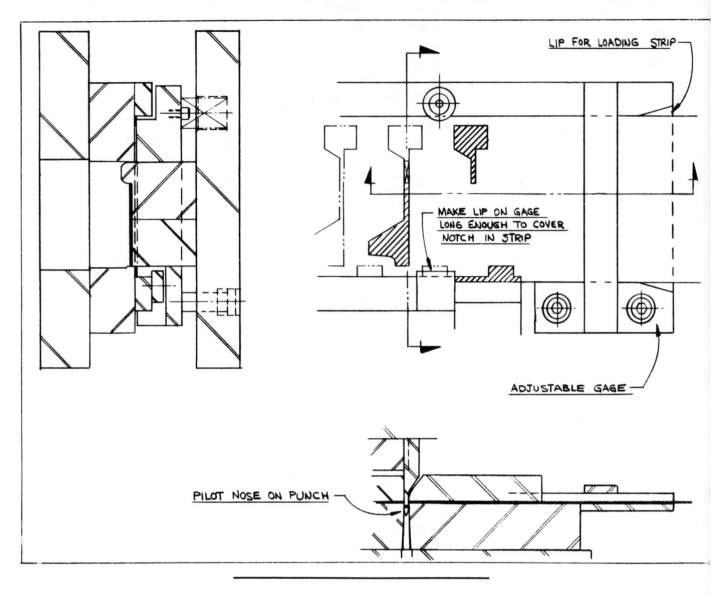

LIP FOR LOADING STRIP

MAKE LIP ON GAGE
LONG ENOUGH TO COVER
NOTCH IN STRIP

ADJUSTABLE GAGE

PILOT NOSE ON PUNCH

STRIP STARTING

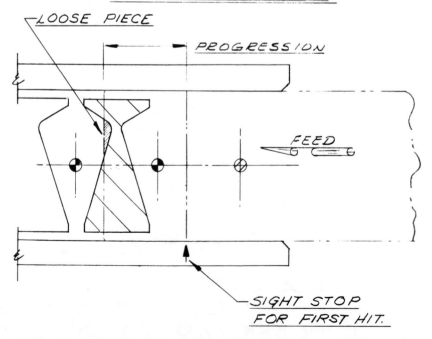

LOOSE PIECE

PROGRESSION

FEED

SIGHT STOP
FOR FIRST HIT.

AVOID LOOSE SCRAP WHEN STARTING OR FINISHING A COIL

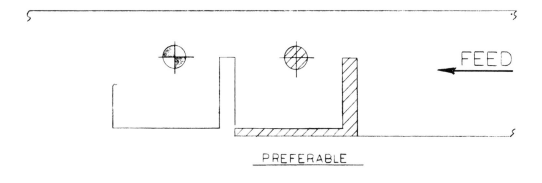

FEED ←

PREFERABLE

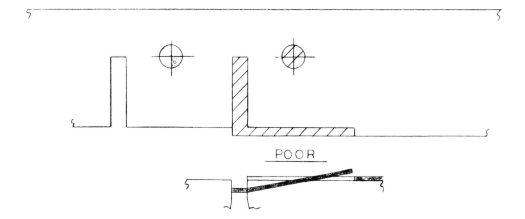

POOR

DO NOT PUT TALL END OF SLUG FORWARD BECAUSE IT CAN LIFT
WITH PUNCH AND INCOMING STOCK WILL CATCH ON SLUG

LIMIT SWITCH PITCH STOP

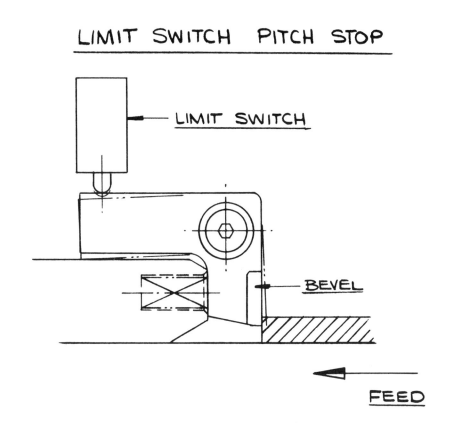

LIMIT SWITCH

BEVEL

FEED ←

STRIP LIFTERS

Spring Pins:

Use punch blanks or ejector pins. - Cut length to suit.

By proper placement of a spring pin, it can be used as a "first stop" instead of using a "slight first stop".
Position spring pins so that a gap in the strip does not allow the strip to fall around the lifter pin.

Bar Lifters:

Use on outside carriers.

Use internally to bridge gaps in the strip.

Pilot Spools can act as a lifter to support the material during pilot entry. Use them especially for high lift conditions and/or thin material.

Air Cylinders may be required for extremely high lift conditions.

Note: No matter which kind of lifters are used, make certain that the strip is properly balanced on the lifters.

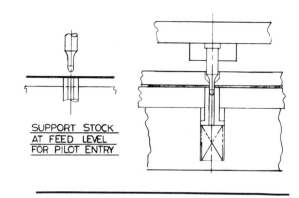

SUPPORT STOCK
AT FEED LEVEL
FOR PILOT ENTRY

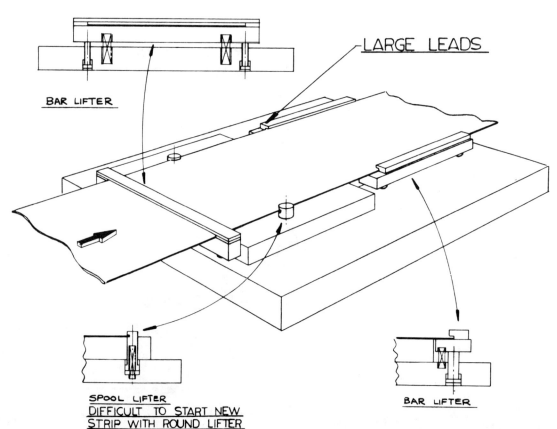

BAR LIFTER

LARGE LEADS

SPOOL LIFTER
DIFFICULT TO START NEW
STRIP WITH ROUND LIFTER

BAR LIFTER

TRIMMING AND PIERCING TIPS

- To eliminate poor punch or die steel conditions, break up the trim into two or more stations.
- For large dies break up the trim areas to permit smaller scrap pieces and to allow for parallels between scrap areas.
- Avoid trimming on a form steel to permit simple sharpening of the steels or provide inserts in the cutting area.
- Do not split a punch steel and die steel at the same point because of burrs.
- Use slug ejectors for trim punches and piercing punches.
- Pierce holes <u>after</u> forming operations if the form will affect the hole locations.
- Pierce all holes, which have a close tolerance relation to each other, in the same station, if possible.
- If the part design will permit, use .020 to .030 mismatch instead of trying to match the trim line.
- Provide pilot ears on thin blades if there is room. The pilot stabilizes the punch and will also help to align the part for match cuts.
- Heel the punch if the cut is not balanced.
- Good scrap ejection is very important.
- When using ball lock punches, use a different shank diameter for each point diameter to prevent inserting a punch in the wrong retainer.
- When cam piercing holes, always use slug ejectors and tapered die button relief hole.

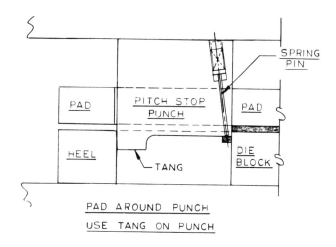

PAD AROUND PUNCH
USE TANG ON PUNCH

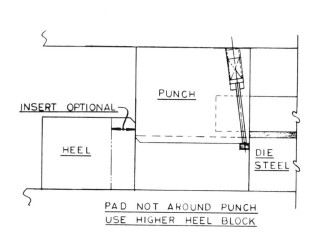

PAD NOT AROUND PUNCH
USE HIGHER HEEL BLOCK

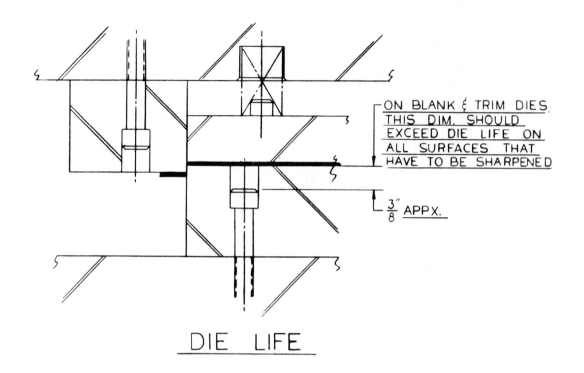

ON BLANK & TRIM DIES.
THIS DIM. SHOULD
EXCEED DIE LIFE ON
ALL SURFACES THAT
HAVE TO BE SHARPENED

$\frac{3}{8}$" APPX.

DIE LIFE

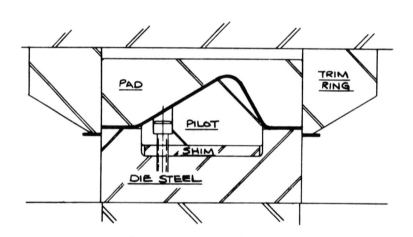

PAD

TRIM RING

PILOT

SHIM

DIE STEEL

PROVIDE GRINDING SHIM TO PERMIT EASIER
PART LOCATOR ADJUSTMENT

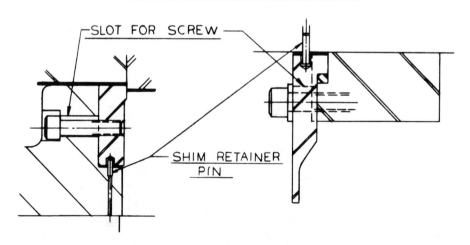

SLOT FOR SCREW

SHIM RETAINER
PIN

SHIM FOR SHARPENING

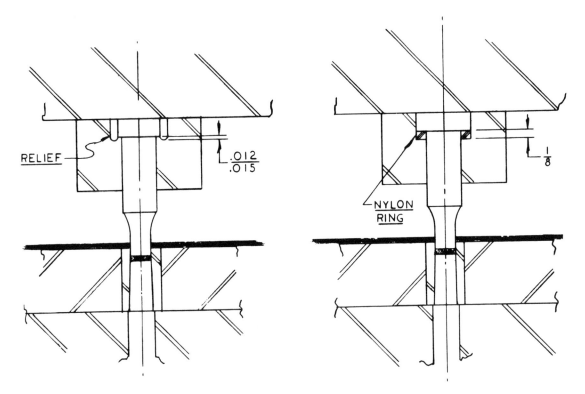

RELIEF

.012
.015

NYLON
RING

1/8

Hints to Reduce Head Breakage Which Takes
Place at "Snap Through" of Punch

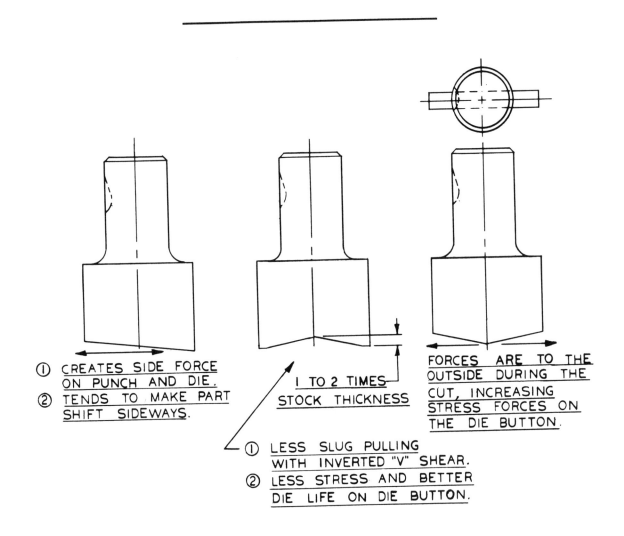

① CREATES SIDE FORCE
ON PUNCH AND DIE.
② TENDS TO MAKE PART
SHIFT SIDEWAYS.

1 TO 2 TIMES
STOCK THICKNESS

① LESS SLUG PULLING
WITH INVERTED "V" SHEAR.
② LESS STRESS AND BETTER
DIE LIFE ON DIE BUTTON.

FORCES ARE TO THE
OUTSIDE DURING THE
CUT, INCREASING
STRESS FORCES ON
THE DIE BUTTON.

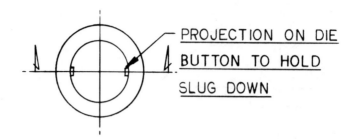

PROJECTION ON DIE
BUTTON TO HOLD
SLUG DOWN

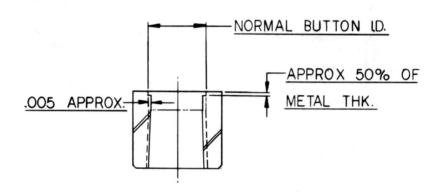

NORMAL BUTTON I.D.

APPROX 50% OF
METAL THK.

.005 APPROX.

CAUTION: ENTER PUNCH ONLY
TO BUTTON FACE

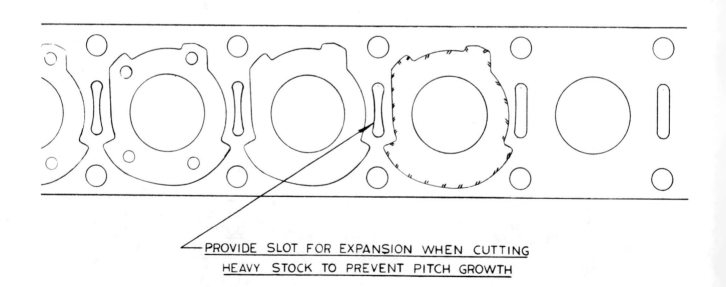

PROVIDE SLOT FOR EXPANSION WHEN CUTTING
HEAVY STOCK TO PREVENT PITCH GROWTH

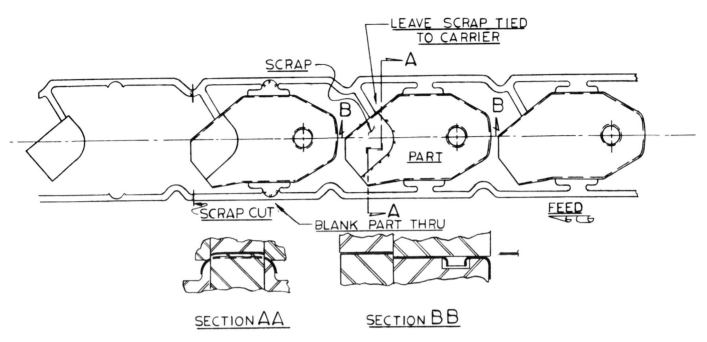

LEAVE SCRAP TIED
TO CARRIER

SCRAP

A

B

B

PART

SCRAP CUT

BLANK PART THRU

A

FEED

SECTION AA   SECTION BB

TRIM "UP" TO PREVENT POOR STEEL CONDITION

LEAVE SCRAP TIED TO CARRIER

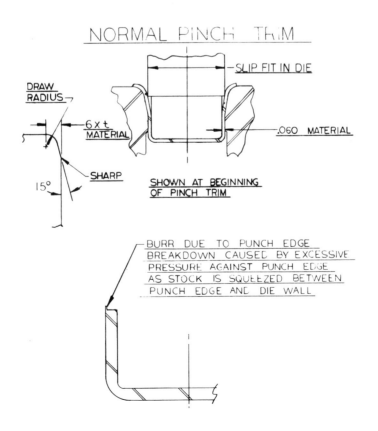

NORMAL PINCH TRIM

SLIP FIT IN DIE

DRAW
RADIUS

6 × t
MATERIAL

.060 MATERIAL

15°

SHARP

SHOWN AT BEGINNING
OF PINCH TRIM

BURR DUE TO PUNCH EDGE
BREAKDOWN CAUSED BY EXCESSIVE
PRESSURE AGAINST PUNCH EDGE
AS STOCK IS SQUEEZED BETWEEN
PUNCH EDGE AND DIE WALL

PINCH TRIM

METHOD PROPOSED BY JAMES ABELLA
FREEWAY CORP.

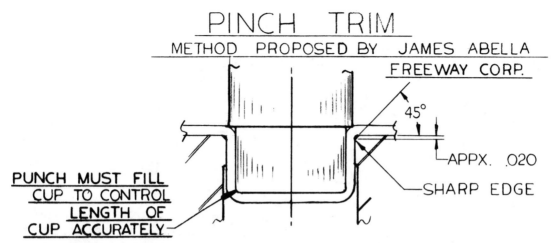

PUNCH MUST FILL CUP TO CONTROL LENGTH OF CUP ACCURATELY

45°

APPX. .020

SHARP EDGE

PUNCH APPROX. 15% TO 20% OF METAL PER SIDE SMALLER THAN DIE

PROPER PUNCH ALIGNMENT IS VERY IMPORTANT IF UNIFORM FRACTURE IS TO BE REALIZED

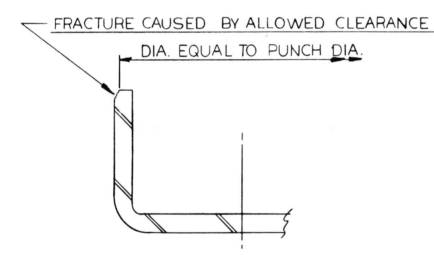

FRACTURE CAUSED BY ALLOWED CLEARANCE

DIA. EQUAL TO PUNCH DIA.

PAST RECORDS INDICATE APPROX. 8 TO 10 TIMES AS MUCH PROD. PER GRIND CAN BE REALIZED IF PROPER PUNCH ALIGNMENT IS MAINTAINED

UPPER PRESSURE PADS

- All upper pads should have the same travels so that the strip and lifters are pushed down evenly.
- Use spools or keepers to prevent breakage (avoid stripper bolts).
- Use different diameter spools, if they have to be different lengths because of more than one pad thickness.
- Provide windows for removal of ball lock punches in high production dies.
- For high pressure requirements, consider nitro-dyne, air cushions, die-draulic, or rubber.
- Use spring cans around springs in any pad that bottoms out.
- Make the pad travel further than the work requires to permit a standard length pilot to be used.

1. If pad "bottoms out", use spring can.

2. If spools are different lengths, use different diameters to prevent mixing at assembly.

3. Provide windows in pad for removal of ball lock punches.

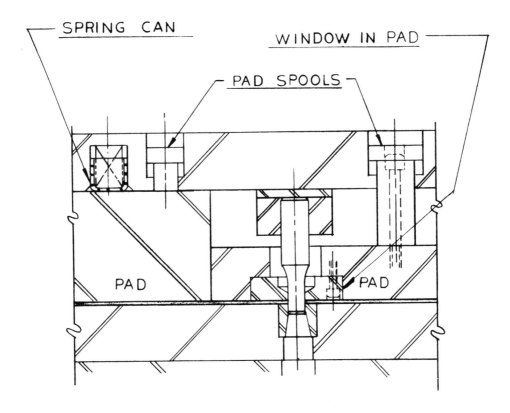

FORMING AND FLANGING TIPS

1. Bottom the pad or coin the corner on all forming operations.

2. Coin all short flanges.

3. Some "up" flanges can be done by forming down.

4. For long double formed flanges use a tangent surface to prevent curling the flange.

5. Provide bevel on punch to prevent whip lash on long flanges.

6. For "up" flanges, flex the web 1/2 above and 1/2 below normal die level to minimize pulling the strip out of position.

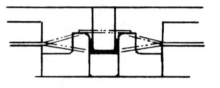

7. Heel wherever necessary to prevent side thrust in the die.

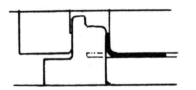

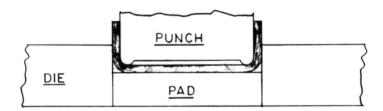

Force required to set corner
F = W x B x S
    W – total length of bend(s)
    B = projected width of beads
    S – setting pressure at 50,000 to 100,000 P.S.I. for mild steel

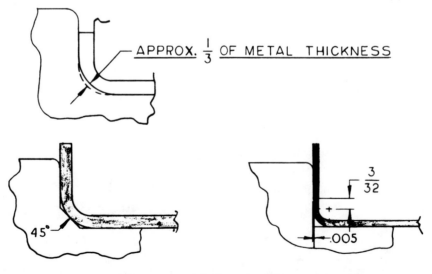

METHODS OF KEEPING FLANGES VERTICAL

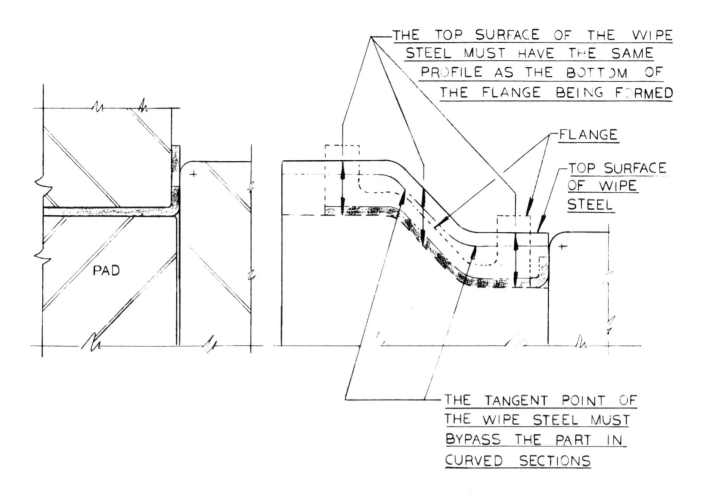

THE TOP SURFACE OF THE WIPE STEEL MUST HAVE THE SAME PROFILE AS THE BOTTOM OF THE FLANGE BEING FORMED

FLANGE

TOP SURFACE OF WIPE STEEL

PAD

THE TANGENT POINT OF THE WIPE STEEL MUST BYPASS THE PART IN CURVED SECTIONS

Pressure Pad Forming A Flange "UP"

· There must be enough preload on the springs to do the forming and also overcome the total lower pad pressure.
· The pad must be properly guided and heeled to hold location and prevent side thrust.
· Use nitro-dyne, die-draulic, or air cushions, if a large force is required.
· Use tool steel inserts, if a large pad is used.

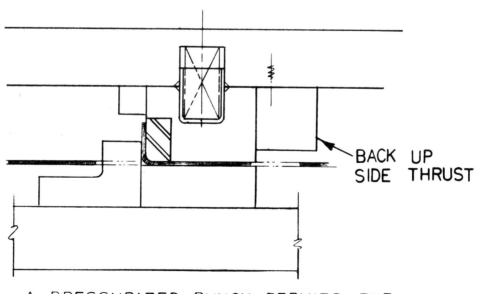

BACK UP SIDE THRUST

A PRESSURIZED PUNCH PERMITS THE STRIP TO BE HELD FLAT DURING ENTIRE DOWN STROKE

CURLING

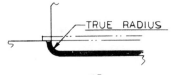

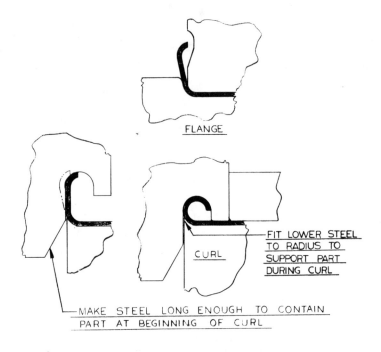

TRUE RADIUS

NIP

FLANGE

CURL

FIT LOWER STEEL TO RADIUS TO SUPPORT PART DURING CURL

MAKE STEEL LONG ENOUGH TO CONTAIN PART AT BEGINNING OF CURL

EXTRUDED OR DRAW-NECKED HOLES

STEPS FOR PROPER HOLE PREPARATION:

1. PIERCE

2. SHAVE

3. RE-SHAVE (IF REQ'D)

4. COIN BOTTOM OF HOLE

5. EXTRUDE IN OPPOSITE DIRECTION OF PIERCE IF POSSIBLE.

PIERCE

SHAVE

COIN

EXTRUDING PUNCH AND DIE

1. PILOT IN PRE-PIERCED HOLE.

2. RADIUS MUST BLEND PERFECTLY WITH STRAIGHT.

3. TAPER DIE BUTTON.

4. RELIEVE PUNCH AFTER STRAIGHT SECTION TO ALLOW FOR LUBRICATION.

5. PUNCH MUST BE HIGHLY POLISHED.

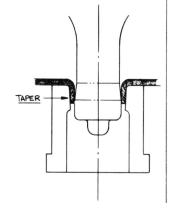

BETTER EXTRUSIONS CAN BE ACHIEVED BY PIERCING IN THE OPPOSITE DIRECTION OF EXTRUDING BECAUSE THE O.D. OF THE NECK WILL STRETCH FURTHER THAN THE I.D.

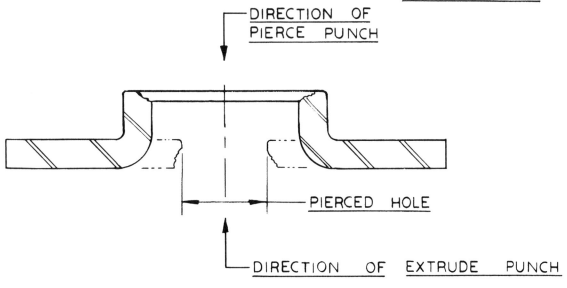

DIRECTION OF PIERCE PUNCH

PIERCED HOLE

DIRECTION OF EXTRUDE PUNCH

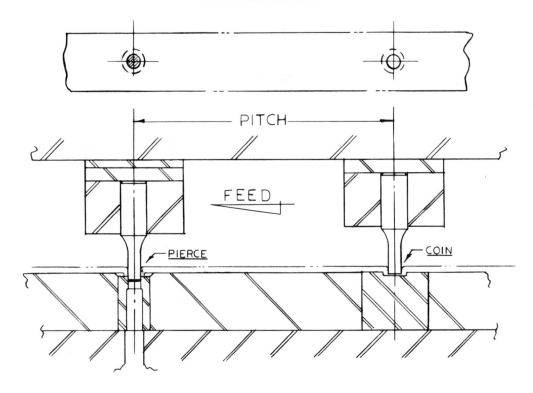

DRAWING TIPS

Area Method of Determining Blank Diameters

To determine the blank diameter of a shell by area method, calculate the of its various sections, the sum of which is equal to the area of the blank.

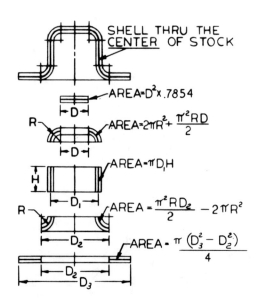

SHELL THRU THE CENTER OF STOCK

AREA = $D^2 \times .7854$

AREA = $2\pi R^2 + \dfrac{\pi^2 RD}{2}$

AREA = $\pi D_1 H$

AREA = $\dfrac{\pi^2 RD_2}{2} - 2\pi R^2$

AREA = $\dfrac{\pi (D_3^2 - D_2^2)}{4}$

Reprinted by permission from:
"Condensed Practical Aids"
"Die Techniques" Publishers
P.O. Box 632
Medinah, Illinois 60157

For calculating maximum percentage of reduction for deep drawing stock, when the blank diameter is 18.000 and the stock thichness .060

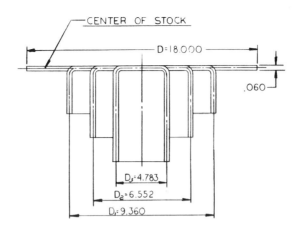

D = 18.000 blank diameter

First Draw:-
48% of 18.000 = 8.640
Subtract 8.640 from 18.000 = 9.360
D_1 = 9.360 diameter of first draw

Second Draw:-
30% of 9.360 = 2.808
Subtract 2.808 from 9.360 = 6.552
D_2 = 6.552 diameter of second draw

Third Draw:-
27% of 6.552 = 1.769
Subtract 1.769 from 6.552 = 4.783
D_3 = 4.783 diameter of third draw

Reprinted by permission from:
"Condensed Practical Aids"
"Die Techniques" Publishers
P.O. Box 632
Medinah, Illinois 60157

Maximum Percentage Of Reduction For "Deep Drawing Stock" On Various Thicknesses Of Material			
Thickness of Material	Percentage of Reduction from Blank to 1st Draw	Percentage of Reduction from 1st Draw to 2nd Draw	Percentage of Reduction from 2nd Draw to 3rd Draw
.010	27%	18%	17%
.015	32%	20%	19%
.020	35%	21%	20%
.025	39%	22%	21%
.030	42%	23%	22%
.035	44%	26%	24%
.040	46%	28%	25%
.045	47%	28%	25%
.050	47%	29%	26%
.055	48%	29%	26%
.060 to .125	48%	30%	27%
.125 to .250	47%	28%	26%

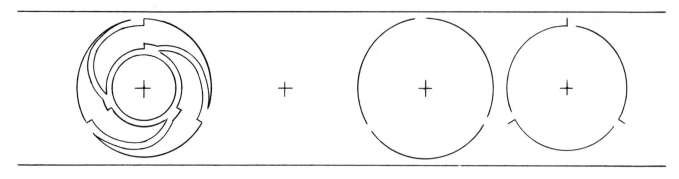

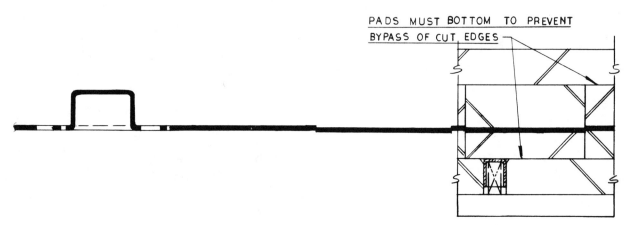

PADS MUST BOTTOM TO PREVENT
BYPASS OF CUT EDGES

SPIRAL WEB FOR DRAWN SHELL

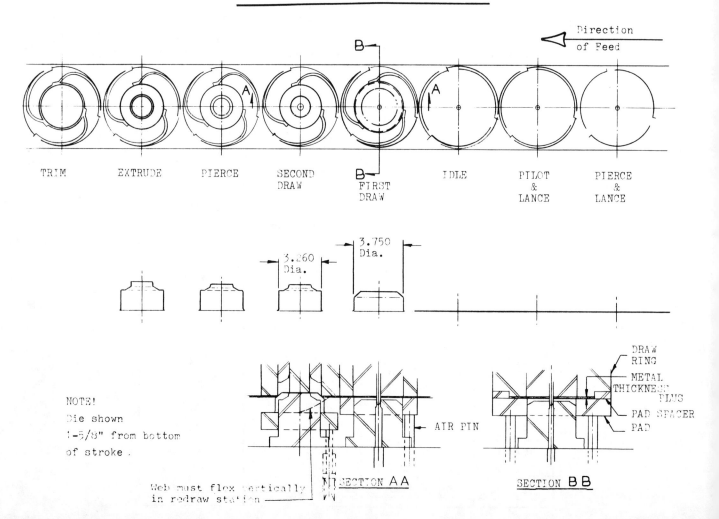

Direction
of Feed

| TRIM | EXTRUDE | PIERCE | SECOND DRAW | FIRST DRAW | IDLE | PILOT & LANCE | PIERCE & LANCE |

3.260 Dia.

3.750 Dia.

NOTE!
Die shown
1-5/8" from bottom
of stroke.

DRAW RING

METAL THICKNESS PLUS

PAD SPACER

PAD

AIR PIN

Web must flex vertically
in redraw station

SECTION AA

SECTION BB

96

PART EJECTION

BLANK THROUGH IS THE
BEST METHOD OF EJECTION.

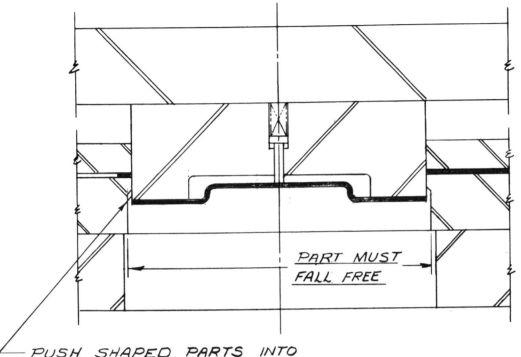

PART MUST
FALL FREE

PUSH SHAPED PARTS INTO
RELIEF IN DIE BLOCK TO PREVENT STACKUP OF PARTS.

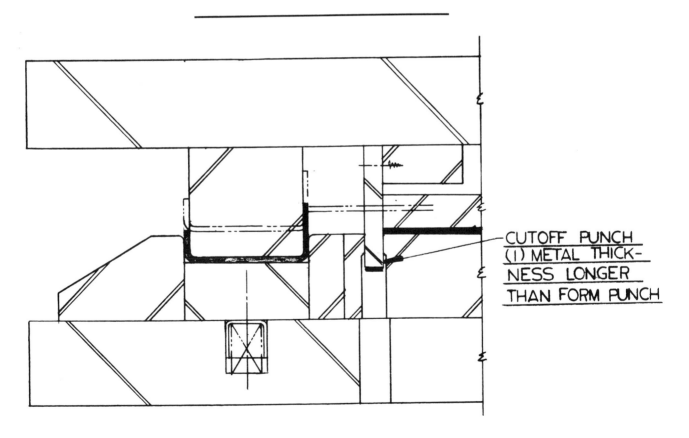

CUTOFF PUNCH
(1) METAL THICK-
NESS LONGER
THAN FORM PUNCH

USE PROGRESSION OF
WEB TO PUSH PART OFF LAST STATION.

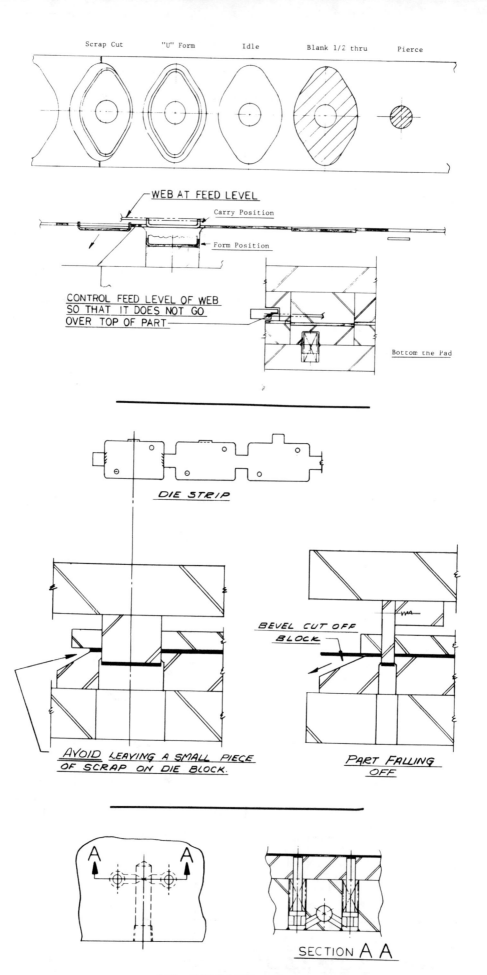

Scrap Cut   "U" Form   Idle   Blank 1/2 thru   Pierce

WEB AT FEED LEVEL

Carry Position

Form Position

CONTROL FEED LEVEL OF WEB
SO THAT IT DOES NOT GO
OVER TOP OF PART

Bottom the Pad

DIE STRIP

BEVEL CUT OFF
BLOCK

AVOID LEAVING A SMALL PIECE
OF SCRAP ON DIE BLOCK.

PART FALLING
OFF

SECTION A A

AIR OPERATED SHEDDER
PINS WITH SPRING RETURN

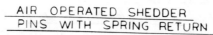

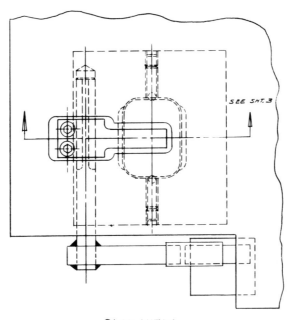

PLAN VIEW

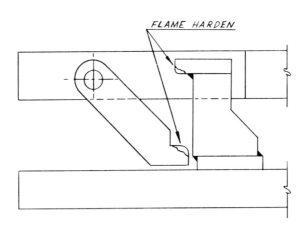

FLAME HARDEN

ELEVATION VIEW

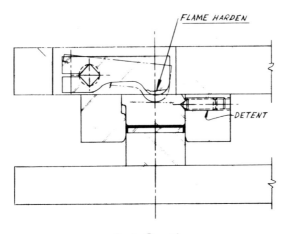

FLAME HARDEN

DETENT

A-A Section

Rotary Knock-Out

Presented at SME's Transfer Die Technology Workshop, February 1970

The Design of Transfer Dies

By S. A. Bianchi
Livernois Automation Co.

INTRODUCTION

The success of any transfer die system is dependent on the use of well established basic design principles and I might add, the application of ordinary common sense.

I have seen and heard of many transfer die applications where the proper approach has not been taken, and consequently, the success of the system has failed. Much time and effort could have been saved and many headaches avoided while still in the die design stages, if more thought were given to the applications.

As best as I can, I will try to convey to you, how some of these pitfalls can be overcome, before the fact, and not during the die tryout period. Before we start any design, we must, of course, begin with the planning and the processing of the operation.

As one of the first steps in planning for a transfer die, we must determine the manner of feeding the raw material into the die. Like progressive dies, transfer dies can be and are often fed from coil material as illustrated in Figure 1.

Figure 1

In this regard, it may be possible to perform certain preliminary operations, such as notching, piercing, preforming,etc., while the part is still contained in the coil strip. Then, at some predetermined point the work piece is cut free of the coil, thereafter being mechanically shuttled from station to station by transfer fingers. Figure 2 shows a good example of this.

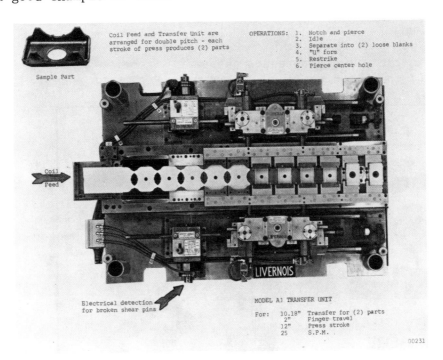

Figure 2

On the other hand, in many cases it has been proven to be more economical to feed pre-cut blanks into a transfer die. There are several ways to introduce pre-cut blanks into a transfer die system. One method is to feed by means of a magazine type feeder as shown in Figure 3. This particular type is used for blanks about .040" thick or greater.

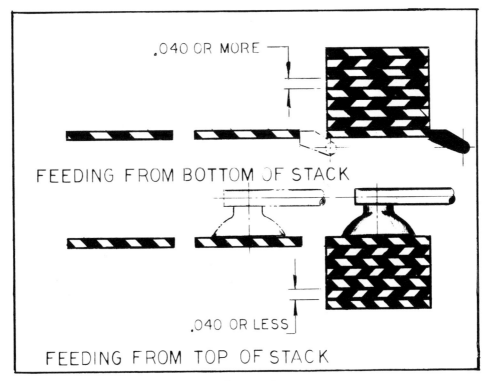

Figure 3

The blanks are removed from the bottom of the stack and are allowed to be "peeled" off through a narrow escapement. This type of magazine feeder can be powered mechanically from the ram of the press or by a cylinder (air or hydraulic) and is very efficient since the magazine may be loaded from the top while the press is continually cycling.

When blanks are thinner than .040 they are best fed from the top of the stack using a vacuum-cup type pick up. Also, blanks with surfaces that cannot be scratched are best handled in this manner.

The coils or blanks can either be fed in the same direction as the transfer feed or at any angle up to 90° to this direction, as shown in Figures 4 and 5.

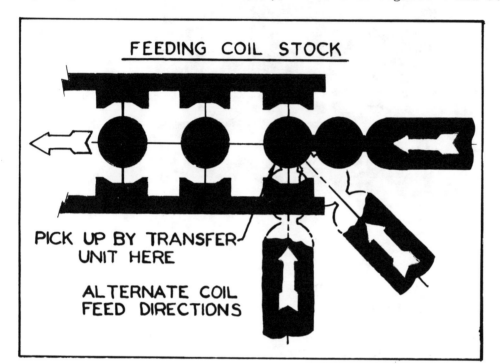

FEEDING COIL STOCK

PICK UP BY TRANSFER UNIT HERE

ALTERNATE COIL FEED DIRECTIONS

Figure 4

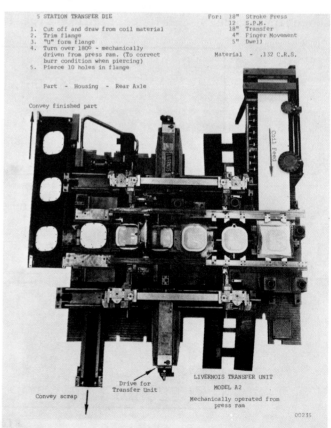

Figure 5

After deciding on the method of feeding we must concern ourselves with the number of die stations for producing a stamping in a transfer die. It is important that the sequence of operations in a transfer system be analyzed and if necessary sketched out roughly before starting on any actual design layout work.

You should remember that the first consideration in a transfer die is that the part must be shuttled or transferred at the same feed level from station to station. This means that, when compared with single stage dies, the performing of multiple functions, such as the combining of trim and pierce operations, sometimes must be separated to accommodate a transfer die system.

Figure 6 illustrates a typical situation. As you will note, this cup shaped part is to be trimmed around its outer flange and pierced in the center. In a conventional single station die, both pierce and trim functions can be performed in the same operation. As the part is taken up with the upper die it is ejected by a positive knock out. In a transfer die we cannot use this type of positive knock out. The part must remain on the lower die. If we were to combine these operations in a transfer die it is apparent that there would be no way to raise or bring the part back to feed level, since the trim section is anchored to the die shoe.

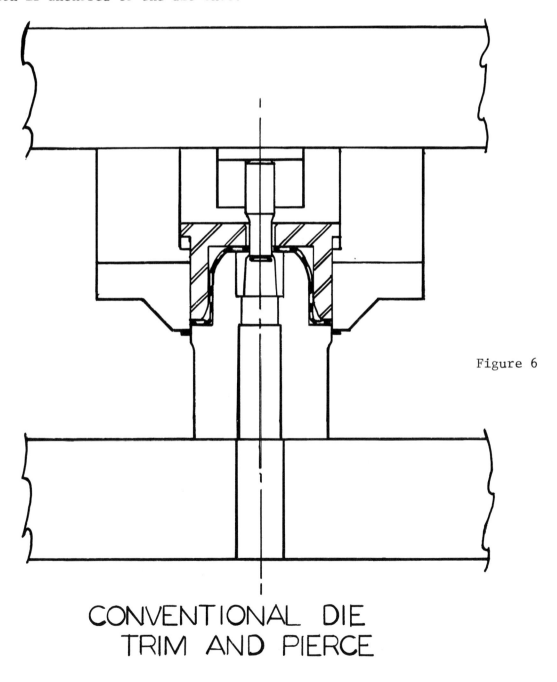

Figure 6

CONVENTIONAL DIE
TRIM AND PIERCE

Therefore, you can readily see in Figure 7 why some operations must be separated in order to effect proper and uninterrupted transfer. In this case the trim line is the feed level, while at the pierce station, the part must be lowered over a post by means of spring pads. Note the upper pins which depress the pad, allowing the part to settle over the post. This is a simplified illustration of one of the basic concepts when planning for the number of stations required. It would also apply to certain forming and trimming operations. Each application and stamping would have its own peculiarities

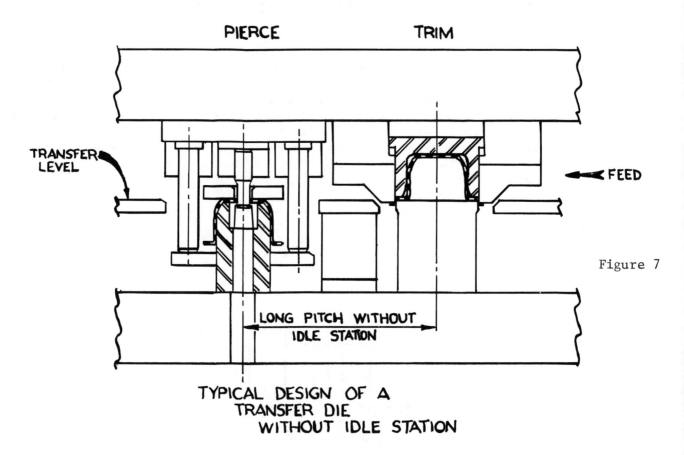

Figure 7

TYPICAL DESIGN OF A
TRANSFER DIE
WITHOUT IDLE STATION

As another consideration during the process and design stage, some thought must be given in determining the transfer pitch, that is, the center to center distance between stations, along with operating speed.

I repeat these two words, pitch and speed, because they play an important part in planning a transfer die system.

Let us then consider these two factors in a transfer system. They are somewhat closely related to each other. By this I mean, the shorter the transfer pitch, the faster we are able to cycle. Generally speaking, the speed of the transfer movement, in terms of feet or inches per minute, is fixed. Visualize a car travelling at a fixed speed of 50 M.P.H. It will take twice as long to travel two miles than going at the same speed for one mile. Therefore, if we apply this reasoning to transfer dies we can understand why the shortest transfer pitch is desirable. It provides the potential to cycle at a greater speed.

Now, we have learned another rule, and that is to keep a minimum distance between working stations, without sacrificing any of the physical strength of the die steels. When the shortening of the pitch adversely effects good design practice, then there are ways to overcome these shortcomings.

In these instances, it is advisable to make use of idle stations. The incorporation of idle stations will give us the desired shorter pitch along with satisfactory die conditions as we illustrate in Figures 8 and 9.

104

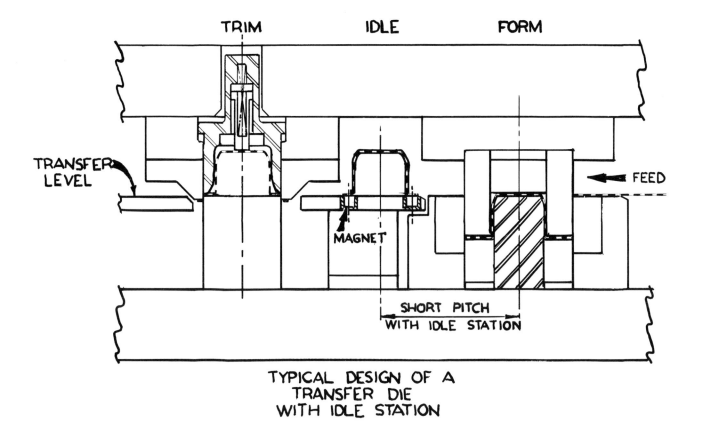

TRIM　　　　IDLE　　　　FORM

TRANSFER LEVEL

FEED

MAGNET

SHORT PITCH
WITH IDLE STATION

TYPICAL DESIGN OF A
TRANSFER DIE
WITH IDLE STATION

Figure 8

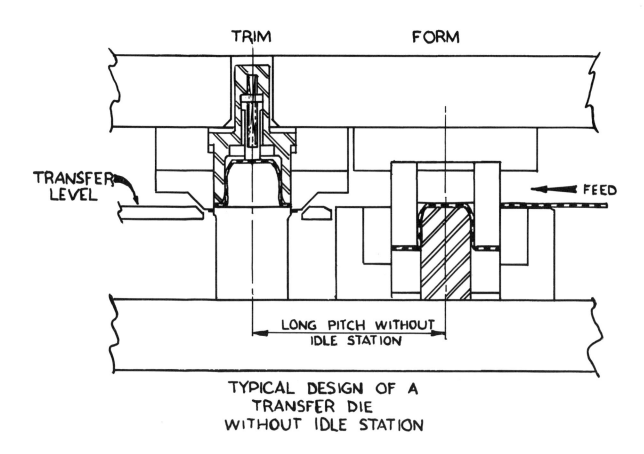

TRIM　　　　FORM

TRANSFER LEVEL

FEED

LONG PITCH WITHOUT
IDLE STATION

TYPICAL DESIGN OF A
TRANSFER DIE
WITHOUT IDLE STATION

Figure 9

An idle station is merely a resting point for the work piece and does not greatly affect the cost of the tooling. There are times when two or more idle stations will be necessary.

Regardless of the number, remember that intelligent use of them is an important means in maintaining as short a transfer distance as is possible. Most of my comments on pitch and speed relate to the use of "portable" transfer units, whereby we can specify the transfer distance to suit the application and have the transfer mechanism built to these specifications.

However, in terms of an existing transfer press, you must live with the pitch and speed as are available.

Remember that a transfer die is no more than a series of single stage dies aligned in a row. If you think of transfer dies in these terms then all the mystery is removed. We can perform all of the types of operations that are performed in conventional dies. We can do cam operations, pierce, trim, draw operations and we can utilize aerial cam types of operations. As I had stated before, we may have to re-align some operations but basically they are still die operations. Use your common sense and be mindful of the important transfer die principles.

Now that we have completed the planning stages I would like to discuss a few of the important techniques of transfer die design and construction, such as the mounting of die stations, volume consideration, finger design, scrap removal, part orientation and other related features.

There are two methods of mounting work stations that are generally used in transfer die construction. In most cases the size of part will govern the selection of the type of design you will use.

Please observe the die construction in Figure 10.

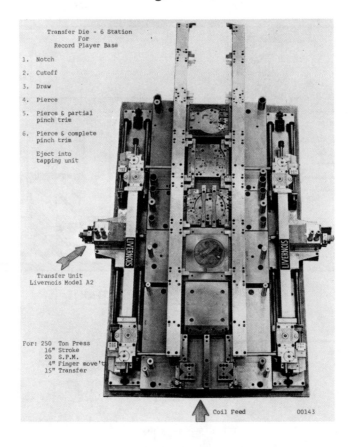

Figure 10

When the part is large enough to permit the use of individual die sets for each station, then it is recommended to follow this practice. Each individual die set would include its own guide pins. This design simplifies the building and facilitates the tryout of each individual station. Another advantage in using this concept is the added flexibility, whereby each station, being a separate die in itself, allows them to be used as single operation dies where the need arises, such as during press breakdowns. Maintenance of the dies is also greatly simplified, since the station can be easily removed as an integral die unit.

The second general type is the use of one single master die set for all stations. This is normally used for smaller stampings. All stations are mounted directly to the master die set and are butted against each other.

You will see a good example of this method in Figure 11.

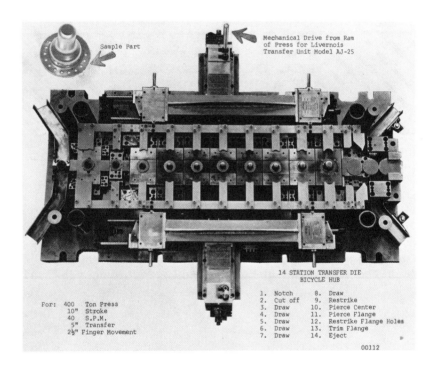

Figure 11

The smaller stampings of course, can also utilize individual die sets at each station. However, this is done at the sacrifice of press-bed area and in most cases, at a greater transfer pitch.

Now, that we have established the method of feeding, planned the sequence of operations, determined the transfer pitch and decided on the type of construction, we are well prepared to proceed with the layout of the design.

In most cases a cross section layout in the direction of transfer feed is the initial step. This will show all stations of the die in a closed position, that is at bottom dead center of the press stroke. Shown in Figure 12. This will allow the design engineer to establish a common feed level for shuttling the part between stations.

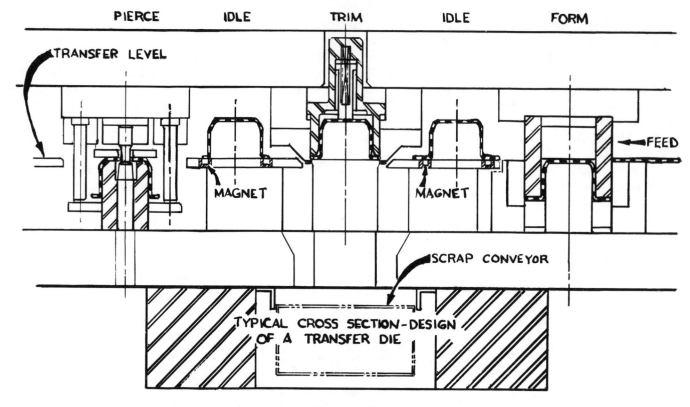

PIERCE   IDLE   TRIM   IDLE   FORM

TRANSFER LEVEL

MAGNET   MAGNET

FEED

SCRAP CONVEYOR

TYPICAL CROSS SECTION-DESIGN
OF A TRANSFER DIE

Figure 12

Notice that the part can be at various levels when the die is in a closed position. However, you will see that in all cases the part is elevated to the same feed level when the die is opened, thus allowing the transfer fingers to engage each part for a smooth and uninterrupted journey to the next station. Also note in Figure 13 that all gaps or spaces between the die station must be bridged, either by rails or the die section themselves.

Figure 13

One of the most important elements, particularly in transfer dies, involves the strip-ping of the part from both upper and lower die. Obviously, if the part does not re-main at feed level on the lower die, we are unable to complete the transfer, but more seriously, it could be the cause of expensive die breakage due to double headers. You can appreciate that stripping be 100% sure with nothing left to chance.

You will notice in Figure 14 that we even make a provision to strip the stripper by means of shedder pins or oil breakers. Unlike manually operated, single stage dies, a transfer die must be able to consistently and positively perform its stripping func-tions, under all conditions. Since in confined areas sufficient pressure for springs may not be possible, we must look to other means such as cylinders or positive mech-anical arrangements, in the nature of cam actuated or solid strippers. As a general rule, where springs or cylinders are utilized, it is good practice to provide somewhat greater stripping pressures then used in standard single operation dies.

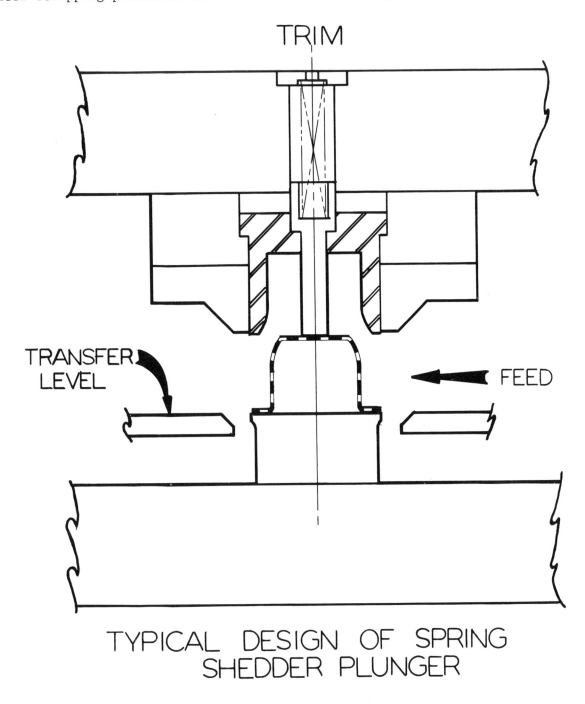

TRIM

TRANSFER LEVEL

FEED

TYPICAL DESIGN OF SPRING
SHEDDER PLUNGER

Figure 14

If stripping cannot be guaranteed with 100% reliability, it is necessary to incorporate a press-stopping circuit into the transfer die. This usually takes the form of a missing parts detection system. If stripping does not take place, the press is immediately signaled to stop by means of electrical circuitry hooked into the press controls.

Now that we have the part properly stripped, how do we stabilize the part from press vibrations? Loose parts are often held in position both in idle and work stations by magnets inserted into the die steels. These are used to maintain the position of the part in the interval after the die opens and before contact is made by transfer fingers, as shown in Figure 15.

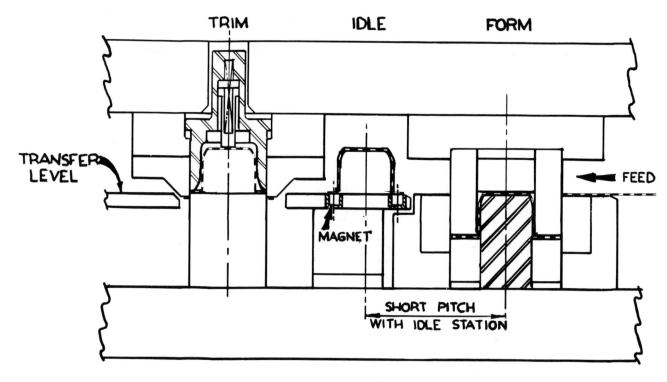

TYPICAL DESIGN OF A
TRANSFER DIE
WITH IDLE STATION

Figure 15

In other instances spring loaded retaining pins from the upper die are used. When stampings of non-magnetic material are being made other means of part retention must be used, such as hold down rails, or mechanical cam actuated bars shown in Figure 16.

110

Figure 16

The next subject I would like to cover deals with the transfer fingers. <u>Finger bars</u> are the connecting link between the transfer unit and the die itself. Since they are to be custom fitted to the progressively changing configurations of the work piece, they must be considered as a part of the die, and very definitely are special tools. The success of the transfer die depends a great deal on the intelligent applications of transfer techniques to finger bar design and construction. The following guides will prove very helpful during the design planning stages.

· The transfer fingers must be able to contain the part surely and safely when transferring.

· They must be able to locate the part precisely and repeatedly in the same spot each time, regardless of press speed or die conditions.

· Finger timing cycles should be engineered to allow enough time for the work piece to settle down at end of transfer stroke so that punches of die can guide the stamping into its proper location.

· Finger bars are to be as light as possible, because, as a rapidly reciprocating member, weight has to be held down to an absolute minimum to minimize inertia. Yet it must be rigid enough to overcome flexing or distortion during transfer operations so as not to lose parts.

· Lightweight hardened inserts may be used when coming in contact with the raw, sharp edges of steel stampings. All possible damage that could occur to a die if finger bars could accidentally be caught between die steels has to be evaluated and eliminated.

Figure 17 illustrates some of the incorrect means for finger construction. Spring loaded fingers will tend to push the part out of location when retracting because of the difficulty of maintaining equal preload on both sides of the fingers. Rubber becomes coated and sticky with oil and die lubricant, which also tends to pull the work piece off center during retraction.

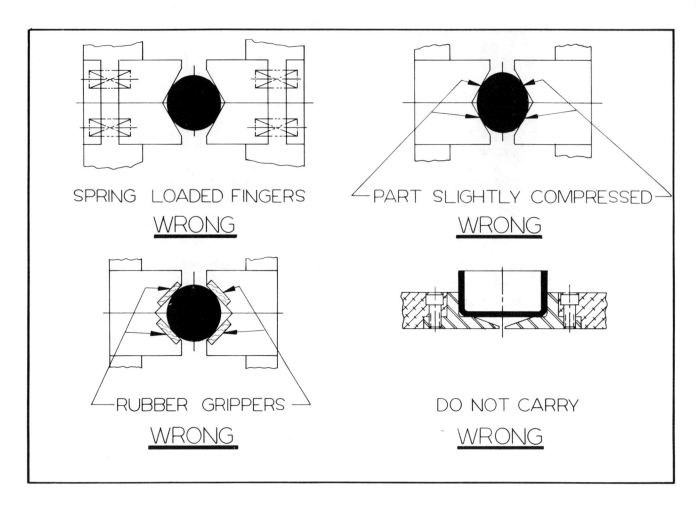

SPRING LOADED FINGERS
WRONG

PART SLIGHTLY COMPRESSED
WRONG

RUBBER GRIPPERS
WRONG

DO NOT CARRY
WRONG

Figure 17

You must never allow fingers to act in the capacity of a clamp or vise. This could result in distortion and marring of work piece and could also contribute to subsequent mislocations and mis-hits further along the progressions in the transfer. Provide clearance between fingers and the work piece. Never make it a practice to use fingers to carry a part over die cavities or other openings. Despite the fact that this is still frequently done, it still doesn't change the fact that it is poor transfer practice, unsafe and unnecessary. Incorporate spring lifter bars and pads to bring parts up to a common level and onto a smooth transfer surface.

Fingers should never be used to take the place of pilots and other precision die locators. Continue to incorporate them in the die where they properly belong.

The next Figure 18 points out two other items of interest.

One shows a simple method of inserting light weight hardened inserts in finger bars when engaging raw steel edges of blanks. The other indicates a smooth contact area of the piece part, where inserts are not necessary. In such instances light weight aluminum construction is very desirable.

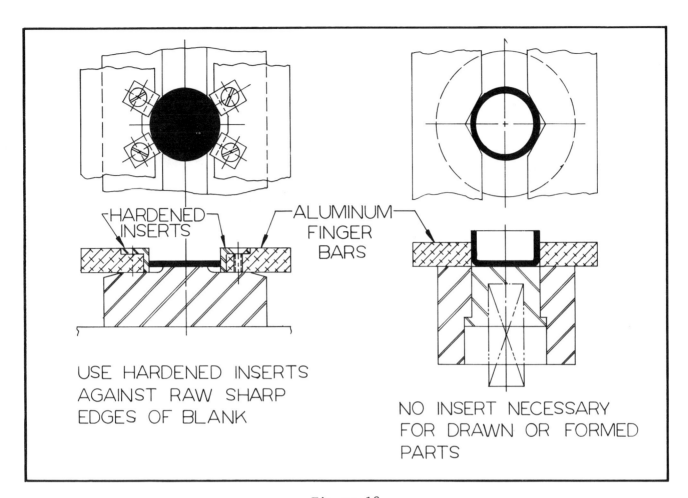

HARDENED INSERTS   ALUMINUM FINGER BARS

USE HARDENED INSERTS
AGAINST RAW SHARP
EDGES OF BLANK

NO INSERT NECESSARY
FOR DRAWN OR FORMED
PARTS

Figure 18

Orientation of parts is sometimes necessary and, when such is the case, provisions must be made by either notching the flange or forming a tab, whereby the fingers can be designed to mate the notch or the tab. At or near the final station the notch or tab is trimmed off.

Another area of concern is the removal of scrap in an automated transfer die, this problem merits serious thought. It is necessary to ensure that all scrap, trim, slugs and offal be satisfactorily disposed of, without intervention of the transfer die cycle. Scrap must be cut into suitable small pieces and shed away from the die station onto chutes or scrap conveyors. Generally, the dies should be designed with enough height to provide proper shedding angles for gravity ejection. Quite often, the scrap and slugs are dropped through the bottom die shoe and carried away by means of conveyors. At times, it may be necessary to separate the trim operation into two stations, in order to effect proper scrap disposal, as shown in Figure 19.

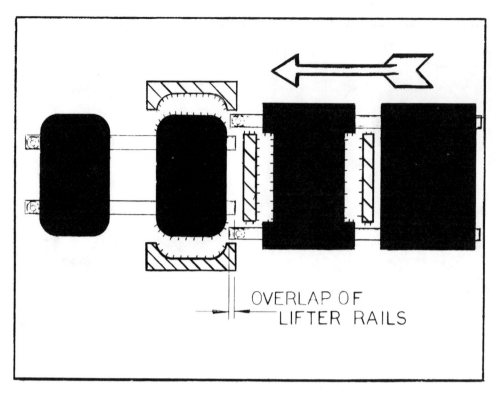

OVERLAP OF
LIFTER RAILS

Figure 19

Finally, consideration should be given to die materials. The use of carbide inserts is advisable if the die is intended for prolonged service or very high volume production. Generally speaking, (with respect to die materials) similar practices to those used in conventional or progressive dies are followed.

All sliding members of the die, such as cam slides, should be provided with lubricant or grease fittings.

Briefly reviewing the main points, bear in mind the following:

·Proper planning will result in successful and trouble free transfer die applications.

·Transfer dies permit practically any manner or method of feeding raw material, whether they be pre-cut blanks, coils or preformed parts.

·Keep the transfer pitch as short as possible to attain the highest operating speed.

·Always maintain an uninterrupted flow of parts by means of common feed levels and bridging of gaps.

·Provide the necessary idle stations for ease of scrap removal and decreasing of transfer pitch.

·Take the necessary precautions to ensure fool-proof stripping.

·Keep the fingers and bars as light as possible and never use the fingers to grasp or squeeze the part. Provide clearance between the part and fingers.

·And, finally, remember that it is much less costly to correct any errors on paper at the design stage than out in the shop. Carefully check each design for proper function before releasing it to the die shop.

Reprinted with permission from Tooling & Production, July 1980

HIGH-SPEED DRAWING

by Thomas M Aurio
Vice President of Manufacturing
RoMatic Manufacturing Co
Southbury, CT

1. New Waterbury Farrel 15-ton DS die set press is designed around a universal transfer mechanism that provides positive part control at high speeds. Photo at right shows antenna ferrule, stock from which it is double-cut blanked, and scrap trimmed in the die. Picture below shows ten-station die set in press.

Although the bulk of our production is in the fabrication of highly polished and carefully lacquered metal closures for cosmetic containers, we also put our tooling and processing know-how to work on other metal specialties for industry. The same multiple-drawing techniques used to make a cap for a lipstick holder can be used to produce other drawn parts.

A good illustration of this capability is the antenna ferrule (a component of the terminal assembly on the cable that plugs into automobile and other mobile radio equipment), which we draw at high speed on our new Waterbury Farrel 15-ton DS die set press, **Figure 1**.

Order quantities are high: 20 to 30 million a year. So rather than tool this part to run on our ICOP presses at 80 to 90 strokes/min we decided to put it on the die set press where we can go to 190 strokes/min. The principal difference in the tooling is that, rather than the punch holders and dies each being separate units for each station, all ten stations for this job are built into one die set, **Figure 2**, that can be removed from the press as one unit.

That is the primary advantage of the die set transfer press configuration. Tooling, which is interchangeable between machines, is set up and proven off

line. Downtime for exchanging one complete die set for another can be as little as 45 min and is rarely over 3 hr. When precision, interchangeable die blocks and punch holders are used within the die set, individual tool changes can be made in a matter of minutes with the die set still in the machine.

In this press configuration all the transfer actuating functions are built into the press rather than into the die. So we aren't talking about complete, more costly, transfer die sets. Only simple punches, dies, transfer bars and fingers are needed for each die set.

The DS press has a cam-driven solid slide that provides a 3 to 1 improvement

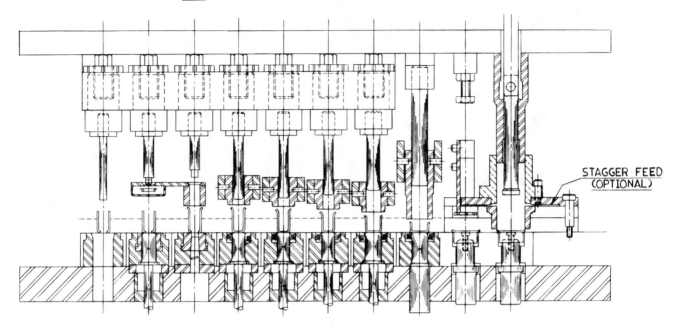

STA. 10	STA. 9	STA. 8	STA. 7	STA. 6	STA. 5	STA. 4	STA. 3	STA. 2	STA. 1
EJECT	TRIM	PIERCE BTM.	REDRAW	REDRAW	REDRAW	DRAW	CUP	HOLD DOWN	BLANK

STAGGER FEED (OPTIONAL)

15 TON DS DIE SET

2. Section drawing of die set developed by user firm to produce drawn antenna ferrules at 190/min on die set press. When job is changed, all of this tooling is removed from the press as a unit—facilitating easier setup.

3. Probing at each die station is by infrared sensors (below) that sense for malfunction at each stroke of the press. In the event of trouble at any station the press is shut down immediately and a signal goes to the appropriate indicator light on the Willtec panel (right) mounted into the front face of the press. Such monitoring systems must be fast and accurate to provide reliable protection for the die set tooling. Modular tooling consists of interchangeable die blocks and punch holders that are easy to replace in the event of trouble.

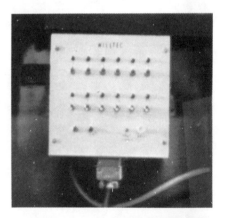

in cycle time over crank-actuated slides. The cam design also provides the timing for the transfer action.

Skills from experience

While such die set tooling can be designed and developed for us by the press builder or by tool and die shops, we prefer to build our own tooling. That is the way our own people can get to understand the machine and its capabilities. When we develop a job ourselves we can get maximum performance from our equipment and remain competitive in quality and price for contract metal fabrications.

This arrangement is part of a larger

concept of value analysis in which our engineers have the capability and experience to develop metal parts from the packaging concept sketch, or detailed industrial blueprint, through to production. We are often able to suggest cost-cutting design variations which will simplify production while retaining functional utility.

This experience has been applied to a wide range of precision parts for industry—electronic parts and assemblies, eyelets, sleeves, ferrules, plugs, shells, contacts, caps, stampings, cases, shields and many other specialized fabrications from a variety of metals—steel or stainless steel, aluminum, copper or brass.

Monitoring essential

At these speeds it is essential that we monitor each station each cycle to be certain that nothing has malfunctioned or broken in the die. Interfacing solid-state electronics to the machine is accomplished by an infrared sensor system rather than the use of a limit switch circuit for this needed protection, **Figure 3**. This system was provided by Willtec, Middlebury, CT.

Each die station's sensor is connected to an indicator light on the Willtec panel. In the event of trouble, the system not only shuts the press down immediately, but indicates by the warning light which station has a problem.

The reliability of the detection system itself is important. Not only do we want

it to protect the operations from trouble, but we want to avoid needless downtime that could occur if the system were overly sensitive and shut down the press when no fault existed except in the detection system itself. When you are going at 190 strokes/min, every minute of downtime is 190 parts of lost production.

In our experience so far, infrared sensors are particularly well suited to high-speed press monitoring.

Coil stock handling

The antenna ferrule is made from 0.0155"-thick brass stock. This is fed from a coil at the rear of the machine into the blanking station (1). In the original proposal stage of this development it is necessary to decide whether to make

4. *Stagger feed attachment is mounted at the rear of the press and moves the strip back and forth laterally so that successive blanking hits are in alternate columns along the length of the strip. Using this option on this ferrule job saves 11.7 percent of the material.*

5. *Processing coil stock through a press at 190 strokes/min could give a lot of scrap to be rewound on the front side of the press. This machine is equipped with a scrap chopper that cuts the scrap into small pieces that are more manageable.*

the parts from a narrow coil strip with a single cut of parts from the width of material or to nest two columns of blanks in a wider strip and stagger the feed as the coil goes into the die.

The stagger-feed attachment, **Figure 4**, shifts the stock to the other column after a hit in either column. The amount of material saved depends on the amount of space between blanks, the edging beside the blanks and the diameter of the blanks. In the case of this part, we have calculated a savings of 11.7 percent (see box) by using the stagger-feed and double-cut layout rather than a single cut.

With high-priced materials, high quantities of production parts and high-speed press operations, the use of such attachments makes sense. This is the kind of purchase that adds to the original capital cost of the machine tool, but can pay for itself in operating savings.

The time involved in handling the material before and after it goes through the press can represent considerable expense. The stagger-feed double-cut method gives more output per lineal foot of coil and thereby reduces the number of times we must load and thread a new coil to complete a production run. On the front side (in this case), rather than rewind the scrap we have a chopper that gives us more manageable small pieces of scrap, **Figure 5**.

Secondary operations

These antenna ferrules get lanced on the side of the cylinder to produce three protruding tabs to hold the assembled connector in the socket. Other designs call for tapered ribs, long and short tabs, and represent different designers' ideas of how to perform the retention function.

While it may be possible to tool the die set in such a way as to complete this requirement while the parts are still in the press, there is no known way to do it at that speed. So we lance them on an automatic setup we have devised off the press. These brass parts get a zinc plating before they are shipped to our customers.

Conclusion

The development of the die set transfer press has presented us with some new challenges and opportunities. The methods and equipment described here are helping us in our efforts to hold the line on costs for the benefit of our customers.

■

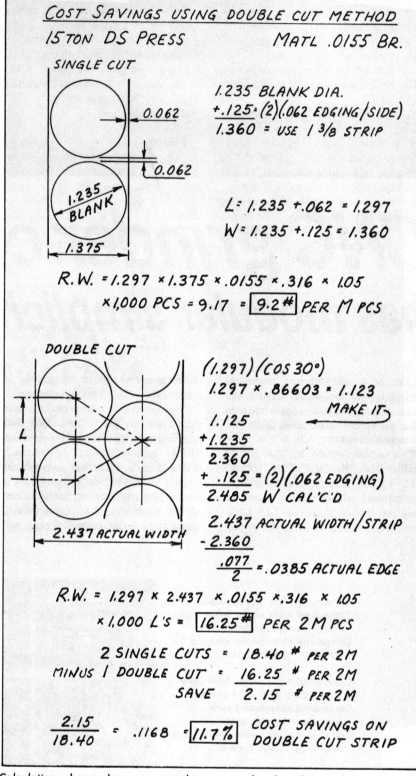

Calculations shown above were used to support the idea of using the stagger feed on this antenna ferrule job. Nesting of the blanks in the double-cut method saves 11.7 percent in this case. Additional savings accrue by getting more parts per lineal foot of strip stock and thereby reloading strip less often.

Reprinted from Manufacturing Engineering, February 1976

SDT—A New Concept in Metal Stamping

Intricate stampings that are impractical to produce on progressive or transfer dies can be made accurately and economically with the Sliding Die Transfer process

CHARLES WICK
Managing Editor

1. MECHANICAL PRESS that has been developed to automatically produce stampings by the Sliding Die Transfer process.

COST REDUCTIONS and higher productivity attained in making complete stampings by combining several operations on a single press, instead of performing the operations on different presses, are well known. For this purpose, progressive and transfer dies, as well as transfer presses, are being widely used for medium to high production requirements.

Selection of the particular process to use depends on many factors, including part design, material, production requirements, and press and die costs. There are some parts, because of their shape or design, that are difficult or impractical to produce on progressive or transfer dies. Now there is a new process — Sliding Die Transfer (SDT), developed by Westberg Tool & Mfg. Co., Stratford, Conn. — for completing such stampings on a single press.

SDT Process. The proprietary SDT process employs a modified mechanical press, *Figure* 1, equipped to combine a series of individual stamping operations into a continuous and automatic method of production. While the tooling is similar in some respects to a combination die, with a number of individual die stations mounted on a common die set, the process differs in the unusual sliding die method of transferring parts from station to station and other refinements.

Essentially, the setup consists of a reciprocating slide carrying a master die set on which individual dies are mounted at each of four or more sta-

tions. The distance that the slide travels during each half of its longitudinal reciprocating stroke is called the lead, and equals the distance between successive stations.

A part is completed every other stroke of the press ram. Operations are performed on each part at the different stations during alternate work strokes. During alternate deposit strokes, *Figure* 2, each part is placed in the die at the next station. Parts are always retained in the upper tool members when the press ram rises after each work stroke, and are ejected by air-actuated shedders into nests in the lower dies at the next stations after the slide has shuttled to the left.

Process Advantages. In addition to the economy and higher productivity resulting from automatic cycling, the process offers the additional advantages of increased versatility and accuracy, plus material and tooling savings. Versatility is gained by the ability to produce parts difficult or impractical to produce on progressive or transfer dies, or those that require a combination of progressive and secondary operations. The SDT process can include additional or secondary operations in

the automatic sequence to produce complex shaped parts with a minimum additional tooling expense. Some of the individual dies can often be used for similar, different-size parts, and changeover to a different part can usually be done in less than one hour.

Superior and consistent accuracy of parts produced, with a minimum of scrap, is the result of several design features. First, the entire part is blanked (and often pierced) in the first station without gutting and potential mismatching of edges. The SDT process eliminates tugging and distortion often contributed by the carrier strip, pilots, stops, and feed errors in progressive dies. Second, the parts are always held under firm control when transferred from station to station. They are never dropped loose in nests, or subjected to distortion or locational errors sometimes produced by carrying fingers in transfer dies or presses. Also, the parts can usually be held in alignment at the exact dimensional points critical to accuracy at the next operation in the sequence.

Users of the SDT process have reported they can maintain tolerances about half those generally held on pro-

2. *FIVE-STATION die for producing bearing retainers. Die is shown in deposit position at left with parts about to be placed in nests at next stations. Work position is seen at right.*

3. *TYPICAL PARTS completely formed automatically by the SDT process with tool cost savings of 40 to 60%, and material savings as high as 75%.*

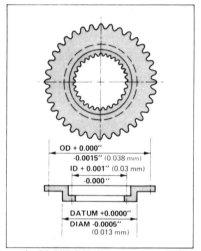

4. *CLUTCH GEAR produced to close tolerances with a four-station die provided savings of 60% on labor and 50% on materials.*

gressive dies. For example, on contours and hole locations, tolerances of 0.001 inch (0.03 mm) or less are being consistently maintained, compared to 0.002 to 0.003 inch (0.05 to 0.08 mm) with progressive dies.

Tooling for the SDT process is generally much simpler than that required to produce the same part on a progressive die, and tool cost savings of 40 to 60% have been reported. Use of an integral master die set on the SDT press, which holds the individual die stations in precise alignment and lead, eliminates the need of a die set for each different part produced. Upper and lower portions of each individual die at the various stations can be easily removed and reset to the dowel locators provided when repair or replacement is required, thus facilitating and reducing the cost of maintenance.

Raw material savings as great as 75% can be achieved because the SDT process does not require a carrier ribbon, guttings, and pilots needed for progressive dies. Users have also reported improved operating efficiencies, with uptimes of 75 to 80% compared to about 60% with progressive dies.

The possible disadvantage of two press strokes being required to complete each part is often far outweighed by the many advantages. Also, the SDT process has been found best for parts not suited to production on progressive dies.

Applications. Most applications for the SDT process so far have been for the production of small and medium size retainers (cages) for precision ball bearings, watch case backs, and similar parts, some of which are shown in *Figure* 3. More recently, the process has been applied to the production of other parts that are fragile or complex shaped, difficult to grip in transfer dies or to hold onto in progressive dies, or that require a combination of progressive and secondary operations. The process seems to fill a gap that exists where volume requirements are large enough to make automation desirable, but not large enough to justify the cost of special higher speed, single-purpose dies and equipment.

The precise clutch gear shown in *Figure* 4 used to be produced in three operations. First, the part was turned, faced, and cut off from steel rods on an automatic screw machine, and then the internal and external gear teeth were formed in press operations. Now, using the SDT process, the clutch gears are produced automatically in a single operation. A four-station die successively blanks each part, coins the offset shoulder, pierces the internal gear teeth, and blanks the external teeth. Savings with this improved method were 60% on labor and 50% on material. Roots of the internal and external gear teeth are held concentric with the datum surface within 0.0010 inch (0.025 mm), full indicator reading.

Presses Used. Crankshaft type mechanical presses, with specially cast gap frames and high-speed clutch/brake units, are used for the SDT process. Westberg adds the vertical drive, cam box, die slide mechanism, varible speed drive, coil stock feed unit, electrical equipment, safety features, and control console, as well as the individual dies, if desired.

A vertical driveshaft, *Figure* 5, is rotated through a 2-to-1 reduction gear set from the press crankshaft. Keyed to the lower end of this driveshaft and rotating with it is a precision sinusoidal cam. Two roll followers in contact with this cam reciprocate a slide horizontally on a way on the press bed.

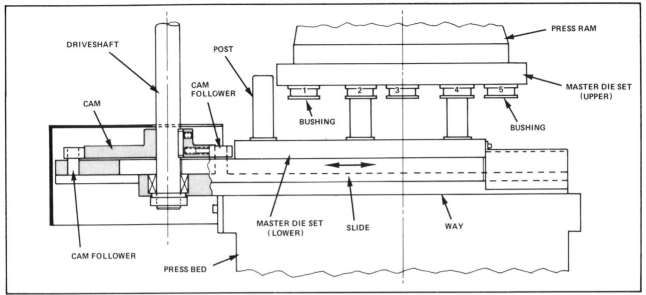

5. *VERTICAL DRIVESHAFT, driven from press crankshaft, rotates cam to reciprocate slide on which the lower half of the master die-set is mounted.*

Mounted on the reciprocating slide is the lower half of the die set, which carries three permanently mounted, hardened steel locating posts. The upper half of the master die set is mounted on the press ram and carries five bronze bushings. On each deposit stroke of the press, when workpieces are placed into nests in the lower dies (not shown) at the next stations, two of the three locating posts enter bushings 2 and 4, as shown. On each alternate work stroke, the three posts enter bushings 1, 3, and 5 to assure accurate alignment.

Also mounted on the upper master die set, in front of each bushing and on the centerline of the work transfer axis, is a pancake type air cylinder for each station. These cylinders are actuated by cams (not shown) mounted on the vertical driveshaft, using shop air for power and plastic tubes to connect the cams to the cylinders. These cylinders are used to eject the workpieces into the nests in the lower dies.

Presses for the SDT process have been built with capacities of 22, 45, and 75 tons (197.7, 400.3, and 667.2 kN), and Westberg is currently building a 100-ton (889.6-kN) machine. The 22 and 45-ton presses operate at 80 to 140 spm to produce 40 to 70 parts per minute, the 75-ton machine runs at 60 to 120 spm, and the 100-ton press will operate at 60 to 100 spm. Standard leads (station spacings) are 3 inches (76.2 mm) for the 22-ton press, 4 inches (101.6 mm) for the 45-ton machine, and 5 inches (127 mm) for both 75 and 100-ton presses. While the lead is fixed on each press, it could be varied when the press is being built to suit specific application requirements. One press has been supplied with interchangeable cams and master die sets to provide two different leads.

Standard safety features provided on

each press include a double control circuit system, Wintriss proximity part detectors, and a Pro-Tek capacitance type (radio frequency) presence sensing device that stops the press if the operator places his hands near the point of operation. The control console, *Figure* 6, includes indicator lights for the proximity detector and safety systems, start-stop pushbuttons, a parts counter, and a tachometer scale to indicate press speed in strokes per minute.

Die Design. Most of the dies that have been built for the SDT process contain five stations, but some have three or four stations, and more than five could be provided if required. Standard master die sets have two locating dowels and two screw sets in both upper and lower members for securing to the press ram and reciprocating slide respectively. Standard dowel locations are also provided on both members of the master die set for the individual die stations, thus simplifying construction. One master die set for each press handles all parts within its size and lead capabilities.

Individual dies are easy to replace in changing production to a different part. Some dies and many of the holding blocks and plates used at the individual die stations can often be used to produce different parts. Air cylinders provided at the individual die stations primarily for ejecting parts into the nests can also be used to perform operations such as coining, piercing, and embossing, especially on small parts, during the work or deposit strokes with proper adjustment of the die levels. Otherwise, such operations might require an additional die station or use of a double-action press method. The SDT process also permits the use of split dies for pushing metal outward, as

6. *CONTROL CONSOLE for SDT press includes indicator lights for proximity detector and safety systems, and a scale to show press speed in strokes per minute.*

required in forming lips on cups.

The first station for most SDT applications is usually a compound die that blanks the OD of each part upward while simultaneously piercing the ID downward, with scrap falling out the bottom. Parts are always retained in the upper dies or on the punches when the press ram rises after each work stroke. This is accomplished by pilots about 0.0005-inch (0.013-mm) oversize entering existing holes in the workpieces, strippers on the upper punches, or shedders in the lower dies, depending on which way the parts are being formed. ∎

Reprinted from Manufacturing Engineering, September 1973

MODERN LAMINATION DIE
in the diemaking process at Lamina, Inc. Details of the construction of dies
of this type are covered in this article and a second article to follow.

Basics of Lamination Dies, Part 1

Lamination dies have evolved from rudimentary dies
into super sophisticated press tools capable of production
runs in excess of 300 million. In this article, the first of two,
details are provided on design and capabilities

DANIEL B. DALLAS
Editorial Director

LAMINA, INC., OF OAK PARK, MICHIGAN, is one of the top designers and builders of lamination dies in the country today. Lamina's large backlog of orders is directly attributed to its extensive experience in building lamination dies, the insistence of Lamina President F. J. Henkel that the company specialize in the construction of lamination dies only, and the concentrated follow-up of engineering and servicing of each order by qualified personnel.

Lamina's customers include some of the top names in the manufacture of electric motors; Emerson Electric, Franklin Electric, General Electric, A. O. Smith, and Westinghouse, among others. Overseas customers are located in Turkey, Egypt, Iran, Mexico, and South America.

To find out what it is that makes this company so successful in the highly competitive field of lamination diemaking, MEM has spent quite a bit of time with Chief Engineer Vic Gross in Lamina's shop and engineering of-

fices. In this article, the first of two on the subject, the Lamina approach to design and fabrication is discussed.

According to Vic Gross, the biggest problem currently facing users of lamination dies is that of insufficient maintenance time. In lamination stamping plants, as in all stamping plants, time allocated to assembly, disassembly, and maintenance is at a minimum. Therefore, Lamina's answer to this problem is to design and build dies in such a way that dismantling for grinding and repairs is held to a minimum.

In many cases the company's design innovations are quite effective. In virtually all cases they can be applied

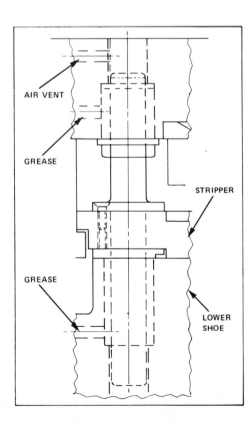

STRIPPERS ARE STABILIZED
by guidepins of this type. During die operation, these pins are never disengaged from the upper and lower shoes. Use of these pins, rather than the die set guidepins, permits use of a thicker stripper that is smaller in overall dimensions.

to many forms of routine progressive dies. Above all—with or without a highly skilled maintenance staff—they can do much to increase the productivity of all your stamping operations.

The Stripper. Design of the stripper has undergone numerous changes in the past twenty years—perhaps more changes than any other part of the die. There was a time when virtually all strippers were bridge type units. Punch openings were hand filed, and the stripper material was soft steel. The limitations of this design were insufficient support of the punches and a tendency for the stock to tip during punch withdrawal. Both conditions led to excessive punch breakage.

Today's stripper is an integral working member of the die. It moves with the upper die on guidepins that are always engaged with the top and bottom members. This design rules out the possibility of any cocking movement in the stripper—movement that could easily snap the punches.

The importance of close control over stripper movement is seen in the tightness of clearance between punch and stripper. The stock normally run in a lamination die is from 0.018 to 0.025 inch thick. This means that the clearance (on one side) between punch and die is in the order of 0.001 inch. In Lamina's die standards, the clearance between punch and stripper must be 50 percent of the punch-die clearance. Thus the clearance between punch and stripper is in the order of 0.0005 inch—far too little to sustain movement or cocking of the stripper.

In many non-Lamina designs, the overall dimensions of the stripper correspond to the dimensions of the top and bottom shoes. In these designs the stripper is guided and supported by the die guidepins. Lamina prefers a smaller stripper containing its own guidepins, since the smaller the stripper, the less the tendency to flexure. Moreover, the reduction in overall dimensions permits greater stripper thickness and this, too, provides greater insurance against tilting and flexure. Additionally, fixing of the guideposts in the stripper provides greater bearing surface than can be obtained in the die set guideposts.

Most Lamina strippers are 1¼ inch thick. They're made of medium carbon steel hardened to $R_c 38$. Stripper inserts which guide the punches are HCHC

hardened to $R_c 60$-62. The stripper guidepins are equipped with flanges and fixed to the stripper with three to four screws per pin.

Preloading the Stripper. Another important design feature of the stripper is the use of preloaded springs. This design—which can easily be adapted to virtually all progressive dies—solves three problems: pulldown; uniformity of pressure; and lost springs.

▶ PULLDOWN. Normally, the job of pulling a stripper down into place presents problems. In the case of a stripper used for punch support and guidance, the problem areas can include broken punches. In many instances the stripper is pulled down by C-clamps for subsequent mounting of hanger blocks. The trouble with this approach is that the C-clamps may be tightened at an uneven rate, in which case delicate punches guided by the stripper can be snapped. But if the springs are preloaded (see drawing), the stripper can be manually set in place without the need to fight the springs. The hangers, which may absorb the last 0.010 inch of load, can easily be bolted in place without endangering delicate piercing punches.

▶ UNIFORM PRESSURE. One of the principal difficulties in the use of conventional blanking or progressive dies is that of timing between punches and stripper. In many cases, the stripper is lowered every time the punches are ground. If the stripper isn't lowered, it may be necessary to shim up the punch sections.

Since shimming up the punches is normally unacceptable when running lamination dies, it's necessary to set the die progressively deeper to compensate for decreasing punch length. This

leads to increased spring pressure and therefore to shortened spring life and greater danger of spring failure. The advantage of the Lamina design is that the service washers (see drawing) can be ground to maintain correct timing of the die and stripper without changing the preload value established in design.

▶ LOST SPRINGS. How much of a problem this may be depends entirely on the quality of the die maintenance staff. In any case, Lamina's design eliminates the problem by holding the springs to the stripper with shoulder bolts. This approach will be of interest to progressive die operators involved in routine sheet metal forming. In many cases it's necessary to use heavy duty springs in certain areas of a stripper, and standard springs in another. This is something the die repairman may not appreciate—and if he doesn't, there's an excellent chance that the springs will be interchanged whenever the die is down for repairs. Obviously, the technique of bolting the springs to the stripper solves this problem.

Stock Centralizers. Lamina die design calls for an intermediate step between the conventional stockguides and the pilots. This step takes the form of a set of "stock centralizers" mounted in the stripper. Since conventional progressive dies, like lamination dies, use guides and pilots for stock control, this approach will be of interest to virtually all stampers.

The advantage of stock centralizers is their ability to align slightly misaligned stock prior to punch and pilot entry. In effect, the stockguides pick up the stock for positioning by the centralizers; the centralizers, in turn, bring the stock into position for pilot pickup.

No more than four centralizers are

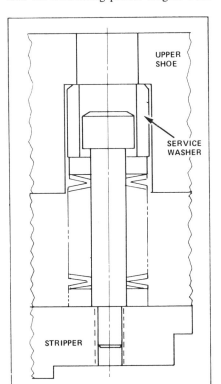

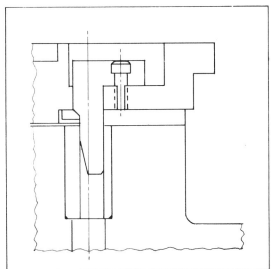

PRELOADING THE STRIPPER PLATE is accomplished with this design. The spring is given predetermined compression by a shoulder screw. Timing is maintained by grinding an amount off the service washer equal to the amount ground off the punches during sharpening.

ALIGNING THE INCOMING STRIP is accomplished with four stock centralizers of this design. Their use relieves the pilots of all work other than that of guaranteeing the progression.

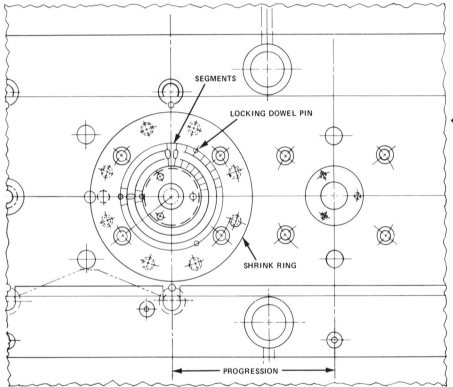

SEGMENTS

LOCKING DOWEL PIN

SHRINK RING

PROGRESSION

shoe, a Meehanite casting, is shaped in the form of an inverted T. Die clusters are fitted into shrink rings which, in turn, are fitted into holes bored on the station lines. Again, design is predicated on the need to simplify die dismantling for grinding or repairs. If a die segment requires replacement, for example, dismantling is confined to the related station. None of the other stations are affected. If die sharpening is required, the guidepins, stock guides and stock lifters are removed, and the entire die is placed on the surface grinder chuck. Subsequent grinding covers the entire die surface.

▶ DIE WITHIN A DIE. In this design concept, one or more stations can be built as individual dies. The lamination die numbered 13568 is an excellent example in that the master die contains two subordinate dies, one of which contains a third die. The nature of the operation performed—notching of large corner sections—precludes the use of self-contained die stations. At the same time, the use of individual dies assures fast teardown and reassembly, as required.

Guidepins. Removal of guidepins for die sharpening or repair is simplified through use of taper-lock guidepins, an item that is commercially available from Lamina. One of the more interesting aspects of this design is that guidepin removal is easier to effect than stripper removal—a condition which some may think contradictory

used—two at the station where pilot holes are pierced and two at the first pilot station. Clearance between the stock and the centralizers is 0.005 inch—a dimension small enough to assure stock alignment with the axis of the die, and large enough to enable the stock to float. Clearance between stock and stockguide is normally ¹⁄₁₆ to ¹⁄₃₂ inch.

To some companies other than Lamina, the use of centralizers is now established practice. To others it's unheard of, since it's assumed that the pilots can handle stock location.

Actually, the concept of piloting does not include the correction of angular feeding, as those who have seen the phenomenon of "pilot pull" can attest. The role of the pilots is simply to guarantee correct advance of the stock—

something it can do most effectively when aided by four stock centralizers.

The Bottom Die. Like numerous other die builders, Lamina formerly pocketed its lower die sections. In theory, at least, there's nothing wrong with a sequence of pocketed die sections, but it can pose problems through accumulated tolerances. These problems can be especially severe when relatively inexperienced personnel dismantle a die for repairs or grinding. To solve these problems Lamina now takes two general approaches to die design. One is a sequence of self-contained die stations nested in jig-bored holes in the lower shoe. The other is the die-within-a-die concept—and sometimes a die within a die that is mounted within still another die.

▶ SELF-CONTAINED STATIONS. The lower

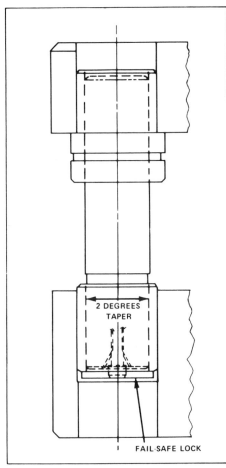

2 DEGREES TAPER

FAIL-SAFE LOCK

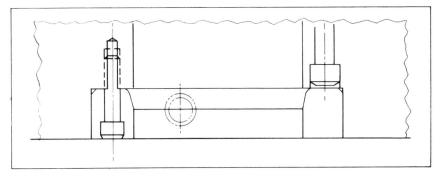

SPONGINESS IS ELIMINATED
by this device, held in the bottom of the lower shoe with one screw. Essentially,
this is a split washer that can be adjusted to part thickness. As such it permits
part passage while taking the pressure of the column of finished parts.

DESIGNED FOR FAST PULLOUT
the guidepins fit into a 2-deg taper
bushing in the bottom shoe.
◀ *This facilitates pin removal for*
sharpening of the die. It also permits
pin pullout in the event of pin freezeup
in the upper shoe.

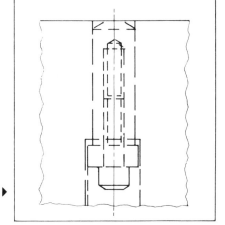

HEMISPHERIC END OF THE LIFTER
need not be ground when the die is
lowered. Instead, the pin is removed ▶
and ground at the opposite
end after removal of the flange.

to the concept of a high precision die. In fact, the end cap used in this design is something of a fail-safe device in that it breaks and allows easy pin pullout in the unlikely event of pin-bushing seizure. Lamina has three answers to those who insist that guidepins should be of massive construction and firmly anchored in the bottom shoe.

The first is that the role of the guidepins is to maintain die alignment at all times except when the die is in actual operation. Their function does not include the maintenance of alignment during operation in the press. For no guidepin—no matter how large in diameter it may be—can overcome any inaccuracy in the slide.

The second is that the taper construction of these guidepins—while providing ease of pin removal—provides absolute accuracy of location, no matter how many times the pins are removed.

The third answer is that the company manufactures conventional press fit guidepins as part of its standard commercial line, and the customer who insists on this type of guidepin in his lamination die can have it. But from an engineering point of view, Lamina definitely recommends taper-lock guidepins for use in all precision dies.

Die Clusters. As the accompanying drawing shows, four dowel pins are used to lock the various segments of a die cluster in place. The rationale for this design is simply that the seg-

ments, if assembled starting and ending at a single dowel pin, tend to accumulate tolerance. This tends to make the last segment difficult to insert. It also makes perpendicularity of the segments more difficult to attain.

But if four dowel pins are used, the diemaker or die repairman can work in quadrants. In effect, he divides the tolerance and problems of perpendicularity by four. Moreover, he saves a great deal of bench time, since only one quadrant need be disassembled if a single segment needs repair.

Stock Lifters. The drawing of the stock lifter shows still another design which can be used to advantage in non-lamination die work. Again, the advantage is simplified maintenance. Stock lifters of this design (i.e., cylindrical) must have hemispheric ends if the die is to function smoothly. But as the die is lowered through continued grinding, the cylindrical portion of the lifter begins to extend above the die surface, effectively blocking stock advance.

Two solutions to this problem are normally followed. The first is to lower the hemispheric tip by machine grinding. The second is to rough grind the circular configuration on a pedestal grinder.

The first alternative is expensive. The second is unacceptable shop practice, although it is a practice followed by an increasingly large number of inexperienced maintenance men. The best answer is the two-part lifter shown.

The repairman removes the head—held in place by a socket head capscrew—and surface grinds the flat end of the lifter by an amount equal to the amount ground off the die surface.

Squeeze Rings. Removal of stampings from a lamination die is accomplished with stacking chutes. Designed to attach to the bottom of the bolster, the chutes keep the stampings in a columnar configuration, although it's a column that can wind and twist. While the design and fabrication of stacking chutes is too complex a subject to be handled in this article, it should be noted that the advance of the column of stampings is effected by the action of the cutoff punch.

The weight of the column, which must be advanced by punch action, leads to a condition in the die that is generally referred to as "sponginess." It can be solved, however, with a device called a squeeze ring, one of which is shown in the accompanying illustration. Because the squeeze ring can be adjusted to precisely the right amount of tension, it can hold a number of laminations—thus assuring their flatness—while simultaneously eliminating back pressure from stampings, retained in the stacking chutes. ◀

Reprinted from Manufacturing Engineering, October 1973

Basics of Lamination Dies, Part 2

In this article, the second of two on the subject, attention is given to the top shoe and press. Emphasis is also given to preferred methods of grinding lamination dies

DANIEL B. DALLAS
Editorial Director

IN DEVELOPING ITS CONCEPT of lamination dies, Lamina, Inc., Oak Park, Michigan, has stressed the need to simplify maintenance. At the same time, it has sought to make the lamination die a far more productive tool than it has been in the past. Its success in the latter is measurable partly by the fact that runs are longer than ever, and partly by the fact that lamination dies have greater capabilities for producing different families of parts.

In terms of production runs, the company's lamination dies can now produce more than 300 million stampings before reaching the end of their useful life. This assumes a carbide die, of course.

In terms of capabilities, the lead photograph presents a good example. This die is designed for the production of a family of parts. It has four different shaft hole sets, two different rotor clusters, and one stator cluster. Conversion of this tool from one part to another simply requires substitution of one set of components for another, a changeover that can be effected in a matter of eight hours.

Most important of all, this die is designed for ease of maintenance. Design aspects of lamination dies pertaining to the stripper and lower die were presented in the first article in this series. (MEM, Sept. 1973, p. 42.) This article deals with the upper shoe, overall die sizes, and the all-important subject of die grinding.

Punches. Normally, long punches equal long die life. But in conventional dies, long perforating punches also equal short punch life. The reason, of course, is that the punches do not have the support necessary to withstand the lateral forces encountered in piercing.

Lamina's solution to this problem is the double spider design shown sectionally and as a photograph. The secret of this design is the second spider, a unit which—for all practical purposes—is a second punch retainer. When the punches have been shortened by a certain amount, the stripper comes into close proximity with the second spider. This problem is solved by grinding the spacers between the spiders. Thus the outer support spider can gradually be retracted to provide space for the stripper. At the same time, it can be maintained in a position that provides maximum punch support. This design feature, more than anything else, accounts for the longevity of these lamination dies.

Slug pulling—always a problem in dies that use small perforating punches —is solved by air pressure, supplied through the punches. Lamina has found that this method of slug disposal is most effective if two sources of air supply are used. If only one is used, the pressure differential that develops between front and back is too great to keep the slugs down on the side opposite to air entry. It would be possible, of course, to increase the pressure, but doing so would lead to a waste of air on the intake side. Accordingly, air is brought in from two diametrically opposed sides. This permits effective blowoff with low pressure—in the order of 2 to 12 psi.

Timing. An interesting approach to punch and stripper timing is seen in the design of the hangers. It will be noted that the hanger in the sectional view is counterbored from both sides. The design rationale is that the original timing can be kept intact if the hangers are ground when the punches are ground. Accordingly, this design permits inversion of the hangers on the shoe. Prior to grinding, they're screwed to the shoe in upside down position, and then finished off with the punches.

It's possible to be critical of this design, since it requires the use of an expensive diamond wheel to grind cold-rolled steel hangers. However, the design is extremely popular with many users of lamination dies, presumably because it enables relatively inexperienced die repairmen to maintain perfect timing with minimum effort.

In line with this, the spacer washers associated with the stripper must be ground by an amount equal to that removed from the punches and hanger blocks. Discussed in the first article, these spacers enable the stripper springs to maintain their original preload. In the event they're not ground—and this is something that should be included on the die maintenance process sheet—spring pressure will build up to dangerously high levels as the die is progressively lowered through sharpening.

This design for timing and preload, like the air blowoff system and the double spider, need not be restricted to lamination dies. These techniques can be effectively used in many ordinary sheet metal progressive dies.

Cam-positioned Punches. Still another design feature which has applications elsewhere is seen in the cam-positioned punch. Its purpose is to bring another punch into play without dismantling the die each time the punch is inserted or removed.

To activate the punch, the setup man or press operator simply loosens a

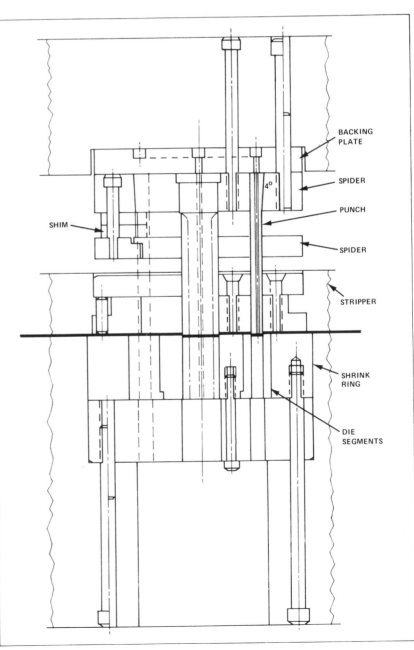

BACKING PLATE

SPIDER

PUNCH

SHIM

SPIDER

STRIPPER

SHRINK RING

DIE SEGMENTS

4°

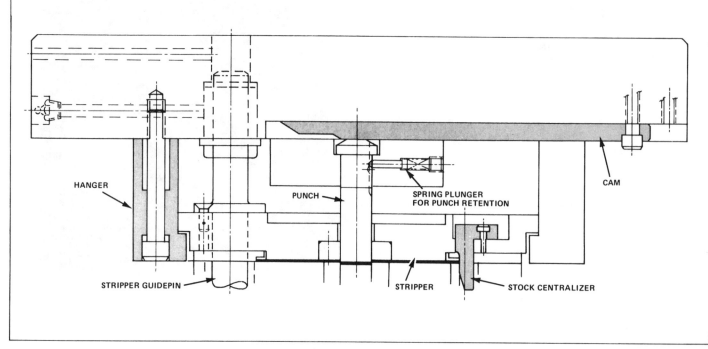

TIMING AND CAM ACTIVATION OF PUNCHES
are shown in this drawing. To maintain timing as the punch is lowered due to sharpening, the hangers must also be ground—from the bottom. The counterbored holes in the hangers permit inversion and grinding during punch sharpening. The punch at the center is activated by forward advance of the cam shown. Retraction of the cam deactivates the punch.

socket head capscrew used to hold the cam in position. He then moves the cam forward and screws the capscrew into the next hole. Advance of the cam forces the punch down for hole trimming in what is an otherwise idle station. When the cam is retracted to deactivate the station, the punch is pushed upward manually. A Vlier spring plunger engages it at this point, holding it up and out of the way.

Specifications. It is Lamina's recommendation that dies be designed to a 12-inch maximum shut height wherever possible. The feed line should be 6 inches above the bolster. The bolster itself should be 6 to 8 inches thick. The importance of maximum heft cannot be overemphasized, since the bolster and die—no matter how thick they may be —tend to bow under the bottoming action of the press.

The thickness of the die sections varies slightly according to material. In carbide dies, the die sections should be 1¼ inches thick. In HCHC dies, the bottom sections can be as much as 1⅜ inches. Relief in the sections should be approximately 0.0015 inch taper per inch of thickness. Because of this taper, it is necessary to plan on more frequent sharpenings as the die is lowered through grinding.

The Press. The stroke of the press should be at least 1 inch. This has nothing to do with die operation—it's simply that a minimum of 1 inch is required for periodic examination of the die. Should

problems of any sort occur in the die, even 1 inch makes for rather tight quarters.

It is Lamina's recommendation that the press in which a lamination die is operated have twice the tonnage actually required. Advantages of "overpressing" include smoother and quieter operation. This stems from the fact that dies can close on the stock without taking up all the slack in the bearings. This, in turn, means that the dies can perform their cutting action without accelerating at the bottom of the stroke due to dropping of the slide.

Parallelism between bolster and slide

SETUP FOR GRINDING A LAMINATION DIE.
Delicate punches are supported by a frame consisting of two strips tack welded together. To facilitate mounting of the frame, the punch openings are filed to a slip fit or etched with muriatic acid.

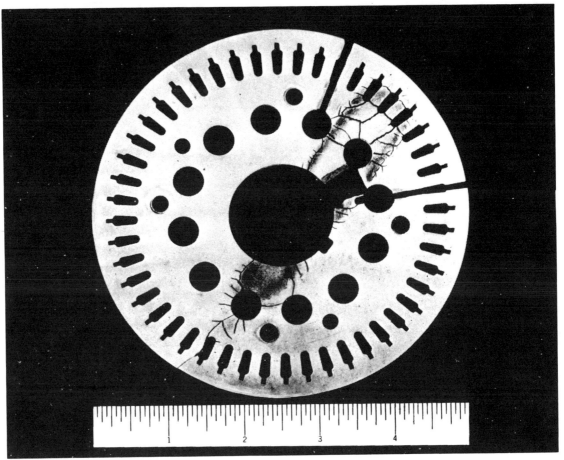

DIE FAILURE DUE TO BURN is seen in this photo. Hardness at the center of this HCHC rotor die is R$_c$60-62. Although burn was camouflaged by subsequent grinding, its effects were brought out, as shown, with a sulfuric acid etch.

is mandatory. Checking for parallelism can be done with an indicator and by attempting to insert a thin feeler gage between lower die and bolster, and between upper die and slide. A secondary advantage of the latter is that it sometimes leads to the detection of foreign objects—slugs, for example—on top of the die. Checking the bolster with a surface gage/indicator setup is beneficial in locating low spots—usually in the center of the bolster—which can and do cause deformation of the die. However, inspection for parallelism must be done under load, since it is a load condition that causes the slide to tip if its gibs and bearings are defective.

Defective gibbing and bearings is a recurrent problem when lamination dies are run. The small amount of clearance in these dies plus the brittleness of tungsten carbide allows for no deviation in the downward movement of the slide. If a slight deviation exists, a lamination die made of high-carbon, high-chrome may be operable, but a tungsten carbide die is not.

One of the more prevalent causes of defective gibbings is lack of perpendicularity in the press itself. In many cases presses are set up at a slight angle to the vertical. When this is done, there is a natural, although often imperceptible, shift of the slide to the low side. This leads to increased wear on one side and subsequently to an out-of-parallel condition when the dies close. And this, of course, is an intolerable

condition when close tolerance lamination dies are operated in the press.

Die Grinding. While Lamina has no special recommendations regarding wheels, the company has found two types highly successful in its own die-making operations. In diamond wheels for tungsten carbide, it prefers an MDW 100P-75-B 1/8. In aluminum oxide, its preference is an LLA-3620-H-8-V-2. These are the wheels selected for final grinding prior to delivery of a die to the customer.

Final dressing is accomplished with a single pass of the diamond. This pass should be fast to minimize the possibility of dulling and polishing the grain. This, in turn, minimizes the possibility of heat buildup.

Wheel speeds should be low. Reason: the slower the speed, the less the heat buildup on the surface of the work.

Shallow cuts are necessary. Again, the objective is to grind with minimum buildup of heat. Accordingly, cuts no deeper than 0.0002 inch are recommended. In contrast, cuts across the face of the work can be quite rapid—in the order of ½ inch or more per stroke of the grinder.

Use strips to support the punches. Two strips, tack welded together, can be slipped over the punches to provide support during grinding. It's important, however, that this support device not be pounded on the punches. Pounding invariably leads to punch chipping. To provide an easy gage fit, the openings

should be etched with acid or filed. In the case of a new die, the stripper must be used to support the punches during the initial grind, but this approach is not recommended for existing dies. One objection is that the stripper acts as a receptacle for diamond grit which eventually erodes the punches and die sections. In line with this, thorough cleansing to remove all traces of diamond dust after grinding is mandatory.

Should the steel inadvertently be burned, it's necessary to grind 0.005 to 0.010 inch below the burn to remove the stressed area. A good example of why is seen in the accompanying photograph. In this case, an operator accidently burned a solid die section by bringing the wheel down too fast. He subsequently camouflaged his mistake by grinding until the area affected "cleaned up." Subsequently, the section broke in service. The reason why remained a mystery until the plant metallurgist applied an acid etch to the surface, at which time the hidden burn emerged.

The cost of grinding is expensive even if considered only in terms of die life. For example, if a die costs $40,000—a figure that is about average for the modern carbide lamination die—and if it has an inch of useful life, the die cost of every thousandth of an inch removed is $40. Accordingly, the greatest of care must be exercised to avoid burning, but if it occurs it must be corrected prior to return of the die to service. ◀

Reprinted from Sheet Metal Industries, April 1980

TOOLING FOR ELECTRICAL STEELS

Carbide tools for lamination blanking - analysis of some basic factors affecting design and use.

by Dott. Ing. Giancarlo Corrada

This report deals with problems and experiences relating to the blanking — with carbide tools — of thin sheet steel (thickness 0.35mm to 1mm) for electrical applications: motors, transformers, watt-meters, reactors and remote-control switches. In view of a rational utilization of tools, some major factors are taken into consideration: the press, the lubricant and more specifically the sheet steel.

In order to obtain the best results and taking into account that speeds of 400-800 blows/min and coil stock feed rates of 50-80m/min are currently considered as normal, the press should feature the following characteristics:

Enclosed structure with the highest possible rigidity;

minimum clearances;

dynamic balancing of the various masses of the upper parts of the tool in order to minimise vibrations at all operating speeds:

thermal stability at all operating speeds in all important areas of the press, *eg* uprights, guides, ram and bolster;

reduction to a minimum of parallelism errors between bolster and ram both statically and dynamically;

very-high-precision coil-stock feeding system;

efficient coil-stock straightener.

The lubricant

Before introducing the sheet steel into the tool, lubrication is performed by using "oil plus kerosene," oil emulsions in water, oil solutions in kerosene and many other systems.

Chemical characteristics and application methods of any lubricating

This article formed part of the programme for the Sheet Metal Conference presented during the 3EMO held in Milan.

L'usage des outils de carbure dans la préparation des flans pour stratification — Analyse de facteurs essentiels en vue d'une utilisation rationnelle.
Karbidwerkzeuge für das Ausstanzen von Lamellenblechen — eine Analyse einiger grundlegender Faktoren in bezug auf die rationelle Verwendung.

system must meet the following requirements, at least as far as carbide tools are concerned:

In addition to its detergent properties, the lubricant must act as a true lubricant. The effectiveness of this action depends on the chemical-physical properties of the lubricating system and, in the case of mixtures, on the percentage of lubricant in water or kerosene.

The *p*H value must be neutral, otherwise the lubricant can initiate chemical corrosion of the cobalt bond in the carbide. This action would result in accelerated wear of carbide punches and dies and, consequently, in their rapid degradation.

The presence of sulphur cannot be allowed, except for traces. The presence of sulphur also can initiate corrosion as described above.

The sheet steel

The mechanical properties of the sheet steel have a direct and substantial impact on the design and performance of a carbide tool. To this end the most important mechanical properties are:

Yield point	Y (kg/mm²)
Tensile strength	T (kg/mm²)
Yield point/tensile strength ratio	Y/T
Elongation	A%
Surface hardness on the two faces of the steel	HV5

In general the determination of these properties in the longitudinal (rolling) direction of the coil stock is sufficient. In this report reference is exclusively made to the above properties.

Their determination in the trans-

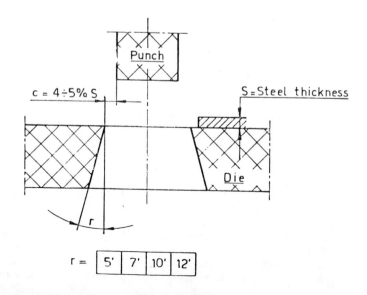

Fig 1
Clearance and die relief.

Punch

c = 4÷5% S

S=Steel thickness

Die

r

r = 5' 7' 10' 12'

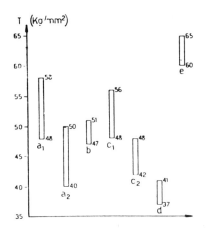

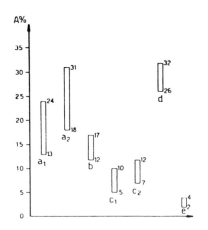

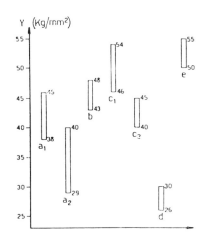

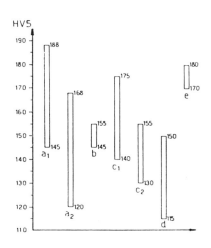

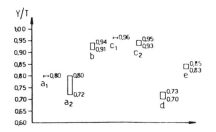

a₁ = Silicon steel
a₂ = Silicon steel

b = Semiprocessed silicon steel

c₁ = Low carbon semiprocessed steel
c₂ = Low carbon semiprocessed steel

d = Fe P01 steel

e = Fully hardened steel

Fig 2 *Mechanical properties histograms.*

verse direction may be necessary only in special cases—for example, when deformation in all directions caused by the release of residual stresses in blanks is to be controlled and reduced to a minimum. In this respect a typical example is the need to minimise the ovalisation error of the internal diameter of the stator of high-performance electric motors (*eg* sealed compressor units).

As regards carbide-tool design a major early decision has to be made on the clearance between punches and dies, die relief and carbide grades for punches and dies.

Fig 1 shows the range of variability of clearance (c) and relief (r) values. The selection of optimal "c" and "r" values for each application depends on the specific mechanical properties

of the sheet steel to be used as well as on other parameters such as the shape of the workpiece to be blanked and its possible critical sections.

The "blankability" of a certain type of sheet steel can be expressed by means of the following factors: number of blows between sharpenings; resultant tool wear and burr height on blanked laminations; obtaining and holding of specified dimensions of laminations; lamination flatness; possible tendency of slugs to lift or to be forced into the die openings.

In 1969 the author began a study of the correlation between sheet steel mechanical properties and blankability factors. To this end, following a specific request, a number of research institutes tested the

mechanical properties of hundreds of sheet steels; results were then compared with design factors ("c," "r," carbide grades) and with the performance of related tools.

The author stresses, therefore, that his research results are not based on theoretical laboratory experiments but on ten years of actual operation of a large number of carbide tools for a total of many hundreds of millions of blows. The final results of the research concern the life of the carbide tool both *up and downstream. Upstream—in relation to tool design*—the clearance "c" between punches and dies and especially die relief "r" must be increased proportionately to the increase of sheet steel elongation A% and to the decrease of Y and T absolute values and of the Y/T ratio.

As the higher or lower value of "r" implies a larger or smaller total useful die thickness to be sharpened, it is clear that the use of sheet steel with a low A% value allows for a longer tool life, provided the tool is properly designed. *Downstream—in relation to tool utilisation*—from the "blankability" standpoint the performance of the sheet steel improves as its A% lowers, as Y and T absolute values increase, and as the Y/T ratio is closer to 1. On the other hand, HV5 surface hardness has no significance because sometimes sheet steel can be surface-hardened but possess a "soft core." Obviously, when a carbide tool is designed and built for a specific type of sheet steel, its performance will basically depend on the *uniformity* of the mechanical properties of the type of sheet steel used as compared with the characteristics taken into consideration in the tool-design stage.

At this point it may be worthwhile providing users of carbide tools and sheet steel with some practical indications based on the application of the above concepts. To this end, the mechanical properties of five types of sheet steel used in electrical applications are taken into consideration.

Fig 2 shows the histograms illustrating the ranges of variability of the mechanical properties of the types of sheet steel taken into consideration as determined on large batches in steel mills. Our considerations exclusively refer to the concepts of good or poor blankability of each type of sheet steel by means of carbide tools.

(a) Silicon steel

This includes traditional magnetic coil stock. Magnetic properties are specified by EU-106 and EU-107

EURONORM standards for normal and oriented-grain magnetic coil stock, respectively. However, none of the Euronorm standards covers the mechanical properties of sheet steel.

(a$_1$) and (a$_2$) sub-types of non-oriented-grain sheet steel are described here:

(a$_1$) Si content is between 2.00% and 2.50% with a core loss reaching values between 2 and 2.3W/kg for 0.5mm-thick sheet steel.

The maximum absolute T value (58kg/mm^2) is excellent while the minimum (48kg/mm^2) can be considered fair. The variability range of T (19%) is acceptable.

The per cent variability range is calculated by dividing the difference between the two extreme values by their arithmetical mean.

Minimum and maximum Y values are relatively low.

The Y/T ratio (about 0.80) is acceptable.

Minimum elongation value (A% = 13%) is good at least for this type of sheet steel; on the other hand, the maximum value (24%) is not so good. The related range of variability (51%) is very wide.

HV5 maximum value can be considered as acceptable; the corresponding minimum value is low.

As to blankability, this type of coil stock is not exceptional but acceptable, especially when T and Y values are close to maximum and A% is close to minimum.

(a$_2$) Si content ranges between 1.00% and 1.50% with a core loss reaching values between 3 and 3.6W/kg for 0.5mm-thick sheet steel. T maximum absolute value (50kg/mm^2) is good while the minimum value (40kg/mm^2) is too low.

Y minimum and maximum values are definitely lower than those of (a$_1$) sheet steel; the Y/T ratio may reach values between 0.80 and 0.72 (the latter value is to be considered low). A% minimum value (18%) is barely sufficient while the maximum value (31%) is very high. The range of variability, too, is very wide (52%). HV5 minimum value is definitely low. As to blankability, the behaviour of this type of coil stock is barely acceptable only when T and Y reach maximum values and A% its minimum. Blankability becomes critical when the values of mechanical properties are reversed.

(b) Semiprocessed silicon steel

As indicated by the definition, this type of sheet steel contains silicon; however, it has to be annealed after blanking. The Euronorm standard for this sheet steel is in the process of being defined. However,

it can be anticipated that this standard too will not deal with mechanical properties. This type of sheet steel has a silicon content ranging between 1.00% and 1.50%. After annealing it shows a maximum core loss of 2.3W/kg. Sheet steel (b) has a chemical composition substantially similar to that of (a$_2$); its processing cycle, however, is different. In Italy, this type of sheet steel is not yet widely used. The following values of mechanical properties relate to a small number of measurements.

T maximum and minimum absolute values (51 and 47kg/mm^2) are good and the range of variability (10%) is narrow.

Y values (48 and 43kg/mm^2) and the variability range (10%) are also good. As a result, Y/T minimum and maximum values (0.91 and 0.94) are excellent.

A% extreme values (12% and 17%) are fair, although a lower maximum value would be preferable.

As to blankability, this type of sheet steel shows good mechanical properties.

(c) Low-carbon semiprocessed steel

After blanking, this silicon-free sheet steel needs annealing at 720°C to 800°C in a controlled decarbonising environment in order to acquire specific magnetic properties. EU-126 Euronorm standard specifies the magnetic properties of this type of sheet steel; once again mechanical properties are ignored. (c$_1$) and (c$_2$) sub-types are described here:

(c$_1$) For a 0.5mm thickness, maximum core loss is 2.8W/kg after annealing.

Fig 3 *Type of tool taken into consideration.*

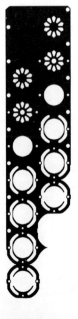

T maximum absolute value (56kg/mm^2) is very good and its variability range is acceptable.

The same considerations apply to Y values.

Y/T values (about 0.96) are very close to 1 and, therefore, exceptionally good.

A% minimum value (5%) is excellent and its maximum (10%) is good. The related range of variability (66%) is wide. However, it is acceptable in consideration of its low absolute values.

HV5 maximum value is good, though the minimum could be better.

As to blankability, (c$_1$) sheet steel is very good.

(c$_2$) For a 0.5mm thickness maximum core loss is 3.60 W/kg after annealing.

T maximum absolute value (48kg/mm^2) is good and its range of variability (13%) is narrow.

Y values are not exceptional even if they are acceptable especially in the high range.

Y/T minimum and maximum values are very good.

A% minimum value (7%) is very good; its maximum value (12%) can be considered fair. A% wide range of variability (52%) is still acceptable in consideration of its low absolute values.

HV5 maximum and minimum values are modest.

As to blankability, (c$_2$) sheet steel is to be considered good.

(d) FePO1 sheet steel for bending and light stamping

The utilisation of this type of sheet steel in the electrical field is inappropriate; the definition itself clearly indicates that the end use of this steel is quite different. Nevertheless its use in the electrical field is widespread and its utilisation is essentially due to its low price. Manufacturers do not officially sell this steel for blanking magnetic laminations for electric motors and, therefore, do not provide any guarantee as to this application.

The analysis of the histograms of this sheet steel shows that T maximum and minimum absolute values (41 and 37kg/mm^2) are very low. Under these conditions, the narrow range of variability (10%) has no positive significance.

The same applies to the very low values of Y (30 and 26kg/mm^2).

In the presence of such negative values, the analysis of the Y/T ratio (0.70-0.73) is not very significant; in any case this ratio features low values.

HV5 extreme values are also very low.

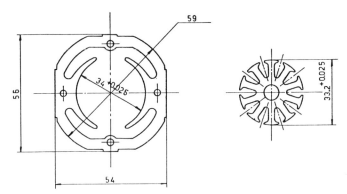

59

56

34⁺0.025

54

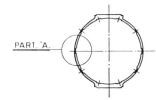

PART. 'A.

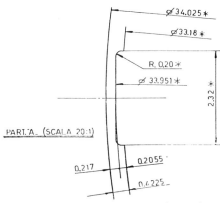

PART.'A. (SCALA 20:1)

∅ 34.025 *
∅ 33.18 *
R. 0.20 *
∅ 33.951 *
2.32 *

0.217   0.2055
         0.6225

Finally, A% minimum and maximum absolute value (26% and 32%) fully justify the designation of this coil stock as sheet steel for "bending and light stamping."

It has also to be pointed out that types of coil stock classified as FePO1 are often available on the market, yet with lower T and Y values than those previously mentioned.

As to blankability, (d) sheet steel is to be considered as not suitable; its utilisation on carbide tools requires the adoption of higher values of clearance between punches and dies and especially of die relief.

(e) Low-carbon fully-hardened cold-rolled steel

This is a low-carbon steel as (d).

	tool 1	tool 2
Blanking blows	45,885,000	18,188,000
Regrinds	14	5
Blows per regrind	3,277,000	3,637,000
Total thickness ground from the die	1.55mm	0.61mm
Thickness ground from die per regrind	0.11mm	0.12mm
Total thickness ground from punches	1.85mm	0.65mm
Thickness ground from punches per regrind	0.13mm	0.13mm

The considerations made for (d) apply to its magnetic properties and to its applications in the electrical field. The analysis of the histograms of (e) sheet steel shows that T maximum (65kg/mm²) and minimum (60kg/mm²) absolute values are excellent; the range of variability (8%) is very narrow.

Y maximum and minimum absolute values 55 and 50kg/mm²) are also excellent; the range of variability (10%) is narrow.

The values of the Y/T ratio are consequently good: from 0.83 to 0.85.

HV5 extreme values (170 and 180) are excellent.

Finally, A% minimum and maximum values (2% and 4%) are exceptionally low.

As to blankability, this type of sheet steel is to be considered excellent. This conclusion finds a confirmation in some data drawn from experience. The following are the excellent operating results obtained with this type of sheet steel. The data refer to two almost identical Stellram carbide tools (tool 1 and tool 2) blanking two sets of motor laminations per press blow. The two tools were supplied with an interval of three years.

Fig 3 shows the type of tool taken into consideration.

Fig 4 shows the sketches of the rotor/stator laminations and of the corresponding air-gap rings blanked by the tool. Blanking conditions in the air-gap area can be considered as "critical" if one takes into account the ratio between the rim blanked in the 10 thinnest areas (0.217mm) and the sheet steel thickness (0.70mm).

The performance data below refer to the latest period of tool utilisation, after both tools were provided with new especially designed air gap blanking punches. Punches are manufactured in a new Stellram carbide grade.

The excellent performance of these two tools, which are still in operation, are strictly related to the excellent mechanical properties of the sheet steel used and to the uniformity of their values in time. These favourable conditions also allowed the adoption of low "c" and especially "r" values in the tool design stage. This choice involves the following positive results: substantial increase in tool life and reduction in the number of tool maintenance and sharpening interventions.

Conclusions

When investigating the development of a carbide tool, it is found that design and manufacture are strictly related to precision criteria and tolerance ranges which should be within one-thousandth of a millimeter.

Clearly, to impose the adoption of such strict concepts on coil-stock manufacturers would be out of place and impossible. However, it is believed that it would be possible and appropriate to define limits and tolerances to the mechanical properties of different types of sheet steel.

In fact, there is no sense in spending several thousand hours of high'y skilled work and of sophisticated machinery to design and manufacture a carbide tool with tolerances of 1/1000mm just to process indiscriminately all available types of sheet steel regardless of their mechanical properties.

A clearer situation in the field would be beneficial to all those who are concerned (tool manufacturers, sheet steel manufacturers, and tool and sheet steel users) and this report is intended to be a contribution to the study and solution of the problem.

Finally, the valuable co-operation of the Falck company in compiling this report is gratefully acknowledged.

Fig 4 * = dimensions of blanking components.

33.2⁺0.025

Reprinted from Sheet Metal Industries, April 1980

FORMING TECHNOLOGY

Deep drawing and ironing - theory and practice - 2

by David Campion (Deepform Technology Ltd)

In this, the second article surveying aspects of combined deep drawing and ironing, the author looks at the considerable progress which has occurred in the design and use of tooling for this process. Similarly, improvements in lubrication have enhanced the result obtained and extended the application of the technique. Equipment available for the DDI process is reviewed in the final section of this article which forms part of a detailed survey of progress in the deep drawing and ironing field.

Tooling for combined drawing and ironing operations has improved considerably in recent years and this is an ongoing situation. An example of this improvement can be shown in the tooling for the DWI beverage can or aerosol can where the final wall thickness of the can is about 0.1mm. This is drawn and ironed from material of 0.3mm thickness at speeds of 150 to 180 strokes/minute. Tungsten carbide is extensively used for such tooling and special high-speed tool steel is used for many parts where high resistance to wear is required.

If drawing of a thick blank without a blankholder is considered, the following component parts will constitute a set of tools.

(a) Punch assembly
The "working" part of the punch assembly consists of the punch or mandrel, commonly of D2 material for non-ferrous work or a high-speed steel such as ASP 23 for use with ferrous blanks. The punch is hardened and ground to give a hardness of 60 to 62 R. and is drilled to provide an air passage to prevent a vacuum build-up during stripping. The flat blank is cupped and ironed on to this punch surface. The punch is bolted to a punch extension, of the same diameter, which runs in guide

bushes of phosphor-bronze. The punch extension is finish ground to size but is not through hardened.

The punch carries the blank through the cupping and ironing tool set and there are good arguments for using a slightly rough punch. With a very smooth punch the friction on the inside walls of the pressing is low and nearly all the punch force is carried on the base of the pressing; this leads to increased tensile forces on the walls of the pressing.

With a roughened punch, there is greater friction between the punch and the inside wall of the pressing and this friction helps to transmit the punch load to the work. This, in turn, lowers the tensile forces in the wall of the pressing. The problem of using a roughened punch lies in stripping the work. Where this high friction exists, stripping will be difficult and if a thin-wall pressing is being made, then buckling of the walls of the pressing could occur on stripping.

(b) Blank locator
It is essential to locate the blank centrally with respect to the axis of the tractrix cupping die. Some designers prefer a stepped profile to the cupping die as shown here in fig 6. However, this is not felt to be as good as a separate mechanism located immediately before the cupping die. Such a separate blank-location device will contain adjustable pins to centralize the blank and can be designed to accommodate blanks of ± 10mm diameter so that it can be used again in conjunction with a different cupping die. The blank locator is fitted with a sensing device to register when

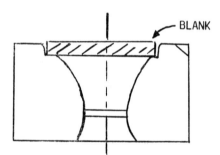

Fig 6.

the blank is correctly located and to signal the punch to advance.

(c) Cupping die
This is possibly the most important part of the tool set when working from flat blanks (see fig 6 (a)). The design of the cupping die is critical since the cylindrical work emerging from the die must be axi-symmetrical, must have minimum eccentricity and should be "square". Although there may well be earing present, the ears should be regular in height and not slope from one side of the pressing to the other.

In addition to all this, the cupping die must not permit folding of the blank and must also offer the least frictional resistance during the passage of the cup. In order to present as little friction as possible the pure geometric tractrix form of the die is modified since the blank thickens during cupping and also lengthens (see fig 7). Both the thickening and lengthening are taken into account in the design of the die.

Finally, the die (fig 8) should be capable of carrying out corrective ironing so that the first ironing die in

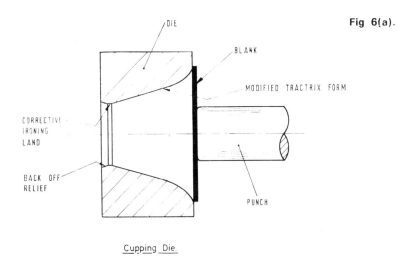

Fig 6(a).

Cupping Die.

the sequence is presented with a uniform wall thickness.

The die must be strong enough to withstand repeated hoop tensile stresses and must also exhibit a good resistance to wear. Materials for dies may be D2 steel through hardened to R_c 60/62 or high-speed steel. Sometimes it is necessary to use a tungsten-carbide tractrix die and in this case an insert of tungsten carbide is shrink fitted into a tough, ductile-steel housing.

The largest tractrix die within the author's experience had an outer diameter of 800mm, a throat diameter of 420mm and a height of 350mm. It was made from D2 steel, hardened and tempered to 60 R_c with a tensile strength of 130 to 140tonf/in² (82 to 89kg/mm²).

Calculations showed that a punch force of 300 000kg (300 ton) would be needed to push a steel blank through this die. The maximum cupping load on a die of *modified* tractrix form occurs when the free edge of the blank has been deformed through 50°.

Using Lamé's thick cylinder equation,

$$\text{Max hoop stress } f = \frac{(R_o^2 + R_i^2)}{(R_o^2 - R_i^2)}$$

where R_o and R_i are outer and inner radii respectively and p is the equivalent internal pressure which can be calculated. From these considerations a maximum hoop tensile stress of 7.0kg/mm² was deduced and a diametral expansion of 0.13mm occurred at the throat of the die.

It is not normally necessary to delve into the theory to this degree and quite often these stress and strain calculations are omitted altogether. In the example quoted above the cost of the tractrix die and its accompanying ironing dies was considerable and breakage of a die for the sake of a few hours calculation would be quite inexcusable.

For corrective ironing, sharp ironing edges are preferred followed by

a parallel land. After the parallel land there is a back-off relief; this is an important feature — without it there would be cracking and failure in the land portion.

If it is considered desirable to provide a tungsten-carbide insert in a cupping die (usually for reasons of wear) then a shrink-fit allowance of 0.045mm/25mm of diameter should be used.

Ironing dies

The function of the ironing die is to reduce the wall thickness of the work as it passes through the throat of the die. In some instances, particularly in elevated temperature working, a set of rollers of concave profile is used to reduce the wall thickness. However, the description here will be limited to circular dies (fig 9).

As with all engineering processes, one must seek the best all-purpose solution bearing in mind problems of cost, life of the part, accuracy of the product, frictional pick-up, and so on. For the majority of ironing dies, tungsten carbide is chosen. This material, being of a very brittle nature must always be used as an insert held captive within a shrink-fit housing. Shrink-fit allowance is normally the same as that previously mentioned, *ie* 0.045mm/25mm of diameter. Different grades of tungsten carbide are available depending upon the duty imposed upon the die but a carbide containing 11% to 12% cobalt is generally used.

Again a sharp ironing edge is preferred with a short land and back-off relief, as in the typical die design

Fig 7.

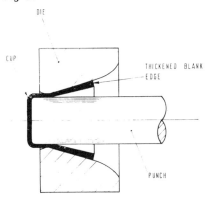

Disc Being Cupped

Fig 8.
Tractrix cupping dies (Courtesy Liebergeld Co).

Fig 9. Punch and ironing dies (Courtesy Liebergeld Co).

shown in fig 10. Eventually with use, the sharp edge becomes dull and the die should then be ground and polished to give a new sharp edge with some sacrifice of the length of the land.

Where multiple dies are used in a single-stroke operation, the dies become progressively smaller in diameter and this sequential ironing demands that the dies be spaced apart an increasing distance, spacing rings being provided for this purpose.

The "know-how" on the individual ironing reductions at each ring is all-important and it is not possible to enter into all the detail in this report. Different alloys and different tempers will demand special consideration. Individual ironing loads must be calculated and a knowledge of the strain-hardening characteristics of the metal being worked must be known. This sounds a complicated procedure but the calculations are quite simple and are explained in the theoretical section. Strain-hardening characteristic curves for almost any alloy may be obtained from data sheets.*

Spacing rings
As mentioned above, the ironing dies are held apart by means of spacing rings, which, made from mild steel, must be accurate and square with respect to their axes. If the face of a spacer is out of square then this will affect the squareness of the adjacent ironing die and this can lead to the development of curvature along the length of a pressing.

The spacers are drilled or milled to allow the coolant to flow on to the work during ironing.

*For example those published by VDI, Germany

Stripper mechanism
A stripper is required at the end of the stroke to draw the pressing off the punch. It is a feature of the process that the work clings elastically to the punch and on smooth punches the stripping load is about 20% of the cupping load.

There are several different types of stripper available, some being pneumatically operated so that the stripper jaws open automatically as the work approaches and then close automatically as the direction of the punch is reversed. Some strippers are actually pushed open by the passage of the work and then spring shut behind the work.

When drawing and ironing relatively thick blanks down to a wall thickness of around 1mm the stripper is a simple robust device of no particular sophistication. If there is a tendency for the open end of the pressing to buckle, then very considerable bursting stresses can be set up within the jaws of the stripper and the jaws must be designed so as to withstand these forces.

In the case of very thin-wall can stripping (ie the tin-plate DWI beverage can) then a large number of pressure fingers are made to contact the irregular form at the open end of the pressing so that the stripping load is "shared" evenly all round the wall.

Lubrication
Ferrous metals
Where the area reduction in a component is greater than about 70% a solid film lubricant of phosphate and sodium stearate is commonly used. This is an excellent lubrication process if coating weights of between 2,5 and 3,0gm/m² are used. An even phosphate coating is essential as bare patches on the steel surface will invariably cause friction welding. In some cases it is advisable to shot or grit-blast the steel blanks prior to application of the phosphate coating. This increases the surface area of the blank as well as removing mill-scale from hot rolled material. Phosphate and sodium stearate treatment is not necessary if metal reductions are less than about 70% as EP oil based lubricants have proved successful. These remarks apply to deep drawing quality mild steel.

A tenacious oxide scale which is difficult to remove by normal chemical pickling is usually a sign that the coiling temperature is too high. Lower coiling temperatures will greatly reduce the mill scale problem. Oxalate coatings have been used successfully on stainless steel but in recent years graphite and molyb-

denum di-sulphate containing lubricants have also found considerable favour.

A totally different solution to the question of lubrication can be adopted by using soft, ductile metal coatings on the surface of the steel blank. Probably the most common metal coating is tin as used in tin-plate for the production, by drawing and wall ironing, of thin wall containers for beverage and aerosol cans. Copper and zinc coatings are also used on steel to assist lubrication but it should be remembered that soft metal coatings do not normally survive inter-draw annealing procedures.

Non-ferrous metals
In the case of non-ferrous metals, good quality EP oil-based lubricants are recommended. The 'tricks of the trade' when considering lubrication are considerable and this is one aspect of deep drawing and ironing where experimentation and development are possible. When all the variable in the process are considered, most of these 'variables' turn out to be quite rigid. The geometry of the component is fixed within narrow limits; the metal of the component is specified; there is a minimum production rate; the work hardening of the metal follows well defined laws and so on. In the case of metal cutting or in a process like flow-forming there is flexibility in the system which is absent in a draw and iron tool set.

General comments
There are probably only two true variables — choice of material from which the tooling is made and lubrication. The author's company was recently involved in a study exercise for one of the metal bellows manufacturers in the UK. The metal being ironed was stainless steel and the problem was one of frictional pick-up.

Fig 10. *Ironing die.*

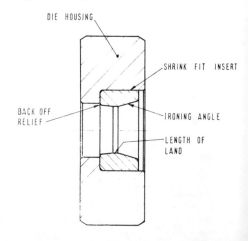

at another installation where incorrect mixing of lubricants led to a bacteria growth which completely blocked the press filters.

Performance of the lubricant does not end with the success of a drawing and ironing operation. The component produced, be it a fire extinguisher body, soda syphon, gas bottle or cartridge case, would normally be cleaned prior to further operations such as annealing, painting or anodising. The degreasing or cleaning of the part must be accomplished satisfactorily even though this is sometimes difficult because of adsorbed chemical coatings. Again expert advice should be sought on this point as some lubricants can leave a permanent stain which may not be acceptable in practice.

The solution to the problem had to recognise that the client did not wish to alter his tooling, his process, labour, blank material, production rate or interfere in any way with the production costings.

To the academic reader, these constraints may appear far too oppresive but when dealing with an industrial problem it is no use asking the client to go back to 'square one' where production schedules have to be met.

In this particular instance the lubrication was at fault as was the tool setting. The tool setting was adjusted and then the lubricant itself was shown to have too low a film strength for this type of work. Frictional pick-up was occurring between the stainless steel component being ironed and the cobalt of the tungsten carbide ironing dies. A heavy duty Acheson lubricant was added to the liquid coolant being pumped through the tool-set and the problem was solved.

There are so many different lubricants available, all claiming to have excellent performance in heavy wall ironing. Phosphate and soap (sodium stearate) is extremely good and for many years was far better

than any other system. Now the gap between the phosphate performance and that of extreme pressure lubricants is closing and companies such as R D Nicol of Sheffield and Achesons of Plymouth are able to offer lubricant systems especially designed to cope with heavy wall ironing.

In addition to the specific properties of the lubricant itself, some common sense must be used in its application. The finest lubricants have been seen to be used in poor shop conditions where swarf and dirt have been applied to the work in addition to the oil. Great quantities of lubricant have been applied to the blank where one tenth of that quantity would suffice. Above all, seek expert advice and accept it. Mixing of incompatible oils can have serious consequences; incorrect dilution can also be serious. To give two examples, assistance was sought at one installation where incompatible oils were being used — one for blank lubrication and the other for cooling the tools. The result was the formation of a weak hydrochloric acid solution which attacked everything within reach, including the press. There were expensive results

Equipment

Deep drawing and ironing can be carried out on long stroking presses, either mechanical or hydraulic. The required force/punch travel characteristics are reasonably flat with respect to travel with the peak load occurring early in the stroke during the cuppling operation. It is quite possible to fit a set of tools to an existing press provided that it has sufficient stroke. Some minor modifications may be required — for instance it will be necessary to provide a cooling system for the tooling but this is not a serious problem.

Tooling can be held in a vertical or a horizontal attitude. Modern presses have been designed to use horizontal stroking and a number of such presses are shown in figs 11 — 14. Double-ended horizontal presses are popular since they use the return stroke to carry out another ironing operation and these presses are all hydraulic. A typical press will have a left and right hand tool chamber with a moving crosshead oscillating between these tool chambers. The press is built on top of a sump containing 2-3000 litres of coolant and within this sump is an immersed pump providing plenty of coolant to the tooling.

Using this system with two sets of tools is efficient and loading and off-loading the work is carried out at a convenient working height. No pit is required for an installation of this kind of machine although the press does require a generous amount of floor space.

High speed mechanical presses of the horizontal type are used in can making, where both tin-plate and aluminium stock is used. Standun/ Metal Box presses are shown in fig 15. These presses are capable of producing 150 cans/min. The Schuler press

Fig 12. Double ended horizontal press (Courtesy Thyssen Industrie AG).

Fig 13.
Double-ended horizontal press (Courtesy SMG).

2,4 metre stroke, then the first draw stroke will also be 2,4 metres.

Fig 12 shows a typical horizontal double-ended, hydraulic deep drawing and ironing press of German manufacture. This particular machine, which is 5800mm long, 2200mm front to back and 1900mm high, has an all-up weight of 16 000Kg. Power is provided by a 110KW, three-phase ac short circuit rotor type electric motor connected by a flexible coupling to a submerged valveless axial piston pump with infinitely variable supply.

The moving cross-head, which has a fully adjustable stroke of up to 1600mm applies an infinitely adjust-

for can making is shown in fig 16. This type of press has been in use for many years. In a survey of the Aluminium Can Industry for food packaging (Alcan Development Bulletin No 8, May 1950) mention is made of the Keller press and tooling where multiple ironing dies are used on a high speed mechanical press. This press and tooling system designed and built by Jacob Keller in Switzerland, was in commercial production of thin-wall aluminium cans in 1940 and so from this example alone it is possible to point to the long pedigree of this system of forming metal.

Over the years, equipment has become more sophisticated and has also been refined to meet the Health and Safety regulations. Electronic control of the press is now very advanced but in essence, a deep drawing and ironing press is simply a means of pushing a blank or cup through a set of tools as economically as possible.

On hydraulic presses, variable delivery pumps are used to give smooth and stepless variation of crosshead speed. With modern hydraulic presses it is also possible to introduce slow speed stripping for the first one or two centimetres of stroke to dis-

Fig 15.
Standun metal box press (Courtesy Metal Box Ltd).

courage buckling of the work on stripping.

Where a double-ended press is being considered, the stroke acting on one tool set is the same as the stroke acting on the other. This is obvious but is sometimes overlooked when calculating production rates. Thus if we have a 2-draw component with the first draw requiring 1 metre stroke with the second draw requiring (say)

able pressing force of between 0 and 1200KN. Speed is variable between 2 and 18 metres/min (1.3 and 11.8in/sec) depending upon load.

A supply of cooling fluid housed in the press bedplate is directed to a tool chamber at each end of the press by means of a vane pump driven by a 3-phase ac 4,0KW electric motor. The press is capable of fully automatic running on continuous cycle or can be inched by means of the mechanical

Fig 14.
Author with double-ended 60ton press showing 1st and 2nd draw shock absorber tubing (Courtesy SMG).

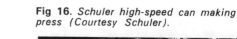

Fig 16. *Schuler high-speed can making press (Courtesy Schuler).*

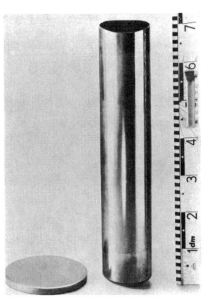

Fig 20. *105mm brass cartridge case (Courtesy SMG)*.

manual override lever at the top-centre of the machine. Both operating speed and crosshead force are adjusted by means of the manually operated control dials on the press front panel.

Fig 17 shows an interesting hydraulic press application using a number of tooling techniques all within the same stroke. A relatively thin blank of aluminium is held by a pressure blankholder and is drawn and re-drawn on a telescopic punch system. A normal cupping die is used — not of tractrix form. Thus a deep component is made in one stroke of the press and within the same stroke, an ironing operation is carried out to give greater length and accuracy.

Where a vertical installation is required, identical tooling can be arranged provided that plenty of

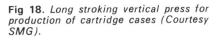

Fig 18. *Long stroking vertical press for production of cartridge cases (Courtesy SMG)*.

Fig 19. *Vertical tool stack for cartridge case production (Courtesy SMG)*.

coolant is allowed to flow over the tooling. Figs 18, 19 and 20 show a long stroking vertical hydraulic press, the tooling and finished component of a brass cartridge case production installation. The finished case as drawn is 700mm long. A smaller vertical press for drawing and ironing saucepans and cooking pots is shown in fig 21.

To take full advantage of modern stock materials, modern lubricants, tooling know-how and other improvements, it is desirable to use long stroking presses and to do as much metal deformation as possible in each draw. This philosophy favours the use of horizontal presses since large vertical daylight can often be a problem. In order to reduce vertical daylight, it is possible to install the tooling within the bottom table and to extract the work below the table, but this would require a deep pit.

A horizontal press, on the other hand, requires greater floor space but does not require a pit. Both entry and exit heights of the work are convenient and, in addition, where there are a number of tools in series, it is

possible to change one tool, say a die or a spacing ring, without disturbing the remainder of the tooling. As both forward and return strokes can be used, one horizontal press has almost the same output as two vertical machines, with only one press installation cost.

The debate between the pros and cons of vertical *versus* horizontal is a complex one where all pertinent facts must be taken into consideration. In general, the author takes the view that for strokes in excess of about 1,2 metre, the argument comes down in favour of the horizontal press.

Fig 21. *Vertical press for production of cooking pots (Courtesy Bruderer UK)*.

Reprinted from the Australian Confrence on Manufacturing Engineering, Adelaide, 17-19 August 1977. Published by The Institution of Engineers, Australia NCP 77/7

Aspects of Draw Die Forming of Sheet Metal

J. L. DUNCAN

Professor, Department of Mechanical Engineering, McMaster University, Hamilton, Ontario, Canada

SUMMARY   A simplified two-dimensional analysis of springback in a shallow, smoothly contoured sheet metal part which is formed in a typical draw die shows that if adequate tension is developed in the sheet, the springback is small and equal to $\Delta h = (P/E) h$, where P/E is the ratio of the plastic to the elastic modulus and h is the total crown of the part. To achieve these conditions, the tensile to yield strength ratio for the sheet material must exceed $\exp (\mu\pi/2)$ where μ is the coefficient of friction between the tool and the plastically deforming sheet. The work is relevant to   forming typical autobody and appliance panels, particularly in high strength aluminum and steel sheet.

NOTATION

a   semi-width of punch
e   engineering strain in plane strain
e_o strain at inner surface of sheet
E   elastic modulus in plane strain
F   applied force
h   crown (sagitta) of profile
Δh springback, change in h on unloading
I   second moment of area of unit width of sheet, $= t^3/12$
M   moment about mid-thickness of sheet
P   plastic modulus in plane strain
q   tool contact pressure
R   radius of curvature
T   tension* (stress resultant) acting in sheet, $= \sigma t$
t   sheet thickness
Y   yield stress in plane strain
y   distance of fibre in the sheet from the inner surface
λ fractional depth of elastic zone
μ coefficient of friction
σ stress in plane strain

*The word "tension" is used throughout in the special sense of force per unit width transmitted by the sheet.

1   INTRODUCTION

The purpose of this work is to develop a rudimentary model of springback in a thin sheet formed over a smoothly curved punch and to use this model for determining those factors which most strongly affect shape control in draw die forming. The type of part considered is shown schematically in Figure 1;this is chosen as a simple representation of many of the parts formed in the automotive and appliance industries.

The forming process is illustrated in Figure 2. The blank is held in a separately actuated binder, draw ring, or blankholder which surrounds the punch and die. Its purpose is to keep the sheet flat and to impose some restraint or tension in the sheet as it is drawn into the die. Various features such as draw beads may be incorporated to improve the control of the sheet. After closing the binder, the punch descends to form the part. If re-entrant shapes are required, these are produced by features on the die which deform the

sheet as the punch bottoms. It is important to appreciate that the sheet is formed by tensile forces in the plane of the sheet. These arise from the lateral movement imposed by the punch and the restraint or resistance to drawing in developed in the binder. In no sense is the sheet squeezed between the punch and die as in a forging process; the pressures exerted, in terms of press load per unit area of punch face, are much too small and typically less than 1% of the yield stress of the sheet. After forming, the metal remaining in the binder is trimmed off as shown. The success of the whole operation will depend very much on the design of the binder and the shape of the blank before forming. Considerable artifice is employed by tool engineers in binder design but in this work we consider only the deformation of the sheet as it is formed over the punch and concentrate on shape control in the finished part after trimming.

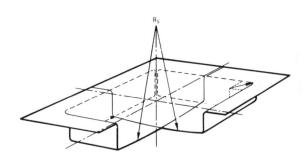

Figure 1   Representation of a shallow, smoothly contoured panel

Shape control is a major problem in forming shallow parts in HSLA steels and high strength aluminum alloy sheet. It has various aspects. One is springback which is an overall change in curvature when the sheet is unloaded after forming. A second aspect is racking or twisting of the part after trimming, and a third can be best described as "slackness." This is probably related to residual stresses in the sheet and causes lack of transverse rigidity-flutter-or in extreme cases, oil-canning.

The problem of shape control in shallow panels was discussed by Sachs (1966), and more recently detail

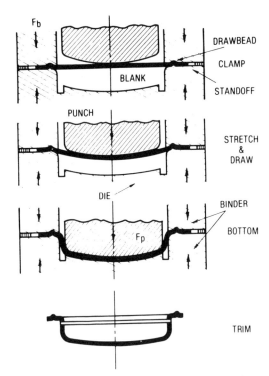

Figure 2 Sectional views showing the
stages in forming a simple part
in a typical draw die process

studies have been undertaken in Japan by Yoshida
et al (1970) and in the USA by Adams, Kasper, and
Kurajian (1973) and (1975). Using the analysis of
Adams et al, it is possible to determine the
"overcrowning" or modification which should be made
to the punch profile to allow for the effects of
springback. The predictive accuracy is likely to
be better than using the relations presented here,
however, the simpler model is useful as a conceptu-
al aid in understanding the major causes of poor
shape control in typical panels.

2   THEORY

2.1   Springback

In the analysis of springback presented here, we
grossly simplify both the part and the deformation
process. We consider a strip of the sheet across
the part near the midsection as shown in Figure 3,
and study the shape of that part, OP, which is to
be formed against the punch face of radius of
curvature R_p.

After forming, the unloaded sheet has a radius of
curvature R_s as shown in Figure 4 and the springback is defined by Δh which is the reduction in the
total crown of the part. The specific assumptions

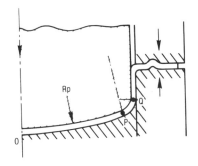

Figure 3 Enlarged view of the parts
of the panel considered

made are:

(a) the problem is a two-dimensional one; i.e., we
assume plane strain deformation and consider that
both the punch and the sheet have a cylindrical
surface;

(b) the radius of curvature of the punch is very
large compared with the thickness of the sheet;

(c) contact between the punch and the sheet is
frictionless;

(d) strains in the sheet are small and we may
neglect changes in thickness;

(e) the material obeys an elastic, linear strain
hardening law;

(f) in bending, plane sections through the sheet
remain plane.

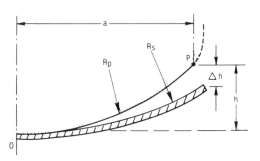

Figure 4 Schematic view of the punch and
part of the panel after springback

In shallow parts, the radius of curvature of the
punch face is much greater than the minimum radius
of curvature to which the sheet can be bent while
still remaining full elastic. As shown in Figure 5
(a), the sheet could be bent to the punch radius
R_p by applying an elastic moment at each end. On
unloading, however, the sheet would spring back
entirely and, hence, in the forming process not only
a moment but also a tension must be applied to the
sheet as shown in Figure 5(b). To preserve
equilibrium, some small contact stress, q, will
exist and for the frictionless case, T, M and q
will be constant across the whole face. T is a
tension (or stress resultant, σt) defined as the
force per unit width acting on the sheet.

As in free bending, we assume that plane sections
remain plane, but in forming on a punch, the radius
of curvature of the inner surface, R_p, remains
constant and an element fgjk in the original sheet

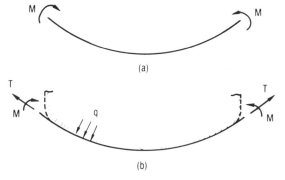

Figure 5 Curvature of the panel by
(a) bending and (b) bending plus tension

will deform to f'gjk' on the punch as shown in Figure 6. By symmetry, we deduce that transverse sections such as fk will be perpendicular to the tool face in the deformed state. Under the action of a moment and some tension, the element may first be considered to deform to $fgjk_1$, where

$$\overline{kk_1} \simeq y \cdot \frac{\overline{gf}}{R_p}$$

If the tension is increased, the element deforms to f'gjk'. The strain at the inner surface, which we denote as e_0, is given by

$$e_0 = (e)_{y=0} = \frac{\overline{f'f}}{\overline{gf}}$$

The strain at a distance y from the inner surface is,

$$e_y = \frac{\overline{kk_1} + \overline{k_1k'}}{\overline{gf}}$$

which we write as

$$e_y = e_0 + \frac{y}{R_p} \qquad (1)$$

We note that (1) is an approximation as $k_1k' \neq ff'$, however, both (t/R_p) and the total strains are very small and the error in (1) is not significant. The strains e_0 and e_y are engineering strains, however, for the same reasons we can equate these with true strains.

The equilibrium equations which apply are:

$$q = \frac{T}{R_p} \qquad (2)$$

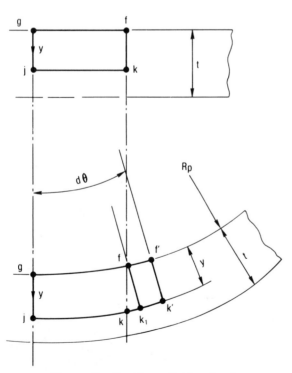

Figure 6 Section of the sheet showing the undeformed and deformed shape of an element

$$T = \int_0^t \sigma \, dy \qquad (3)$$

and

$$M = \int_0^t \sigma \left(y - \frac{t}{2} \right) dy \qquad (4)$$

where M is the moment about the midthickness.

It is convenient to describe the material behavior in terms of plane strain parameters; i.e.,

$$\text{for} \quad e \leqslant Y/E \qquad \sigma = Ee \qquad (5a)$$

$$\text{for} \quad e > YE \qquad \sigma = Y \left[1 - (P/E) \right] + Pe \qquad (5b)$$

The plane strain yield stress, Y, and elastic and plastic moduli E and P may be derived readily from uniaxial parameters, or alternatively and without great loss of accuracy, they may be equated with the uniaxial values. The assumed stress strain curve is shown in Figure 7.

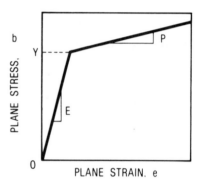

Figure 7 The assumed stress strain curve for plane strain

We now consider the case when the strip is partially plastic; i.e., the tension has increased to the point where the outer region is plastic and the inner surface is elastic as shown in Figure 8(a). The elastic plastic interface is at a fractional depth λ from the inner surface. The strain at the elastic-plastic interface is equal to the yield strain, i.e., in Figure 8(b)

$$e_y = \lambda t = e_Y = \frac{Y}{E} \quad ,$$

and hence, from (1), the strain at the inner surface is

$$e_0 = \frac{Y}{E} - \frac{\lambda t}{R_p} \qquad (6)$$

The strain distribution, as shown in Figure 8(b), is given by

$$e_y = \frac{Y}{E} + \frac{y - \lambda t}{R_p} \qquad (7)$$

and using 5(a) we obtain the stress distribution for the elastic region, as shown in Figure 8(c); i.e.,

$$\sigma = Y + \frac{E}{R_p} (y - \lambda t) \qquad 0 < y < \lambda t \qquad (8)$$

and in the plastic region,

$$\sigma = Y + \frac{P}{R_p} (y - \lambda t) \qquad \lambda t < y < t \qquad (9)$$

142

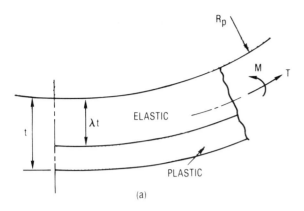

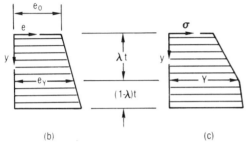

Figure 8 Schematic showing
(a) a section of the sheet in the elastic-plastic
state during forming and the corresponding strain
distribution, (b), and stress distribution, (c)

Substituting the above relations in the equilibrium
(3) and (4), we obtain:

$$T = \int_0^{\lambda t} \left[Y + \frac{E}{R_p} (y-\lambda t) \right] dy + \int_{\lambda t}^t \left[Y + \frac{P}{R_p} (y-\lambda t) \right] dy$$

$$= Yt - \frac{Et^2}{2R_p} \left[\lambda^2 - \frac{P}{E} (1-\lambda)^2 \right] \tag{10}$$

and,

$$M = \int_0^{\lambda t} \left[Y + \frac{E}{R_p} (y-\lambda t) \right] (y-\frac{t}{2}) \, dy$$

$$+ \int_{\lambda t}^t \left[Y + \frac{P}{R_p} (y-\lambda t) \right] (y-\frac{t}{2}) \, dy$$

$$= \frac{EI}{R_p} \left[(3-2\lambda)\lambda^2 + \frac{P}{E} (1+2\lambda) (1-\lambda)^2 \right] \tag{11}$$

where I is the second moment of area of unit width
of the strip; i.e.,

$$I = t^3/12$$

The salient cases are when the strip has just
reached the limit of elasticity; i.e., $\lambda = 1$ and
when it has just become fully plastic, $\lambda = 0$. The
values of the applied loads in these cases can be
found from (10) and (11).

We now consider the unloading of the strip. When
the tension T is removed, the strip will slide
around the punch; there will be some slight change
in the radius of curvature as in the radial
shrinkage of a thin-walled cylinder, but this may be
neglected. We assume then that there is no springback, Δh, due to unloading the tension force. To
unload the moment, we superimpose a moment M_e
associated with an elastic strain and stress
distribution which is equal in magnitude to the
moment of (11) but of opposite sense. Following
elastic bending theory, this will lead to a change
in curvature of

$$\Delta \left(\frac{1}{R} \right) = \frac{1}{R_p} - \frac{1}{R_s} = \frac{M_e}{EI} \tag{12}$$

The geometric relation between the variables in
Figure 4 is

$$R = \frac{h^2 + a^2}{2h}$$

from which, for $h \ll a$, we obtain

$$\frac{1}{R} \simeq \frac{2h}{a^2} \tag{13}$$

thence for a given value of a, we obtain the
approximation,

$$\Delta \left(\frac{1}{R} \right) = \frac{2}{a^2} \Delta h \tag{14}$$

Combining (11) to (14) and utilizing the relation

$$h \simeq \frac{a^2}{2R_p}$$

we obtain

$$\frac{\Delta h}{h} = 1 - (1+2\lambda)(1-\lambda)^2 \left[1 - \frac{P}{E} \right] \tag{15}$$

For the fully elastic case, $\lambda = 1$, the strip
springs back entirely and $\Delta h/h$ in (15) is, of
course, unity. For the fully plastic case, $\lambda = 0$,
the springback is

$$\Delta h = \frac{P}{E} h \tag{16}$$

It may also be shown that if the strip is strained
beyond the point where it has just become fully
plastic, the springback is unaltered and remains as
given by (16). The situation is illustrated in
Figure 9, in which we plot the springback per unit
depth of the part, $\Delta h/h$ against the tension
expressed in nondimensional form, T/Yt. The term
Yt is the tension necessary to yield the flat
sheet. In typical materials, the plastic modulus
is about two orders of magnitude smaller than the
elastic modulus (5% of E is a reasonable figure
for aluminum body sheet) and, hence, the springback
in a panel made fully plastic is quite small and,
surprisingly, is independent of yield stress, the
absolute value of the elastic modulus and the
amount of plastic strain produced in the part.

This analysis indicates that it is only necessary
to exceed the yield state slightly to reduce
springback to a small and probably negligible
amount. It becomes difficult to understand then
why springback should present difficulties and
in order to investigate this, we consider the
situation as the metal flows around the punch
corner radius; i.e., PQ in Figure 3.

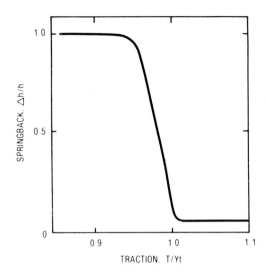

Figure 9   Nondimensional springback
versus tension curve for typical
conditions in shallow panels

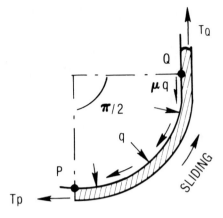

Figure 10   Enlarged view of the
punch profile radius, PQ, during forming

2.2   Friction and Sidewall Failure

The contact stress, q, over the face of the punch is quite small; less than the pressure one's foot exerts on the ground in many cases. Friction is probably not an important factor over the gently curved regions but in the corner, PQ, in Figure 3, the radius is generally small, and from (2) we deduce that the contact pressure could suddenly increase by several orders of magnitude.

In order to develop the required tension in the sheet at the point P, the sheet must slide around the radius as shown in Figure 10 and it will be acted on by friction forces μq as shown. The relationship between the tension T_q in the vertical part of the sheet and that at the punch face T_p is well-known*; i.e.,

$$\frac{T_q}{T_p} = \exp \frac{\mu\pi}{2} \qquad (17)$$

As may be seen in Figure 3, the sheet at Q is virtually unsupported and the maximum stress it can sustain would be equivalent to the ultimate tensile strength. By definition then,

$$(T_q) \text{ max} = (TS) \text{ t} \qquad (18)$$

From the previous section we note that T_p must exceed Yt by some small amount. Hence utilizing (17) we obtain a useful inequality, namely that in order to obtain shape control and form a shallow panel successfully, the ratio of the tensile to yield stress in the sheet must exceed the value given by

$$\frac{TS}{Y} > e^{\mu\pi/2} \qquad (19)$$

where TS is the plane strain tensile strength. The material parameters in the relation (19) strictly refer to plane strain deformation and to be more rigorous we should investigate more closely the relationship between plane strain and uniaxial

* Well-known to mechanical engineers who were fortunate enough to study their mechanics in a traditional form--it is the formula for a flat belt on a pulley.

parameters, particularly the tensile strength. We neglect also the fact that in reaching the state shown in Figure 10, the strip will have been bent around the corner radius under tension and may be thinned more than in a plane strain tensile test. For these reasons, we should consider the relation (19) as a lower bound for the required material characteristics and the actual tensile to yield ratios may have to be significantly greater.

3   DISCUSSION

As already stated, the simple theory suggests that springback in typical panels should be small and independent of the material yield stress and elastic modulus (but dependent on the ratio of the plastic to the elastic modulus). This is contrary to the view of many practitioners who consider that springback is directly related to the elastic modulus and the yield stress of the sheet. In an attempt to resolve this dichotomy, we consider springback curves similar to Figure 9 but plotted in absolute values for various sheets having slight differences in yield stress as shown in Figure 11. If the tooling is set up so that for the given binder design, binder load and friction conditions we obtain a tension over the face of the punch of T_A in Figure 11, then the springback Δh will be appreciable and will vary significantly with small changes in yield stress. Alternatively if the operating tension is at T_B, we expect the springback to be small and independent of material strength. Thus both views can be correct but clearly it is more desirable to operate with the higher tension, T_B. (It should be pointed out that the above comments present a rather simplified view. If the material hardness increases, the tension necessary to draw the sheet through the draw bead will increase and hence the tension on the punch face is not entirely independent of material behavior.)

In considering the influence of strain on springback, we note that the bilinear stress strain curve in Figure 7 is a poor approximation at low strain values for many materials and that the value of P will depend on the strain range over which the line is fitted. This point is discussed by Yoshida (1976).

The relationship derived between the tensile/yield ratio and the coefficient of friction is useful conceptually even though it is only a lower bound. It is well-known that materials with low tensile/yield ratios can be adequately deep drawn into a

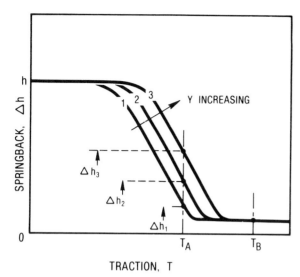

SPRINGBACK, Δh

Y INCREASING

Δh_3

Δh_2

Δh_1

T_A T_B

TRACTION, T

Figure 11 Schematic diagram showing the springback in different sheets, 1 to 3, having slightly different values of yield stress

cylindrical cup but without relation (19) it is not immediately obvious why these materials cannot be used in draw die forming of shallow parts. The material which slides around the punch profile radius, PQ in Figure 3, is at a state of yield and very little information exists about friction coefficients under this situation. Slider contact measurements on a strip, which is not plastically deforming, are probably not applicable. An ingeneous technique for obtaining the appropriate friction coefficient has been suggested recently by Marciniak (1976).

4   CONCLUSIONS

A simplified two-dimensional analysis of forming a shallow, smoothly contoured part in a draw die leads to the following conclusions:

(i)   if the tension forces over the face of the punch are sufficient to cause all of the material to reach the plastic state, the springback should be small and repeatable;

(ii)   under these conditions the springback is

independent of the material yield stress and the plastic strain produced and is given by the relation,

$$\Delta h = \frac{P}{E} \cdot h$$

where the ratio, P/E, of plastic to elastic modulus typically has the magnitude of 10^{-2};

(iii)   in order to achieve these conditions, the ratio of tensile to yield strength in the sheet must exceed the value, $\exp(\mu \pi/2)$;

(iv)   if the above conditions are not fulfilled, the springback is likely to be large and very sensitive to changes in material properties.

5   ACKNOWLEDGMENTS

This work was performed during the author's sabbatical program at the Alcoa Technical Center. The author would like to thank the Aluminum Company of America for the opportunity of engaging in this work and for their kind permission to publish this paper; in particular he would like to thank J.W. Clark, J.G. Kaufman and F.G. McKee of Alcoa for their help and support.

6   REFERENCES

ADAMS, D.G., KASPER, A.S. and KURAJIAN, G.M. (1973). Springback analysis of biaxially stretched panels. SAE Paper 730529.

ADAMS, D.G., KASPER, A.S. and KURAJIAN, G.M. (1975). The effects of mechanical properties on the elastic recovery of biaxially stretched panels. SME Technical Report MFR75-07.

MARCINIAK, Z. (1976). A new method of assessing sheet metal formability. Private communication.

SACHS, G. (1966). Principles and methods of sheet-metal fabricating. 2nd ed., New York, Reinhold Publishing Company, p 167.

YOSHIDA, K. et al. (1976). Strain propagation behavior in metal sheet. Proc. 9th IDDRG Congress, Ann Arbor, October, 1976.

Reprinted from Manufacturing Engineering, February 1977

Cooled Punch Increases Drawability

Here's how a small amount of punch cooling can increase the drawability of carbon steel from 10 to 25%

COOLING PRESS PUNCHES during drawing operations can increase the drawability of carbon steel from 10 to 25%. A relatively small amount of punch cooling, ±40°F (4.4°C) from normal room temperature, has this significant effect. Research engineers at Armco Steel Corp. made this discovery after a study of how steel's tensile and yield strengths are affected by temperature. Armco considers this to be a proprietary process and is seeking a patent. However, the company indicates it will make the process available to any interested stamper or fabricator at no cost.

How It Works. Since friction generates heat during a drawing operation, the strength of the steel varies during that critical time. The effect of temperature on the tensile strength of a typical low-carbon steel is shown in *Figure* 1. As can be seen, a relatively small change in temperature has a significant effect on the steel's strength. By allowing the blank to soften due to friction-induced heat be-

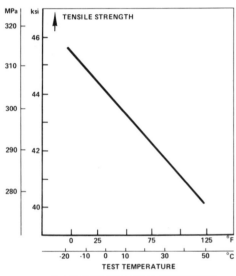

1. SIGNIFICANT EFFECTS of small temperature changes on the tensile strength of low-carbon steel.

2. CUP DIE with punch modified for cooling to increase drawability.

3. CUPS DRAWN to their limits before failure with constant die temperature but different punch temperatures.

DIAMETER OF THE LARGEST BLANKS THAT COULD SUCCESSFULLY BE DRAWN INTO CUPS AT THE TEMPERATURES NOTED

Die Temperature °F (°C)	Punch Temperature			
	40°F (4.4°C)	65°F (18.3°C)	100°F (37.8°C)	125°F (51.7°C)
Max. Diam. Blank, Inch (mm), "C" Grade Steel				
70 (21.1)	8.75 (222.3)	8.50 (215.9)	8.25 (209.6)	8.25 (209.6)
100 (37.8)	8.75 (222.3)	8.50 (215.9)	8.25 (209.6)	8.25 (209.6)
125 (51.7)	9.00 (228.6)	8.75 (222.3)	8.50 (215.9)	8.25 (209.6)
Max. Diam. Blank, Inch (mm), "B" Grade Steel				
70 (21.1)	9.50 (241.3)	9.00 (228.6)	8.50 (215.9)	8.50 (215.9)
100 (37.8)	9.25 (235.0)	9.00 (228.6)	8.75 (222.3)	8.50 (215.9)
125 (51.7)	9.25 (235.0)	9.25 (235.0)	8.75 (222.3)	8.75 (222.3)
Max. Diam. Blank, Inch (mm), "A" Grade Steel				
70 (21.1)	9.75 (247.7)	9.75 (247.7)	9.00 (228.6)	9.00 (228.6)
100 (37.8)	10.00 (254.0)	10.00 (254.0)	9.50 (241.3)	9.00 (228.6)
125 (51.7)	10.00 (254.0)	10.00 (254.0)	9.50 (241.3)	9.00 (228.6)

tween the blankholder and die — and subsequently strengthening the sidewalls of the part by chilling against the cold punch — the depth of draw can be increased.

Test Procedure. Using a hollow punch configuration, the test dies were a 4″ (102-mm) diameter cup with a 0.375″ (9.53-mm) radius, and a 6″ (152-mm) square box with 0.250″ (6.35-mm) radii. Heaters were attached to the periphery of the die and the blankholder to simulate the normal heat buildup that occurs in commercial operations. The hollow punch had fittings for flexible tubing coolant connections, and an internal baffle to force water to the bottom for improved cooling, *Figure* 2.

Three grades of cold-rolled an-nealed, low-carbon sheet steels were tested. A petroleum-based lubricant containing EP additives was brushed on each blank before forming. The three cups shown in *Figure* 3 were drawn to their limits before failure at a constant 75°F (23.9°C) die temperature. Punch diameters, however, were varied — 100°F (37.8°C), 65°F (18.3°C), and 40°F (4.4°C) from left to right. Blank diameters from left to right were 8.5″ (216 mm), 9.0″ (229 mm), and 9.5″ (241 mm).

The accompanying table demonstrates how critical the punch temperature is to the cup forming results. Cup depth of the cold-rolled steels was increased at least 10% by cooling the punch from 100 to 65°F, and 25% by cooling it from 100 to 40°F.

Applications. Wayne Granzow, Armco researcher who made the invention, explained "The punch can be cooled by any convenient method. A simple way is to drill a hole in the punch, run a flexible water line down inside the punch to cool it, and provide another line to remove the water. The procedure can be used either with an entire punch or with selected problem areas within the punch."

Mr. Granzow added "While our tests with the procedure were with low-carbon steel and Type 304 stainless steel, the method should also work in drawing other stainless steels and possibly other materials. We see the method being widely used by metal stampers to reduce rejects." ∎

Presented at SME's Modern Can Manufacturing Clinic, January 1981

Two-Piece Can Manufacturing: Blanking and Cup Drawing

by Cor Langewis
Langewis Consulting & Engineering Inc.

INTRODUCTION

The earliest cans made were cans with a soldered side seam and a separate bottom. Because the completed can consists of three pieces (body, bottom and top cover) these cans are commonly known as three piece cans. During the last half century, drawn and ironed (D&I) cans have replaced a large portion of the three piece cans on the market. The D&I cans are known as two piece cans because the bottom is an integral part of the can body and the completed can has only two parts.

The first steps in D&I can making are blanking and drawing. Continuous efforts are being made to reduce the amount of metal in the can. One way to reduce the over-all cost of the can is to reduce the thickness of the starting metal. For a given can size, thinner and harder starting metal means larger blank size and this combination makes the drawing operation more difficult and critical.

Tooling lay-out for blanking, metal economics, draw dies and metal behavior during drawing are discussed in detail.

HISTORY OF CAN MAKING

> "Find a need and fill it"
>   Henry J. Kaiser

The large Kaiser empire is a good example of what the results can be if such an advice is followed. In order to survive--against competition or during the ultimate competition (war), certain needs require immediate solutions.

Napolean faced a problem to feed his roaming armies and large rewards were offered for the development of methods to preserve food. A Paris champagne bottler turned candy maker, named Nicolas Appert, was experimenting with food preservation in 1794 and discovered preservation by heat. His containers were champagne bottles and he bottled milk, soup and vegetables. After closing, the bottles were put in boiling water for some time. He was quite successful and soon employed fifty people. In 1807 the French Navy took bottled vegetables to the Caribbean with very good results. Appert got a reward of 12,000-Francs for his efforts.

It was an Englishman, Peter Durant, who introduced canning in England. He got a patent which was an English version of the Appert system, but he was smart enough not to limit the patent to glass bottles. The patent reads: "Enclose the said food or articles in bottles or other vessels of glass, pottery, tin or other metals or fit materials."

England was in a good position to carry on with the development. Tin plate was produced in England, where the tin mines in Cornwall had been producing tin for centuries. In France, tin plate was practically non-existent.

In 1811 Durant sold the patent rights for one thousand pounds and the new owners soon thereafter started the first commercial three-piece can business. Cans were made by hand with soldered on bottoms and tops. Production was slow--at first ten cans per man per day, later on increasing to 5-6 cans per man per hour.

Customers were polar expeditions and the military. The English Navy bought 23,779 cans of meat and vegetables in 1818. Canned food became available in England to the general public in 1830. High prices held sales back--canned salmon cost as much as the weekly rent for an ordinary house. Convenience was also a factor as these cans required a hammer and chisel to open.

Sales to the military represented a booming business and soon competitors entered the market. The newcomers apparently did not fully understand food preservation and the work of Pasteur was not known at that time. Large numbers of cans spoiled and many people got sick. A few died and in Europe this turned public opinion against cans and this was to last until the end of the nineteenth century.

In the U.S.A. William Underwood produced the first cans in 1819, but can making did not really take off until the mid 1800's when Borden started to can condensed milk.

The lead in the solder joints caused little concern in those days, but seams can leak and the advantages of the two-piece can were recognized early. In the late 1800's Luigi Stampacchia hit upon the idea of using a double action press for producing a double drawn can, which after draw and redraw was pushed through a die of slightly smaller inside diameter than the outside diameter of the can. Thus the first attempts were made to iron drawn tin plate cans in Italy. James Rigby got a U.S. patent in 1904 for tin plate cans with the wall thickness reduced by "burnishing." His patent shows basically the same method as the Stampacchia patent, which was issued in 1894.

However, tools, die materials and production machinery were ill-suited for this technology at that time and commercial use of the draw and iron process for cans started many decades later.

In Switzerland, Jacob Keller obtained patents on drawing and ironing methods in 1944 and Willem Van Leer described ironing in detail in a British Patent issued in 1949.

After this, the development of tools and machinery for draw and iron can manufacturing advanced rapidly and D&I beverage cans appeared in quantity on the market in the early sixties. First in aluminum, but quickly followed by tin plate.

Since then, efforts have continuously been made to reduce the cost of cans. More than half of the can cost is the cost of the metal and reducing the amount of metal in a can is the most effective way of cost reduction. This has led to the use of thinner and harder metal, which for a given can size means a larger blank size. A larger blank size means more multiple and more difficult draws.

BLANKING

The first step in cup drawing is the punching cut of a circular blank or cut edge. A typical 5-out pattern is shown in Figure 1. Five blanks (shown cross-hatched) are punched out simultaneously. The cut edge should contain enough metal at minimum thickness to produce the desired can. After the blank diameter has been established, the required width of the sheet can be calculated as shown in Figure 1.

Modern cam-driven stock feeds are very accurate and a skeleton width of .040" is possible. The edge clearance depends on the overall width tolerance the metal supplier requires, but usually .060"-.065" will be sufficient.

The number of blanks to be stamped out simultaneously should be chosen to suit production requirements as well as coil widths available. Some coil widths can be had only at a premium price and should be avoided.

The number of blanks produced per stroke has a distinct effect on the overall metal economics (Fig. 2). For a given cut edge the amount of skeleton scrap will be reduced by $1\frac{1}{2}$% if the number of blanks per stroke is increased from five to ten. Metal savings here can be substantial; for aluminum, the above savings of $1\frac{1}{2}$% represent more than $100,000.-per year.

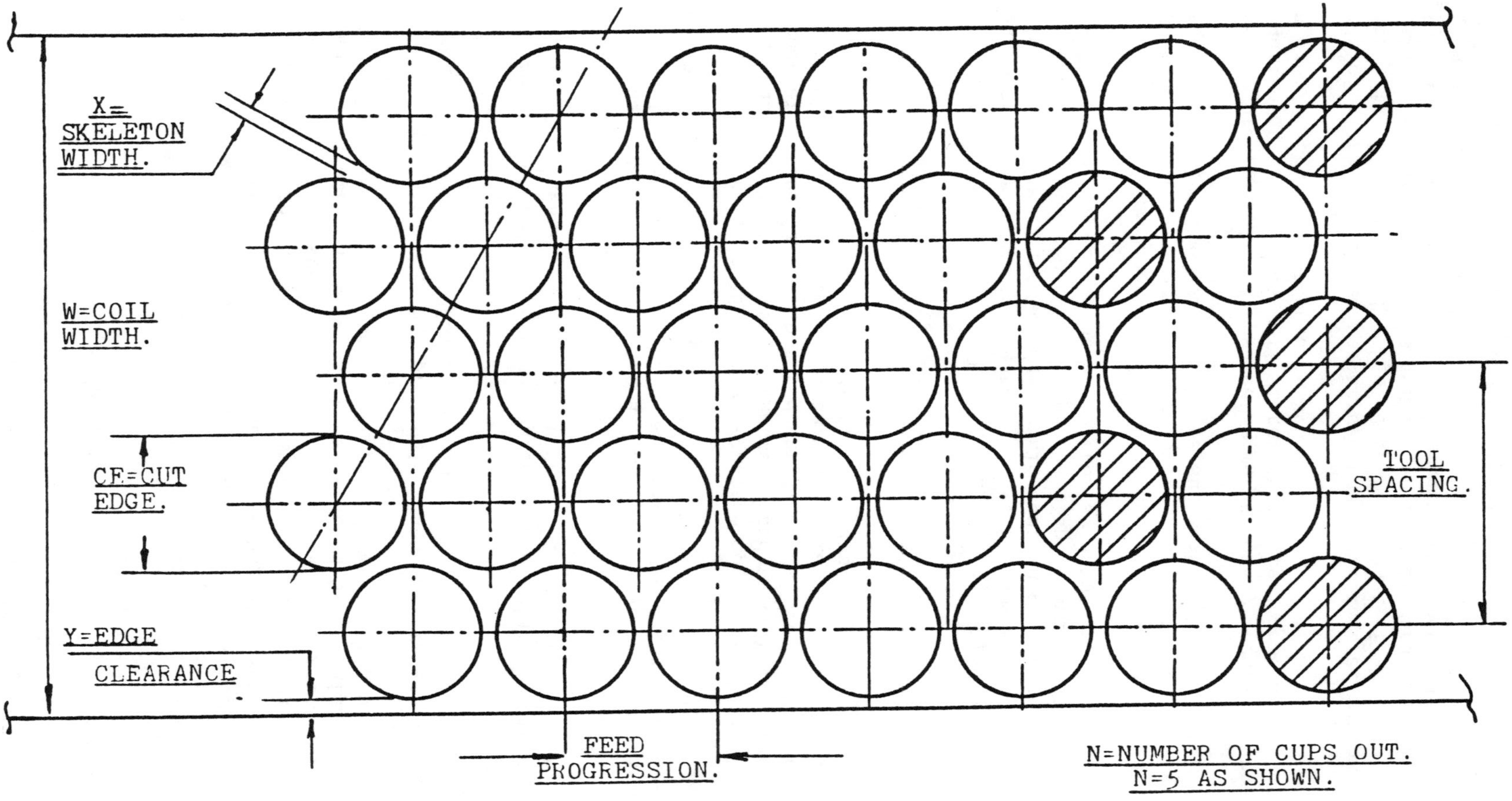

FIGURE 1.

X = SKELETON WIDTH.

W = COIL WIDTH.

CE = CUT EDGE.

Y = EDGE CLEARANCE

FEED PROGRESSION.

N = NUMBER OF CUPS OUT. $N=5$ AS SHOWN.

TOOL SPACING.

COIL WIDTH = $W = SIN.60^{\circ}(N--1)(CE+X)+CE+2Y$.
FEED PROGRESSION = $CE+X$.
TOOL SPACING = $2Sin.60^{\circ}(CE+X)$.

150

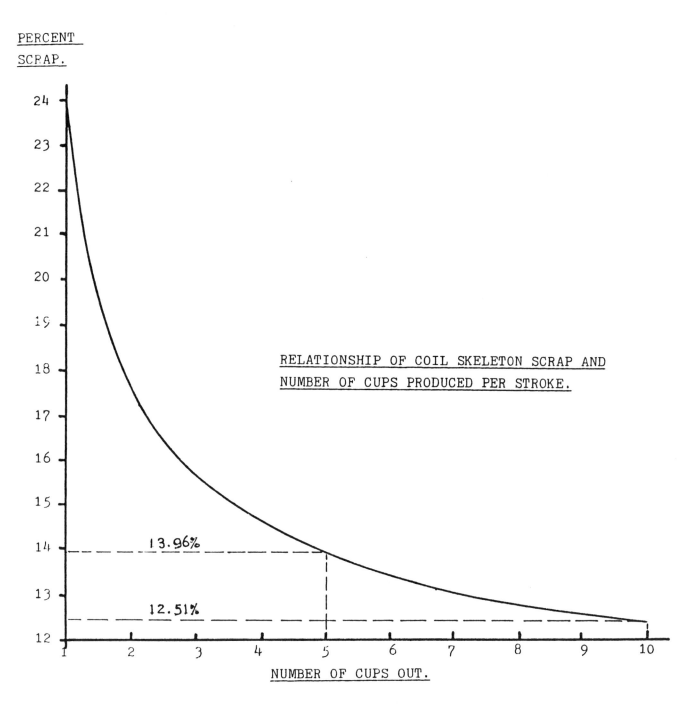

PERCENT
SCRAP.

RELATIONSHIP OF COIL SKELETON SCRAP AND
NUMBER OF CUPS PRODUCED PER STROKE.

13.96%

12.51%

NUMBER OF CUPS OUT.

FIGURE 2.

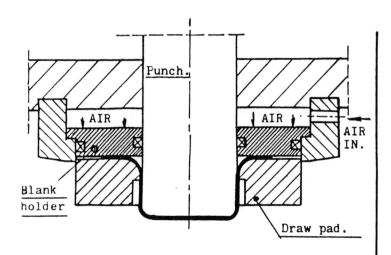

Figure 3.

BLANK & DRAW.

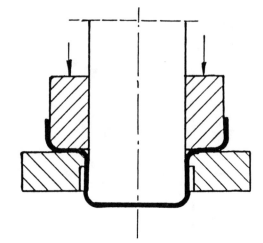

Figure 4.

DIRECT OR STRAIGHT REDRAW.

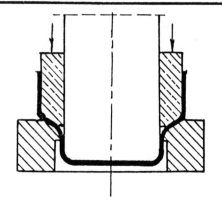

Figure 5.

DIRECT REDRAW-INCLINED PLANE.

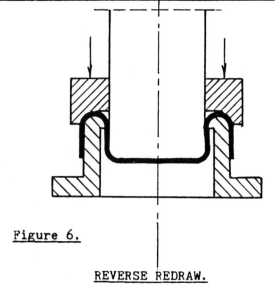

Figure 6.

REVERSE REDRAW.

DRAWING

The next step in can making is to form the flat, circular blank into a cup shaped container. This is accomplished by clamping the blank between two disc shaped dies (blankholder and draw pad, see Fig. 3) and an advancing punch then draws the blank into a cup.

There are limitations how much work can be done in a single drawing pass. The work done can be expressed as the reduction in diameter from blank to inside cup.

$$\text{Percentage Reduceion} = \frac{\text{Blank Diameter - Cup Inside Diameter}}{\text{Blank Diameter}} \times 100\%$$

The maximum reduction with ordinary tools is about 48% for aluminum, but with tin plate 52-56% reductions are possible.

The maximum reduction possible is sometimes called the limited draw ratio (LDR) and is calculated as follows:

$$\text{L.D.R.} = \frac{\text{Maximum Blank Diameter}}{\text{Cup Inside Diameter}}$$

It can be seen that a 50% reduction means an L.D.R. of 2 and therefore the L.D.R. for aluminum should be less than 2 (1.923 for 48% reduction) and the L.D.R. for tin plate should be higher than 2--for example, 2.174 for 54% reduction.

If a can diameter is required that is smaller than the one that can be obtained with a maximum reduction in one pass, then multiple draws are needed.

This can be done with a straight redraw (Fig. 4) or with a reverse redraw (Fig. 6) where the cup is actually turned inside-out. With a straight redraw, the metal is severely worked as it is bent 90° in two different directions during the redraw. In general, stresses are less severe with a reverse redraw where the metal is formed in one direction only. A compromise is shown in Fig. 5, where the bottom of the cup of the first draw has a taper and the metal does not have to make two 90° bends during the redraw. This method, however, puts a limitation on the amount of reduction in the first draw. At the beginning of the draw, the metal around the tapered nose of the punch is not supported and also, the draw reduction at that moment is much larger than the final one. The unsupported metal can easily wrinkle and the amount of reduction and the angle of the punch nose are very critical--especially when the blank diameter/ metal thickness ratio is large.

CUP HEIGHTS

The height of the drawn cup can be calculated as follows: (See Fig. 7)

$$\text{Cup Height First Draw: } H1 = \frac{D1^2 - D2^2}{4(D2 + T)}$$

Where: D1 = Blank Diameter
D2 = Inside Diameter Cup, First Draw
T = Metal Thickness

The cup height of the second draw can be computed in the same way:

$$\text{Cup Height Second Draw: } H2 = \frac{D1^2 - D3^2}{4(D3 + T)}$$

153

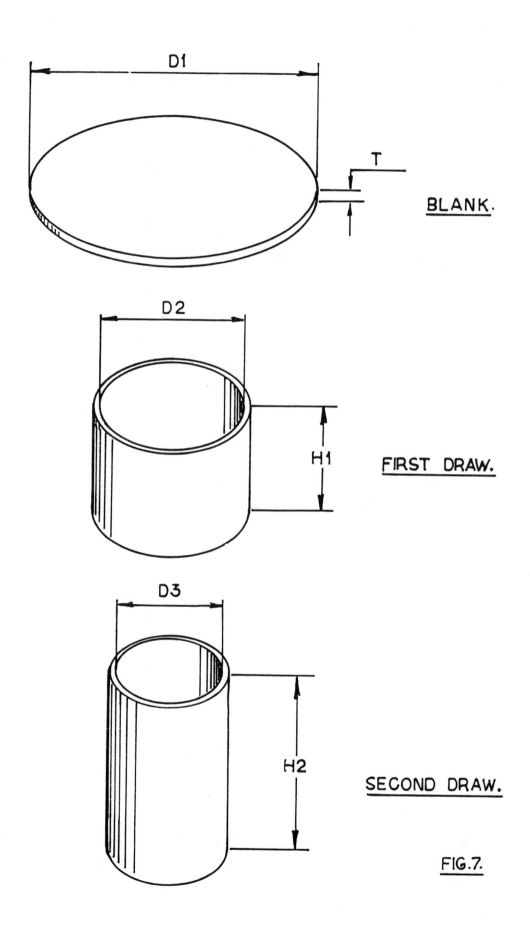

D1

T

BLANK.

D2

H1

FIRST DRAW.

D3

H2

SECOND DRAW.

FIG.7.

154

D3 = Inside Diameter of the Second Draw

If the first reduction is R1 (for instance .4 for 40%) and the second reduction is R2, then the final reduction RF - R1+R2-R1R2 by using these equations it can be calculated that for a 48% maximum reduction in aluminum the maximum cup height will be .35 D1 or .675 D2.

This means that if the desired height of the cup exceeds 67½% of the inside diameter, more than one draw will be required.

For a double draw with a 40% reduction in the first draw and a 30% reduction in the second, the final reduction from blank size D1 is: .4 + .3 - .4 x .3 = .58 or 58%.

$$\text{Then: } D1 \ (1 - .58) = D3$$
$$.42 \ D1 = D3$$

$$\text{Or: } D1 = \frac{D3}{.42} \qquad D1 = 2.381 \ D3.$$

Ignoring metal thickness, then:

$$H2 = \frac{D1^2 - D3^2}{4D3} = \frac{(2.381 \ D3)^2 - D3^2}{4D3} = H2 = 1.672 \ D3.$$

This means that if the height of the final cup exceeds 1.67 x cup inside diameter either more than two draws will be required or larger reductions should be used.

EARING

As a circular blank is drawn into a cup, the metal between draw pad and blank holder (Fig. 3) is subjected to radial tensile stress as well as compressive hoop stress.

Unfortunately, no can stock is strictly isotropic--which means that the strength of it would be the same in all directions.

The metals used in can making have mechanical properties that are not the same in different directions and this is called anisotropy. There are two kinds to consider:

1. Planar Anisotropy

    Here the properties vary in the plank of the sheet--in other words, the tensile strength in the rolling direction might vary from the tensile strength perpendicular to the rolling direction.

2. Normal Anistropy

    In which the strength of the material across the thickness direction differs from the properties in the plane of the sheet.

During the drawing process, material in the flange of the cup between draw pad and blank holder has to move from a large diameter (blank size), to a much smaller size, i.e. the cup diameter. The metal is subjected to a compressive hoop stress as well as a radial tensile stress and can deform in various ways:

1. By Buckling;
2. By Elongating;
3. By Thickening.   (See Fig. 8)

Buckling, of course, is to be avoided by proper die design.

A test sample in a tensile tester will elongate under load and the specimen can do so by getting narrower or thinner. A measurement of a good drawing material would be the so-called "R" value, which is the ratio of the width strain to the thickness strain. It is also called the plastic strain ratio. A high "R" value means that the test strip gets narrower rather than thinner. A good drawing metal would be one with a high "R" value (greater than 1), which means that it flows easily in the plane of the sheet but not in the thickness direction.

A material that flows easily in the thickness direction ("R" smaller than 1), would have the undesirable tendency to thin under the influence of the wall tension during drawing and thinning of the cup wall could lead to metal failure.

Typical "R" values run from 1.0 to 2.0 for various steels and usually below 1.0 for aluminum.

The planar anistropy and variations inthe normal anistropy cause the very un-desirable earing of the material during drawing.

Earing goes usually together with partial wrinkling of the cup wall. Between the ears of the cup are the valleys where the material has thickened under the compressive hoop stress instead of elongated under the radial tensile stress. This thicker material forces the dies open against the blank holder pressure and this can allow the metal in the thinner sections around the ears to wrinkle. The die design, die radii, draw reduction and lubricant all can have an effect on earing.

For aluminum, grooving of the blank holder can reduce earing and wrinkling. Sometimes the use of a lower grade lubricant will reduce the amount of wrinkles. Earing can be reduced by ironing the top of the cup in the draw pad which will reduce the thickness of the valleys between the ears. Earing can be expressed as a percen-tage and is calculated as follows:

Average Height of Ears Minus Average Height of Valleys
Average Height of Valleys   x 100%

A good drawing material should exhibit less than 4% earing. Earing is very un-desirable as it can lead to "clipping" in draw dies and wall ironer. Clipping can occur in the cupping press when at the end of the draw the full blank holding load is concentrated on the tip of the ears. These can be then pinched off due to the high unit load and an accumulation of these clippings in the dies can be a very serious problem.

Various ways can be employed to prevent ear pinching. In double or triple action presses, the dies can be so designed that the blank holder is lifted off the flange of the cup just before the end of the draw. This requires a precise setting of the dies and shimming of the dies after re-grinding to maintain the same and original die height. Also, in double action presses with a cam actuated blanking ram, the dies can be so designed so that the blank holder cannot snap shut at the end of the draw.

A positive gap then remains between blank holder and draw pad--usually between 60 and 80% of the metal thickness. Sometimes the draw pad or blank holder are tapered, but this could lead to wrinkling of the flange with thin material and high

156

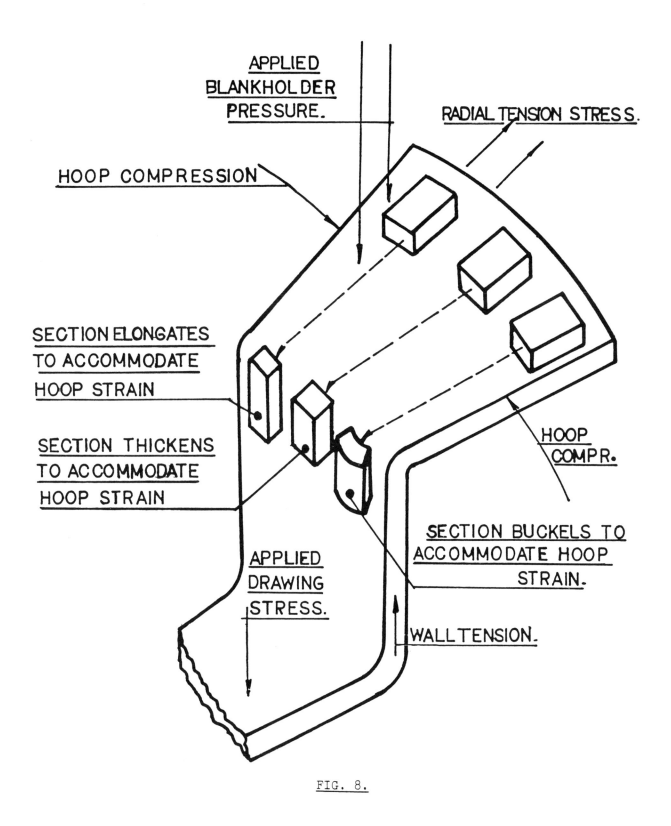

APPLIED
BLANKHOLDER
PRESSURE.

RADIAL TENSION STRESS.

HOOP COMPRESSION

SECTION ELONGATES
TO ACCOMMODATE
HOOP STRAIN

SECTION THICKENS
TO ACCOMMODATE
HOOP STRAIN

HOOP
COMPR.

APPLIED
DRAWING
STRESS.

SECTION BUCKELS TO
ACCOMMODATE HOOP
STRAIN.

WALL TENSION.

FIG. 8.

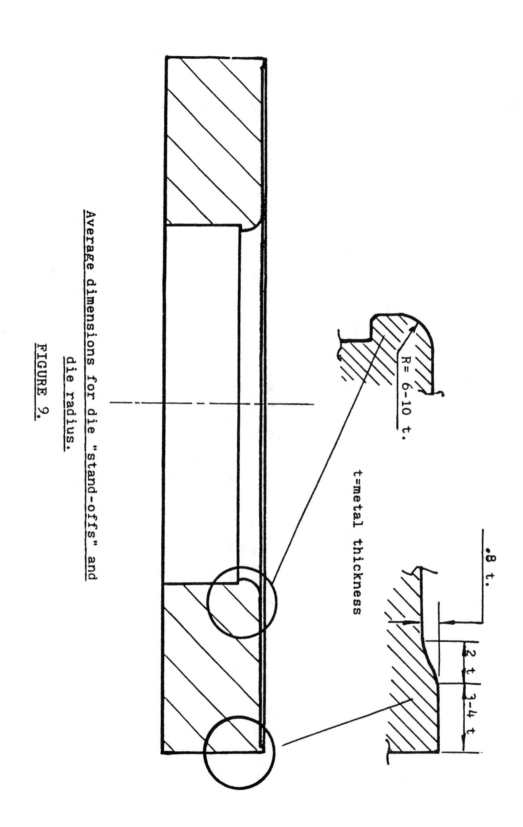

Average dimensions for die "stand-offs" and die radius.

FIGURE 9.

R= 6-10 t.

t=metal thickness

.8 t.

2 t

3-4 t

drawing reductions. A stand-off as shown in Fig. 9 can work satisfactorily if a controlled gap or timed lift-off are not possible.

Two successive draws can be made in a double action press equipped with cushions to provide the required third action--or a triple action press can be used. Also, the second draw can be performed by the wall ironer if this machine is equipped with a suitable blank holding mechanism.

Determining the "R" value of aluminum can stock is a time consuming procedure, that requires several tests with a tensile tester. The "R" value of tin plate can be determined in minutes by electromagnetic means.

BLANK HOLDING PRESSURE

This is, to say the least, a very controversial issue. Handbooks show rules of thumb, charts, graphs, etc.--most values are found empirically. The writer found for a given material, punch and blank size four different answers from four different sources. They varied between 5500 and 23,000 lbs. A more than four to one ratio leaves some doubts about the validity of these figures. A formula that seems to give dependable results for blanks with a blank diameter/thickness ratio up to 400 is:

$$P = .0025 \, (\beta_0 - 1)^2 + \left(\frac{.5d}{100t}\right) \sigma b$$

where: P is the blank holding <u>pressure</u> in psi at the flange area:
σb is the tensile strength in psi;
β_0 is the ratio $\frac{\text{blank diameter}}{\text{punch diameter}}$;
d is the punch diameter;
t is the metal thickness in inches.

However, it was found that for large blanks with a diameter/thickness ratio of 700, the calculated blank holding pressure was much higher than actually needed.

Cups that are double drawn in the cupping press are usually made in such a way that a small amount of redraw in the wall ironer is needed to set the material on the punch before the wall ironing starts. For instance, for a 211 size container and .0165" material, a $7\frac{1}{2}$% redraw reduction can be made without a blank holder. For .0135" thick material, the maximum reduction is about $3\frac{1}{2}$-$4\frac{1}{2}$%.

REFERENCES

E. Siebel: "Der Niederhalterdruck Beim Tiefziehen"
Stahl und Eisen, 74, 1954, pages 155-158

Prof. J. Wright: "The Phenomenon of Earing in Deep Drawing"
Sheet Metal Industries, November 1965

Dr. G.L. Montgommery: "Deep Drawing and Anisotropy"
Stamping and Die Making, September/October 1972.

S.Y. Chung and Prof. H.W. Swift: "Cylindrical Shells--An Investigation Into Redrawing". Iron & Steel, February 1953.

James Burke: Connections. 1978

Reprinted from Manufacturing Engineering, January 1974

Fill Your Draw Die With Water

More than double the depth, sharper corners, and smoother surfaces can be obtained in drawing sheet steel by using water in the die cavity to provide forced lubrication.

WAYNE GRANZON
Research Metallurgist
Armco Steel Corp.
Middletown, Ohio

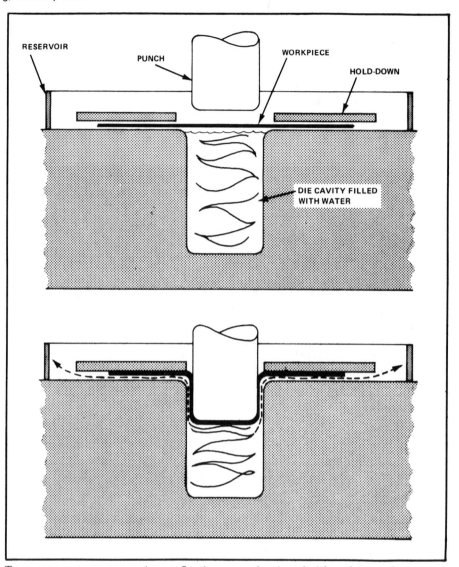

TESTS BEING CONDUCTED at Armco Steel Corp's. Research Center indicate that sheet steel can be drawn significantly deeper by using water in the die cavity to provide forced lubrication during the drawing operation. Sharper corners can also be produced, and, since friction between the die and blank is greatly reduced, there is practically no scoring.

Additional benefits of the so-called Aquadraw process include eliminating the cost of lubricant and its application, removal, and disposal, and reducing the number of draws needed to make parts, thus saving on die costs. Other potential advantages include the possibilities of using lower cost and/or thinner steel, drawing parts previously considered impossible, and reducing reject rates.

Process Details. The die cavity is simply filled with water, a blank is placed on the die, and the press cycle started. At the start of the cycle, the hold-down plate causes the blank to seal the water in the cavity. When the punch starts deforming the blank, hold-down pressure is reduced slightly and water is forced upward between the blank and die-wall to the surface. The high pressure developed lifts the workpiece slightly off the top surface of the die to allow water to escape, *Figure* 1. As a result, the workpiece actually rides on a thin sheet of water under pressure, thus reducing friction.

Back pressure created by the water necessitates increased tonnage (up to three times that normally used) for forming. Oil could be used instead of water, but the only advantage appears to be rust prevention. This can be achieved equally well by adding a small amount (less than one percent) of rust inhibitor to the water. Providing a dike around the die serves as a reservoir for containing and recycling the water. When the punch is raised, the water flows back into the cavity.

Limitations. Since the blanks create a seal over the die cavity, they must not contain any holes. Also, the formed parts must have flanges. A less obvious limitation is on the shape of the punch. If any of the metal in the workpiece is not supported by the punch, that area may be prematurely deformed by the water under pressure. If such deformation becomes too great before the punch provides support, the metal may rupture.

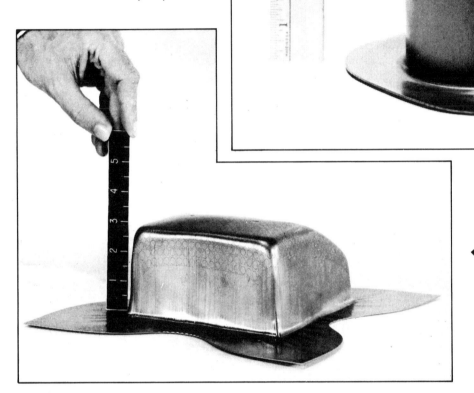

*1. IN AQUADRAW PROCESS,
water is forced upward between
workpiece and die, and friction
is greatly reduced.*

*2. DRAWN CUP,
4 inches in diameter and
4 inches deep, is formed
in a single stroke with bottom
radius of only ⅛ inch.*

*3. UNSYMMETRICAL PART
that could not be formed
with conventional lubricants
is successfully drawn
with Aquadraw process.*

Applications. When using properly designed dies, the performance in any drawing operation is determined by the properties of the metal and the quality of lubrication used. Testing at Armco is done on a 75-ton press, using dies that form a 4-inch diameter cylindrical cup. Blanks of increasing size are used until the maximum size that can be drawn to full depth without breaking is determined. The ratio of that blank diameter to the diameter of the cup being drawn is the limiting draw ratio.

Results of 25 tests are summarized in the accompanying table. Using a conventional oil-type drawing compound, the limiting draw ratio ranged from 1.87 to 2.25 for four different qualities of steel. With the Aquadraw process, this ratio varied from 2.37 to 2.62. This process does not eliminate inherent differences among the several grades of drawing steels. Rather, it enhances the drawing capabilities of each, including even commercial quality steels.

A 4-inch diameter cup drawn to a depth of 4 inches in a single stroke, and having a bottom radius of only ⅛-inch is shown in *Figure* 2. The starting blank of DQ grade steel was 10 inches in diameter. Unsymmetrical parts have also been successfully drawn with this process. One such part formed from DQ grade rimmed steel is seen in *Figure* 3. This part cannot be made with this grade steel using conventional drawing compounds or oils for lubrication. Although interrupted draws have shown there is some early deformation in this part due to water pressure, it is not severe enough to interfere with forming the part.

Details of the simple new process are being offered by Armco to any stamping plants that find they can adapt it to their drawing operations. Although the company has applied for a patent, any fabricator is free to carry the development work further in his own plant. No royalty fees or licensing arrangements will be required. ◄

Comparison of Effectiveness of Lubricating Processes

Limiting draw ratio	Quality of Armco Steel Tested				Max. Blank Diam. (inch)	Max. Cup Height (inch)
	CQ	DQ	DQSK	I-F		
1.87	Drawing Compound				7.5	2.0
2.00		Drawing Compound			8.0	2.5
2.12			Drawing Compound		8.5	3.0
2.25				Drawing Compound	9.0	3.5
2.37	Aquadraw				9.5	4.0
2.50		Aquadraw	Aquadraw		10.0	4.5
2.62				Aquadraw	10.5	5.0

Presented at SME's Manufacturing of Wire III Clinic, April 1978

Techniques In Drawing Brittle Materials

by George W. King
Westinghouse Electric Corp.

I. Introduction

The wire drawing process is one that necessarily requires yielding and considerable plastic flow of the material being drawn. On the other hand, a brittle material is by definition one in which only a negligible amount of plastic flow occurs prior to fracture. Therefore, the basic requirement in drawing a brittle material is to first make it sufficiently ductile to withstand the drawing process without fracturing. There are two practical approaches available by which a brittle material can be made to become ductile. The most direct approach is to draw the material at a temperature above its ductile to brittle transition temperature (DBTT). The other is to improve the ductility of the starting material by prior deformation processes which essentially involve compressive forces (e.g. swaging, extrusion, rolling). In actual practice, such as in the tungsten lamp filament industry, a combination of these steps are involved and will serve as a basis for this paper.

The grade of tungsten used for lamp filaments is powder metallurgy tungsten doped with additives of K, Al, and Si compounds which greatly affect its recrystallized grain structure. This is illustrated in Figure 1 which compares the recrystallized grain structure of both undoped and doped tungsten (Fig. 1A and 1B) at a large wire size ($\geqslant$ 2.0 mm) and shows that the equiaxed grain structure of undoped tungsten is converted to a coarse elongated grain structure by the presence of the dopants. On the other hand, the unrecrystallized structure of either material shows a much finer and more highly elongated grain structure as depicted in Figure 1C for doped tungsten. The latter is quite important to overcoming the problems in drawing tungsten as will be now described in more detail.

II. The Effect of Prior Deformation on the Wire Drawing Process for Tungsten

A typical sequence in the fabrication of powder metallurgy tungsten would be as follows. The metal powders are pressed into an ingot and sintered to about 90% of theoretical density. The ingot is then swaged at elevated temperatures to a size of about 2.0 to 3.5 mm at which point wire drawing begins. Anneals are employed during the primary fabrication process which are mostly important to the wire properties at use sizes. The more important aspects of swaging or rolling prior to wire drawing is that it fully densifies the sintered ingot and reduces it to a size more suitable for drawing, while also enhancing its low temperature ductility. The latter effect is illustrated in Figure 2 in which the low temperature tensile ductility of tungsten (expressed as % Red. in area) is plotted as a function of test temperature for both fully recrystallized doped and undoped tungsten and for doped tungsten which has been swaged to a total deformation of about 93% but only 65% after recrystallization at a prior size. The corresponding microstructures of the recrystallized and un-recrystallized materials were those shown in Figure 1. It can be seen that the fully recrystallized tungsten of both grades has a ductile to brittle transition temperature (DBTT) of about 300°C, although their microstructures are quite different, whereas the DBTT of the worked material is only about 150°C. As a matter of interest it might be noted that continued deformation of the doped material by swaging and drawing further improves ductility to the point that the wire is fully ductile at room temperature

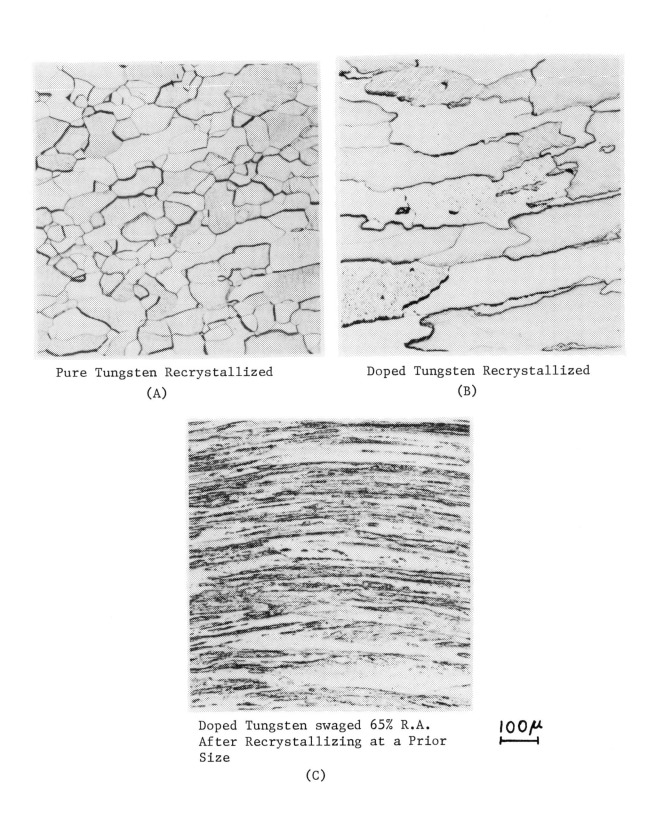

Pure Tungsten Recrystallized

(A)

Doped Tungsten Recrystallized

(B)

Doped Tungsten swaged 65% R.A.
After Recrystallizing at a Prior
Size

(C)

100μ

Figure 1. Microstructures of Recrystallized and Deformed Power
          Metallurgy Tungsten.

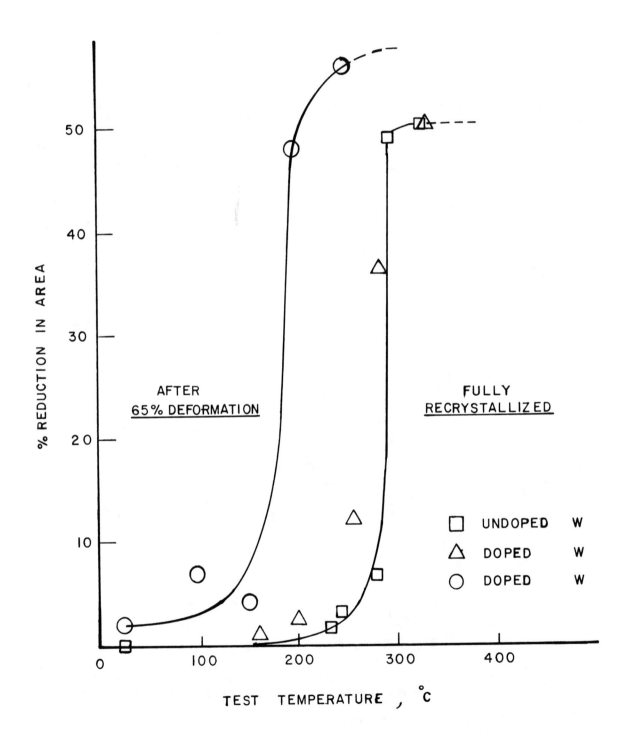

Figure 2. Effect of Deformation by Swaging or Rolling on
the Ductile to Brittle Transition Temperature
of Powder Metallurgy Tungsten.

(Fig. 3) because of the development of long fibrous grains. However, drawing begins while the material is still brittle at room temperature and it is this aspect of the process which we will now examine.

III. <u>Pre-Heating and Lubrication Problems in Drawing Tungsten with Poor Low Temperature Ductility</u>

In the commercial production of tungsten wire, practical considerations require that the wire is drawn onto a capstan. Consequently, unless the capstan is unusually large, most of the problems in drawing will occur as the wire is cooling on the capstan because of the poor low temperature ductility of the starting material. A lower estimate of the strain which develops in the outermost fibers of a 2.0 mm to 3.5 mm dia wire as it is wound onto a capstan is shown in Figure 4. Here the strain due to bending alone is given as $E = r/R$ where r is the radius of the wire and R is the radius of the capstan. The total strain will actually be greater because of the tensile force in the wire imposed by drawing it through the die. None-the-less, the results show that the strains which develop are in excess of the strain at the conventional 0.2% yield strength of tungsten, and hence will cause fracture if the material is in a brittle state. It is largely for this reason that the pre-heat temperature at the outset of drawing is as high as $1000^{o}C$, and also that the capstan is heated to prevent too rapid cooling of the drawn wire. This fact also emphasizes the importance of the prior deformation which lowers the DBTT from $300^{o}C$ to about $150^{o}C$. Not only does it reduce the temperature required to maintain the material in a ductile state, but it also greatly reduces handling problems for the operator. However, with each drawing pass the low temperature ductility improves to the point that the capstan size can be gradually reduced to much smaller sizes causing the maximum strain due to bending to rise to about 0.7%. Concomitantly, the drawing temperatures are reduced and pre-heating of the capstan is eliminated after about 90% deformation by drawing.

The fact that high temperatures are necessary at the start of the drawing process brings about a severe problem in lubrication. Graphite powder suspended in an aqueous solution is used as a lubricant throughout the drawing process. The exact composition is proprietary to the supplier, but different grades are used depending on wire size. In order for the lubricant to be most effective it must be applied to an oxidized wire surface, and must be dried during pre-heating without the lubricant itself being oxidized. This requires that the temperature of the heat source is varied so that the lubricant is first dried at relatively low temperatures, then the temperature of the heat source increased so that the wire is rapidly heated to the drawing temperature just before entering the die. Under these conditions, the coefficient of friction, u, for drawing 0.86 mm dia tungsten wire has been determined in our laboratory, and has also been determined independently by Dr. R. N. Wright for drawing 2.0 mm dia tungsten wire when he was formerly at the Westinghouse Research Laboratory in Pittsburgh, Pa. The details of the results will be jointly published at a later time, but were found to be in substantial agreement with the results shown in Figure 5 for the case of drawing 0.86 mm dia tungsten wire. These results based on equations developed by several authors (1, 2, 3) show that at a temperature of about $600^{o}C$. the coefficient of friction is about 0.05 when using short bearing dies. On the other hand,

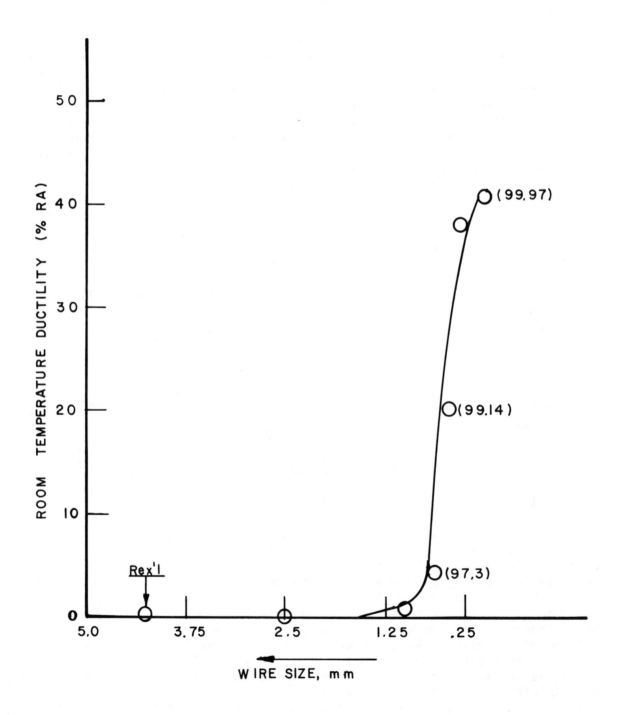

Figure 3. Effect of Deformation on the Room Temperature
Ductility of Power Metallurgy Tungsten (Numbers
in Parenthesis Represent Total % Deformation).

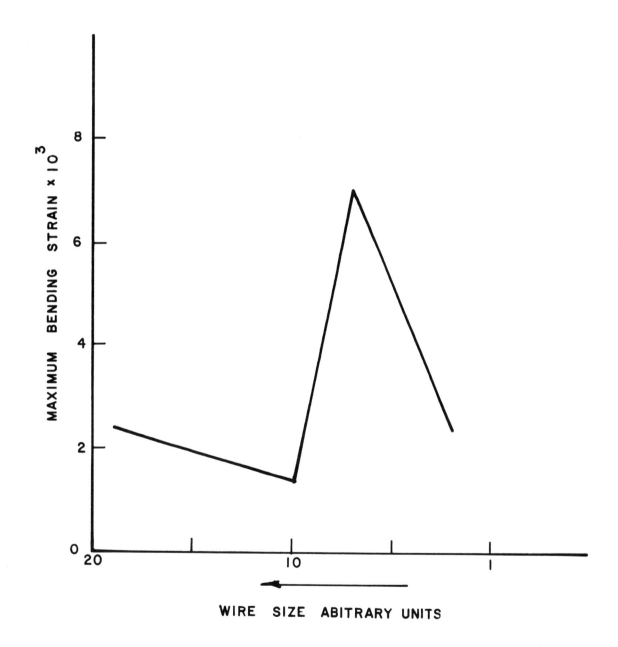

Figure 4.   Maximum Bending Strain (E = r/R) Caused by Winding
             Wire on a Capstan: r = Wire Size, R = Capstan Size.

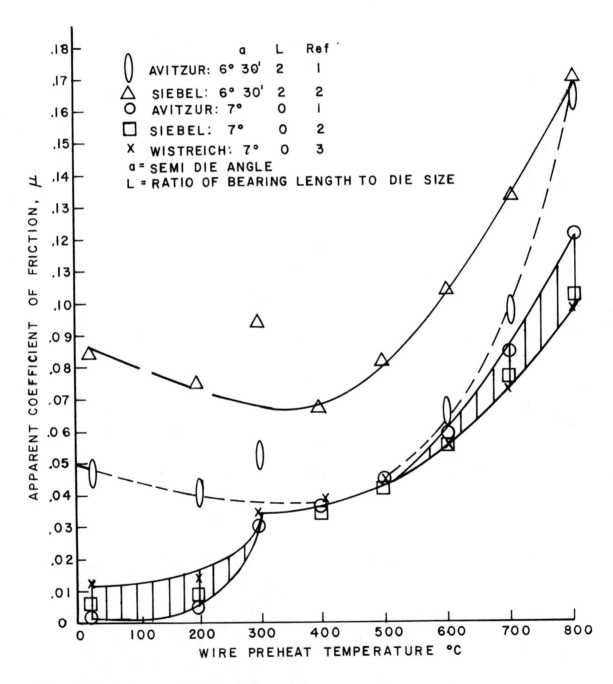

Figure 5. The Apparent Coefficient of Friction for a 29% Reduction
in Area of 0.86 mm Dia. Tungsten Wire Plotted as a Function
of Pre-heat Temperature and Die Contour. Die Temperature
$\sim$ 300°C.

as the pre-heat temperature is increased or if the wire is allowed to remain at high temperatures for a prolonged period of time, oxidation of the lubricant causes the coefficient of friction to rapidly increase and eventually results in the wire breaking in the die. Likewise the data in Fig. 5 show that if long bearing dies are used the apparent coefficient of friction increases more rapidly at high temperatures.

IV. Other Considerations in Drawing Brittle Materials

At the temperature at which tungsten that is still brittle or semi-brittle at room temperature is drawn, the ultimate strength is only about 25% greater than the yield strength of the material (Fig. 6), and therefore any factor which causes an increase in the drawing force is undesirable. Thus the tungsten carbide drawing die should be selected so that the die angle and bearing length is optimized with respect to the drawing force, without sacrificing control over wire uniformity. Also plotted in Fig. 6 is the drawing force for a 30% reduction of 0.86 mm dia tungsten wire as a function of temperature and die contour. It can be seen that at the higher temperatures the drawing force is almost equal to the ultimate strength of the wire in uniform tension when long bearing dies are used, but is substantially lower if short bearing dies are used. Other data not shown also indicates that the optimum included die angle is between 16° and 18°. Thus the optimum die profile would be about a 17° included die angle with a bearing length of 75% to 100% of the wire size (since a shorter bearing would cause difficulty in controlling wire size uniformity because of excessive die wear).

Since lowering the drawing temperature causes the coefficient of friction to decrease, it also causes the drawing force to decrease to a minimum at about $400^{\circ}C$, at which point the rapid increase in yield strength of tungsten causes an increase in the drawing force at lower temperatures. Because of this effect of temperature on the draw force, there is a tendency for operators to want to draw at lower than recommended temperatures once the wire is sufficiently ductile to not break on the capstan at the lower drawing temperatures. However, even after the material has developed sufficient ductility to be drawn at low temperatures, the drawing temperature must remain above $600^{\circ}C$ in order to avoid the development of extended longitudinal cracks (splits) and surface defects which can cause wire breaks in subsequent drawing passes. An example of one type of surface defect which develops as the result of low temperature drawing is shown in Figure 7. Defects of this type can bulge back in the die in subsequent drawing passes as a result of surface friction and thereby result in wire breaks in the die.

Materials which have poor ductility are very notch sensitive. Therefore, the presence of surface defects in a brittle type material greatly aggravates problems in wire drawing. An extreme sample is the case of drawing the high strength alloy W-Hf-C (W - 0.35Hf - 0.026C) developed at NASA-Lewis for fiber reinforcement of super alloys. The starting material is a vacuum arc cast alloy which is extruded with molybdenum cladding and swaged without removal of the cladding. During the extrusion process a heavily corrugated surface structure develops which remains after swaging (Fig. 8A). After swaging the cladding has thinned to the point that it must be removed before wire drawing can begin, but in order to draw this

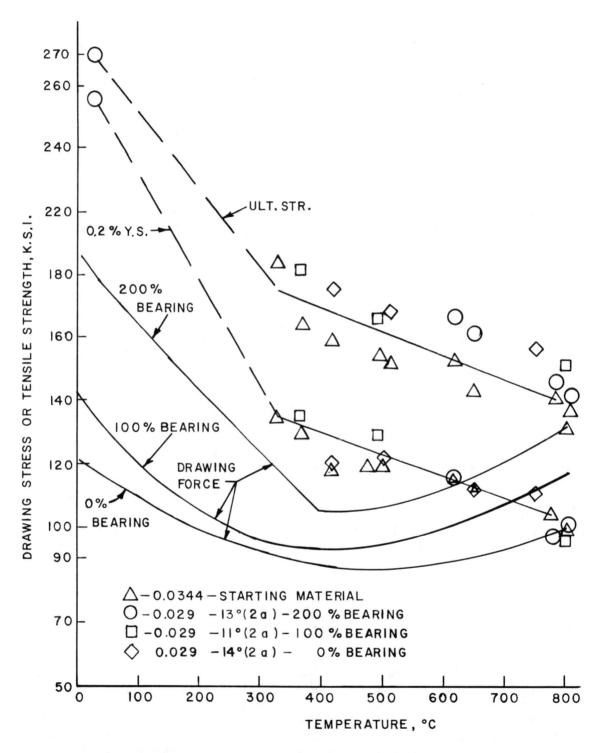

Figure 6. Tensile Properties and Drawing Stress (29% RA) Plotted as a Function of Temperature (2α is the Included Die Angle).

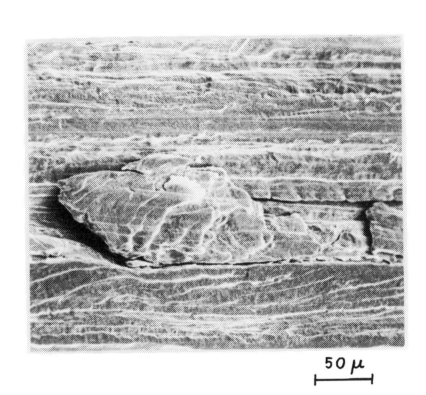

50 μ

Figure 7.   SEM Micrograph of a Surface Defect by Drawing
            Tungsten at Low Temperatures (< 600°C).

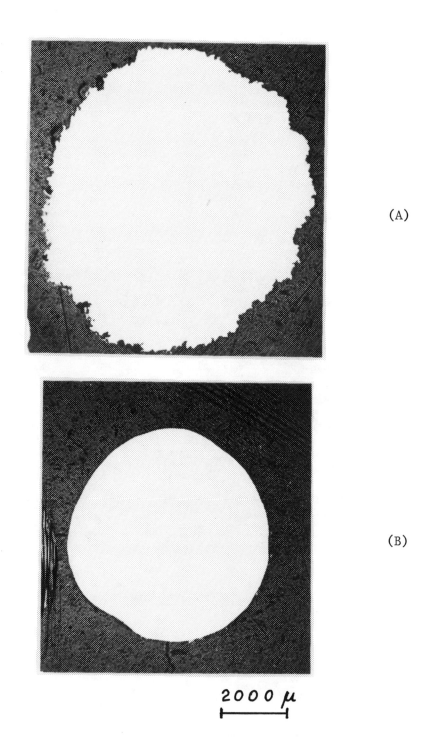

(A)

(B)

2000 μ

Figure 8.   Photomicrographs of W-Hf-C Rod Swaged With Cladding
            After Extrusion. (A) As Swaged, (B) After Surface
            Removal of Unclad Rod in Fused Salt.

material the surface defects shown in Figure 8 must be removed. The most efficient means of removing the surface is by immersion in a fused salt bath of sodium nitrate salts which react rapidly to produce a surface which is still irregular but relatively smooth (Fig. 8B). After this treatment the material can be drawn in a manner similar to that described for doped tungsten wire drawing except that the first few passes are made on a straight draw bench.

Another example of the deleterious effects of the surface condition on wire drawing is the case of a material which reacts with the atmosphere to form a brittle surface layer. In this instance the material is a columbium base alloy B88(Cb-28W - 2 Hf - 0.07C) which was swaged after being vacuum clad in molybdenum tubing. Before drawing the cladding is removed and it is found that the material is completely brittle. A micrograph of the longitudinal cross section of a swaged rod which includes the cladding is shown in Figure 9 and reveals the presence of numerous transverse cracks which were the cause of the extreme brittleness. Further evaluation of the surface condition by X-ray analysis and other techniques strongly indicated that excessive oxygen contamination was responsible for the surface embrittlement. In any event, after chemically removing only a few tenths of a mm from the surface of the rod, it becomes completely ductile and could even be drawn at room temperature, although the actual drawing temperature was maintained at about $500^{o}C$ in order to minimize split formation.

V. Conclusions

The most important considerations in drawing a material with poor low temperature ductility are the following:

1. Draw the material at a temperature at which it remains ductile throughout the drawing process.

2. Introduce sufficient deformation prior to drawing to improve the low temperature ductility.

3. Control the heating rate of the wire for drawing in such a way as to not destory the lubricant by oxidation.

4. Surface condition the material if needed to remove surface flaws and contaminants.

5. Minimize surface strains in the drawn wire by control of the capstan size.

6. Exercise close control over drawing dies.

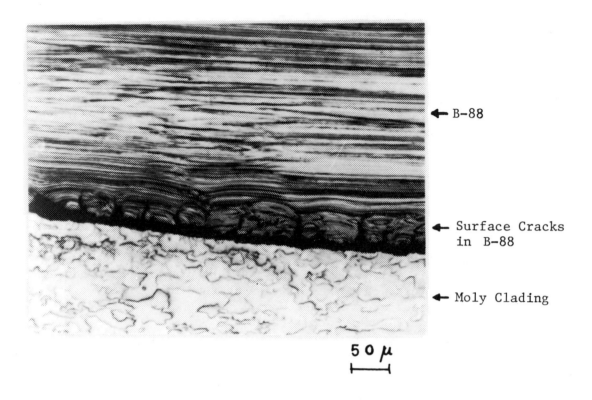

Figure 9. Photomicrographs of Surface Cracks in B-88 Rod
Swaged Clad to 3.7 mm Diameter.

References

1. B. Avitzur: J. Eng. Ind. Trans. ASME B, 1963, Vol. 85, pp. 89-96.

2. E. Siebel: Stahl and Eisen, 1947, Vol. 66-67, No. 11-22, pp. 171-180.

3. J. G. Wistreich: Proc. Inst. Mech. Engrs., 1955, Vol. 169, pp. 654-665.

CHAPTER 3

FINEBLANKING DIES

Fine blanking

by Ing. A. Guidi
Brugg-Biel
Switzerland

Introduction

A German patent issued March 9, 1923, describes a hydraulic cutting and punching device. It describes clamping the workpiece during the process on both sides of the cutting line. And in a German publication, the patent (371004) is referred to and the remark is added that it might be necessary to "tooth" the stripper for clamping the material.

Basically the prime requisite for fine blanking is to control metal flow in the shear zone. How to fulfill this requirement has long been known, but still the use of fine blanking did not begin until much later. The reasons delaying the spread of this interesting process are various, but probably the one foremost deterrent has been the extra precision of press and tooling

---

The terms of origin, such as fine punching, fine cutting, fine stamping, etc. will be either used in these articles or changed to fine blanking.

necessary. It is remarkable that the inventor brought the fine blanking process to maturity, before the machine tool was available for production work.

Fundamental considerations

Suppose a disk several times as large as its thickness is cut out, in a fall-through way, without a pressure pad. The return forces (fiber tension) will increase the tension at the shearing zone. And increased pressure means separation of disk to make a hole, but the sheet will have been bent at the beginning of the cutting operation between the punch and the die.

When a tool has a pressure pad, the sheet cannot bend—since it is clamped between the pad and the die or between the punch and the ejector, respectively. To be effective great force is required to clamp the sheet.

Also the amount of clearance between the punch and die is known to influence the surface quality of the sheared faces. When the ratio of clearance between punch and die to the thickness of the sheet is diminished, the ratio of land area to the fracture zone on the sheared surface

Figure 1

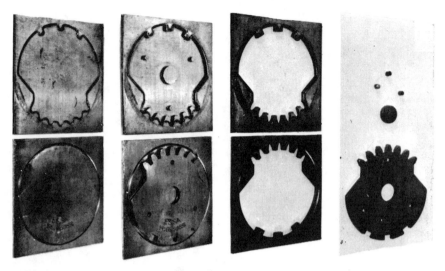

Figure 2

is increased. When clearance between punch and die is small, the surface quality of the sheared face on the blanked part and the pierced sheet is often improved.

The depth of the tear, as well as the number of tears in the direction of cut may be smaller on the pierced sheet than on the blanked part. Furthermore, the surface quality of the sheared face of various materials, cut under the same conditions, may be different; this depends to a great extent on the deformability of the mat'l.

The bending mentioned above is not related to the fact that one edge at the shear face of every fine blanked part is slightly rounded. The rounded edge of the blanked part lies in the plane, which during the cutting operation rests on the die. The rounded edge that lies in the sheet plane during the cutting operation is directed to the punch side; this rounded edge is on the waste strip. The amount of this roundness (draw) depends on the geometric form of the cutting line and other considerations. These rounded edges are formed during the first part of the cutting operation **(Figure 1)**.

The volume of blanked part is decreased due to the shear radius and this amount is, in all cases, displaced into the scrap strip. This swelling of the partly cut sheet will, after the maximum cutting power has been exceeded, cause tensile stresses in the shearing zone that may in turn tend to form cracks.

There should be no cracks in the shearing zone during cutting so in a fine blanking operation the sheet is clamped on both sides of the cutting line, with virtually no clearance between the punch and the die. This hinders the flow of metal in the shear zone. For most effective clampings, a knife edge ring is pressed into the scrap strip along the cutting line of the blanked part.

Figure 2 shows the separation of a ⁵⁄₃₂ thick fine blanked part. As both the pressure pad and

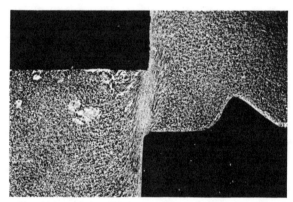

Figure 3

Figure 4

the die were provided with an impingement ring, the strip is shown as seen from the punch side above and from the die side below.

Figure 3 shows a normal section through the shearing zone of a fine blanked part which has not yet been entirely separated from the scrap strip. The penetration of the punch already amounts to 75 percent of the thickness and the shearing zone does not show any cracks.

Impingement ring

Fine blanked parts generally have inside shapes such as holes and recesses, which are produced at the same time:

1) Inside shapes: The shearing faces of inside shapes are in most cases good if there is virtually no clearance between the hole-punch and the outside-contour-punch; hole punches ride in main punch. This is so if the part to be blanked is clamped between the punch and the ejector or counter-punch. As mentioned before, the slight radius indicates a flow of material from the radius area to the part being separated from it. In the instances where holes are being punched, this volume is so small it is not usually necessary to press an impingement ring along the shear line. The shearing faces of "small" holes being punched out are, however, often torn, as seen in **Figure 4**. As the punched out

piece is scrap, the surface quality of the face is of no importance.

If dimensions of an inside shape is in all directions several times greater than the thickness of the sheet, it too should be clamped, during the cutting, between the punch and the ejector.

2) Outside shape: The impingement ring which is pressed into the strip at the beginning of the cutting operation, along the outside shape, hinders the flow of crystals in that zone. Thus, the depth of this zone is diminished.

Dimensioning the impingement ring along an outside shape is a matter of experience. Factors of consequence are described below.

A small ring near the shear line may have the same effect as a large ring further from the shear line. Also if the ring of the pressure pad is too near the cutting line, material may be "removed" from it—when the shear radius is formed—so that its efficiency is impaired. The greater the distance the ring is from the shear line the greater the consumption of material; moreover, the pressure required becomes greater, and the efficiency of the press is impaired.

Where it is necessary to impinge a recess in the blanked part this can be tolerated more readily than protrusions. These recesses in a blanked part will be one-and-a-half times as wide as the sheet is thick, and flow in the sheared zone will be minimal. In certain instances, it is not necessary that the impingement ring follow the shear line exactly.

The area of the blanked parts located at the yet full strip feed side can be subjected to the

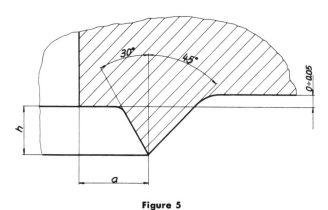

Figure 5

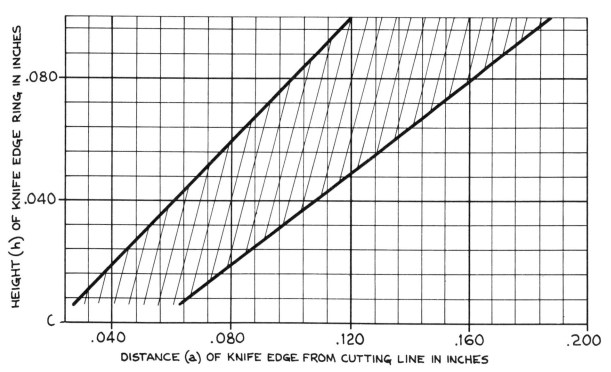

Figure 6

fine blanking operation more easily than the portions located at the edges or the web end. Large rim and web widths are uneconomic, and so it is often necessary to also provide the die with an impingement ring as mentioned earlier. To avoid extra impingement rings, the important portions of a blanked part may therefore be arranged, when possible, on the strip feed-end.

The influence of a ring on the die, on the shear radius, is greater than the influence of the ring on the pressure pad. In other words, the knife edge on the die reduces die roll (or draw) along the sheared edge of the part, more than the ring on the pressure pad.

Dimensioning of the impingement ring is, as inferred, dependent upon the thickness of the sheet and the properties of the material. **Figure 5** shows a ring profile used frequently. The profile height "h" corresponds to the penetration of the "knife ring" into the material. The penetration of the knife should be one-fifth of the thickness of the stock for materials of low deformability. For materials easy to deform, up to one-third of the thickness of the stock is used. If the pressure pad and the die are both provided with an impingement ring, the penetration should correspond to the sum of the two ring heights. In general, knife edge rings should be used as per the thickness of the stock. Up to ⁵⁄₃₂ stock only use a ring on the pressure pad. From ⁷⁄₆₄ to ⁹⁄₃₂, a ring may be needed on the pressure pad and partly on the die. For stock more than ³⁄₁₆, a ring on pressure pad and also on

cutting die plate, may be necessary.

The distance "a" **(Figure 5)** of the tip of the "knife" from the cutting line is shown in the diagram of **Figure 6.** The contour of the knife ring at the pressure pad approximately follows the shear contour of the blanked part, which would be obtained from normal blanking. In certain instances the ring cannot practically follow the exact part outline. **Figure 7** shows the course of the knife edge ring, by examples. The fine line shows the impingement ring, and the shaded line represents the die cutting line.

If the die is provided with a closed ring, its contour is generally identical with the contour of the ring on the pressure pad. As the ring of the die is a hindrance to resharpening, it may be practical to compromise the design.

The pressure required for pressing one linear

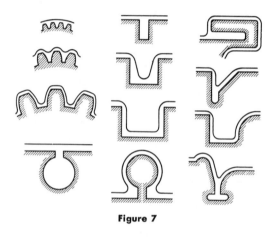

Figure 7

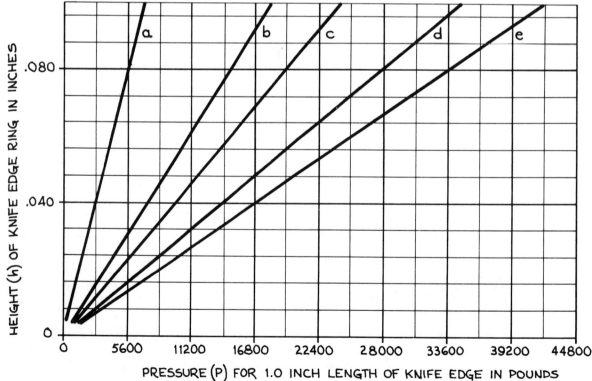

a) Charts pure aluminum (hard); b) copper (soft) AlMgSi (half hard); c) mild steels, half hard brass, AlMgSi (hard), copper (hard); d) alloyed case hardened steel; and e) stainless steel.

Figure 8

inch of knife edge into various materials can be taken from **Figure 8**. If the pressure pad and the die are both provided with a knife edge ring, the fine blanking press will only have to provide the maximum pressure to press in one knife edge ring or the other. The combined pressures are not required.

Cutting work and cutting speed

During the cutting operation the cutting work required for cutting out the blanked part is converted into heat. The major part of this heat is formed in the shearing zone in which the crystals are deformed.

Figure 9 shows schematically the force-distance diagram for the cutting out of a blanked part with normal cutting clearance (curve "a") and for fine blanking (curve "b"). The area between the abscissa and the curve "a" corresponds to the "coarse cutting work" and the area between the abscissa and the curve "b" to the "fine blanking work." The work required and consequently the quantity of heat liberated during the fine blanking operation is about twice as great as in the case of cutting with a normal cutting clearance.

According to **Figure 9** the cutting work "L" for fine blanking is approximately

$$L = \frac{1}{2} \cdot P_{max} \cdot s = \frac{1}{2} \cdot 1 \cdot s^2 \cdot t, \qquad (1)$$

L being the cutting work in mkg,
P the cutting force in kg,
s the thickness of the sheet in m,
l the length of the cutting line in m, and
t the shearing strength in kg/m²
The quantity of heat equivalent to the cutting work is

$$Q = A \cdot L = \frac{1}{2} \cdot A \cdot 1 \cdot s^2 \cdot t, \qquad (2)$$

Q being the quantity of heat in kcal and
A the mechanical heat equivalent in $\frac{1}{427} \frac{mkg.}{kcal}$

Dissertation pertaining to heat generated during cutting operation, formulae etc., has been left in the metric system for convenience of use.

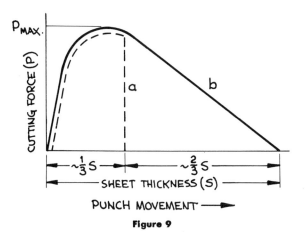

SHEET THICKNESS (S)

PUNCH MOVEMENT ⟶

Figure 9

If the cutting operation is carried out very quickly, i.e. if the cutting speed is high, the heat formed is accumulated in the shearing zone of the blanked part and the strip. The temperature increase in the shearing zone will then be

$$\Delta t = \frac{\Delta Q}{V \cdot \gamma \cdot c} = \frac{A \cdot 1 \cdot s^2 \cdot t}{2 \cdot 1 \cdot s \cdot b \cdot \gamma \cdot c} = \frac{s}{b} \cdot \frac{A \cdot t,}{2 \cdot \gamma \cdot c} \qquad (3)$$

Δt being the temperature increase in °C,
V the volume of the shearing zone in m³,
γ the specific gravity in kg/m³,
c the specific heat in kcal/kg °C and
b the depth of the shearing zone of the blanked part and the strip in "m".
Example: Material: A1S1-C1010 thickness:
    $s = 4$ mm, shearing strength: $t = 30$ kg/mm², depth of the shearing zone: $b = 0.5$ mm (measured according to Fig. 5).

According to equation 3 it follows that:

$$\Delta t = \frac{4 \cdot 10^{-3} \cdot 30 \cdot 10^6}{5 \cdot 10^{-4} \cdot 2 \cdot 427 \cdot 7,85 \cdot 10^3 \cdot 0,11} = 325°C. \qquad (4)$$

Therefore, the temperature increase in the shearing zone is 325°C.

The author is very well aware of the shortcomings of this calculation; assumptions have been made here which are not, or not in this simple form, fulfilled in practice. In any case, the temperature increase in the shearing zone is considerable and, particularly when fine blanking thick sheet, of great influence on the efficiency of the cutting elements of the fine blanking tool.

According to equation 3, the temperature increase Δt is proportional to the quotient $\frac{s}{b}$. The temperature in the shearing zone increases with a decreasing depth of the sheared zone. Since the depth of the sheared zone is influenced by the knife edge, the connection between knife edge ring and tool wear is justified.

The maximum temperature reached in the shearing zone during the cutting operation is also dependent upon the cutting speed. When the cutting speed is low, the quantity of heat continuously formed in the shearing zone during the cutting operation is partly dissipated.

At all times during the cutting operation, the quantity of heat obtained corresponds to the cutting work performed. In accordance with **Figure 9,** the greatest quantity of heat is obtained during the first half of the cutting operation. A relatively low temperature increase in the shearing zone can therefore be achieved by low cutting speed, during the first half of the cutting operation. For judging the cutting speed, not only its initial value or any mean value is decisive, but its course as a function of the sheet thickness. The lower "heat load" of the cutting elements, at lower cutting speed in general and in particular, during first half of the cutting operation can multiply efficiency. ∎

Reprinted from "Fine-Blanking Practical Handbook", courtesy of American Feintool Inc., Cincinnati, Ohio

Construction of Fine-Blanking Tools

The design and construction of fine-blanking tools can be best compared to the conventional type of compound tools. The fine-blanking tool is, however, more rigid. The major differences between a fine-blanking tool and a conventional press tool are:

- The spring elements providing force for stripping the skeleton strip and for ejecting the blanked piece-parts are not required. These forces are transferred by the pressure pins which are actuated directly from the hydraulics in the machine.

- The clearance between punch and die plate has a total dimension (i. e. relative to the diameter) of approximately 1% of the material thickness to be worked. (See also section 5.31.) In conventional press tools the clearance is approximately 5–10%.

- Due to the reduced clearance the guidance and centering of the main punch relative to the die plate must be more exact.

- The 'vee-ring' which follows the outer periphery of the piece-part form is machined on the surface of the guide plate (also termed stripper plate or pressure plate) and is imbedded into the material to be worked through the hydraulics in the machine. This prevents a material flow away from the main punch and thereby prevents fractures occurring over the sheared surface.

- The main punch for the outer piece-part form is at the same time 'die plate' for the inner configurations. The inner form slugs do not fall through the main punch. They are ejected upward out of the punch with ejector pins actuated by the hydraulics in the machine after the blanking operation is completed.

These punch inner forms do not run through the whole of the height of the punch, which enables the punch base to be far more rigid. Because of this rigid punch base, piece-parts with many complicated inner forms lying close to each other may be produced in one operation, without the danger of punch breakage occurring.

In fine-blanking two tool systems may be used:

– Tools with sliding (moving) punch (picture 44b)
– Tools with fixed punch (picture 44c)

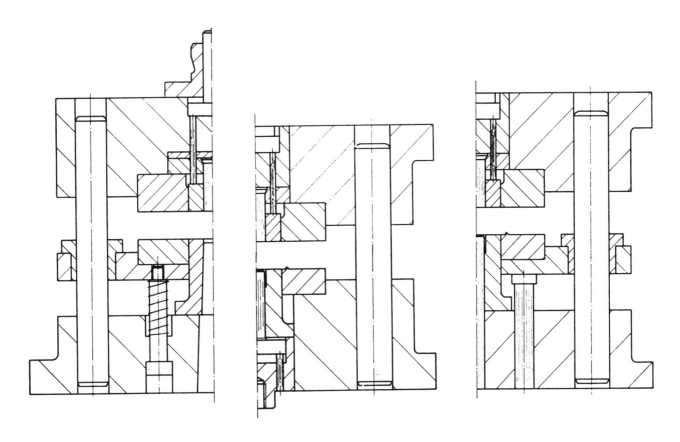

Picture 44

a) conventional compound press tool

b) fine-blanking tool with sliding punch

c) fine-blanking tool with fixed punch

Fine-blanking tools with sliding punch (pictures 45–47)

In order that fine-blanked components may be produced with minimum difficulty, an exact centering of the punch to the die plate is required. This centering can only be guaranteed when the main punch is correctly located and guided.

In the so-called 'sliding punch' type of fine-blanking tools both the die plate and guide plate (pressure plate) are fixed in the die-set bolsters (die-shoes). The punch is guided through a bore in the lower die-set bolster and the guide plate. The punch movement is always equal to the material thickness being worked. If the largest punch dimension exceeds the punch height the exact centering location required can no longer be guaranteed. From this it may be noted that the 'sliding punch' tool system is applied mainly to small and medium sized parts.

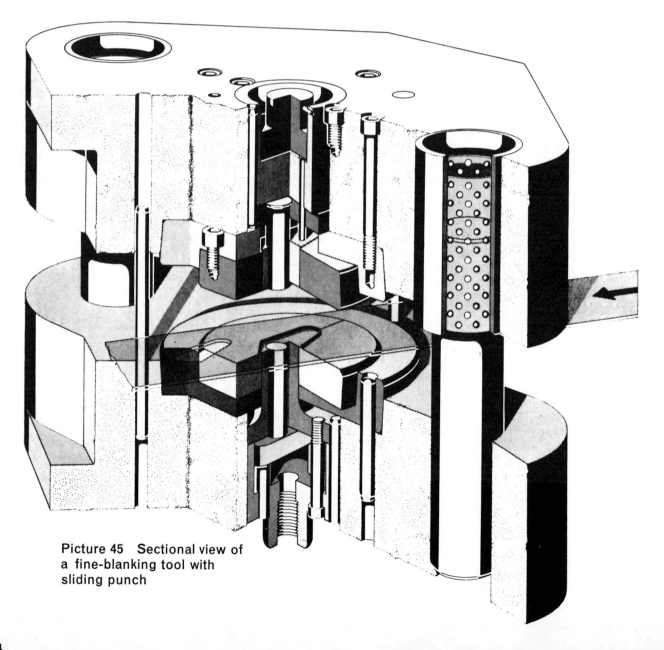

Picture 45   Sectional view of
a fine-blanking tool with
sliding punch

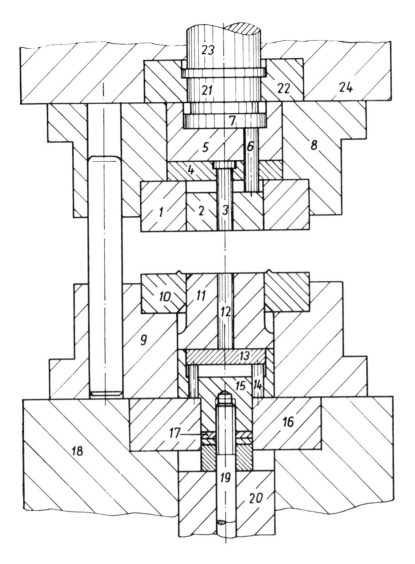

Picture 46 Fine-blanking tool with sliding punch. Standard design

Upper half of tool

1 Die-plate
2 Ejector (counter-punch)
3 Piercing punches Piercing punch retaining plate
5 Back-up plate
6 Pressure pins
7 Pressure pad
8 Die-set bolster

Lower half of tool

9 Die-set bolster
10 Guide-plate (pressure plate)
11 Main punch
12 Ejector pins
13 Ejector bridge
14 Pressure pins
15 Punch base

Lower table (for sliding punch)

16 Adaptor-ring
17 Spacer discs
18 Press table under hydraulic pressure for imprinting 'vee-ring'
19 Tie-bar (clamping punch)
20 Press ram

Upper table

21 Pressure pad
22 Adaptor-ring
23 Hydraulic piston for counter pressure
24 Press table

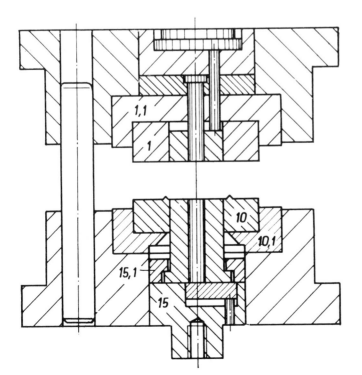

Picture 47 Sliding punch retained through coupling-ring

1   Die-plate
1.1 Shroud-ring
10   Guide plate (pressure plate)
10.1 Shroud ring
15   Punch base
15.1 Coupling/clamp plate

Fine-blanking tools with fixed punch (pictures 48–50)

Using this type of tool construction the punch is screwed and dowelled to the die-set bolster. The punch is guided through the stripper plate which also functions as the pressure plate carrying the 'vee-ring'. For these reasons it is essential that the stripper plate is securely retained and for this purpose is guided over the die-set pillars (guide-pins).

This basic tool design system is best suited for:

- large, long and narrow parts
- asymmetrical parts where there is a danger of side pressures occurring
- parts with many inner forms where a sliding punch arrangement would not prove strong enough due to the positioning of the ejector-pin bridge in the punch base.
- thick parts which require an exceptionally stable tool design and where high pressures are to be used. In such cases a special adaptor ring is used to give extra support to the die-set (and thereby also to the punch). The 'vee-ring' and ejector pressures are transferred over pins.

Tools with sliding punches are automatically centered in the machine through the punch base. Fine-blanking tools with fixed punches have to be centered relative to the adaptor rings in order that the pressure pin positions correspond. This is achieved most easily by introducing two dowel pins into the lower adaptor ring and a slot through the bottom die-set bolster (die-shoe).

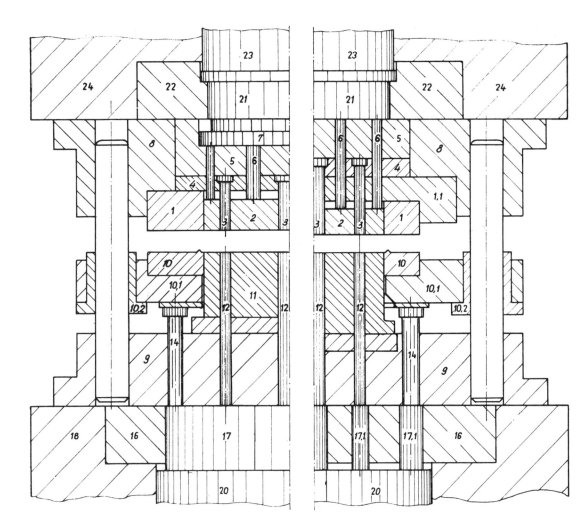

Picture 48 Fine-blanking tool with fixed punch. Standard design

Picture 49 Die-set given extra support through special adaptor-ring design

Upper half of tool

1	Die-plate
1.1	Shroud-ring
2	Ejector (counter punch)
3	Piercing punches
4	Piercing punch retaining plate
5	Back-up plate
6	Pressure pins
7	Pressure pad
8	Die-set bolster

Lower half of tool

9	Die-set bolster
10	Stripper plate (pressure plate)
10.1	Shroud ring for pressure plate
10.2	Guide-bush

11	Main punch
12	Ejector pins
14	Pressure pins

Lower table (for fixed punch tools)

16	Adaptor-ring	
17	Pressure pad	actuated hydrauli-cally for 'vee-ring' pressure
17.1	Pressure pins	
18	Press table	
20	Piston for 'vee-ring' pressure	

Upper table

21	Pressure-pad
22	Adaptor-ring
23	Piston for opposing pressure
24	Press table

Basically it can be stated that for large parts with complicated forms tools of fixed punch design are better suited than sliding punch tools. The maintenance and setting of these tools, however, takes somewhat longer. As opposed to the sliding punch tool, where the punch has always to remain in the lower half of the die-set, the fixed punch may be set in the upper die-set bolster (picture 50). The die plate is then located in the lower die-set bolster and the piece-part is ejected from below. This system is applied generally when a removal arm has to be used (large, heavy parts or multi-punch tools) and also for progressive fine-blanking tools.

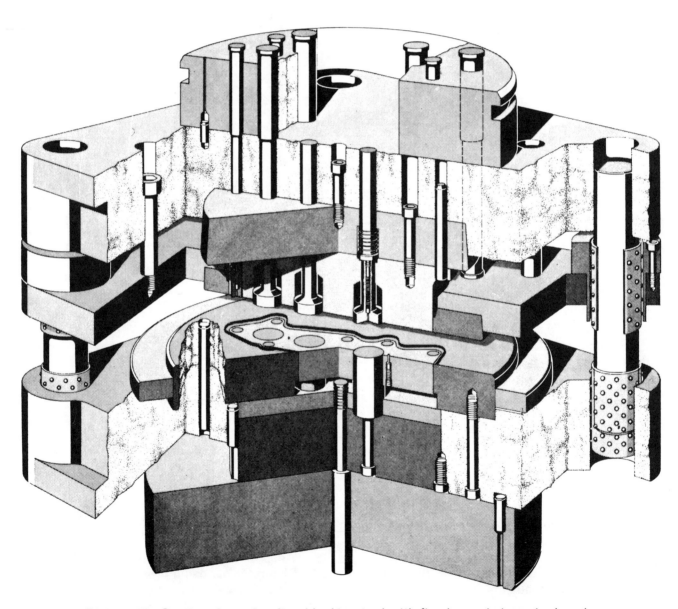

Picture 50   Section through a fine-blanking tool with fixed punch (punch above)

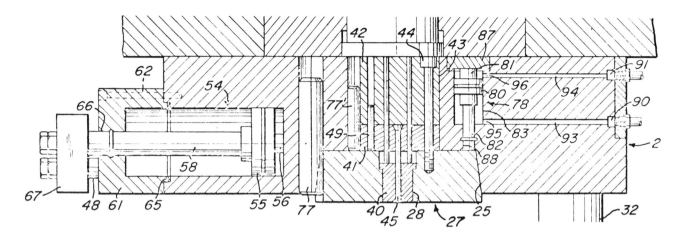

Die Components Make for Economic Fineblanking

by Karl A. Keyes
International Fineblanking Corp.

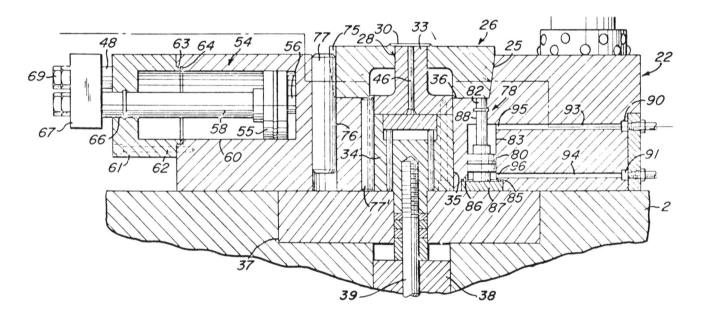

THE SYSTEM

The IFC quick change die system is made-up of a precision-built master die set with cavities that accept quick change components in both the upper and lower shoe in precise alignment with each other. With the use of hydraulics for locking, it is possible to use a calculated preload upon both the stinger plate and die plate to counteract the internal pressures involved when blanking and ejecting parts. Then when the die components are unlocked from the master set, an ejection system pops the components from their cavities; and they are removed by hand, leaving the master set ready to accept other IFC components. The entire tooling system is built around the master die set that works as shown in the above drawing.

The die block, a small component no larger than necessary
to contain the part configuration; the punch retainer;
and the adaptor, the spacer and guide for ejector pins;
make up major top components. There is, of course, the
shedder (or ejector) that works in the die cavity to
eject the scrap and/or workpiece, as the case may be.

The lower components consist of the stinger ring which
in turn guides the blanking punch, and immediately below
is the adaptor for the punch; it acts as a guide for pins
that support the stinger ring. And, that's it! Basically, what is seen in the explored view becomes what you
pay for.

The real advantage is the fact that you don't have to pay
for a whole die set and all it's special components to
have your parts produced; you pay for only the guts, and
the master die set remains intact in the press.

ABOUT COST

On an average, these quick change parts cost you about
$4500, as compared with a complete die in the range of
$7,000/$10,000. There are many advantages, but the most
immediate and obvious one is that you can actually afford
to go to fineblanking when you have only a 500-piece requirement.

Die cost has almost always cancelled out the possibility
of buying fineblanked parts when low-volume production
was concerned. Now purchasing as few as 500 pieces per
year is practical. In most cases, a fifty percent (50%)
savings over a conventional fineblank die can be expected.

THE 20-MINUTE CHANGEOVER

The photos shown, of the piecepart, and the parts that are
changed in the master die were taken at an exact twenty-
minute (20) time interval. Within this time frame, one
part was being blanked and then the press cleared and
similar components were "popped" into place to run the
other part shown. Beautifully simple, quick, inexpensive
and highly accurate. The components have precise accuracy
because the die parts are actually nested into a hardened
and ground cone-shaped cavity in the master die which
provides positive alignment.

The setup time of twenty (20) minutes is compared with
hours, in most cases, at least one-and-one-half (1-1/2)
hours, when using conventional fineblanking dies.

Also, if a punch has to be reground, you can be out and in,
and running again, in the same short time-span. As the
punch is sharpened away, spacers of known increments are
inserted to put back the height lost in regrinding.

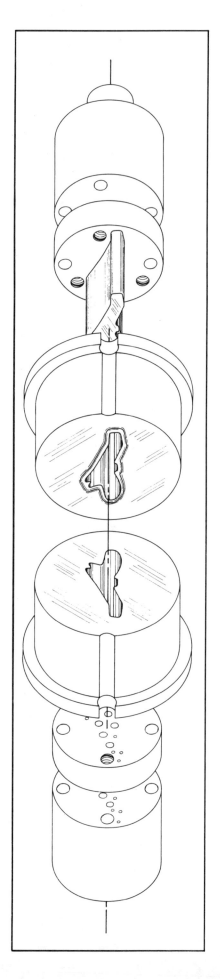

Machine operator holds portion of strip skeleton while the production superintendent holds a fineblanked part. Immediately after this photo, the components were changed to produce a different part.

IFC components released from hydraulic clamping (built into the master die set) actually pop out into the operator's hand.

IFC components for lower and upper master die shoes will be installed to fineblank a different part.

HIGH VOLUMES, TOO

Fineblanking has been accepted where part volumes are high enough to support original die cost. But every part does not deserve the sophistication of a complete fineblanking die, no matter what the volume might be. Contracts for as many as four million pieces per year have been completed by this system. Parts in these numbers could justify any reasonable die cost, but the parts couldn't care less if they are stamped on a quick change die or conventional fineblanking die. The big advantage in the joyous situation of having part contracts in the millions would be quick change dies because these quantities are not produced in one press run. So, changing dies quickly is important here, too.

FINEBLANKING

Fineblanking is known as a slow process, but slow is a relative term. It all depends on how much work you are doing with one stroke of the press. In most cases, fineblanking can hold much closer tolerances than a conventional progressive or compound die, and at the same time produce a one-hundred percent (100%) sheared edge - no die break.

When a conventional stamping is used, and many times operations, such as: broaching, reaming, drilling, boring, grinding, milling, countersinking, and coining, are necessary to finish the part; a fineblanking can be very competitive by giving you all that in one hit.

The field of fineblanking involves mainly mechanical components. If you look through the vast array of fineblanked parts being produced, you will find most of them are involved in some mechanical assembly as an end use. This is because in most cases when the mechanical movement is involved, there is a close tolerance required, or a camming surface that requires a high degree of accuracy and good finish. Before high-tonnage fineblank presses were introduced in the U.S., parts such as side frames, were flat plates numerically

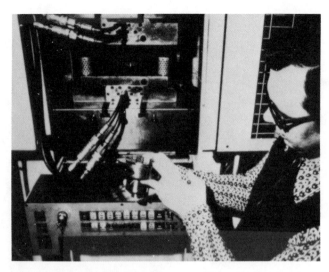

The components for the lower master shoe are already assembled to a standard ring that is part of master die set. You can see the precision groove a hydraulic pin will plunge into (one on both sides) to seat and lock-in the bottom components. Principle is the same for locating and locking the upper components.

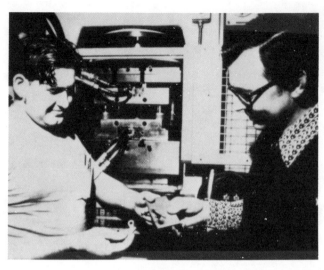

Twenty minutes later an entirely different fineblanked part is being blanked. The stock coil was also changed within this time frame.

controlled, drilled and jig bored. Now these parts have become practical, cost-saving applications for the fineblanking process. It is common knowledge that drilling can take up to thirty (30) minutes to make a series of holes in a flat plate. A fineblanking press can do it in seconds (one stroke); the actual cost savings available can be fantastic.

Fine blanking
...tool construction

PRIME CONSIDERATION associated with the manufacture of fine blanking tools is to build the four main parts (punch, pressure pad, die, and ejector), with virtually no deviation in mating fits so that the parts can be properly matched in the assembled tool.

Figure 23
Depth of the partly-cut profile is 0.160″. Inset shows magnified view.

The oldest and least expensive manufacturing method is to transfer the cutting profile into the pressure pad and die with the punch by shearing-in. This operation permits standardization of the fine blanking die set kits, which are produced in production with built-in tool elements (pressure pad, die, hole punch plate, base, punch, and ejector).

Fundamental sequence of operations for this production method:

1) Machine the punch.
2) Harden and temper the punch.
3) Rough machine pressure pad opening and die opening.
4) Shear-in pressure pad opening with punch.
5) Machine knife edge ring on pressure pad.
6) Harden and temper the pressure pad.
7) Install pressure pad in upper part of die set.
8) Shear-in die opening by means of punch guided in pressure pad.
9) Harden and temper the die.
10) Install die in lower part of die set.
11) Rough-machine outer contour of ejector.
12) Shear ejector into die.
13) Rough-machine inside shapes of ejector (hole punch passages).
14) Shear-in inside shapes in ejector by means of auxiliary punches (from inside shapes of punch).
15) Harden and temper the ejector.
16) Machine, harden, and temper the base and hole punch plate.
17) Assemble tool; install ejector pins, slug ejectors, hole punches and other components.

If the die is also to be provided with a closed knife edge ring, it should be put on after heat treatment of the die. Sharpening and resharpening is done by EDM with a suitable electrode. Partial knife edge ring on the die can be ground in most cases.

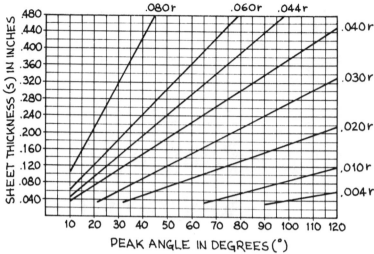

Figure 24
Recommended values (in inches) for the radii at corners and peaks.

Sheared-in process

The pressure pad opening and the die opening as well as the internal and external contour of the ejector are finished to size by means of the sheared-in process. The allowance of 0.002″ to 0.007″ of the rough-machined opening is removed with the punch or auxiliary punch. The punch or auxiliary punch is driven into the opening with a slight advance per blow; the chips should be removed after each advance. **Figure 23** shows a sectioned die that is partly sheared-in.

In this method, since heat treatment is the last important operation, it governs usability of the four main parts of a fine blanking die. The main parts must therefore be produced from tool steel that will, after proper heat treat, return to its original size. The mechanism of dimensional change of these steels has been made the subject of thorough investigations. In these studies, a distinction is made between dimensional changes (unavoidable) and distortion (results of inexpert handling). The restriction being that the separation of dimensional change and distortion is not unequivocally possible in all cases. When the main parts of the fine blanking die are heat treated with particular care, dimensional differences between the soft and the hardened condition can be largely avoided. However, heat treatment will then be correspondingly more expensive.

Approximately 80 percent of the dies built for fine blanking are constructed in the above manner or a variation of that sheared-in process. There are several other processes for building fine blanking dies, including the total grind or the EDM process. However, this method should be avoided by newcomers until they have acquired experience in both design and construction. The conventional sheared-in process allows entering the fine blanking process with the least amount of learning curve and minimum of capital equipment. Dies shown in this article were built from die set kits by the conventional method using only equipment found in the average toolroom.

Unfortunately, fine blanking tools are not normally ready for production when they leave the toolmaker's bench. The first trial in the press will in most cases show inconsistencies (dislocations, measuring errors, etc.), the removal of which requires subsequent treatment. The sources for trouble include:

- Improper tool construction.
- Asymetric deformation of the press upright and shifting of the press ram under load.
- Deformation within the tool under load.

The source of trouble mentioned under the second item is particularly disagreeable. When working with unsuitable fine blanking presses, the subsequent treatment is directed to the use of a particular press and its momentary condition (ram guide). Contradictory error indications when clamping the tool several times often render satisfactory subsequent treatment impossible. The efficiency of a fine blanking die between tool regrinding operations is, in this case, also subject to great variations.

Carrying out the functions of die correction and improving efficiency are a matter of experience. What is most difficult is recognizing and interpreting error indications. Significant error indications on the fine blanked part include: Fractures in the sheared surface, different burr formations, sheared surfaces which are not plain in the direction of cut, and sheared surfaces which are not vertical to the plane of the part. Depending on distribution of error over the entire "blanking picture," the die should be corrected according to the interpretation. Certain

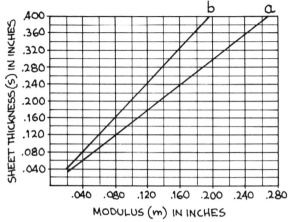

Figure 25
Limit values (in inches) for toothings—"a" for materials with normal deformability, "b" for materials with great deformability (relatively great cutting roundness).

production and tooling problems can be avoided when the workpiece is designed by specifying the largest radii possible at all corners of the fine blanked part. Apart from the fact that the sheared surface at sharp corners of the outside shape invariably break out, the tool's cutting components become highly stressed and are subject to great wear. The weakest point of the cutting element therefore becomes the most critical in performance. Minimum recommended radii are shown in **Figure 24**.

Performance of tools

Performance of fine blanking dies between two resharpenings and consequently, the total performance of their cutting elements depend on the following:
- Construction and condition of the press.
- Cutting speed.
- Correct adjustment of the press.
- Type of construction and condition of the tool.
- Properties of the material, its thickness, and shape of the blanked parts.
- Specifications of the blanked parts (tolerances and surface property).
- Lubrication.

In order to judge performance of a fine blanking die, a reference point for permissible wear of cutting edges at the punch and die should be laid down. For ordinary blanked parts, permissible burr height is often used at the reference point. It is impossible to get fine blanked parts without some burr. In most cases they are easily belt-sanded and tumbled. Burr height is therefore no appreciable hindrance in the production of fine blanked parts. Increased height of the burr, however, provides an indication as to the wear of cutting edges of the punch and die.

Under favorable conditions the performance of the cutting elements of a fine blanking tool for a part 0.100″ thick of AISI 1010 steel is at least 40,000 parts per resharpening. At this point, only the punch need be sharpened; the die will be resharpened at 80,000 parts. As a rule, the punch wear is approximately two to one to the die. For complete restoration of the cutting conditions, a loss of 0.005″ to 0.007″ per regrind must be expected at the punch and die.

Materials which are suitable for fine blanking are those with great deformability. These mainly include mild steels from C-1010 to C-1050, stainless steels 302-303 and 410-430, alloy steels 4140-8620, copper, brass from a copper content of 67 percent upward, aluminum, and some aluminum alloys. Many other materials will fine blank well but the inexperienced person should refrain from attempting them until he has the ability to relate chemical and structural property of the material to the process.

However, because of sturdy construction of fine blanking tools, and because slugs are always ejected after every cut, some very difficult parts can be made. For example, tiny configurations, such as holes, slots, teeth, and noses may be produced from comparatively thick stock. It is possible to provide holes of 0.080″ in a 0.160″ thick soft-annealed case-hardened steel. And gear teeth may also be produced in small sizes as shown in the diagram of **Figure 25**.

Although the widths of edges and webs of waste strip should be somewhat greater for fine blanking than for overall cutting, these dimensions may be reduced. In many cases, it is possible to grind a partial ring denticulation on the tool to blank parts within small edge and web widths. Note resultant indents produced in the waste strip shown in **Figure 26**.

Calculation of tonnage

The statement that the required total force of a fine blanked part amounts to 1½-2½ times the cutting force is not sufficient for determining correct press size. The cutting force, the press force, and the counter-force should be calculated individually for each fine blanked part. Example: All forces for the production of an eccentric disk made of C-1010 are to be calculated. Diameter of the eccentric disk D=1.575″, diameter of the eccentric shaft bore d=0.787″, thickness of the disk S=0.157″.

Cutting force Ps: According to the most frequently used equation,
$$Ps = 0.8 \times \sigma \times l_s \times s$$
The cutting force will be:
$$Ps = 0.8 \times \sigma \times (D+d) \times \pi \times 5$$
$$= 0.8 \times 64,000 \times (1.575 + 0.787) \times \pi \times 157$$
$$= 27.1 \text{ metric tons}$$
σ being the tensile strength in PSI (64,000).
l_s the area of cut in sq inches (1.165 sq in)

Pressure Pp: According to the diagram in **Figure 6**, the mean distance of the knife edge ring tip from the shear line is for a knife edge ring height of 0.047″ about 0.086″. The length of the

knife edge ring will thus become
$$lr = (D + 0.172'') \times \pi = 5.488''$$

According to the diagram in **Figure 8**, the pressure wil be about 5.61 metric tons per inch of knife edge ring. The pressure will thus be:
$$PF = lr \times P = 5.488'' \times 5.61 = 30.78 \text{ metric tons}$$
lr being the knife edge ring length in inches and P the related pressure in metric tons per inch.

Counter-force P_G: The counter-force is determined in accordance with the area of the fine blanked part. The specific counter-force generally lies between 3000 to 10,000 lbs per sq inch of the blanked part area. Unless there is some coining or embossing operation during the cutting cycle.

$$P_G = F \times g = \frac{\pi}{4} \times (D^2 - d^2) \times g = \frac{\pi}{4} \times$$
$(2.5 - 0.62) \times 6400 = 9652$ lbs or 4.3 metric tons; F being the blanked part area in square inches and g the specific counter-force in lbs per sq inch.

The total force P_{TOT} will thus be:
$$P_{TOT} = P_s + P_p + P_g = 27.1 + 30.78 + 4.3 =$$
$$62.18 \text{ metric tons}$$

If, in this case, not only the pressure pad but also the die should be provided with a knife edge ring, then in order to achieve about the same effect, the heights of the knife edge rings would be only one-half of a single ring. This will also change the distance of the knife edge rings from the openings and therefore shorten the total length of the ring from 5.488″ to 5.313″. The related pressure for a ring 0.024″ high according to **Figure 8** would then become about 2.8 metric tons per linear inch.
$$P_s = 5.313'' \times 2.8 = 14.87 \text{ metric tons}$$
The total force required will then be reduced to:
$$P_{TOT}: 27.1 + 14.87 + 4.3 = 46.27 \text{ metric tons}$$

This tonnage reduction method is often made use of when a single ring calculation exceeds the available press tonnage.

Final remarks
The three most critical steps in fine blanking are as follows and in appropriate order:
1) Selection of the fine blanking press. Construction must be such that the rams remain in a positive position at all times regardless of tonnage requirements. This means that any defect in the tool construction can be con-

Figure 26
Waste strip of 0.120 thickness has edge width of 0.120″. Top view shows punch side; and bottom, the die side.

tributed and traced to the tool without considering any misalignment of press.
2) Tool design and construction—this should always begin with conventional type of tool design and build. This allows both the designer and tool maker to cover the greatest range of experience with a minimum amount of time and expense.
3) Support personnel—good designers and toolmakers go a long way to make the process a success. However, if they are not available, it is possible to purchase a press with the necessary proven dies.

Some companies who have entered the fine blanking process are either not satisfied with it or have abandoned it completely. Others have succeeded so well that their products are now being designed with fine blanking as one of the primary considerations. In either case, success or failure is directly attributed to the three critical considerations mentioned above. ∎

Reprinted from "Fine-Blanking Practical Handbook", courtesy of American Feintool Inc.,
Cincinnati, Ohio

Preparation for the Design of a Fine-Blanking Tool

Calculation of the required pressures

Calculation of the blanking (shearing) pressure

The most important factor for determining the type of machine to be used
is the shear pressure. In practice the formula used is as follows:

$$F = L \cdot s \cdot \sigma_B \cdot 0.9$$

F = Blanking or shearing pressure (tons or kp)
L = Total of outer and inner shear periphery lengths (in. or mm)
s = Material thickness (in. or mm)
σ_B = Tensile strength (t./sq. in. or kp/mm²)

It will be noted that instead of τ_B (shear strength) 90% of σ_B (tensile strength)
is given. The reason for this is that the shear strength (τ_B) is only rarely
given by material suppliers.

The exact shear pressure is influenced by the following factors:

- condition of the edges of the cutting elements (punch and die plate)
- size of punch-die clearance
- shear speed
- geometric form of the part
- metallurgical structure of the material
- type and amount of cutting lubricant
- surface finish of the cutting elements
- tolerance of the material being worked

As it is impossible to always take every factor into account the formula
given previously supplies a more than adequate basis for the calculation of
the basic shear pressure concerned.

Calculation of the 'vee-ring' and counter pressures

The calculation for determining the 'vee-ring' pressure is comparable to that for the shear force. Various formulas have been created to determine the theoretical 'vee-ring' pressure, none of which have proven to be 100% accurate in practice. A fixed ratio of 'vee-ring' pressure to shear pressure does not apply. When working soft materials of between 19 and 32 t./sq. in. (30–50 kp/mm²) tensile a ratio of 30 to 50% may be applied. When working extremely hard materials the 'vee-ring' pressure may be 100% i. e. equivalent to the shear pressure. The Feintool presses have the ratio of maximum shear pressure to maximum 'vee-ring' pressure independently and infinitely adjustable so that in practice the size of press required may be decided by the formula given under 4.11. The actual 'vee-ring' pressure required is noted when the first sample parts are produced and then recorded on the tool card.

The same approach is used for the counter pressure.

When repeat series of parts are to be produced the respective pressures are set on the machine and checked on the pressure gauge (manometer).

Calculation of the ejection pressure (for piece-parts) and the stripping pressure (punch)

In order to eject the piece-part from the die plate aperture (ejector pressure) and to strip the material from the punch and eject the inner form slugs out of the punch (stripping pressure) experience indicates 10 to 15% of the shear pressure is required.

Calculation of the resulting actual shear line force

In order to achieve optimum shear load conditions, the actual line of force from the ram should coincide with the shear line force required in the tool as closely as possible. The more exact these requirements can be held in practice, the better will be the expected result. Excessive shear pressure which must be applied to areas outside the actual line of ram force can lead to increased tool wear.

To determine the resulting shear line force the center of gravity of the part must be calculated from the contour of the piece-part inner and outer form.

For calculation purposes two methods may be applied:

– arithmetic using moments relative to a given axis
– from a graph using polygon of forces

Arithmetic determination of the resulting shear line force

To determine the center of gravity of the part the various edges (or lines) are divided into individual lengths with a known center of gravity. (For the calculation of the center of gravity of lines as radii this information may be found in practical hand-book literature concerning the subject.) Co-ordinates x and y are to be assumed and the distance of each respective lineal center of gravity measured from the x and y axes (picture 51).

The resulting distances of the lineal centers of gravity from the y axis can be calculated with formula 1.

Formula 1: $$x_s = \frac{l_1 \, x_1 + l_2 \, x_2 \ldots + l_6 \, x_6}{l_1 + l_2 \ldots + l_6} = \frac{\Sigma \triangle \, lx}{\Sigma \triangle \, l}$$

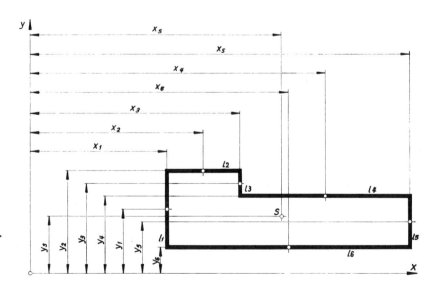

Picture 51
Arithmetic determination of the resulting shear line force

The resulting distances of the lineal centers of gravity from the x axis can be calculated in the same manner.

Formula 2: $y_s = \dfrac{l_1\,y_1 \; + \; l_2\,y_2... + \; l_6\,y_6}{l_1 \; + \; l_2... \; + \; l_6} = \dfrac{\Sigma\triangle\,l\,y}{\Sigma\triangle\,l}$

At the point of intersection of the lines x_s and y_s is the resulting shear line force. For l, x, and y in the above example the actual measured lengths may be applied.

Graphic determination of the resulting actual shear line force (picture 52)

The piece-part in question is drawn exactly to an enlarged scale (see picture 52) and the various edges (or lines) divided to give known centers of gravity. The lines 1 to 18 in the plan show the various lengths, the circles in the various lengths indicate the center of gravity of these lines. Basically the numbering may be started with any desired length. In the example given here numbering was begun with the length furthest from the x axis (line 1) and continued counter clockwise from this point.

The triangular representation of the forces used to determine the resulting lines of force of the x axis is drawn as follows: The separate lengths of the lines (edges) already established are relative to the shear forces to be employed. These lengths are set together proportionally on an x axis (picture 52b) and marked (i. e. 1...18). These distances/forces are best marked on the x axis line formed in order of the line center of gravity positions measured from the x axis—in this case then 1, 2, 14, 13, 12, 6, 11 etc. The lineal centers of gravity for points 16, 17, and 18 all lie on the same line. These forces can then of course be calculated together as one unit. After all distances/forces have been introduced an 0 point in any position may be chosen and the positions marked on the x axis joined by lines 0′, 1′, 2′...4′ to the 0 point. The triangular representation diagram is then set so that axis x (picture 52b) is parallel to axis x in the plan (picture 52a). First line 0′ is extended to intersect the line 1x at any point. The line 1′ is then also extended and arranged to pass through the intersection 0′ 1x. This in turn gives an intersection of the line 2x which forms a new intersection 1′2x. The line 2′ is extended and arranged to pass through 1′2x which forms a new intersection 2′14x. This method is followed until all the lines in the triangular representation diagram have formed new locations on the plan (picture 52a). The last line 4′ is to be arranged to intersect the first line 0′ which determines the resulting actual shear line force parallel to axis x.

The triangular representation diagram for determining the resulting line of force on the y axis (picture 52c) is drawn with the lengths/forces drawn proportionally on a y axis. The forces should be marked on the drawing in order of the line center of gravity positions measured from the y axis—in this case 3, 16, 2, 11...5. An 0 point is chosen, lines drawn to this point and the positions transferred to the plan as already explained for the x axis.

Through intersection 0″,5″ passes the resulting actual shear line force parallel to axis y.

The resulting actual line of shear force lies at intersection S of the axes x and y.

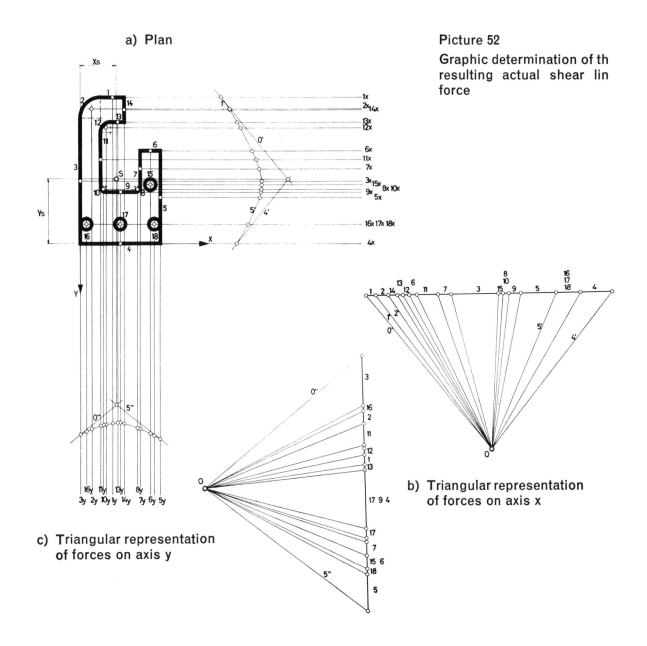

a) Plan

Picture 52

Graphic determination of th resulting actual shear lin force

b) Triangular representation of forces on axis x

c) Triangular representation of forces on axis y

Selection of the tool system

From the data given in sections 3.1 and 3.2 the tool system can be selected.

Methods of die plate manufacture

When building fine-blanking tools two basic methods of die plate manufacture can be applied, namely grinding and/or spark eroding (E. D. M.). As both methods have no influence upon the tool life and production volume per regrind the choice of manufacturing method to be applied is mainly dependent upon the geometric form of the part, and of course the types of machine tools available.

Ground dies are generally produced with two or more sections (split-die). Due to the pressures imposed during the shearing operation this can lead to a small 'thread like' deformity occurring as a protrusion on the sheared piece-part surface at the point where the die sections meet (picture 53). For this reason split dies must be suitably retained in order to prevent 'breathing', or at least to reduce it to a minimum.

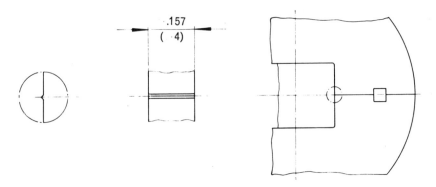

Picture 53   Thread-like deformity over thickness of part

For piece-parts which have a function to fulfill over their whole perimeter, for example cams and gear-wheels, etc., eroded (E. D. M.) dies can be used to great advantage.

When producing piece-parts more than 0.118″ (3 mm) thick, where possible, only solid die plates should be used. These die plates are primarily eroded (E. D. M.) or produced on a jig grinder. The second method takes somewhat longer and is therefore more expensive.

Selecting the die-set size

From the calculation of the actual shear line force the center point of the tool has been determined and the die plate will be laid around this point. The method of manufacture for the die is also decided and from this the size of the die plate can be established. Using a standardization system the size of the die-set required is also given.

When determining the size of the die plate for ground/split dies it must be noted that the distance from the most extreme section of the die aperture to the die plate circumference be not less than 0.98″ (25 mm) (picture 54a). For eroded (E. D. M.) or other solid die plates this distance should be a minimum of 1.37″ (35 mm) (see picture 54b). These values are applicable for materials of approximately 0.059″–0.118″ (1.5–3 mm) thickness and should be increased proportionally for thicker materials. For smaller thinner parts these values may of course be reduced slightly.

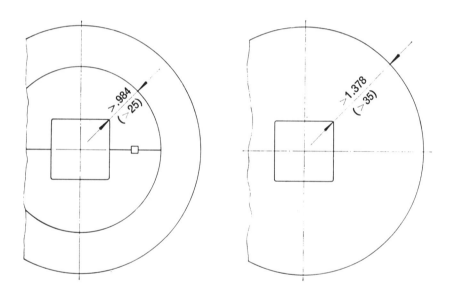

Picture 54   Minimum distance from die aperture extremes to die plate perimeter

a) for ground/split dies   b) for solid/eroded (E. D. M.) dies

Reprinted from "Fine-Blanking Practical Handbook", courtesy of American Feintool Inc., Cincinnati, Ohio

Fine-Blanking Tool Design

Calculating the strip width and length of feed

When the grain direction of the material is not related to any function of the part, the part configuration is located in the strip to ensure the minimum amount of scrap or waste material. Complicated forms, tooth forms or areas which require a completely fine-blanked surface should be laid to correspond with the infeed side of the material in order that they may be sheared from the fullest possible section of material (picture 55).

The necessary strip width is calculated using the following rule: Piece-part width measured at right angles to the direction of feed plus four times material thickness.

The length of feed per stroke is derived from the dimension across the piece-part measured in the direction of feed plus 1.5 to 2 x material thickness.

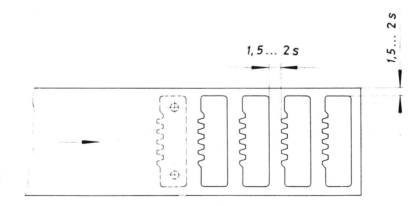

Picture 55 Strip lay out (s = stock thickness)

The distances from the piece-part to the outer edge of the material and from part to part should be 1.5 to 2 s (s = material thickness). For thin materials the higher value and for thicker materials the lower value is recommended. The minimum values between parts and the outer edge of the material should never be less than 0.039 (1 mm).

These are minimum values to enable perfect fine-blanked parts to be produced.

Purpose and determination of the 'vee-ring'

The most noticeable difference between a fine-blanking tool and a conventional press tool when first viewed is the 'vee-ring'. This 'vee' form runs as a raised ridge on the guide plate around the shear periphery at a prescribed distance from the cutting edge. The 'vee-ring' function is to confine the material outside the shear zone, and to prevent the material flowing away from the punch during the blanking/shearing operation. On small inner forms this flow of material away from the shear zone does not occur so that a 'vee-ring' is not usually required. For large inner forms (diameter of 1.18″–1.57″ [30–40 mm] and more) it is often advisable to machine a 'vee-ring' on to the ejector pins. This is always the case when working with fixed punch type tools, but with sliding punch tools only when absolutely necessary since the bridge section of the tool must then be greatly strengthened in order to transfer the required pressures.

When the material is thicker than 0.157″–0.196″ (4–5 mm), or exceptionally tough materials are being worked, then two 'vee-rings' are usually required, i. e. one on the pressure plate (guide plate) and one on the die plate. In this case the re-sharpening of the die cannot be carried out by surface grinding, but requires a milling turning or eroding (E. D. M.) operation. The size and distance ratios of the 'vee-ring' are determined from the material thickness and can be read from the pictures and tables 56–59.

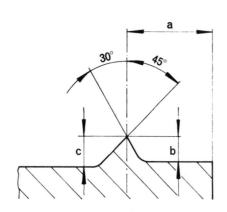

Picture 56   Milled 'vee-ring' profile

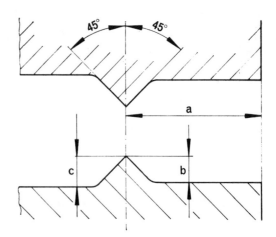

Picture 57   Eroded 'vee-ring' profile

Table 58   'Vee-ring' dimensions for materials up to .158 in. thick

Material Thickness	a	b	c
inches			
.020	.020	.008	.010
.040	.028	.012	.014
.080	.055	.016	.018
.118	.083	.018	.020
.158	.110	.020	.022

Table 59   'Vee-ring' dimensions for materials over .158 in. thick

Material Thickness	a	b	c
inches			
.177	.126	.020	.022
.197	.146	.022	.024
.236	.165	.024	.026
.315	.197	.028	.030
.394	.236	.033	.035

'Vee-ring' dimensions for materials up to 4 mm thick

mm			
0.5	0.5	0.20	0.25
1	0.7	0.30	0.35
2	1.4	0.40	0.45
3	2.1	0.45	0.50
4	2.8	0.50	0.55

'Vee-ring' dimensions for materials over 4 mm thick

mm			
4.5	3.2	0.50	0.55
5	3.7	0.55	0.60
6	4.2	0.60	0.65
8	5.0	0.70	0.75
10	6.0	0.85	0.90

The life of the 'vee-ring' on the pressure plate is in general that of the life of the tool. A certain blunting is expected and can be tolerated.

Determining the size of the cutting elements

When the ejector and inner form piercing punches are removed from the die the blanked part can generally be pressed back into the die plate aperture without exerting too much pressure. This shows that the outer contour of the part tends to become somewhat smaller than the die aperture.
This difference is a maximum of 0.00039″ (0.01 mm) and generally much less.
If the part cannot be pressed back into the die plate the clearance between the punch and die is too small or the accuracy of the part form is influenced by internal material stresses.
Following blanking, inner forms tend to shrink slightly, i. e. they become somewhat smaller than the inner form piercing punches.
Due to these tendencies the die plate and inner form piercing punches should, in the ideal case, be 0.00019″–0.00039″ (0.005–0.01 mm) above the required finished piece-part dimension.

However, practical experience shows that it is more advantageous to manufacture the die plate section for outer contours in the lower third of the piece-part tolerance band. One advantage of this is that should the sample parts be too small the die plate can be enlarged. Also the dimension of the die plate, and thereby the size of the piece-parts, increases slightly in the course of high volume production. Where forms re-enter the piece-part it is logical that the process is reversed, and that in these areas the die plate dimension is produced within the upper third of the tolerance band.
Where round inner forms are required, or inner forms with protruding sections, the piercing punch dimensions are set in the upper tolerance range. Normally the inner forms close slightly and shrink to the ideal dimensions. If this should not be the case then the piercing punches can be reworked to make them slightly smaller. As already explained, precisely the opposite conditions apply to inner forms with sections which re-enter.

Punch-die clearance

Definition: Under clearance between punch and die a dimensional difference between the die contour and the punch contour is implied, measured over the diameter. Ideally then, the distance between the punch and the die at any given position is ½ of the punch-die clearance.

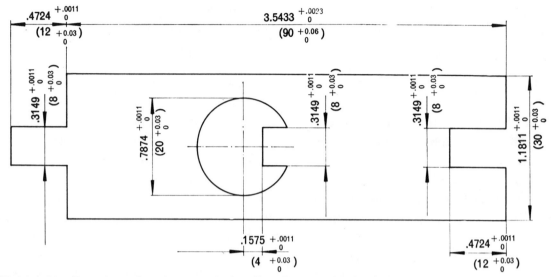

Picture 60   Drawing of a piece-part showing the required tolerances

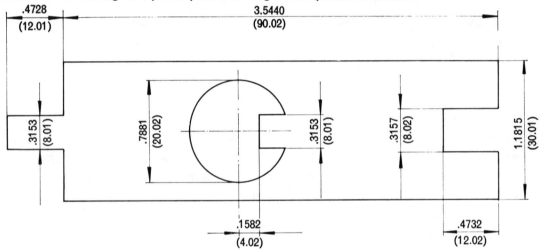

Picture 61   Dimensions of the cutting elements which determine the size of the finished part (die-plate and inner form piercing punches)

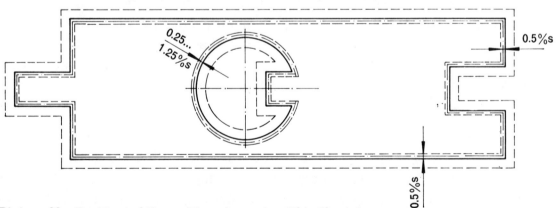

Picture 62   Position of the cutting elements within the tolerance band

    – – – – –   Tolerance band

    ————   Die-plate and inner form piercing punches

    – · – · –   Punch and punch inner forms (for slugs)

In the chapter 'Construction of Fine-Blanking Tools' the reduced punch-die clearance is mentioned. The value given of 1% of the material thickness is an indicative value which requires some further explanation. The variance of clearance between inner and outer contours must also be differentiated.

It must be noted that the following tendencies and values given are to be taken purely as indicative guide lines. In a very few cases, for reasons which today still remain unexplained, better results can be achieved with other values. This is especially noticeable when tough materials which do not correspond to the optimum fine-blanking structure have to be worked. Basically materials having poor formability characteristics require less punch and die clearance than materials with a high degree of formability. Production between regrinds varies directly with the amount of punch and die clearance. Greater clearance means more production. For this reason the greatest possible punch-die clearance should be applied. When the clearance is too great a certain degree of break-out becomes visible on the punch side of the sheared part, and increases directly with the punch-die clearance. In many applications a small degree of break-out on the sheared surface (on thin parts hardly visible and on thicker parts a maximum of 10% of material thickness) is accepted in order to achieve higher production rates per regrind. For piece-parts which do not require a fine-blanked finish on the entire periphery the punch-die clearance is often increased in some areas. In these cases it must be especially noted that the punch retains 100% positive guidance. This requirement can best be met by reducing the punch size only at its tip. To what depth the tip of the punch is reduced is dependent on the material thickness worked and the effective length of the guide plate, but should be at least $1\frac{1}{2} \times$ material thickness. The following data is based on the production of fully, cleanly sheared surfaces over the whole material thickness, with high production per regrind as a requirement. The values given refer to non-alloyed steels with optimum fine-blanking metallurgical structures.

– Outer periphery:

   The punch-die clearance is normally calculated at 1% of the material thickness to be worked.

   For gear-wheels the clearance in the areas of the tooth crest and tooth root are doubled. This also applies to forms which re-enter into the piece-part.

   Slots or other similar forms which re-enter on parts where the 'vee-ring' does not follow the outer shear periphery, are to be treated as inner forms.

– Inner contours:

Concerning inner form contours the diameter, or length and width of the form, also play an important part in determining the clearance together with the material thickness. Indicative values are to be found in the table.

Table 63 *Punch-die clearance as a % of material thickness (s)*

Material Thickness		Outer Forms	Inner Forms $\varnothing < s$	Inner Forms $\varnothing = s$ to $5s$	Inner Forms $\varnothing > 5s$
inches	mm				
.020	0.5	1%	2.5%	2 %	1 %
.040	1	1%	2.5%	2 %	1 %
.080	2	1%	2.5%	1 %	0.5%
.118	3	1%	2 %	1 %	0.5%
.158	4	1%	1.7%	0.75%	0.5%
.240	6	1%	1.7%	0.5 %	0.5%
.394	10	1%	1.5%	0.5 %	0.5%
.590	15	1%	1 %	0.5 %	0.5%

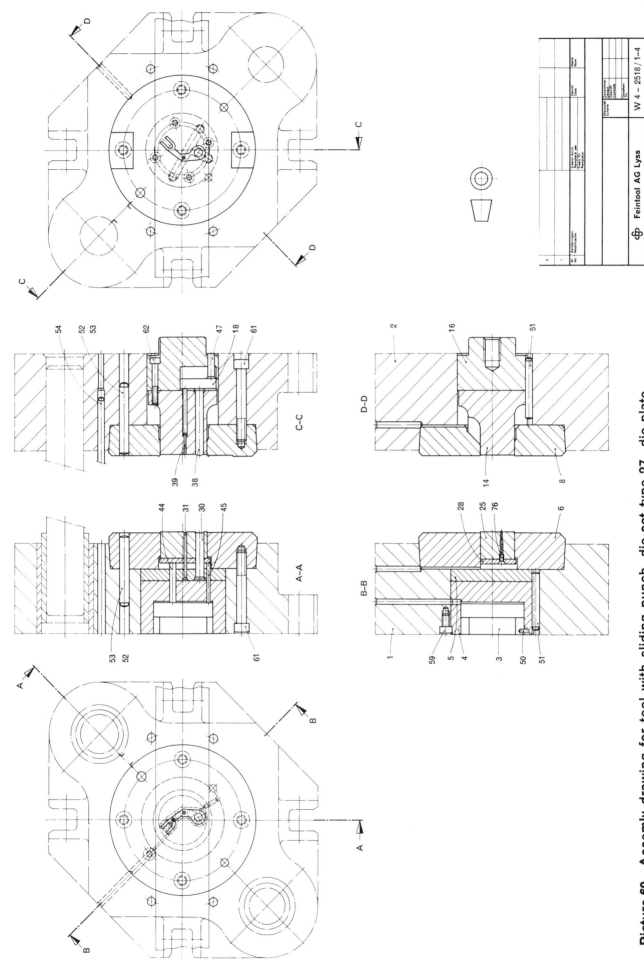

Picture 69 Assemly drawing for tool with sliding punch, die-set type 27, die-plate and guide plate eroded

211

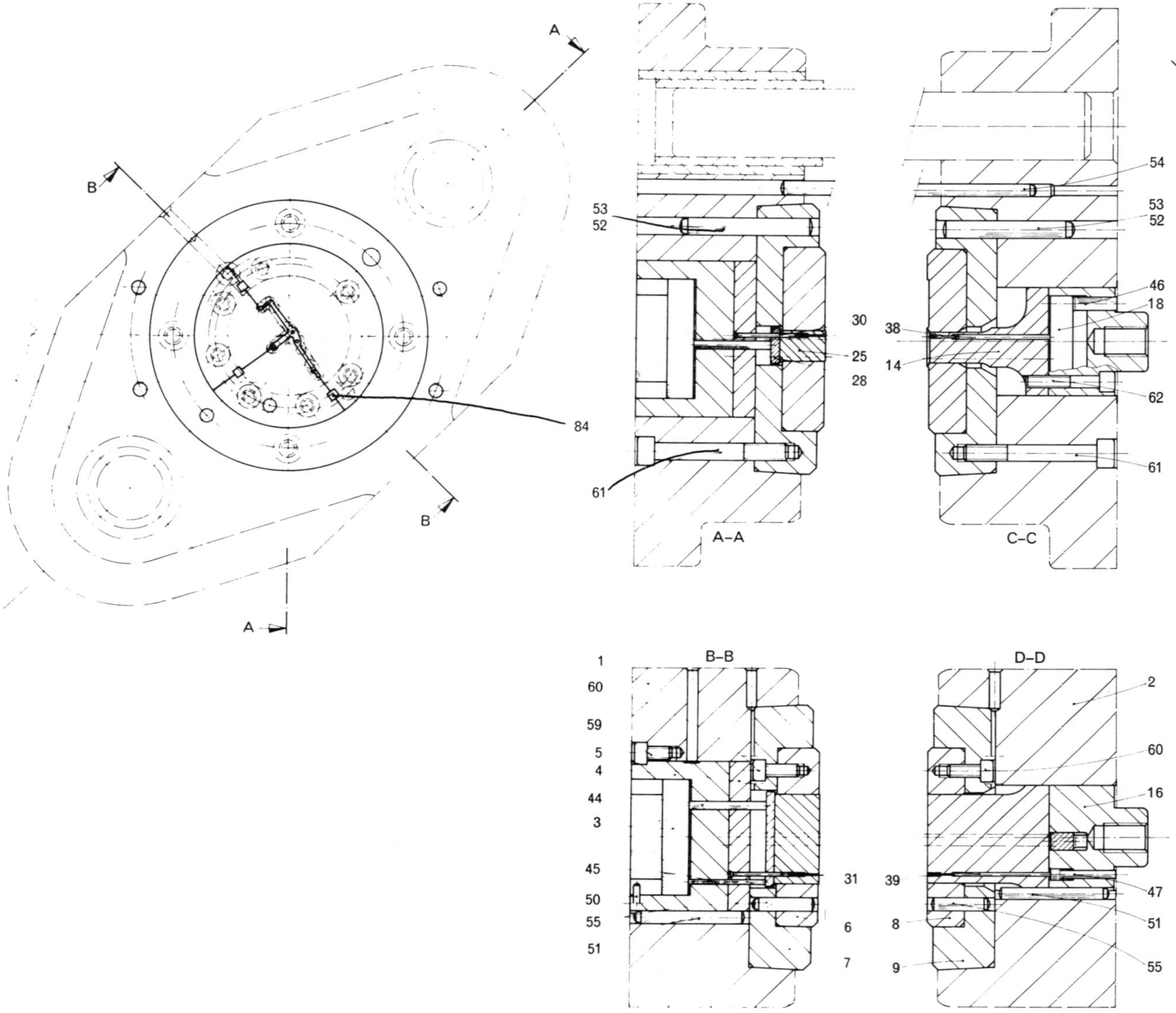

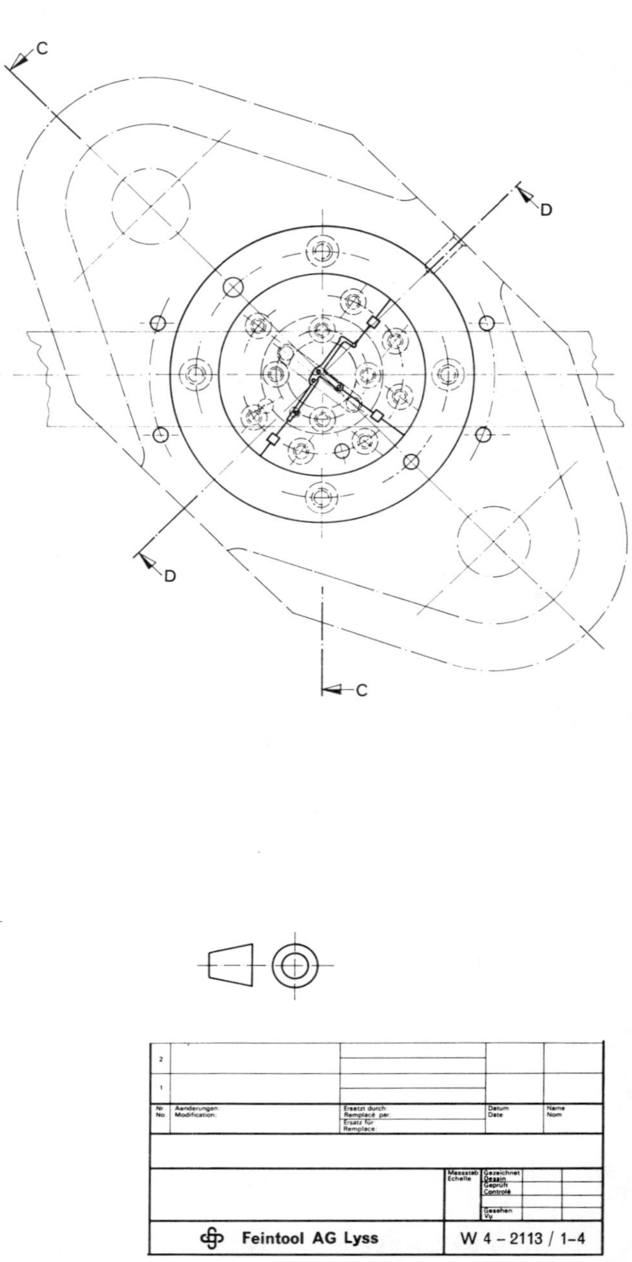

Picture 70 Assembly drawing for tool with sliding punch, die-set type 24, die-plate and guide plate ground

212

Fine blanking
...sequence of operations

THE SEQUENCE OF OPERATIONS in fine blanking may be subdivided into three sections: 1) the closing stroke where the press ram places the tool in working position; 2) the cutting stroke where the knife edge ring is pressed into the material and the part is cut out; and 3) the opening stroke where the press ram returns to its initial position and the tool opens.

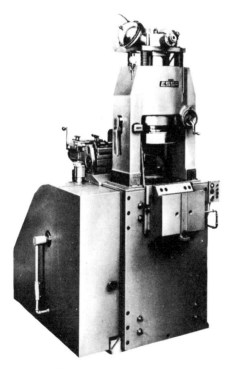

Figure 10
Fine blanking prototype press used for development.

The time during which the press ram travels through the cutting stroke is determined by the "permissible" cutting speed and the thickness of the stock. During the opening stroke (return of the ram) the strip stock is stripped from the punch, the slugs are ejected out of the punch, and the blanked part is ejected out of the die.

The strip stock, the slugs, and the blanked part cannot be stripped or ejected, respectively, before the tool has opened by at least twice the thickness of the stock. This delay prevents the recharging of the slugs and blanked part into the strip stock. During the remaining opening stroke of the press ram, up to the end of the following closing stroke, the strip must be fed and the blanked part and all slugs must be removed from the tool.

Thin and relatively small fine blanked parts with little inside shapes are blown out of the tool together with the slugs while large and thick fine blanked parts, with many inside shapes, are removed together with the slugs by mechanical means. The stroke of the press ram is relatively long in order to allow the part and the slugs to be removed without any difficulties.

In permanent operation, the number of strokes of the press ram is dependent upon the time the ram needs to cover the working travel, and upon the time required for the strip feed for safe removal of the blanked part and the slugs from the tool. Thus, the number of strokes depends upon the cutting speed, the thickness of the stock and the geometrical shape (dimensions, number of slugs, size) of the blanked part. The output normally is from 10 to 90 parts/min.

The cutting punch is installed in the upper part of the tool, and the strip stock is firmly

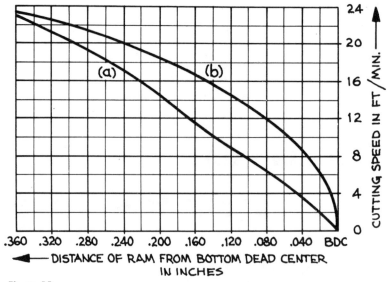

Figure 11

Speed of the ram as a function of its distance from bottom dead center. With a stroke of approximately 2.36" and a speed of 50 rpm, "a" is for double toggle press (Figure 10) and "b" for an eccentric press (Figure 12).

attached to the punch during the first part of the opening stroke, until it is stripped off. There should be ample space between the strip stock and the lower part of the tool, so that the blanked part and the slugs can be removed without any difficulty. Because of this, the strip stock should follow the movement of the upper part of the tool.

The press

As there is virtually no tolerance between the punch and the die in fine blanking tools and as the forces applied to the tool elements are generally one-and-a-half to two-and-a-half times as great as the cutting force, the press is built to work stable and precise under a very high load. This load on the tool elements is met to a large extent by special design (supporting of the die, stationary pressure pad, movable punch), so that the heft of a fine blanking die is not much greater than the weight of a conventional die.

The weight of the fine blanking die shown in **Figure 16** is 80 lbs. The diameter of the gear segment is 2.62. The leader pins of the die set are to help in making the tool and for installing it in the press. Even when oversized die sets are used, they are not intended to balance asymmetrical deformations of the press, dislocations of the press ram and the like.

Figure 10 shows a double toggle press with two built-in hydraulic-pneumatic attachments. This press was a prototype from which analysis was made. The press ram is designed into a closed frame; it is guided in the press upright in wide apart gibbed ways. The lower part of the press has the die fixed on the press table while the upper part of it has the movable

punch on the press ram. This press is equipped with either one or two stationary feed devices.

Even where a relatively low load is applied to this press, the performance of the fine blanking tools ranges up to 10,000 parts before the cutting elements must be resharpened. Even if this performance can be increased with stock more suitable for fine blanking, it must nevertheless be looked upon as insufficient. The low efficiency of fine blanking dies is due to high cutting speed, and ram guiding is poor for fine blanking purposes. The deformation of the press is vertical with the driving elements under load.

Figure 12

Hydraulic production fine blanking press of FSA 100-ton capacity.

Figure 13
Press ram of a production fine blanking press with ball cages in position.

In **Figure 11,** the theoretic ram speed of the double toggle press is plotted (curve "a") as a function of the distance from the bottom dead center. In comparison is curve "b" of an eccentric press with the same stroke of the ram, the same speed, and the same connecting rod ratio of 0.075. Owing to the deformation of the ram frame, the driving elements, etc., the actual ram speed is lower than the theoretical speed, until the maximum of the cutting force is reached. The ram speed is greater if the maximum cutting force is exceeded, because the deformations are reduced again.

The guiding of the ram frame is clearly determined by the two gibbed ways that can easily be adjusted. There should be a certain tolerance (at least 0.001") in order to ensure that a lubricating film can form in the bearings which are also deformed under load. Displacements of 0.002" were found at the tool of this press.

It would be possible to build mechanical fine blanking presses with ram guiding to meet requirements for a single purpose in which the upright deformation is very low. It will, however, hardly be possible to solve the problem of the cutting speed mechanically.

It may be conceivable however to arrange elongation elements in the driving parts, so that the initial cutting speed would be considerably reduced. A calculation shows that the cutting speed will multiply after the maximum of the cutting force has been exceeded. In addition, the elongation should not be greater than the stock thickness remaining after the maximum cutting force. Otherwise the punch would plunge into the die, which should be avoided for obvious reasons.

Figure 12 shows a hydraulic fine blanking press. Here the ram is located in the lower part of the press and works upwards. The bottom of the die set is secured to the press ram, and the upper part to the counter pressure ram.

This press is provided with a two stationary gripper-feed device, the height of which can be

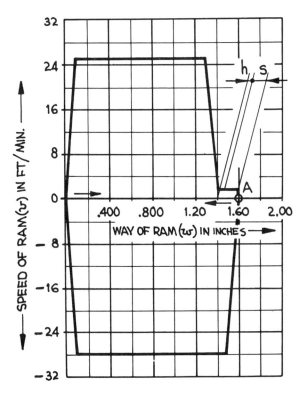

Figure 14
Working diagram of a job run on the press shown in Figure 12. Where "h" is profile height of knife edge ring, approximately 0.031" and stock thickness is 0.120". The ram stroke is 1.56.

adjusted. If the strip stock is clamped between the die and the pressure pad of the tool, prior to the beginning of the cutting operation, the grippers will lift and the feed carriages run back over the stock. Then during the return of the ram, the grippers close the strip and advance it the required length.

The height of feeding devices is so adjusted that the strip is passed through right at the pressure pad height. This arrangement allows the feeding devices to convey thick sheets while the upper part of the tool is cleared of slugs that might still stick to it. Thin and light-weight parts and slugs are blown out of the tool, but the press may also be provided with a unit for the removal of thick or heavy parts and slugs.

The ram of the press is supported by ball guides in two areas. **Figure 13** shows the ram with the ball cages in position. The large bearing with a great number of balls will result in a low load on each individual ball for precise guiding even in the case of extra axial forces.

The theoretic cutting speed of the hydraulic fine blanking press is only about 1.5 ft/min. In order to achieve fast stroking, the opening and closing strokes are run at high speed. Number of strokes is dependent on the ram stroke adjustment and on the cutting stroke (thickness of the stock). Thin parts with few or no slugs are cut out with a short ram stroke; and thick parts with many slugs with a longer ram stroke. The working diagram of an example of the fine blanking of a 0.120″ thick part is shown in **Figure 14** in which the ram speed was plotted over the press stroke. The number of pieces in this case is about 54 per minute.

Design of dies

When designing a die, the following points should be given careful consideration: the construction, the production method, the highest load, and the small (practically nonexisting) clearance between the punch and the die. Various types of construction are conceivable for these dies. Those predominantly built today are built with a movable punch and a stationary pressure pad. Owing to the high loads, the tool elements should be constructed so that they are stable and supported so as not to bend. Also the small clearance between the punch and die re-

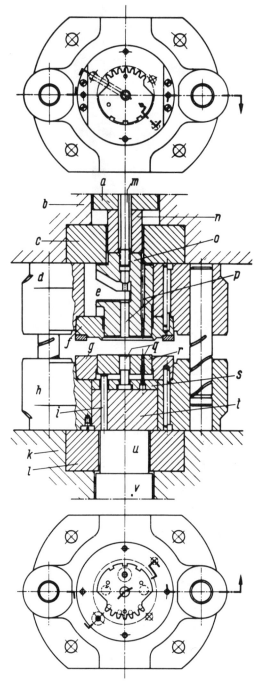

Figure 15
Die for gear segment of a 2.6″ OD where "a" is fixed ram head, "b" is counter pressure ram, "c" is pressure ring, "d" is upper die set, "e" is ejector bar, "f" is pressure pad, "g" is the die, "h" is the lower die set, "i" are ejector pins, "k" is main ram, "l" is pressure ring, "m" is punch take up spindle, "n" is pressure ring insert, "o" is punch, "p" is slug ejector, "q" is hole punch, "r" is ejector, "s" is hole punch plate, "t" is the base, "u" is pressure ring insert and "v" is the ejector ram.

quires "perfect" alignment of pressure pad and die and between punch and hole punch (piercing punch) in the die set.

The location of these tool elements, with respect to one another, should be maintained even if they are removed and installed again and again in the die set. It should also be taken into account that the punch and the die may be exposed to high transverse forces. The alignment of the die and the punch or the pressure pad, respectively, must be able to absorb these transverse forces without the die and the punch shifting in the die set.

Figure 15 is a drawing of the tool, pictured in **Figure 16**. All the individual parts are shown in **Figure 17**. The round body of the punch is guided in the upper part of the die, and the round pressure pad is centered in a slightly conical seat (3 to 5°). The profile part of the punch is guided in the pressure pad. The upper part of the die set is supported at the press counter pressure ram on a thick and hardened pressure ring (thrust ring), and the punch on the pressure ring insert (support ring), which is also hardened.

The standardized pressure rings and pressure ring inserts can be exchanged according to the tool since a slot is milled into the punch body. The support for the slug ejectors of the center hole, which is fixed between the pressure pad and the pressure ring, protrudes into this slot. The punch shaft is provided with a shoulder where it is fastened.

The pitch circle diameter of the three small holes of the gear segment is greater than the diameter of the pressure ring insert. It is therefore possible to have the slug ejectors of the small holes directly supported on the pressure ring. In the lower part of the die set, the die is also centered in a conic seat. The die, like the pressure pad, is installed with a preload of approximately 0.012″. Preload here means the distance between the bearing faces of the die set and the die or the pressure pad, respectively, with the die and the pressure pad inserted into the conic seat. The die is supported through the hole punch plate (piercing punch plate) and the base (base pad) on the pressure ring in the lower part of the press. These parts are all made of hardened steel.

The base should protrude 0.001″ to 0.003″ over the bearing face of the lower part, so that when the die is mounted, it is slightly preloaded, vertically. The ejector is guided in a profiled passage of the die, and is supported through the ejector thrust pins on the pressure ring insert.

Distribution of the pressure pins under the

Figure 16
The fine blanking die that's sectioned in Figure 15.

Figure 17
Individual parts of die illustrated in Figures 15 and 16.

Figure 18
Test part for load test of die being discussed. Die side of workpiece is up. Refer to copy for clarification.

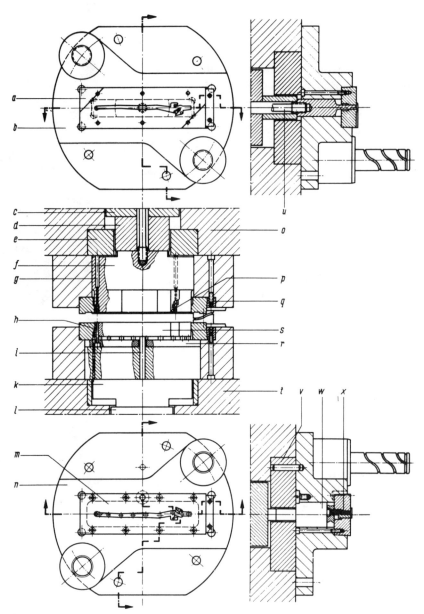

Figure 19
A drawing of die for producing long narrow parts. The nomenclature here is the same as that used for Figure 15.

ejector is very important, particularly if the cutting out is simultaneously combined with embossing or coining operation. The ejector thrust pins should be distributed over the ejector area as uniformly as possible, and the embossing or coining areas be supported to a correspondingly greater extent—in order to avoid deformations of the ejector or differential stresses in the ejector pins. Whenever possible, the mean compressive stress in the hardened ejector pins should not exceed 71,000 psi.

The ejector guides the hole punches and the retaining head of the hole punches, in the hole punch plate, should have a vertical clearance of 0.0010″ to 0.0015″. Horizontally they should have sufficient clearance on all sides, so that the hole punches can align themselves with respect to the ejector. The base, the hole punch plate, the

hole punches and the ejector can be pulled out of the lower part of the tool without removing the die, for easy exchange, and resharpening the die is thus simplified.

Unlike most die sets, the leader pins of the blanking dies are always pressed into the upper part of the die set. For resharpening, the punch is pulled out of the upper part of the tool and ground separately. The die and the hole punches can be resharpened without disassembling the lower part of the tool. With this arrangement the leader pins are not in the way during resharpening.

How safe fine blanking dies are against fracture is proven by **Figure 18.** Before cutting out a 0.160″ thick gear segment made of steel, a 0.080″ thick gear segment (previously blanked) was added off center. After this "accident," it

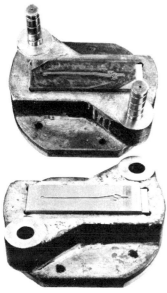

Figure 20

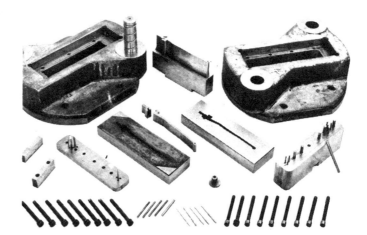

Figure 21

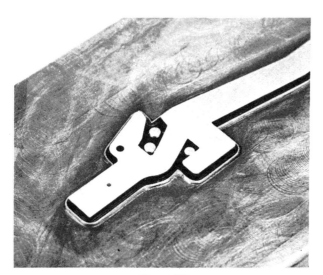

Figure 22

was still possible to use the undamaged die.

Fine blanking tools with rectangular pressure pad and die are easily produced for long narrow parts. **Figure 19** is a drawing of a fine blanking die for a lever. The two long sides, and one short side, of the pressure pad are slightly "conical" and in the upper part of the die the long sides of the recess (into which the pressure pad is inserted) are also milled "conical." But the two short sides are parallel.

Location of the longitudinal axis of the pressure pad is determined by the "conical" seat of the long sides. On the "conical" short side of the pressure pad, a wedge is inserted into the upper part of the die set together with the pressure pad; the latter is pressed on by means of the wedge at the opposite short side. The die in the lower part of the column frame is centered in the same way. Pressure pad and the die, as

well as the two wedges, are installed under a preload. **Figure 20** shows the tools and **Figure 21** its individual components.

The profile of this lever is simple with the exception of the two narrow recessed areas. It is not necessary at these areas to press an impingement ring into the strip. Therefore, the knife edge ring leads past the entrance of the recessed areas and simplifies the shape of the pressure pad passage **(Figure 22)**. The waste stock is stripped off by means of ejector pins, which are supported like the slug ejectors, on the pressure ring.

In order not to weaken the punch unnecessarily, the cutting profile of these areas was worked into the punch only $7/16''$ deep. The form of the die passage was also simplified for safety reasons. Two inserts like hole punches replace the profile missing on the die. ∎

Reprinted from "Fineblanking: An Efficient Production Method", courtesy of Schmid Corporation of America, Goodrich, Michigan

Fixed Punch Fineblanking Tools

by Heinrich Schmid
Schmid Corporation of America

Tool systems

There are two tool systems in use:

a) tools with fixed punch

b) tools with sliding punch

Fineblanking tools with a fixed punch are suitable for any application.

The sliding punch system is limited to relatively thin parts with few punched holes.

The decision to use only the fixed punch system makes the design and manufacturing of fineblanking tools simpler. Therefore, we take a look at this system only.

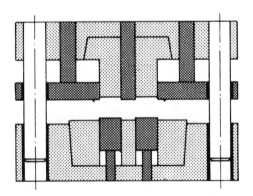

Tool with
fixed punch

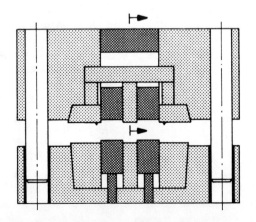

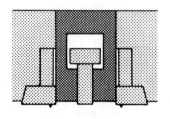

Tool with
sliding punch

Fineblanking tool with fixed punch

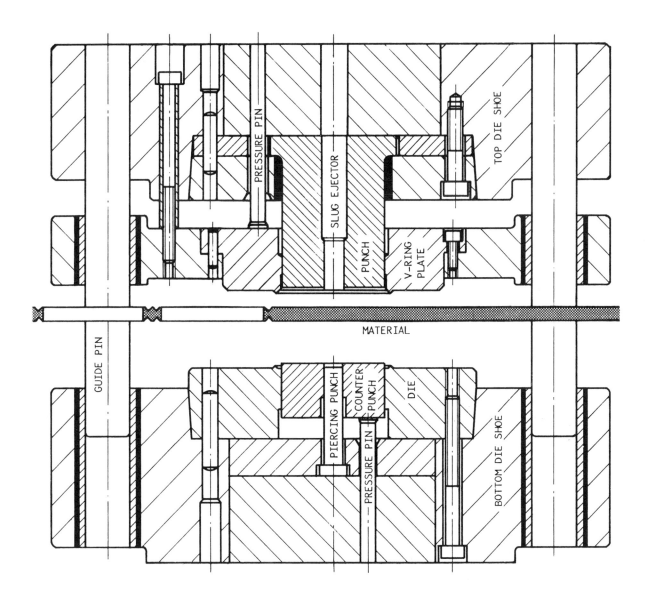

Lateral forces occur during fineblanking. It therefore makes sense to absorb these lateral forces in large size die sets with plain or roller bearing bushings. The initially higher costs are easily compensated for by the longer tool life.

The blanking force is directly transferred to the die plate by the bottom die shoe.

The V-ring force (stripper force) is transferred to the V-ring plate (stripper) by pressure pins. The counter force (ejection force) is also transferred by pressure pins to the counter punch (ejector).

Tool standards

The most economical manufacturing of fineblanking tools can be done if the die sets and their components are manufactured in series.

Therefore, SCHMID has designed a standard line of die sets, which is available from stock. A full set of detailed drawings is provided with each press.

For each type of press, SCHMID has different sizes of standard die sets. The choice depends on the size of the fineblanking component.

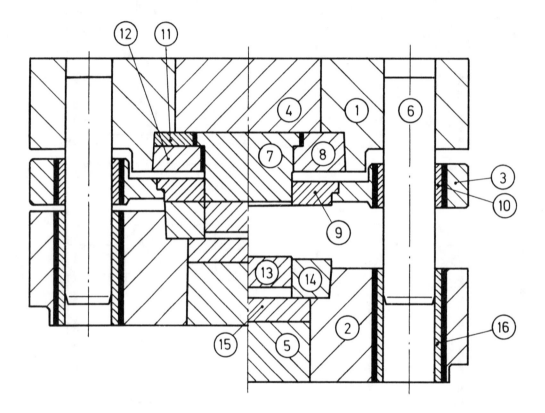

1. Top die shoe
2. Bottom die shoe
3. Guide plate
4. Top back-up block
5. Bottom back-up block
6. Guide pin
7. Punch
8. Punch retainer without adjusting plate
9. V-Ring plate
10. Guide bushing
11. Adjusting plate
12. Punch retainer with adjusting plate
13. Ejector
14. Die
15. Piercing punch retainer
16. Guide bushing

Tool material

The choice of the tool steel and its hardness can differ from case to case. A continuous development of new cutting steels as well as new experience in the application of those tool materials do not allow to make general indications.

Today, for cutting elements, high speed steels are often used with a hardness of 61 - 62 HRC.

Tool manufacturing

To avoid distortion due to heat treatment, the cutting elements are made by ED (Electric Discharging) or grinding after hardening. The other tool components are turned, milled, planed or ground.

The following cutting elements determine the dimensions of the part:

      outside contour   -   die

      inside contour   -   inner form punch (piercing punch)

In order to obtain correct parts with smooth edges, it is important to maintain the proper punch-to-die-clearance and to have the same clearance everywhere.

MANUFACTURING OF THE CUTTING ELEMENTS BY USING AN ELECTRIC DISCHARGE MACHINE-TOOL

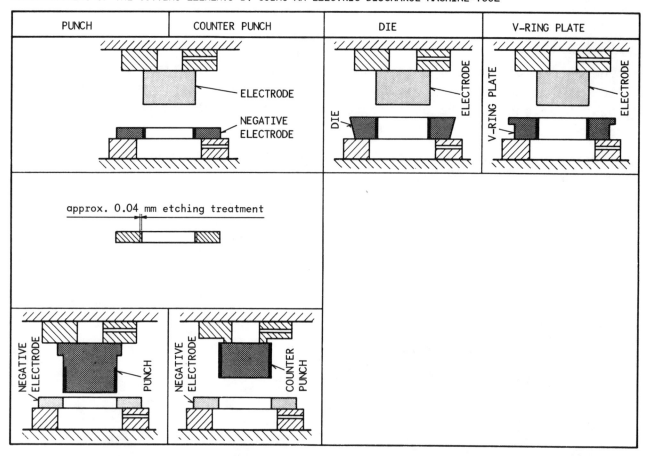

MANUFACTURING OF THE CUTTING ELEMENTS BY USING AN ELECTRIC DISCHARGE WIRE CUTTER

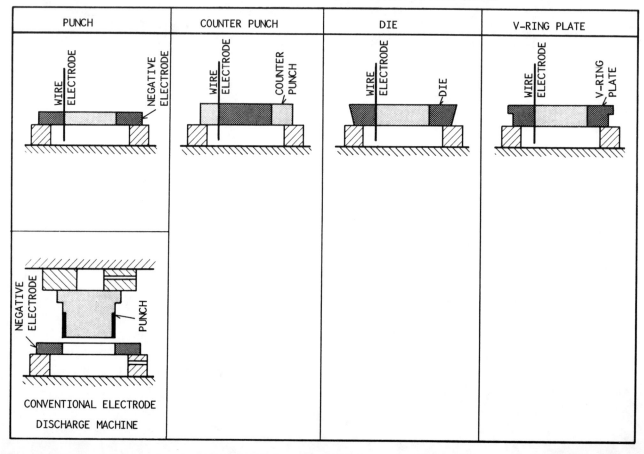

V-rings

For a material thickness of approximately 4 mm or less, the V-ring (stinger) is only on the V-ring plate (stripper), for thicker material a second V-ring is also on the die.

The die as well as the V-ring plate are subject to wear and can be re-worked several times. Therefore, the V-ring is machined into the hardened steel.

Two methods are used to make the V-ring (stinger):

    a) by EDM (electrical discharge machining)
    b) milling with tungsten carbide cutter

Experience has shown that milling the V-ring is not only very economic but also provides a better quality, as no changes occur in the metallurgical structure.

Milling the V-ring is done as follows:

    I   milling of the inside
    II   milling of the outside
    III   milling or grinding of the remaining surface

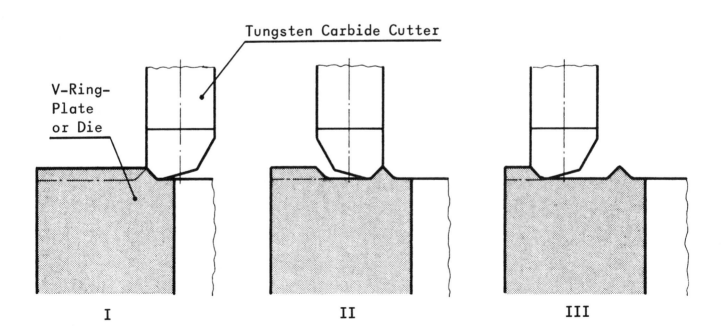

V-ring dimensions

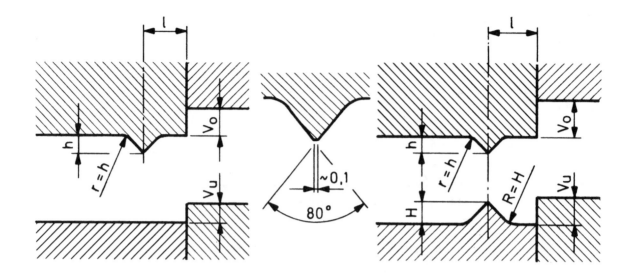

Material Thickness	l	h	V_o	V_u
1.0 - 1.6	1.2	0.4	1.0	1.0
1.6 - 2.5	1.5	0.7	1.2	1.0
2.5 - 3.2	1.9	1.0	1.5	1.1
3.2 - 4.0	2.4	1.2	1.8	1.2

Material Thickness	l	h	H	V_o	V_u
4.0 - 5.0	2.3	0.7	0.9	2.1	1.3
5.0 - 6.3	2.9	0.9	1.1	2.3	1.4
6.3 - 8.0	3.6	1.1	1.4	2.5	1.5
8.0 - 10.0	4.5	1.4	1.7	2.7	1.6
10.0 - 12.5	5.6	1.7	2.1	3.0	1.7
12.5 - 16.0	7.1	2.2	2.7	3.4	1.8

Die with milled
V-ring

V-ring plate
with milled V-ring

Reprinted from "Fine-Blanking Practical Handbook", courtesy of American Feintool Inc., Cincinnati, Ohio

Progressive Fine-Blanking Tools

Parts with certain bends or forms often require several working operations. Where small series of parts are concerned, these operations can be carried out in separate tools. This leads to high production costs and a lengthy processing period through the shop, as the loading of the parts generally has to be done by hand.

Regarding high volume production, the parts are usually manufactured in a progressive tool where the various operations are made consecutively at different stations in the tool. The die-plates in such tools are often sectioned and set together, normally so that there is a non-productive station between the various stages in order to ensure maximum stability of the tool. The extreme lengths of such tools, due to the various stations required, often means that the line of shear force from the press ram does not coincide exactly with the line of shear force required in the various tool stations. Exact guidance of the tool itself can therefore be guaranteed only by exact and play free ram guidance. The fine-blanking press is well suited for the use of progressive tools. Practice has shown that normal progressive dies used in fine-blanking presses ensure higher production between tool re-grinds. This is due to the maximum support of the tool and accurate ram guidance.

The design of a fine-blanking progressive tool is similar to that of a conventional progressive tool. The forces to clamp and retain the material as well as eject the part or slugs are provided by the hydraulics in the machine. These pressures are transferred through pins eliminating all springs which are normally required for these purposes. The cutting elements are all produced cylindrically (no backing off) which guarantees not only a higher degree of stability in the tool, but also ensure piece-parts of the same dimension for the life of the die-plate.

Plunger, scale 1:1

Plunger	Conventional		Fine-Blanking
– Blank (single punch tool)	20	– Fine-Blank (twin punch tool)	14.3
– Shave	150		
– Mill	300		
– De-burr	30	– De-burr	30
	500 min./1000 parts		44.3 min./1000 parts

Production time for tools

	Conventional		Fine-Blanking
– Normal blanking tool (single punch)	150	– Progressive fine-blanking tool (twin punch)	
– Shaving tool	120		
– Milling jig	50		1100
	320 hours		1100 hours

Manufacturing the 'Plunger' parts in a progressive fine-blanking tool eliminates the time consuming shaving operation required to achieve cleanly sheared surfaces. As the chamfers are coined in a station before shearing the costly milling operation could also be excluded. From the table above it can be seen that approximately 7.6 hours manufacturing time can be saved in the production of 1,000 parts. The extra tooling costs (780 hours for building the progressive fine-blanking tool) is amortized after the production of 100,000 to a maximum of 200,000 parts—dependent on the hourly rates involved. As at least 500,000 Plungers have to be made each year the change of working method paid for itself in a short period.

As an example, the design of the twin punch fine-blanking progressive tool for 'Plunger' will be explained.

Requirements of the part:
The outer and inner perimeter surfaces are guide surfaces.
The 'shaft' is formed thinner than the initial material thickness.
In the slots there are bevels for engagement purposes.

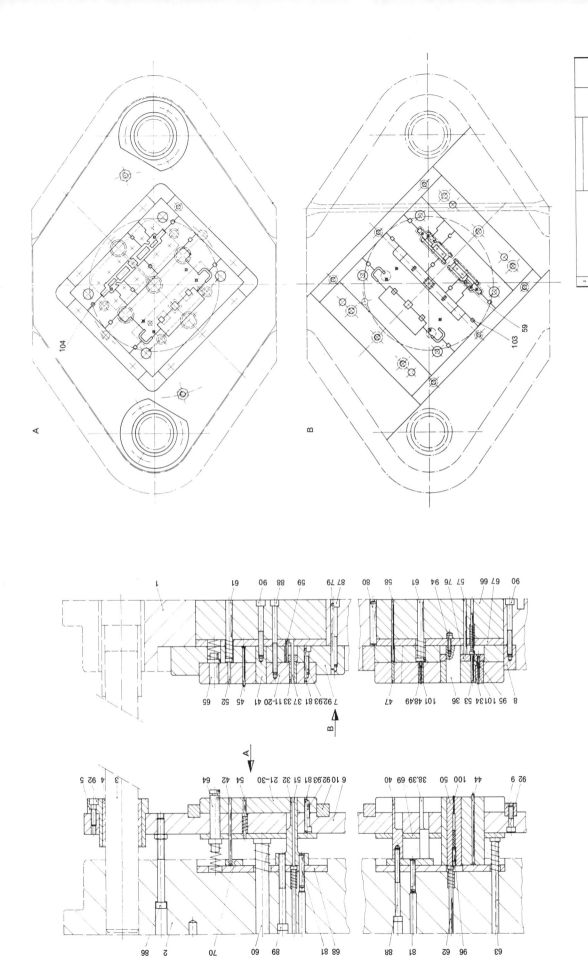

Picture 180 Fine-blanking progressive tool for 'Plunger' (twin punch)

Feintool AG Lyss

W 4 -1689/1-13

229

Station 1   Pierce two (2) pilot holes.
             'Gut-out' around the shaft (two [2] 'U' forms).
             Pierce three (3) forming slots (for coining of the
             engagement bevels).
Station 2   Free station with pilot pins.
Station 3   Locate on pilot.
             Coin the two bevels in each part.
             Coin down the thickness of the shaft.
Station 4   Free station with pilot pins.
Station 5   Pilot from pilot pin in main punch.
             Blanking of the inner and outer forms.

The assembly drawing W4-1689/1-13 shows the design of the tool. The springs under the pressure pins serve only to prevent the pins falling down below the surface of the die set when setting the tool in the press.
Progressive fine-blanking tools of this type require a high standard of tool design capability and a good tool room. The maintenance of such tools also requires considerable effort and care on the part of the toolmaker. For high volume production, however, this type of tool provides the only reasonable economical method of manufacture.

Reprinted from "Fineblanking: An Efficient Production Method", courtesy of Schmid Corporation of America, Goodrich, Michigan

Progressive Tools for Fineblanking

by Heinrich Schmid
Schmid Corporation of America

Many parts have to be manufactured by different forming operations besides fineblanking. These operations can be done either one after another in individual tools or automatically in several stages as strip progression. With this progressive tool system the part remains in the strip webbing up to the last stage and falls out as finished component.

Diagram of fineblanking sequence with a progressive fineblanking tool:

Stage A: cutting of pos. 1, pos. 2 as well as pilot hole pos. 3

Stage B: pos. 4 cutting, pos. 5 coining both sides, pos. 6 bending

Stage C: pos. 7 coining both sides pos. 8 cutting

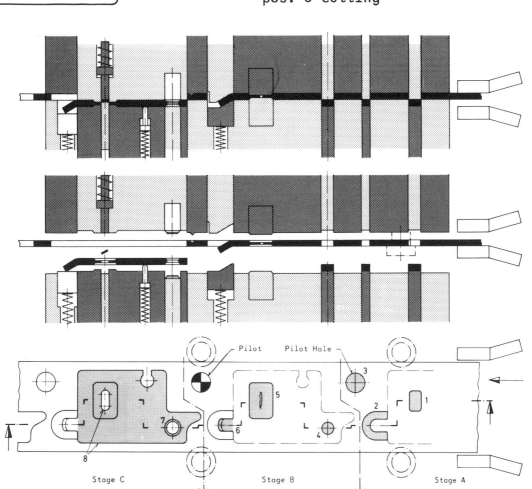

CHAPTER 4

DIES FOR SINGLE PURPOSE MACHINES

Reprinted from Manufacturing Engineering, April 1978

Four-slides, Forming at the Kingpost

Forms made at the kingpost of a four-slide machine vary from the simple to the exotic. In this article MANUFACTURING ENGINEERING starts its study of the forms, beginning with the most fundamental

DANIEL B. DALLAS
Editorial Director

THE MAJORITY OF THE PARTS FORMED in the kingpost area of a four-slide machine are extremely complex. Because of their complexity, the designer with the greatest experience is generally the one who can use the slides most effectively. Accordingly, while this article (and the article to follow) presents a great number of slide layouts, it would be physically impossible to catalog all possible layouts and part designs. Therefore, the purpose of this article is not to provide answers to specific problems, but to give the novice (and possibly the experienced) designer an insight into slide capabilities. The basic designs, which tend to be repetitive, will be reviewed first.

The Basic U-form. Only three slides are required in this design, which is shown in *Figure* 1. The three views presented are plan views (i.e., the viewer is looking down on the mandrel, the slides, and the cutoff). At view *A* the stock advances a predetermined distance. At the completion of this movement, the front slide and the cutoff tool begin their advance toward the strip.

The timing of the cams is such that the pressure pin in the front slide contacts the strip and holds it against the mandrel *before* the cutoff tool makes contact. Again, it is necessary to refer to a previously stated rule: *the stock must be under control at all times*.

With the workpiece firmly pinned against the mandrel, the cutoff blade advances and severs the strip. The front slide continues its forward movement, contacts the strip, and forms it

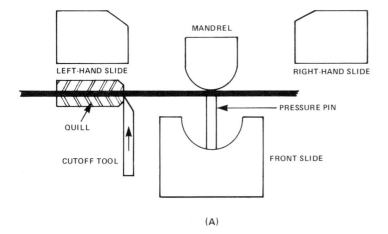

(A)

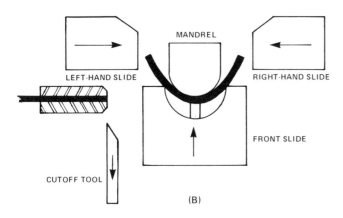

(B)

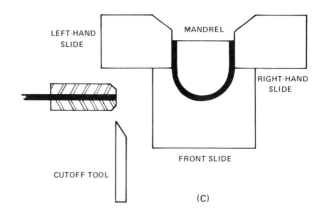

(C)

1. SEQUENTIAL MOVEMENTS when producing a basic U-form on the four-slide are illustrated in these plan views. Only three slides are needed.

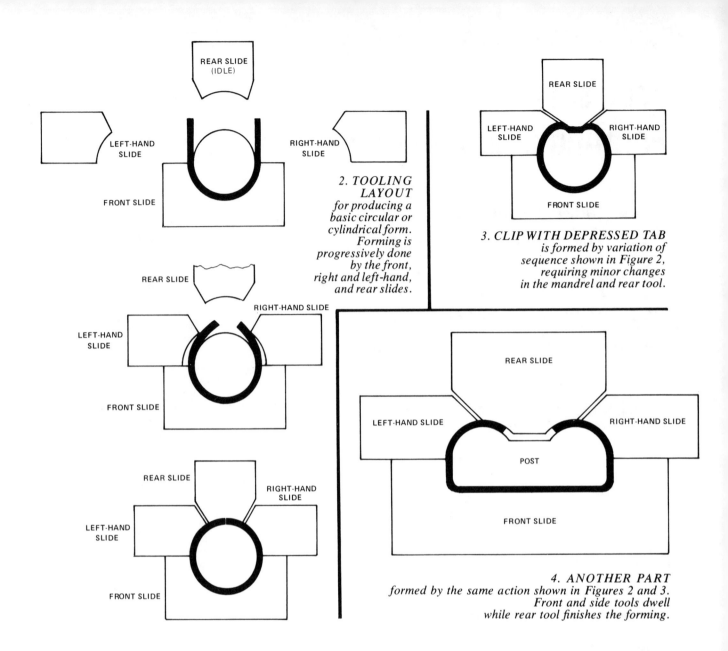

2. TOOLING LAYOUT
for producing a basic circular or cylindrical form. Forming is progressively done by the front, right and left-hand, and rear slides.

3. CLIP WITH DEPRESSED TAB
is formed by variation of sequence shown in Figure 2, requiring minor changes in the mandrel and rear tool.

4. ANOTHER PART
formed by the same action shown in Figures 2 and 3. Front and side tools dwell while rear tool finishes the forming.

against the mandrel, view *B*. The right and left-hand slides now advance and complete the forming of the part into a U-shaped channel, as seen at *C*.

With the part fully formed, the three slides begin their retraction. The stripper (not shown) descends and pushes the part down and off the mandrel.

The slide movements described in this sequence are integrated for maximum utilization of available time. For instance, the front slide and the cutoff blade advance together with the cutoff slightly behind the pressure pin. Just as soon as the pin has firmly grasped the workpiece, the cutoff blade severs the strip and immediately retracts.

Similarly, the right and left-hand slides begin their inward movement before the front slide has completed its preliminary form operation. The reason for this integration of slide movements is that time is limited. More specifi-

cally, all forming must be done within 180° of the machine cycle. With multiple slide movements to be completed within this time interval, it is necessary that slides at 90° to each other be moving simultaneously with one slightly ahead of the other. At this point it is worth noting that The A. H. Nilson Machine Co. has developed a new feed mechanism in which retraction takes place in 90° of the machine cycle. This greatly expands the machine capabilities, since 170° are now available for forming action.

The Basic Circular Form. The tooling layout for a basic circular or cylindrical form is shown in *Figure 2*. The sequence followed is simply an extension of the sequence shown for the U-form. First, the pressure pin grasps the work and the strip or wire is severed. Next, the front slide advances to form one-half of the cylindrical shape, as seen at

the top. It then enters a dwell phase. Meanwhile, the right and left-hand slides are advancing to close the form still farther, shown at the center. When these two slides have completed their advance, they too enter a dwell phase. The rear slide now advances and completes the circular (or cylindrical) form, as seen in the bottom view.

A variation of this layout is seen in *Figure 3*. In this instance a clip with a depressed tab is formed. This necessitates minor changes in the mandrel and rear tool. Otherwise, the sequence is the same.

In *Figure* 4 the same action takes place. The front tool forms, then dwells (a movement that is characteristic of virtually all four-slide forming operations). The side tools then accomplish their forming operations, then dwell. The rear tool advances to finish the part, then retracts. The side and front

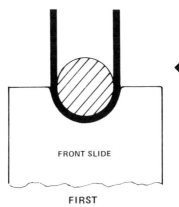

FIRST

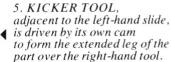

5. KICKER TOOL,
*adjacent to the left-hand slide,
is driven by its own cam
to form the extended leg of the
part over the right-hand tool.* ◄

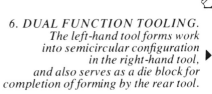

6. DUAL FUNCTION TOOLING.
*The left-hand tool forms work
into semicircular configuration
in the right-hand tool,
and also serves as a die block for
completion of forming by the rear tool.* ►

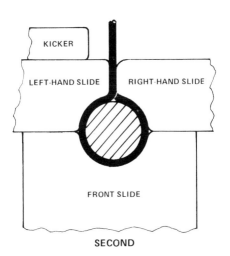

SECOND

FEED →

CUTOFF

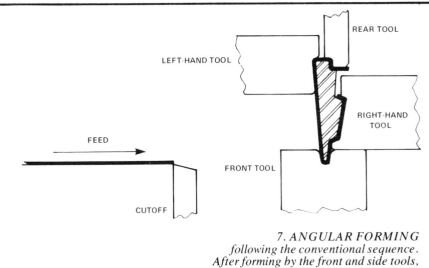

7. ANGULAR FORMING
*following the conventional sequence.
After forming by the front and side tools,
the rear tool makes the final two bends.*

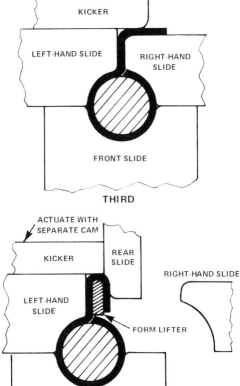

THIRD

FOURTH

MATERIAL FEED →

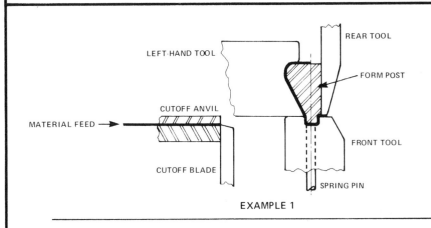

EXAMPLE 1

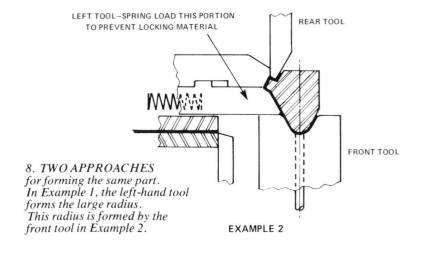

8. TWO APPROACHES
*for forming the same part.
In Example 1, the left-hand tool
forms the large radius.
This radius is formed by the
front tool in Example 2.*

EXAMPLE 2

237

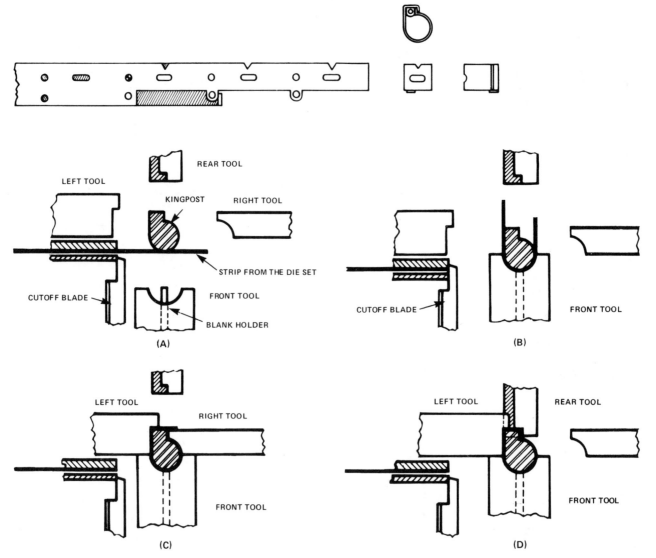

(A)

(B)

(C)

(D)

9. *REAR TOOL has two working levels —
the upper level closes the part,
and the lower level (indicated by cross hatching)
moves under the mandrel to form tab.*

tools also retract. The finished part is stripped from the mandrel and the cycle is complete.

Kicker Tools. The preceding are the basic forming operations. It is now possible to build on these operations through the addition of a tool called the kicker, *Figure* 5. A kicker is simply an auxiliary tool that is carried in — or adjacent to — any of the basic slide tools previously discussed. In some instances a kicker is a spring-loaded addition to one of the slide tools. In other instances, a kicker is independently driven by its own cam. The one shown in *Figure* 5 is independently driven.

In forming the circular segment of the desired part, the front and side cams follow the established sequence (i.e., the front tool advances and dwells; the side tools then advance and form). First, the front tool contacts the work to form half of the cylindrical configuration. Next, the side tools enter and finish the cylinder — leaving

one leg extended, however.

At this point the kicker — driven by its own cam — forms the extended leg over the right-hand tool. The right-hand slide now retracts, withdrawing the tool, and a mandrel fixed to the form lifter descends. The kicker now retracts and a form tool mounted on the rear slide completes the forming operation.

Tool Against Tool. Four-slide tooling is not limited to the forming of work around a mandrel. In a good many instances a tool which pushes metal into a form can also act as a form block. A good example is seen in *Figure* 6.

First, the front tool advances to form half the cylinder. It then dwells. Next, the right-hand tool advances and closes the cylinder on one side. It, too, dwells at this point. Subsequently, the left-hand tool advances and forms the work into a semicircular configuration in the right-hand tool, which is still in its dwell phase. At this point, the rear tool

advances and completes the form against the left-hand tool. Thus the left-hand tool is not only a forming tool — it is also a die block. This provides but one more example of the amazing versatility and forming potential of the four-slide machine.

Forming an Angular Part. Again, the part in question — shown in *Figure* 7 — follows the conventional sequence. First, the front slide forms the part into a radial configuration, then dwells. The right and left-hand tools then contact the work and dwell. The last movement is that of the rear tool coming in to make the final two bends.

Had it been necessary, the tab formed by the rear tool could also have been formed down. This could have been accomplished at the second forming level, a subject yet to be discussed. Or it could have been done at the level shown through a kicker .tool design. This, of course, would have required provision for clearance — for the flange

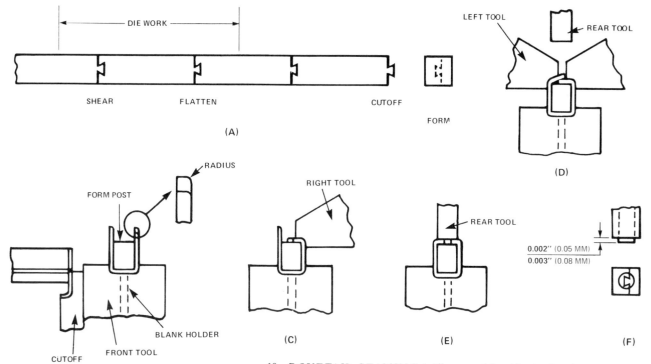

10. *DOVETAIL SEAMING is illustrated by this six-drawing sequence. Seamed edges are sheared – with punch penetrating only partially through the stock – in the progressive strip (A).*

to form down — in the right-hand tool.

Two Approaches to One Part. That two or more different tooling approaches can be taken for one part is shown in *Figure* 8. In Example 1 the front slide makes the initial form, then dwells. Simultaneously, the left slide and the rear slide advance to finish the part.

Precisely the same part is produced in Example 2, but with totally different tooling. In this case the front tool forms the large radius, then dwells. Next, the left-hand tool — equipped with a kicker — advances to form the side and part of the rectangular formation. The rear tool then enters and finishes the part.

Use of the kicker eliminates the possibility of material locking, a condition that could happen if the forming done on the left-hand side were done with a single tool. It should be noted that when the left-hand tool seats on the workpiece, the kicker is bottomed in the upper portion of the tool. At this point the two tools are acting as one, thus assuring a solid bottoming effect on the workpiece.

Forming Under the Mandrel. All kingpost forming operations discussed up to this point have related to forming against a mandrel held in the kingpost. The next example, *Figure* 9, shows how a slide and its tooling can form a part *under* a post as well as *against* it.

The progressive die operation is relatively straight-forward — a V-notch on one edge, several hole piercing operations, and a tab on the other edge.

When the part is severed from the strip, it must also be formed into a locked configuration. Simultaneously, the tab, shown at the lower edge in the progressive sequence, must be formed toward the center of the closed configuration.

The operation begins with cutoff of the part from the progressive die strip, shown at A. The front tool advances and makes a 180° radial form in the workpiece, B. The left-hand tool now advances and forms the extended leg over the mandrel, seen at C. The part is ready for closure, an operation that is effected by the rear tool as the right-hand tool retracts, D.

The rear tool has two working levels. The upper level of the tool closes the part; the lower level — indicated by cross hatching — moves under the mandrel to form the tab.

Lower level tabs of this type could also be produced with the front or left and right-hand tools. However, kicker tools would have to be employed. The kickers would be spring loaded rather than independently driven, however.

Dovetail Seaming. Another capability of the four-slide lies in its ability to perform seaming operations. The six-drawing sequence in *Figure* 10 illustrates the standard four-slide technique for performing a dovetail seaming operation.

The progressive strip is shown at A where the seamed edges are sheared. This shearing operation does not completely separate the two adjacent parts; the punch penetrates no more than

two-thirds of the way through the stock. The stock is then brought back into alignment at the next station with a flattening punch.

In drawing B the part is separated from the strip by the cutoff punch and formed into a U-shape by the now familiar front-tool movement. At C the right-hand tool forms the male portion of the part over the kingpost mandrel. At D the left-hand slide brings the female portion of the part into position over the male. At E the rear tool advances and finishes the operation by locking the dovetail.

The drawing at F illustrates a technique frequently used to tighten the locking action in a dovetail seaming operation. The part shown at the top is a small punch that extends 0.002″ to 0.003″ (0.05 to 0.08 mm) beyond the surface of the rear tool. Because the diameter of the working portion of the punch is slightly larger than the dovetail, it acts to tighten the seam.

Lockseaming. The lockseaming concept shown sequentially in *Figure* 11 brings three new four-slide concepts into play. The first is the use of a stationary tool; the second is the camming of one tool off another; and the third is the double acting slide.

Starting at A, the stock advances slightly past the stationary tool. The broken outline of the work shows the first flange, formed when the front tool advances toward the mandrel. Formation of this flange is a simple wiping action. It does require plenty of blank-

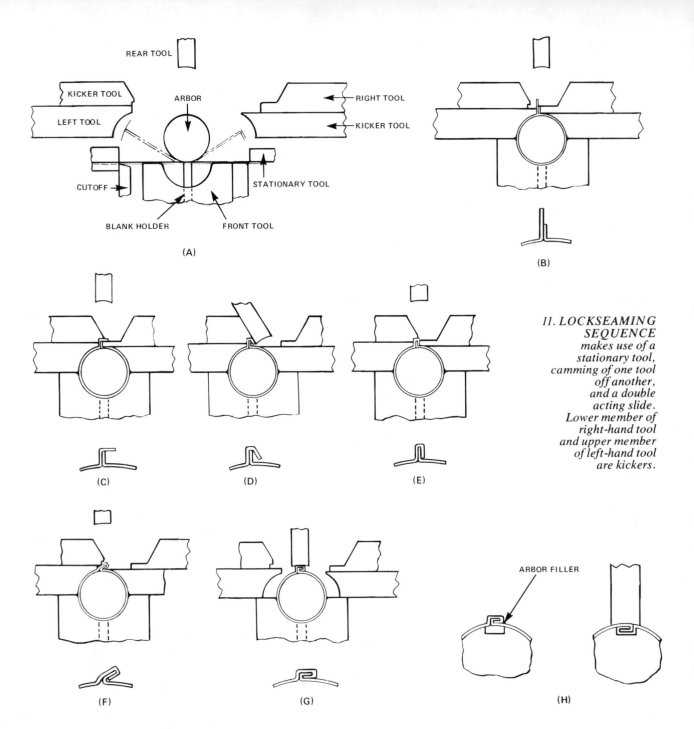

REAR TOOL

KICKER TOOL

ARBOR

RIGHT TOOL

KICKER TOOL

LEFT TOOL

CUTOFF

STATIONARY TOOL

BLANK HOLDER

FRONT TOOL

(A)

(B)

(C)

(D)

(E)

11. LOCKSEAMING SEQUENCE makes use of a stationary tool, camming of one tool off another, and a double acting slide. Lower member of right-hand tool and upper member of left-hand tool are kickers.

(F)

(G)

ARBOR FILLER

(H)

holder force to prevent slippage, however.

At drawing B the front slide tool and side tools have advanced to close the cylinder. It should be noted that the lower member of the right-hand tool is a kicker, as is the upper member of the left-hand tool.

At drawing C the left-hand kicker advances and forms the work into a 90° bend over the right-hand tool. When this operation is complete, the right-hand tool retracts — leaving its kicker in place — and the rear tool begins its advance.

Unlike any of the tooling previously discussed, the rear tool is designed to pivot. It maintains its normal position

(as shown at C) through spring pressure. But when it contacts the left-hand kicker it cams into an angular position and forces the seam flange down at an angle of approximately 45°, as seen at D.

At drawing E the rear tool quickly retracts and the right-hand tool quickly advances to complete the flanging operation. This is an example of double action in a slide, for this is the second time the right-hand tool has advanced in a single cycle of the machine. Double action is effected by a double-lobe cam, a subject to be discussed in Part 5 (June) of this series.

At drawing F both the right and left-hand tools are retracting, and the rear

tool — also driven by a double-lobe cam — is again advancing.

At drawing G all side tooling has retracted and the rear tool is contacting and closing the rear seam, thus completing the job of forming an external lockseam.

Precisely the same tooling can be used to complete an internal lockseam, although changes in the mandrel are required. If both forms of lockseaming are to be done, the arbor must be equipped with a filler, as is shown at H. This filler is removed and a slightly longer, somewhat wider rear tool is used. This tool drives the externally formed seam into the recess, thus producing an internal seam. ∎

240

Reprinted from The Tool & Manufacturing Engineer (Manufacturing Engineering), August 1969

No matter how effective your four-slides are, your production and efficiency depend largely on cam design. This article discusses the fundamentals of four-slide camming

Designing Cams for Four-Slides

ROBERT E. CARLSON, Chief Applications Engineer, Machine Division, Torin Corporation[*], Torrington, Connecticut

Four-slide machines are particularly suited to forming intricately shaped parts from metal strip or ribbon at high production rates. Following what can be numerous die operations in the four-slide's press section, the machine's slide forming tools may be called on to make a variety of closely timed precision bends in the strip material before the finished part is ejected. As a result, slide tools in a four-slide are likely to be advancing and retracting at very high velocities during the machine cycle.

High velocities mean that severe, repetitive impacts occur at many points in the drive system between the main cam shaft and the strip material being formed. When improperly designed cams are run at high speeds, the useful life of the cam rolls and pins can be drastically cut because of the jarring shock that takes place periodically as the cam roll follows a steep cam contour. Too steep a cam contour can also result in freezing or locking the cam, a condition that can severely damage the machine. While most four-slides are ruggedly built to withstand high impact, the repeated shock is harmful to many parts of the machine.

An equally important consideration is the effect of the forming process on part control as bending takes place around the centerform. If the tools strike the strip material at an excessively high rate of speed, the material can easily be distorted or even fractured if the material is in the high tensile range. Materials with low formability may not flow fast enough to respond properly to

forming motions. Such conditions can produce a high reject rate because of high dimensional variation or excessive breakage. And yet speed—number of machine cycles per minute or parts produced per minute—is one of the main reasons for making parts on a four-slide.

The design of the cams controlling the action of the slide forming tools in four-slide machines is then very important to the tool engineer who is planning production of a part. The optimum cam in four-slide tooling therefore might be defined as one which performs its forming action successfully and yet in minimum time so that all forming operations can be conveniently completed during the 360 degrees of one machine cycle at the highest possible production rate. While this is hardly a convenient, easy-to-remember definition, it encompasses all the elements of good cam planning.

Before discussing in more detail specification of forming cams for four-slides and planning the cam cycle, it may be useful to review the types of cams presently used in four-slides and the relative characteristics of the most commonly encountered cam motions.

Formerly The Torrington Manufacturing Co. Illustrations and examples in this article will refer to the vertical-type four-slide machine, such as the Torin Verti-Slide, although the concepts apply to all types of four-slides as well as to other types of mechanically controlled machines.

Types of Four-Slide Cams

There are three basic types of four-slide cams -- the barrel cam, the plate cam, and the box cam. The barrel cam (*Figure* 1) is used for controlling the stock clamp in the centerform area and for actuating other auxiliary mechanisms such as welding attachments. When used to produce angular movement, as in a four-slide, the barrel cam should be designed to insure roller contact on the cam track throughout the complete motion.

Plate cams (*Figure* 2) are used for the stock check in the feed mechanism, where a helical spring return is satisfactory and no locking can occur. Plate cams are also used in four-slides to activate limit switches and to cycle protective devices in the tooling, which are functions in which load is transferred to the cam through the cam follower.

Box cams (*Figure* 3) are available in both the offset cam roll form and the heavy duty form, which has a straddle-mounted roll along with the offset for positive return. The forming slides and retractable centerforms of vertical four-slides are operated by box cams. The box cam in *Figure* 3, which has a pivot arm like the cams in *Figure* 1 and 2, is used for the retractable centerform. The forming slides instead have in-line arms, without pivots, and the cams have two lobes.

The plate cam was the first and most commonly used cam for producing timed tool motions in machinery. The cam follower pushes the slide or lever, and a spring returns it to the rest position. Freezing or locking can occur in this design due to the back pressure of the tool on the centerform or material being formed. It is often difficult to design compression springs with a high enough return load to entirely eliminate the possibility of locking. Therefore, plate cams have been widely changed over to box cams, which provide positive return while preventing the possibility of locking. With further modification, the heavy duty box cam has an extended center portion cam-shaped the same as the inside track. The cam directs power through the straddle-mounted cam roll for pushing or forming power and an offset cam roll for returning the cam to rest.

The most important of the three types of cams to the tool engineer planning four-slide production is the box cam used for the forming tools. While he may never feel it necessary to specify barrel or plate cams other than those provided on the machine, he is concerned with specifying new box cams for the forming tools whenever he plans production of a new part. In doing so, he has the choice of using either a standard cam made by the four-slide manufacturer or a special cam designed for a particular part.

Standard cams are advantageous, of course, because they cost less and are likely to be immediately available, particularly if the four-slide user has built up a library of standard cams. Quite complex parts can be produced with a variety of tightly interlaced forming motions entirely with the use of standard slide cams. On the other hand, special cams may be worth the investment—whether it be to make it possible to form the part at all or to attain certain operating advantages that outweigh the additional cost. For example, relatively simple parts to be produced in high volume quantities can often be run at substantially higher speeds and with longer tool life by installing cams specially designed to minimize tool impact and forming velocities.

Standard cams are designed by four-slide manufacturers to utilize the maximun capabilities of the machines both with regard to structural stresses in operation and available tool stroke to clear material during forming. Special cams, on the other hand, are designed to fit the needs of the particular part within the range of the machine capacity. For

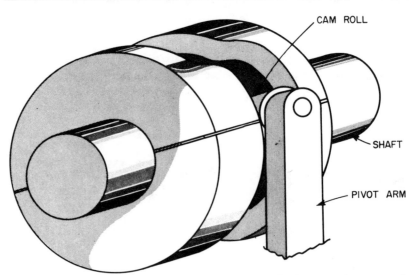

1. BARREL CAM used to control the stock clamp in the centerform area of a four-slide. Barrel clamps are also used to actuate auxiliary mechanisms.

most effective production on four-slides, the tool engineer must know how to take advantage of available standard cams and how to design special cams to meet special needs.

Forming Cams in Action

The application of cams in controlling forming tools is demonstrated in the typical four-slide machine cycle described in *Figure* 4. A ring is being formed from metal strip on a vertical four-slide machine. In *Figure* 4a, the strip—fed in from the press section at left—has stopped over the centerform and has been bent down over the top of the centerform by the top tool. In *Figure* 4b, the left side tool and right side tool have advanced together to bend the two ends of the strip around the bottom of the centerform, while the top tool continues to dwell at its maximum advance.

While a ring has already been formed, precise ring diameter control is provided in this tooling sequence by having the side tools retract from their positions in *Figure* 4b while the bottom tool advances for final forming of the ends of the strip against the circular centerform. The bottom and top tools then retract and the centerform withdraws into

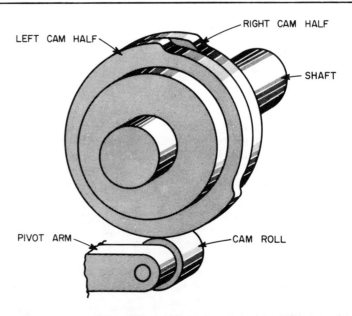

2. PLATE CAM used in the feeding mechanism. Also used to activate limit switches and various protective devices, this cam makes use of spring return.

the vertical tooling plate of the four-slide to eject the finished ring. (A common alternate arrangement is to provide stripping rods to advance out of the tooling plate to eject the part.) The centerform then advances out of the tooling plate again while the next section of strip material is being fed in, at which point the next forming cycle begins.

Standard cams are provided by the four-slide manufacturer for controlling the motion of the four major forming tools (top, left side, right side and bottom), as well as for the centerform, stock clamp (which operates through the top tool to hold the strip on the top of the centerform), rear motion cutoff and stripper rods. A variety of strokes is available for each of these tools—at least up to the physical capacity of the machine

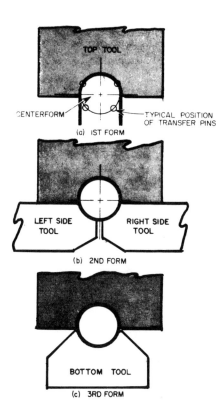

3. BOX CAM—the heavy duty device needed to actuate the forming slides and retract the centerform. This is the most important of the four-slide cams.

—to best match the needs of the part. Similarly, numerous dwell times (expressed in degrees) in the positions of both maximum advance and maximum retract are available for selection to best match the forming sequence. The advance dwell and retract dwell on a cam may vary from zero to nearly 300 degrees.

Planning of the forming cycle is limited by the fact that there are only 360 degrees available in the machine cycle for completing all forming operations. Since tool interference can occur in many parts of the cycle, the engineer is concerned both with the total angle of tool motion (proportion of the machine cycle

consumed) and the segments of the machine cycle in which various tools are moving.

Types of Cam Motions

Once a cam (such as the box cam) has been selected, design of its contour determines the nature of its motion during its period of activity in the machine cycle. The nature of cam motion has an important effect on the degree of impact shock, effective tool life, and dimensional control of the part.

The most widely used general-purpose type of cam motion for standard box cams on four-slide machines is the simple harmonic. As shown in *Figure* 5a, the displacement of the simple harmonic cam increases and decreases sinusoidally throughout the angle of cam rise and fall. In *Figure* 5b, the curve of tool velocity vs. angle of cam rise for the simple harmonic cam shows that its peak velocity is in the center of the rise, with a gradual reduction to zero at

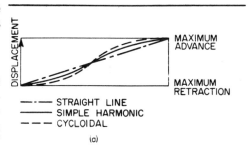
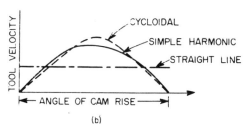

5. THREE TYPES of cam action—cycloidal, simple harmonic, and straight line. The simple harmonic is the most widely used in four-slide applications.

the beginning and end of the tool motion. With harmonic motion on the cam fall, too, there are smooth increases and decreases in tool velocity as the tool reaches maximum advance and maximum retract.

The cycloidal cam motion offers even lower velocities at the beginning and end of the angles of cam rise and fall than simple harmonic motion. Because of this advantage, cycloidal motion is frequently used for extremely high machine cycle rates to reduce noise level and shock at the beginning and end of the stroke. However, as often happens, this advantage is attained with the accompanying disadvantage of higher tool velocity in the middle of the cam rise (*Figure* 5). If work is being performed by the cam in the center of the rise, the cycloidal cam therefore may be expected to cause greater shock to the tools and metal being formed. However, if tools with large strokes are used to make relatively small parts, the contact of tool and part may occur near the top of the advance, where velocity is low.

As an example, the cycloidal cam is used on a vertical four-slide to control the rear-motion cutoff. This tool moves out from the tooling plate and, at maximum advance, serves as a die for cutting off the material via a vertical cutoff mounted on the top tool. Since no forming is done in the middle of the

4. FORMING SEQUENCE for tubular part. Forming is completed by the top and side tools. Precise dimensional control is obtained from bottom tool.

cycle, there is great advantage in minimizing the shock as the rear motion cutoff die stops suddenly at the end of its advance.

The straight line cam, whose contour is linear throughout the length of the stroke, provides constant tool velocity. Moreover, its velocity is low —lower than either the simple harmonic motion or the cycloidal motion through most of the cam rise angle. But it is a high-shock cam, because the acceleration from zero to the full tool velocity at the beginning of the cycle, and deceleration from full velocity to zero at the end are extremely high. If straight line cam motions are used at high production speeds, the operating life of the cam roll and pins is usually relatively short. A box cam will deteriorate very fast at the point of impact at the start of the rise and on the outside of the track. With a spring return on a plate cam, the cam roll will bounce away from the cam face when it is run even at low speeds, resulting in erratic tool action.

A straight line cam can be modified with small radii at both ends of the stroke to smooth out the rapid changes of velocity. Because they are easy to make, the straight line or modified straight line cams are widely used where machine manu-facturers or job shops do not have facilities to produce properly engineered cams. In general, successful application of straight-line cams requires substantially slower speeds.

Cam Pressure Angles

Avoiding abrupt changes in velocity by selecting a simple harmonic cam does not in itself guarantee that tool velocity will not be excessive. The velocity at the center of the angle of cam rise (*Figure 5b*) can be high enough to cause early tool failure and poor dimensional control of the part, despite smooth transitions at the ends of the rise or fall. Therefore, the tool engineer must be concerned with still another characteristic of cams—pressure angles.

Cam pressure angle (α), as shown in the schematic harmonic cam in *Figure 6a*, is defined as the angle between the line of motion of the cam roll (and slide) and a normal to the cam surface at the point of contact. Without offset, the line of motion is through the cam roll center (O_R) and cam center (O_C) and the pressure angle is α_1. By offsetting the line of motion through the offset angle (γ) towards the normal, the pressure angle on the rise portion of the cam is reduced to α_2, which is equal to $\alpha_1 - \gamma$. (Note that α is increased to α_2, which equals $\alpha_1 + \gamma$, on the fall portion of the cam.) When offset is used to decrease the pressure angle on the rise portion of the cam, it simultaneously causes an increase in pressure angle on the fall portion of the cam. This should be considered to avoid difficulty when rotating a cam opposite to its normal direction during setup. For the sake of clarity, it will be assumed in the remainder of this article that there is no offset angle.

If the pressure angle (α) is large enough and the force exerted by the cam roll on the cam contour is high enough, side loading on in-line motions for forming slides (as in *Figure 6*) may jam the tool slide in its ways. On pivot motions, on the other hand, any jamming will occur in the pivot itself. Serious problems of excessive tool velocity can be encountered at far lower pressure angles; therefore, the fact that a four-slide cam may not lock doesn't mean that it has been properly designed.

The schematic cam in *Figure 6a* is a standard harmonic cam designed for operating the left and right side tools on a V-82 Verti-Slide machine. This cam has a stroke h equal to 2¼ inches and equal cam rise and fall angles β of 75 degrees. The out-dwell at maximum advance is 5 degrees, while the in-dwell of 205 degrees occupies the rest of the cam.

The complete rise and fall of the single-lobe harmonic cam in *Figure 6a* has been plotted as tool displacement vs. cam angle in *Figure 6b*. Here, it can be seen that the pressure angle is largest ($\alpha_{max} = 38$ degrees) midway in the rise and fall cam angles, dropping to zero at the out and in dwells. Therefore, the maximum pressure angle itself is a critical characteristic in four-slide cam selection.

The three simple harmonic cam curves in *Figure 7* show how maximum pressure angle (α_{max}) is affected by the angle of cam rise (β). The dimension R_p (distance from cam center to cam roll at mid-stroke) equalling 3⅛ inches, and h (length of stroke) equalling 2¼ inches are constant for all three cams. The cam rise angle has been increased to $\beta = 175$ degrees in *Figure 7b*, so that α_{max} has been reduced to 20 degrees. In *Figure 7c*, the cam rise angle has been reduced to $\beta = 65$ degrees, so that α_{max} is now 45 degrees. If the forming motions for a particular part are simple, and plenty of forming

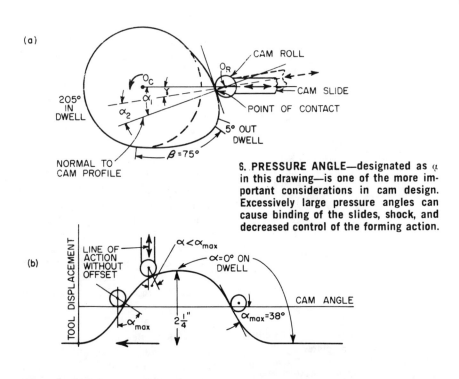

(a)

205° IN DWELL

O_C

α_1

α_2

O_R

CAM ROLL

CAM SLIDE

POINT OF CONTACT

5° OUT DWELL

$\beta = 75°$

NORMAL TO CAM PROFILE

6. PRESSURE ANGLE—designated as α in this drawing—is one of the more important considerations in cam design. Excessively large pressure angles can cause binding of the slides, shock, and decreased control of the forming action.

(b)

TOOL DISPLACEMENT

LINE OF ACTION WITHOUT OFFSET

$\alpha < \alpha_{max}$

$\alpha = 0°$ ON DWELL

α_{max}

2¼"

CAM ANGLE

$\alpha_{max} = 38°$

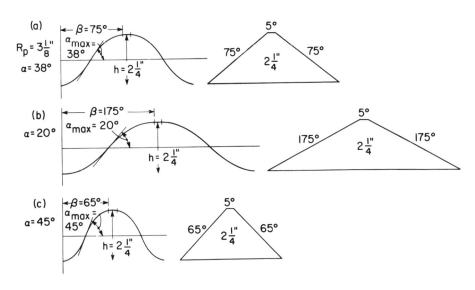

7. PRESSURE ANGLE is a function of β, the angle of cam rise. The top and middle curves are acceptable—the third may cause locking. However, the third, with its alpha max of 45 degrees, may be necessary in complex forming.

time is available in the machine cycle, it is preferable to specify a cam with the lowest available α_{max}. Thus, even though $\alpha_{max} = 38$ degrees in *Figure 7a* is acceptable, $\alpha_{max} = 20$ degrees offers reduced shock and improved part control at the same machine cycle rate. Perhaps more important, the machine cycle rate may then be substantially increased for a higher four-slide yield.

While $\alpha_{max} = 45$ degrees in *Figure 7c* is liable to cause locking, shrinking the cam rise angle in this manner may be attempted in order to minimize the space needed for the side tool advance and retract in the forming cycle; this might be necessary in forming complex strip parts, but in any case would require a relatively low machine cycle rate. It is also probable that such a cam would

be special, in that standard cams are designed with maximum pressure angles that provide acceptable operation within the four-slide's normal range of machine cycle rates. At the right of each harmonic cam in *Figure 7*, the schematic form of representing the cams on cam charts is given. Angle of cam rise is given by

$$\beta = \frac{180\ fh}{\pi R_P}\ \text{degrees}$$

where f is cam factor, (which depends on the maximum cam pressure angle for the particular type of cam), h equals length of stroke, and R_P equals distance from cam center to minimum cam radius in inches. The cam factor, which is $f = 1.6\cot \alpha_{max}$ for simple harmonic cams, is plotted in *Figure 8* for maximum pressure angles from 20 degrees to 45 degrees.

Effective dimensional control of parts depends only on the tool velocity during the time that the forming tools are in contact with the strip metal; therefore it is often important to observe the point in the forming cycle at which the tools first strike the part. Assume, for example, that the standard harmonic cam previously described is being used for the left and right side tools in forming the tubular part drawn in *Figure 9*. The sketches A, B and C in *Figure 9b* show three different points in the forming sequence (also described in *Figure 4*). These points are also labeled in the harmonic cam diagram in *Figure 9a*.

In Sketch A, the side tools are at full retraction in out-dwell, while the top tool has just begun advancing down as the four-slide has almost completed feeding the strip in from the press section at left. In Sketch B, the top tool has formed the strip around the top of the centerform and, allowing clearance for the ends of the strip to move down, the side tools have started their advance toward the centerform. The tool velocity diagram shows that at point *B* the tools are moving relatively slowly. The instant of contact of the side tools with the strip is shown in Sketch C; as illustrated in *Figure 4*, the side tools then continue in to form the strip around the bottom of the centerform.

It is clear in the velocity diagram that the speed of the side tools is quite high (very near maximum) at the time they first contact the part at point *B*, as often happens in four-

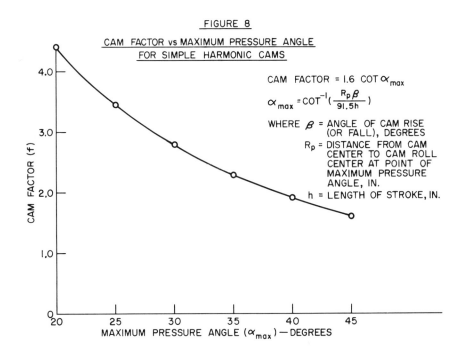

FIGURE 8

CAM FACTOR vs MAXIMUM PRESSURE ANGLE
FOR SIMPLE HARMONIC CAMS

CAM FACTOR = $1.6\ \text{COT}\ \alpha_{max}$

$\alpha_{max} = \text{COT}^{-1}(\frac{R_p\beta}{91.5h})$

WHERE β = ANGLE OF CAM RISE (OR FALL), DEGREES
R_p = DISTANCE FROM CAM CENTER TO CAM ROLL CENTER AT POINT OF MAXIMUM PRESSURE ANGLE, IN.
h = LENGTH OF STROKE, IN.

slide forming. If a special cam with $\alpha_{max} = 45$ degrees were substituted for the standard cam, it is apparent that the speed at the moment of contact would be much higher and probably unacceptable, resulting possibly in distortion of the strip at the two points of contact. With a lower pressure angle, on the other hand, the speed would be reduced, although it was near the maximum.

If the standard cams were used to form a tubular part with a smaller diameter (say, 1 inch instead of 1½ inch), the side tools would not contact the part until later in the rise angle, perhaps at point D in *Figure* 9. The tool velocities for all pressure angles are lower at point D, so that even the high pressure angle cam may be acceptable now, since there is no contact with the part at the

peak tool velocity. Therefore, long-stroke tools are often used in forming small parts in order to begin contact late in the cam rise angle.

While in theory it would be beneficial to operate at point D on a special cam with $\alpha_{max} = 20$ degrees in *Figure* 9, there is no strong reason to do so if the standard cam ($\alpha_{max} = 38$ degrees) performs successfully at the same constant machine cycle rate. There is a very strong reason to do so, however, if the reduction in maximum pressure angle permits the tool engineer to increase the machine cycle rate significantly with the same (or even lower) tool velocities. This actually occurred in practice in producing the banding strip clip in *Figure* 10. With standard side cams ($\alpha_{max} = 38$ degrees), the machine cycle rate had to be limited to

10. STRIP CLIP produced in a four-slide operation at 300 parts per minute.

175 parts/minute in order to maintain proper control of part dimensions. Special side cams with pressure angles of 21 degrees were therefore specified, and it was possible to run the machine at 300 parts per minute with the same degree of dimensional control. At 300 parts per minute with the standard size cams, the tool velocities would have been excessively high. Since this was a high-volume part, the substantially increased production rate provided an excellent return on investment in the special side tools.

Preparing a Cam Chart

The selection of four-slide forming cams and timing of the cam motions in the machine cycle are most conveniently done together on a cam chart. As shown in *Figure* 11, a cam chart is simply the record of the relative timing of the cam motions in the 360 degree machine cycle, with major cam characteristics labeled for convenient reference. Once such a chart has been prepared for a particular part, the four-slide machine can be set up again with correct tooling whenever the part is to be run again. If the cams are part of a standard cam library, as the stock clamp cam and rear-motion transfer cam are in *Figure* 11, the cams can be used in the meantime to make entirely different parts.

The cam chart in *Figure* 11 was used to make the banding strip clip in *Figure* 10 on, in this case, a Verti-Slide V-81 four-slide machine. In addition to forming the part from 0.030 x 1 inch strip material, the machine cycle was planned so that the parts would be transferred off the centerform to a specially designed stacking unit in which the clips interlock together for later insertion into automatic equipment. The press in the four-slide machine was used to stamp an emblem on the top sur-

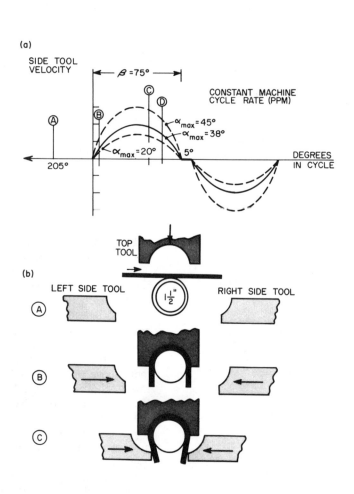

9. THREE POINTS in the forming sequence discussed in Figure 4 and their corresponding points in the harmonic cam diagram shown at the top.

face of the clip (*Figure* 10) and then to supply the driving force for the stacking unit.

When the feed stroke of the four-slide has been completed, the strip comes to rest on top of the center-form and the stock clamp descends to hold the strip down firmly against the centerform. The top tool then moves downward, acting as a cutoff and also making the initial form. The stock clamp and the top tool dwell in the maximum advance position as both side tools move in to complete the forming of the inter-lock against the bottom tool and centerform. All tools retract after which the completed clip is trans-ferred forward into the stacking unit by stripper rods advancing out of the vertical tooling plate.

Preparation of the cam charts for producing the banding strip clamp proceeds roughly as follows:

Cam Pressure Angle. Since the stand-ard cams ($\alpha_{max} = 33$ degrees, includ-ing a 5-degree roll offset) would not permit a speed above approximately 175 parts per minute, it was decided to reduce the α_{max} to 16 degrees (in-cluding a roller offset of 5 degrees). As it turned out, it was then possi-ble to run the parts successfully at the high speed of 300 parts per min-ute. Since the length of stroke (h) on all forming tools for this part is quite small, it was not necessary to go to extremely large angles of cam rise (β) in order to obtain the small cam pressure angle. (See equation for α_{max} in *Figure* 8.)

A rather large value of R_p was also selected for all forming cams in order to help reduce the pressure angle. Therefore, the required stroke for each forming tool was deter-mined on the basis of the part di-mensions; since h equals ½ inch for all forming cams, the calculated an-gles of cam rise and fall (assumed equal for any given cam) are all equal to 30. Much of the rest of the cam chart preparation is then con-cerned with the relative timing of the cam motions and dwell lengths.

Stock Clamp Cam. Since the stock is moving during the feed cycle from zero to 180 degrees, it was decided to have the stock clamp contact the part at 190 degrees—10 degrees after the material stopped on the top of the centerform. The angle of the in-dwell had to be such that the stock clamp held the strip throughout all the forming processes and retracted just before the stripper pins begin moving the part out on the center-form. Since the stock clamp cam is to be a standard cam, the final se-lection is held until the transfer cam has been decided.

Top Cam. The top cam is arbitrarily planned to begin its advance at the point that the stock clamp cam con-tacts the strip material. It must begin to retract a safe angle before the transfer cam starts the stripper rods advancing.

Bottom Cam. This cam is timed to reach its maximum advance, where it acts as a forming arbor after the stock clamp has contacted the mate-rial and just before the top tool reaches the material.

Side Cams. As long as the bottom tool is in position, the side tools can reach the material at almost any point. Very little in-dwell is needed.

Transfer Cam. A standard transfer cam with an intermediate dwell is selected to reduce inertia as the part is transferred out on the center-form. Since the rise, dwell and fall of the transfer cam occupy a rela-tively large total angle of 245 de-grees, motion of the transfer cam is begun at 310 degrees so that the stripper rods will be fully withdrawn a safe margin (25 degrees) before the top cam reaches the material at 220 degrees.

Since the transfer cam begins moving the stripper rods at 310 de-grees, the stockclamp cam is timed to be fully retracted at 310 degrees, making its total in-dwell 110 degrees. The in-dwell angles of the top, bot-tom, and side cams are then ar-ranged so that these tools are out of the way by the time the stripper rods begin advancing.

With the schematic cams drawn in on the cam chart in *Figure* 11, plan-ning of the forming cycle has been completed. The tool engineer has all the information needed for selecting standard four-slide cams and specify-ing or making special simple har-monic cams to make this part.

Making one's own four-slide cams is economical, particularly if a large number of parts are being made on four-slides. All the economies are lost, however, if poor cam manufac-ture results in short tool life and in-adequate quality control. The combi-nation of standard cams provided by the manufacturer and specially made cams, which may also be use-ful in making other parts, can grad-ually grow into a cam library that of-fers immense flexibility in planning production of four-slide parts. ◄

11. CAM CHART developed to record cam operations involved in running the strip clip job. This chart is used as a setup guide whenever part is run.

Reprinted from Manufacturing Engineering & Management (Manufacturing Engineering), May 1970

Cams for Four-Slides: Part 2

In selecting cams for four-slide operations, an engineer can draw from his library, buy standard models—or make new specials. This article provides information on the third option

ROBERT E. CARLSON

Torin Corporation

FOUR-SLIDE MACHINES are among the most productive and versatile machine tools available for the forming of metal. However, their productivity depends largely on the design and manufacture of the cams that control their forming tools movements. Without proper design and manufacture, the machine performs poorly and is subject to permanent structural damage. Additionally, the parts produced tend to run out-of-tolerance, and tool breakage becomes excessive. All of which is unnecessary, since the designing and fabricating of the right cam for the job at hand is a comparatively simple task.

Manufacture of four-slide cams begins when an engineer works out the tooling sequence required, a task described in the first article in this series. If part design and production requirements permit, the engineer need not develop new cams—he need only specify standard units maintained in his cam library. If his company has been operating one or more four-slides for some time and its cams have been wisely selected, it is likely that the library contains an assortment of cams that adequately fits the needs of his company.

In some instances the engineer may find that a standard cam not in his library will do the job. In such cases he can often obtain one directly from a four-slide manufacturer who maintains an adequate inventory. Buying a standard cam has the advantages of faster delivery and lower cost than are possible when specially made cams are specified. But on the other hand, a complete set of special cams may be necessary, either to make the part in the first place or to obtain a production advantage such as higher output or longer tool life. Normally, however, a part can be produced with several standard cams and perhaps one or two specials.

Standard or special cams

The choice of standard or special cams can be demonstrated with regard to production of the banding strip clip shown in *Figure* 1. This part, first introduced in Part 1 of this series on cam design, re-

quires the tooling arrangement shown in *Figure* 2. The cam chart developed for this part is shown in *Figure* 3.

The pressure angle α_{max} (equal to 33 degrees including a 5-degree roll offset) in the available cams does not permit a speed above approximately 175 parts per minute. Therefore, special cams were specified for the top tool, bottom tool, and side tools, the objective being to obtain a lower pressure angle and consequently a higher production rate. It was still possible to use standard cams for the stock clamp and standard part transfer rods (extending out of the vertical machine bed parallel to the centerform) because the actions of these tools do not

involve part forming, and a higher pressure angle would be unlikely to cause excessive shock to either the part or the machine. The logic involved in determining the cam characteristics required to reduce the pressure angle adequately is somewhat as follows.

MAXIMUM PRESSURE ANGLE. The machine used to produce the banding strip is a V81 Verti-Slide four-slide machine in which the maximum standard stroke h equals 1½ inches, and the maximum pitch radius R from the cam center to the cam roll center at the maximum pressure angle R_p—at midpoint of the stroke—equals 3⅛ inches. In an available cycloi-

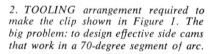

1. *WORKPIECE discussed in this article on four-slide tooling. This component is a banding strip clip, introduced in the first article in this series.*

2. *TOOLING arrangement required to make the clip shown in Figure 1. The big problem: to design effective side cams that work in a 70-degree segment of arc.*

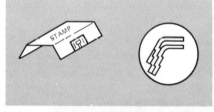

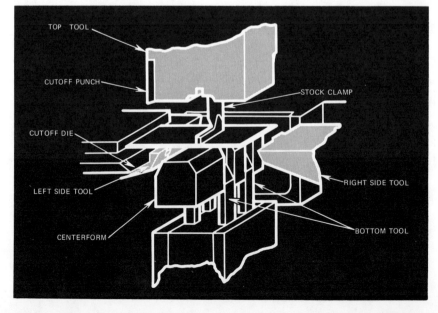

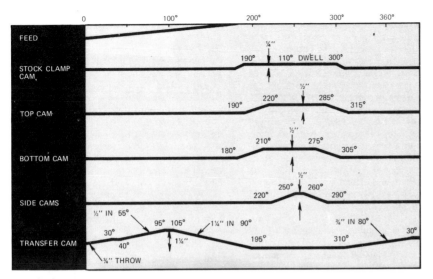

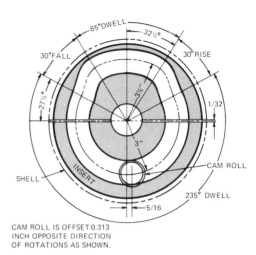

3. CHART developed for design of the cams in the strip clip problem. Basically, this chart is designed to show what the complete set of four-slide cams will look like.

4. SHELL CAM consists of an outer shell and four inserts bolted to shell.

dal cam designed for the side tools on this machine h equals $1\frac{1}{2}$ inches, R_p equals $3\frac{1}{8}$ inches (both are as large as possible) and angle of cam rise β equals 75 degrees. The maximum pressure angle α_{max} equals 33 degrees, including a 5-degree cam roll offset. That the pressure angle is relatively large is partially due to the fact that the available cam is cycloidal and thus steeper than an equivalent simple harmonic cam. Therefore, the first decision the engineer makes is to change to a simple harmonic cam. Review of the formula for maximum pressure angle of such a cam then indicates the alternatives in further reducing its magnitude:

$$\alpha_{max} = \cot^{-1} R_p \, \beta / 91.5 \, h$$

SIDE TOOL CAMS. Since the maximum pressure angle increases as the angle of cam rise (β) decreases, another problem arises—the fact that it will be necessary to reduce the angle of rise in the special side tool cams. As *Figure* 3 shows, the standard stock clamp and transfer cam selected do not allow a total of more than approximately 115 degrees of rise, fall, and forward dwell for the top, bottom, and side cams. In particular, there is only about 70 degrees total available for the side cams. Therefore, taking β at 30 degrees for both the rise and fall (which are usually made equal) of the side, top and bottom cams, the maximum pressure angle calculated in the preceding formula for a simple harmonic cam is 51 degrees, which is much too large.

ALL THREE CAMS. In reviewing the forming sequence, however, the engineer notes that the full standard stroke ($h = 1\frac{1}{2}$ inches) is not necessary, and that a stroke of h equal to $\frac{1}{2}$ inch would be more than adequate for all three cams. Secondly, R_p can be increased slightly from $3\frac{1}{8}$ to $3\frac{3}{8}$ inches. Therefore, with h equal to $\frac{1}{2}$ inch and β equal to 30 degrees, the

maximum pressure angle is equal to 24 degrees. The mathematics involved are as follow:

$$\alpha_{max} = \cot^{-1} (3.375)(30)/(91.5)(0.5)$$
$$= 24 \text{ degrees}$$

Allowing for a 5-degree cam roll offset, α_{max} becomes 19 degrees. This change has reduced the effective maximum pressure angle from 33 degrees to 19—the largest possible reduction within dimensional limitations. All three cams were then specified with R_p equal to $3\frac{3}{8}$ inches, β equal to 30 degrees, and h equal to $\frac{1}{2}$ inch.

The type of cam selected depends on its service in the four-slide, although all normally have simple harmonic shapes. For example, while the transfer cam for the banding strip clip is usually a standard box type, the side cams will probably be specified as heavy duty box cams because of the high forces involved in forming this part.

Making the cam

Once the cam characteristics have been determined—with the help of the cam-timing chart—it's necessary to generate the dimensional data needed to control the machine that makes the cam template. The traditional method is layout by coordinates. While the physical shape of the cam may be drawn for reference, all that is really needed is a table that gives the coordinates of the cam contour around the cam blank in the rise and fall sectors, all of which can be taken from a standard cam manual. Common procedure is to tabulate the coordinates at 1 degree intervals, although $\frac{1}{2}$-degree intervals are recommended on steep portions of a cam.

A toolmaker fabricates a cam template from a cam blank, using an indexing table or dividing head. This involves

moving a cutter a specified distance—usually a few thousandths of an inch—for each unit of rotation. At the completion of machining, the template is filed manually for removal of the cusps, after which the template is ready for use on a cam miller.

At Torin, the cam track is milled to a width 0.030 inch smaller than the cam-roll diameter. If the cams are steel, they are subsequently hardened and tempered. If they are ductile iron, their tracks are flame-hardened to a depth of approximately $\frac{1}{16}$ inch. Final operation is grinding on the cam miller, now equipped with a grinding attachment in place of the end mill used to machine the track. Both contours are ground to a total clearance of 0.002 to 0.003 inch greater than the cam roll diameter. It is good practice to use a grinding wheel with a diameter as close as possible to that of the cam roll. Doing so ensures proper bearing of the cam roll on the cam contour, particularly in the rise and fall sectors. It should be noted that since the cam roll is part of the machine, it is always the same for a particular four-slide.

Because the quantity of cams made at Torin is relatively large, cam blanks with tapped mounting holes are maintained in stock. The blanks for heavy duty box cams that activate the forming slides and retract the centerforms, for example, are $1\frac{1}{8}$ inches thick and $9\frac{1}{4}$ inches in diameter. The maximum cam radius from center to contour surface should be the same wherever possible for all cams used on a machine of given size.

The final step in fabrication is to split the cam so that the edges of the split are in idle segments, preferably in the retract dwell range, so that the cam follower does not cross the split while a forming tool is in contact with the work. If the cam must be split in a forward dwell segment, the split should be located where

249

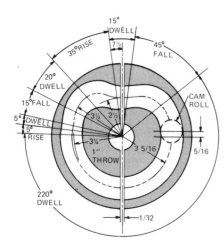

5. SOLID CAM, unlike the shell type, is machined from a solid piece of steel.

the least amount of work is being performed. Otherwise, serious damage may result from cyclic exciting forces developed at the split. If the split is located in a rise or fall segment of the cam, the roll is likely to hit the edge, producing undesirable vibration and reducing tool life.

Cams and the computer

Calculation of cam coordinates, a relatively simple task for single-lobe harmonic cams, is far more time-consuming

with cycloidal cams. Similarly, it can become quite complex in cams with more than one lobe, or more than one motion per lobe, and in instances in which the cam follower is mounted on a pivoted cam arm. Additionally, the formula for coordinates is more complex in the case of a pivoted cam arm. In these cases, a great deal of time can be saved by assigning the cam calculations to a computer, either at a central corporate computer installation or at a time-sharing terminal.

An alternate approach is to have the entire cam template made from original specifications by a firm specializing in cam manufacture. These firms—an example is Cam Technology Inc., Elmsford, N. Y.—generate the coordinates of extremely complex cams by computer, automatically punch all machine instructions on paper tape, and then machine the template on a numerically controlled mill. While the cost of a computer-produced cam is higher, it can be delivered faster, and its accuracy is better. For example, manual filing of the cusps in the example previously cited doesn't provide precise curvature between the points milled to tabular coordinates. In contrast to this, a computer program utilizes curvilinear interpolation to generate the N/C tape required for accurate smoothing of con-

6. BACK-CUTTING, the inevitable result of an attempt to mill a lobe having a radius of curvature smaller than that of the cutter. The result is excessive play.

tours. To obtain a computer-generated cam template, it is necessary only to provide information on the type of cam, pitch radius (R_p), the angle of cam rise and fall (β), and the stroke (h) given on the cam chart. If a duplicate of a particular cam is needed, of course, the machining instructions are already available on paper tape.

Some metalworking companies which have continuing requirements for new cams use special machines designed for mechanical reproduction of cams. Systems of gears and levers in these machines are arranged to create the desired motion mechanically and thus produce a finished cam directly, therefore eliminating the need for templates.

Shell cams and solid cams

Two types of box cam construction are commonly used on four-slide machines—the shell cam (*Figure 4*) and the solid cam (*Figure 5*). The shell cam, which in this case happens to have a simple harmonic contour with a 65-degree forward dwell, and rises and falls of 30 degrees each, consists of an outer shell and four contour inserts bolted to the shell. On the other hand, the solid cam in *Figure 5* has been machined in one piece. This particu-

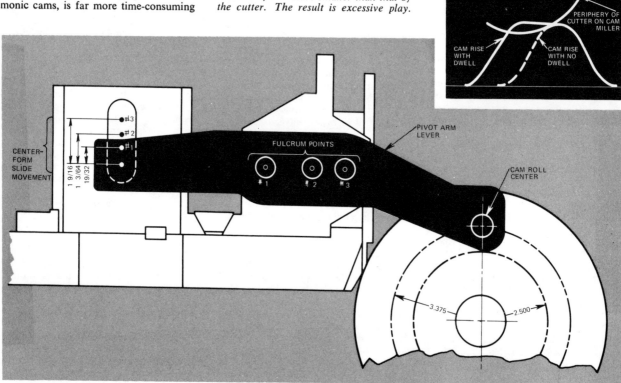

7. PIVOT ARM in a modern four-slide. To minimize the force transmitted through the arm, the fulcrum offering the shortest arm on the slide side should be specified.

lar cam rises to dwell for 20 degrees at 1-inch stroke, drops to ¾ inch to dwell for 5 degrees, and then rises again to dwell for 220 degrees at $1^{13}/_{16}$ inch before dropping for only 15 degrees to the dwell position in *Figure 5*.

A tool-steel contour of a shell cam is useful under relatively heavy loads when production requirements are high. They extend cam life and reduce the frequency of replacement. Additionally, it may be that the cam is being developed along with the forming tools (an unlikely event in the case of a simple harmonic cam), in which case it is more convenient to make contour changes in the toolroom rather than go back to the cam miller. Convenient replacement of the cam may also be helpful when producing a family of four-slide parts, where perhaps only one or two inserts need be replaced for part changeover.

Shell cams have drawbacks too, mainly because the inserts are replaceable. If the inserts are improperly aligned in the shell, damage can occur at the rolls, pins, slides, slide bases and forming tools. Even slight misalignment of an insert can result in wide dimensional variations in the part, particularly if the machine is running at high speed. Even if the first set of cam inserts is correctly made and aligned, machined replacement inserts tapped and bolted in place separately may not precisely duplicate the original cam contour. As a result, there may be variable play (either too much or too little) between the cam roll and cam track.

On the other hand, a solid cam is used until it is worn to the point where dimensional control of part size is lost. At this point the cam is replaced by an exact duplicate made from the same template. Thus, while solid cams have less flexibility, they offer minimal possibility of uncontrolled variation.

In general, tool-steel shell cams last about three times as long as ductile iron solid cams, but they also cost about three

times as much, whether made by the user or purchased from a four-slide manufacturer. Assuming that cam inserts are properly made and bolted into the shell, the principal question for the user to decide is whether the extra flexibility and extended life of shell cams are worth the additional investment. It is likely that any particular metalworking firm might use both shell and solid cams, depending on the parts it produces. In Torin's experience, over three-quarters of either wire or strip parts on four-slides can be made at lower cost with solid cams.

Back-cutting

A sharp peak on the convex contour of a box cam (a sharp peak can be defined as a lobe having a radius of curvature' smaller than the radius of the cutter or cam roll) will be milled off by the cutter by back-cutting, *Figure 6*. The result is excessive play between the cam roll and track at that point. Even if the sharp peak could be properly cut, as in using a cutter much smaller than the cam roll, the convex cam contour (*Figure 6*) could not make the path of the cam-roll center precisely follow a radius of curvature smaller than that of the cam roll. Both these possible conditions can be eliminated by providing for at least a 5-degree dwell at the end of each cam rise or fall on the inner contour. This is also necessary on the fall because a concave contour on one cam surface is a convex contour on the other.

Locking on barrel cams

In a barrel cam in which both the track and roll have flat sides, it is possible that the roll may lock on a rise or fall where there is sufficient force through a swinging pivot arm perpendicular to the sides of the cam track. One possible solution is to make the sides of the cam convex so that there is only point contact rather than

surface-to-surface contact between the roll and track. The one drawback to this solution is that force is concentrated at a single point between the cam roll and cam track instead of being broadly distributed over a line contact. As a result, the mechanical linkage system may be exposed to excessive strain.

Another solution is a cam-miller attachment which provides that the cutter operate from a fulcrum point equivalent to that of the pivot arm of the cam follower of the four-slide. Thrust of the cam roll will then always be parallel to the flat surfaces of the track.

Multiple fulcrum points

When the motion of a cam roll is transmitted to a tool slide through a pivot arm (rather than along a straight line), the design of the four-slide machine may permit the choice of two or more fulcrum points. In *Figure 7*, for example, the pivot arm fulcrum permits the use of any of three fulcrum points between the cam roll at right and the centerform slide at left. For a stroke of ⅞ inch of the cam roll in the box cam at right, the slide arm at left may move $1^{9}/_{32}$, $1^{3}/_{64}$, and $1^{9}/_{16}$ inches.

To minimize the force transmitted through the pivot arms to the cam roll, the fulcrum offering the shortest possible arm on the slide side should be specified. Therefore, whenever possible, the fulcrum point to use is the one for which the slide stroke needed is closest to the maximum stroke available. Specifically, if h equals ¾ inch, Fulcrum 1 should be used rather than Fulcrum 2. If h equals 1 inch, Fulcrum 2 should be used rather than 3. With this approach, unfortunately, the cam stroke h—and therefore the maximum pressure angle (α_{max})—are both larger for a given angle of cam rise (β) and pitch radius (R_p). However, a shorter arm on the slide-tool side is relatively more effective in minimizing the reaction force at the cam roll. ◄

Comments on Four-Slide Tooling

by George Dibble
Vice President, Manufacturing
Small Parts, Inc.

WHEN TO USE THE FOUR-SLIDE

Ten Reasons to Use a Four-Slide Over a Press

· When part would require more than one operation to complete.

· When extra slides are needed in the die to make form.

· When thin material is used that would need to be pulled through a punch press.

· When angle forms are needed over or under 90 angles.

· When close tolerance is needed on angular forms.

· When adjustment is needed for material thickness and hardness variation.

· When finished part on punch press die is hard to eject.

· When the part requires a carrying strip to progress it through the die.

· When burr direction is needed on inside or outside of form.

· When the part has small hole or no holes that could be used for pilots.

Increasing competition and a shortage of skilled labor have combined to put pressure on tool and die makers, tool designers, and plant engineers to produce parts faster and cheaper and, at the same time, save on material.

That is why the ever increasing demand for stamping work is being done on four-slide machines. The objective being to increase production and decrease cost.

Four-slides are not new to industry. Their use dates back before the turn of the century. Early designs of the four-slide machine featured four tool holding slides -- each at right angles to the adjacent slides and move to and from a centrally held arbor (center former) by cams.

The first four-slides built were built out of a need for a machine to form wire parts. They were square and had no room for a press head.

Later, when strip became better rolled and slit to width, the four-slide machine was improved and coiled strip was cut and formed. At this time the four-slide machine became longer than it was wide. Two die heads could be added to the bed. Using the punch press concept, along with the four-slides, each year new ideas of creative tooling has opened up new prospects for the use of this machine.

After the press or die head was added on the front of the machine, there became a need to put the press or die head on the rear of the machine. This was the beginning of the symmetrical four-slide. On this type of machine, the burr can be put on the inside or outside of formed parts.

Practical knowledge on the production of parts formed from metal strip and a knowledge of the punch press is valuable in the use of the four-slide machine.

The designing of tools and the various techniques available, how to choose or adapt the tooling, which is most economical and efficient, and how to get the best out of such machines are the principles used for the four-slide profitability.

Basic operations on all four-slide models are the same. Because of the four-slide's versatility, the tool designer is able to develop simple tooling for forming parts whether they're made from strip or wire.

Design and development of the tool blocks is the key to success with a four-slide where tools can be laid out completely by the tool engineer. In most cases, the tool maker must make alterations to suit the forming characteristics of the metal.

Successful four-slide operation is dependent upon the cams that control the slide motions. That is why it is important that the blueprint be properly designed. When laying out tooling for a complicated part, it is necessary that a cam chart be drawn up showing the sequence of operation for the slides.

The many different approaches in four-slide tooling make it possible to select a simple one. In addition, the designer may employ the use of split slides to get a compound motion that is often helpful in forming some complex shapes.

Production can be doubled by running two strips at a time with no reduction in speed.

Final costs and delivery depends on the time it takes to design, make, and set up the tooling.

The modern stamping plant of today that has four-slides, can now accept jobs that formerly were turned away.

It is also advantageous to have both four-slides and punch presses. By possessing both types of machines, it gives more flexibility and allows the shop a greater variation in jobs than a shop limited to one type machine.

Achievement is the best word to describe the four-slide. Achievement occurs at all stages of development.

In the final analysis, the greatest limitation of the four-slide machine would be the lack of understanding of the various units.

It is understood by all that the best designed machine can not function efficiently without properly designed tooling.

The basic four-slide machine, when arranged for forming either wire or strip components is capable of being tooled to produce hundreds of different forms which are too numerous to illustrate.

It is because of the inherent possibilities of the machine that a warning must be given not to assume that all bent-up components made from wire or strip can be produced on a basic machine, even though the dimensions and tonnage of the part may be within a machine's rated capacity.

Each of the sketches which follow has been selected to try and give the reader a better understanding of the four-slide.

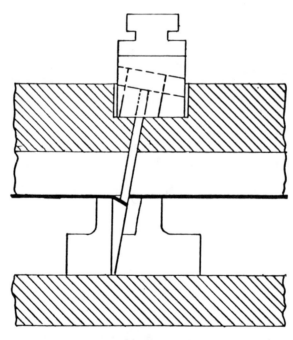

**Shaving With
Rear Auxiliary
Slide**

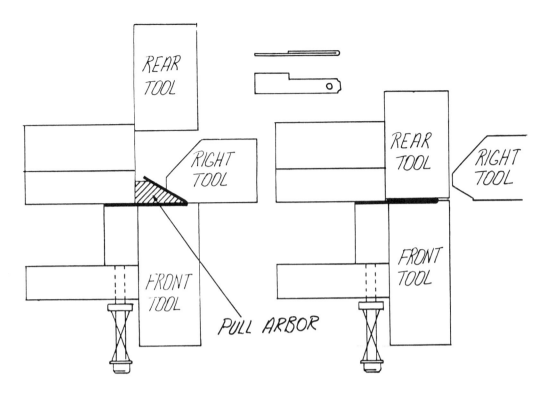

Over The End Die Forming

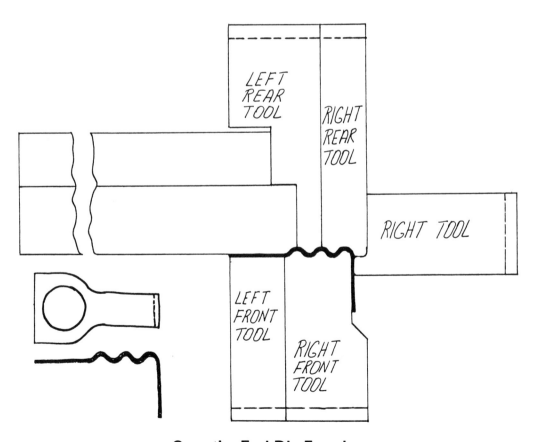

**Over the End Die Forming:
Split Front and Split Rear Slides**

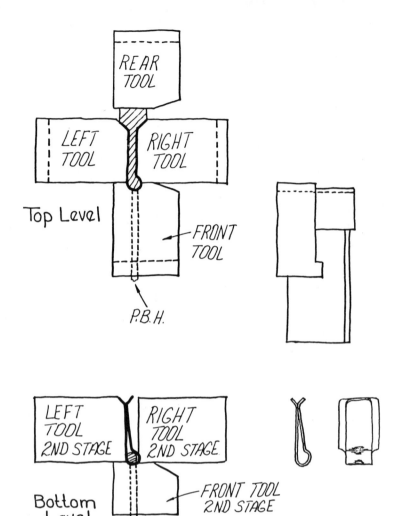

REAR
TOOL

LEFT
TOOL

RIGHT
TOOL

Top Level

FRONT
TOOL

P.B.H.

LEFT
TOOL
2ND STAGE

RIGHT
TOOL
2ND STAGE

Bottom
Level

FRONT TOOL
2ND STAGE

Two Stage Forming

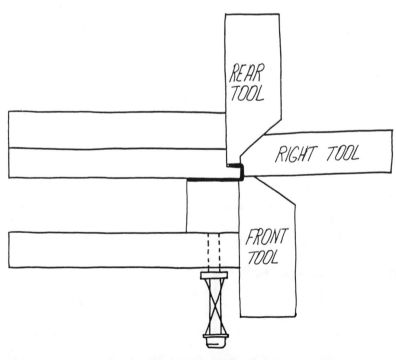

REAR
TOOL

RIGHT TOOL

FRONT
TOOL

**Over The End Die Forming
Three Tools**

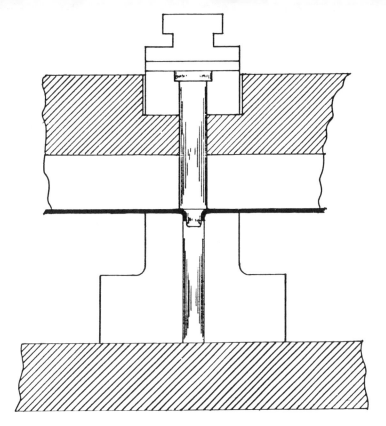

Extruding With Rear Auxiliary Slide

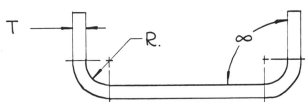

⅓ Stock Thickness	½ Stock Thickness
1.5708 x (R + T/3) ÷ 90° x ∞ = B.A.	1.5708 x (R + T/2) ÷ 90° x ∞ = B.A.
C.R. Steel	Spring Steel
Annealed Sp. Steel	Blue Temp. Sp. Steel
Brass, ¼ ¦ ½ Hard	All Stainless Steel
Copper, ¼ ¦ ½ Hard	Brass ¾ ¦ Full Hard
Berylco, ¼ Hard	Phos. Bronze
Nickel Silver, ¼ Hard	Berylco Sp. Temp.
	Berylco ½ ¦ Full Hard
	Nickel Silver ½ ¦ Full Hard
	¦ All Bends Over 180°

Bend Allowance Chart

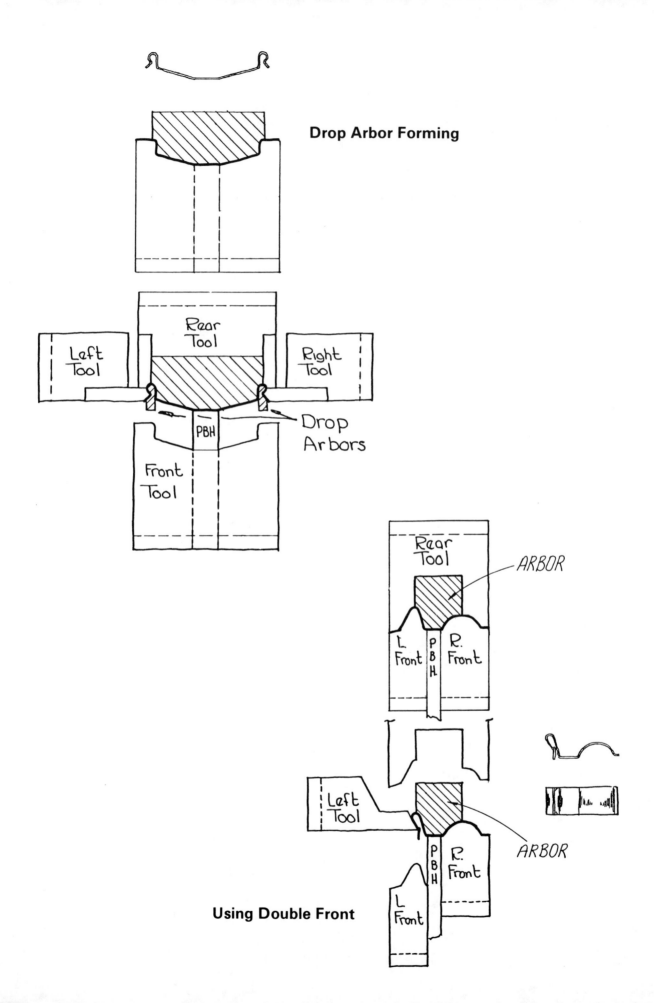

Drop Arbor Forming

Rear Tool

Left Tool

Right Tool

Drop Arbors

PBH

Front Tool

Rear Tool

ARBOR

L Front

P B H

R. Front

Left Tool

ARBOR

PBH

R. Front

L Front

Using Double Front

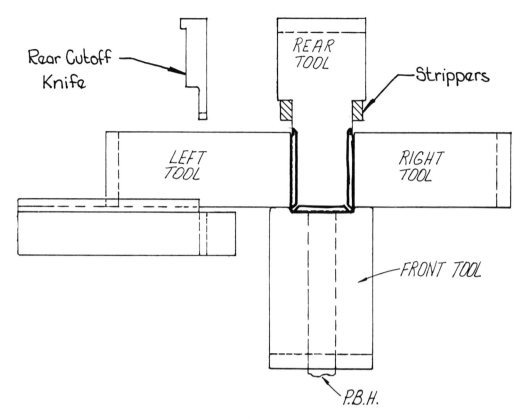

Rear Cutoff Knife

REAR TOOL

Strippers

LEFT TOOL

RIGHT TOOL

FRONT TOOL

P.B.H.

Forming Over Rear Tool

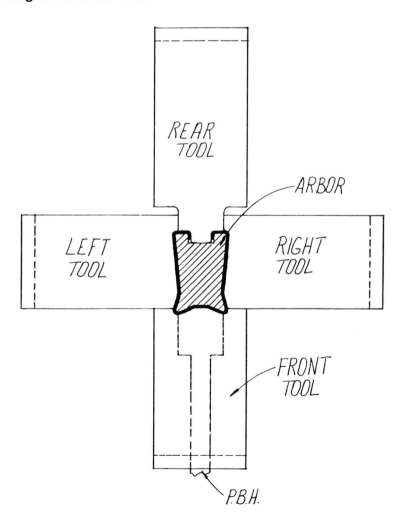

REAR TOOL

ARBOR

LEFT TOOL

RIGHT TOOL

FRONT TOOL

P.B.H.

Four Tool With Blank Holder

259

Reprinted with permission from Tooling & Production, December 1967

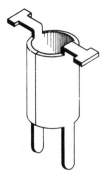

Figure 1
Small stamping will be made on multi-slide machine.

Design for multi-slide tooling

Basics of designing multi-slide tooling are explained step by step by developing a set of tools for a small stamped part.

by Richard Kreutter
Design Engineer
Seneca Metal Products, Inc.
Rochester, N. Y.

ALTHOUGH we have selected a relatively simple part to demonstrate our procedure of designing multi-slide tools, some very intricate parts may be stamped with the process. Here we have chosen to develop tooling to mass produce a small brass terminal post stamping **(Figure 1)**. The part, made from 0.030″ thick brass, is to have a diameter of 0.250″, a length of 0.500″, two mounting lugs, and two T-shaped connector lugs.

General design sequence

1) Determine bend allowances and make a dimensional drawing of the part in the flat **(Figure 2,** upper left**)**. This will give the size of brass strip and amount of advance or pitch of material required.
2) Make strip layout **(Figure 2)**.
3) Select size of multi-slide machine that will produce the part most efficiently.
4) Combine following steps:

a) Figure out cam timing.
b) Determine sequence of operations for notching, perforating and forming **(Figure 2)**.
c) Draw rough layout of complete set of tools.
5) Have rough designs checked and approved by supervisor, and make revisions or changes. Finally, draw details, including dimensions; and then forward completed drawings to toolroom.

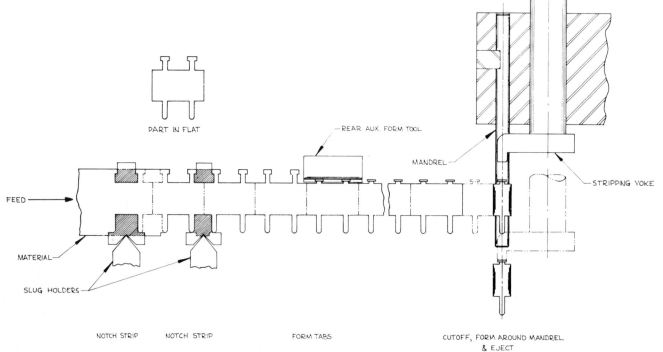

PART IN FLAT

REAR AUX. FORM TOOL

MANDREL

STRIPPING YOKE

FEED

MATERIAL

SLUG HOLDERS

NOTCH STRIP   NOTCH STRIP   FORM TABS   CUTOFF, FORM AROUND MANDREL & EJECT

Figure 2
Elevation view of the strip layout.

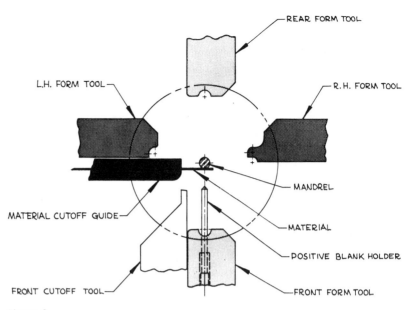

REAR FORM TOOL

L.H. FORM TOOL

R.H. FORM TOOL

MATERIAL CUTOFF GUIDE

MANDREL

MATERIAL

POSITIVE BLANK HOLDER

FRONT CUTOFF TOOL

FRONT FORM TOOL

Figure 3
Four major cam-driven forming tools are shown in retracted position. Material is in position for cutoff and forming.

Figure 4
A) The positive blank holder contracts the material while the right-hand forming tool is moved into position to support the mandrel. The part is separated from the strip by the front cutoff tool. B) Front forming tool puts initial 180° curl on part. C) Left-hand forming tool has moved across and against the right forming tool to put additional curl on the part. D) Rear forming tool is moved forward to add final curl and complete the part.

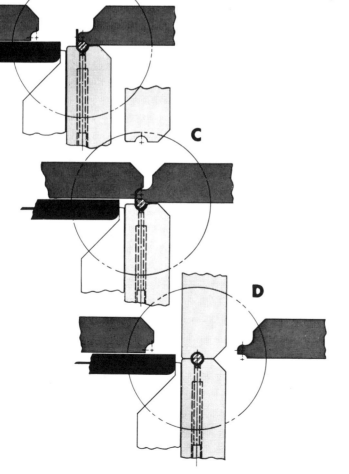

Actual procedure

From initial layout of the workpiece, it has been determined that its dimensions are 0.625″ wide by 0.500″ long. This calls for the use of strip brass 0.680″ wide, which is fed through the multi-slide machine in a vertical position from left to right. Because the material is worked from the upright position, it is necessary to incorporate slug holders in the notching dies. Thus the slugs are prevented from falling back into the tools at the notching stations **(Figure 2,** left center).

After notching, the two T-tabs are formed by a cam-driven rear auxiliary forming tool. At the final station the part is cut off from the strip and finish-formed around a mandrel. After being formed, it is stripped from the mandrel by a yoke that is mounted on the stripping head. **Figures 3 and 4** show the various steps in final forming of the part into its cylindrical shape. (For the sake of clarity, the T-tabs have not been shown on these five views.)

Figure 5
Author checks machine function during production run.

Since timing is of such vital importance to the successful operation of a multi-slide stamping, it is necessary to work out an accurate cam chart in the earliest stages of the planning. This will show the rise, dwell, and return of the cam for each tool. In actual operation all tools will be operating much closer together than shown in the illustrations. These drawings show the tools opened up for easier understanding of the sequence of operations.

As mentioned before, the part selected has been a relatively simple one. However, multi-slide stampings of much more intricate and complex parts are possible, with great advantages in accuracy, efficiency, volume production, and cost reduction. Such in-process operations as tapping, staking hopper-fed rivets to stampings, running screws into tapped holes, and many others are also possible.

Seneca Metal Products, Inc., has been building multi-slide dies and tools for many manufacturers for the past 12 years, and has just expanded its operations by the addition of two new U.S. Baird multi-slide machines (one shown in **Figure 5).** This additional equipment now permits high-volume production runs of parts by Seneca for smaller companies. They can thus benefit from cost savings possible through multi-slide stampings, if they don't have their own production machines. ■

Verti-Slide Engineering Development Report

Control Plate

The Problem:
To produce the control plate (Figure 1), complete with three tapped holes.
Stock size: 3-15/16″×.060″ strip
Material: cold-rolled steel

Figure 1

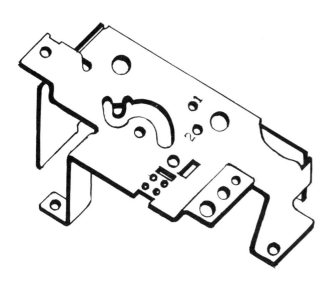

The Solution:
The control plate, which previously required several secondary operations to complete, is made on a V83 Verti-Slide machine. One bottom auxiliary press motion is used to preform the part in the press area. Three air-operated lead screw tapping heads are mounted between the press and forming areas to tap the three holes. In the forming area, a special three-lobe top cam and a long-dwell bottom cam control the forming motions.

The Press Tools:
Two 30-ton presses have a die length of about 42″. The press work is completed in six progressions:

First Progression/Blank and Trim

Figure 2

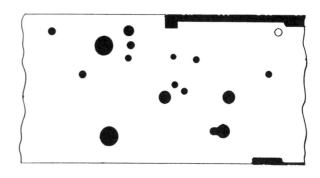

Fourteen round holes of various diameters and one key-shaped slot are pierced, and the edges of the strip partially trimmed.

Second Progression/Coin, Pierce, Trim and Pilot

Figure 3

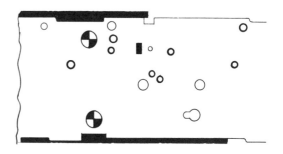

Eight holes are coined on both the top and bottom to eliminate burrs, one small rectangular slot is pierced, and trimming of the edges is completed.

Third Progression/Coin, Size, Blank and Pilot

Figure 4

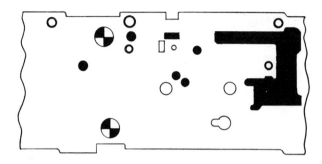

One additional hole is coined on both top and bottom, and five holes are sized. A small rectangular slot and a large irregularly shaped section are blanked.

Fourth Progression/Blank, Size, Coin and Pilot

Figure 5

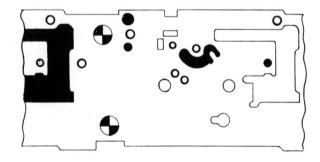

A semicircular shape is blanked, three holes are sized, and the small hole located near the rectangular slots is coined.

Fifth Progression/Blank, Size, Stamp, Emboss and Coin

Figure 6

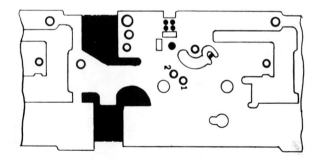

Two irregularly shaped sections are blanked, the last hole is sized, two numbers are stamped, four dimples are embossed, and a small V-shaped notch is coined.

Sixth Progression/Coin and Preform

Figure 7

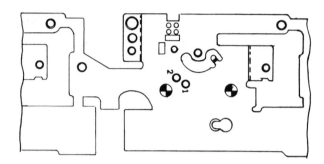

A circular shape is coined into one side of the key-shaped slot, and two sections (see edge view) are formed up, using the bottom auxiliary press motion. By preforming with the bottom auxiliary motion, the strip is fed through the press section and into the tapping position entirely at die level.

Seventh and Eighth Progressions/Tap

Figure 8

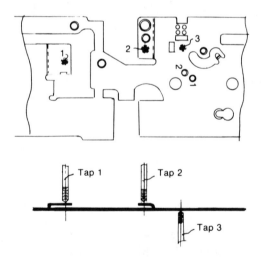

Three holes are tapped by three tapping heads, two mounted above and one mounted below the die level. The single tapper is mounted below to increase the speed at which the part can be tapped. If mounted on the top, it would require at least a 3/8″ stroke, with 1/4″ of the stroke being wasted motion.

The Form Tools:

Figure 9

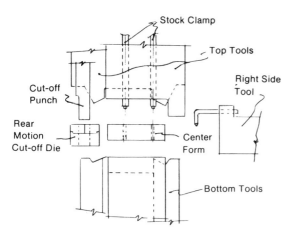

A rear motion cut-off die, twin stock clamps, stationary centerform, top tool, bottom tool and a right side tool were used in forming this part (Figure 9).

The Cut-Off:

Figure 10

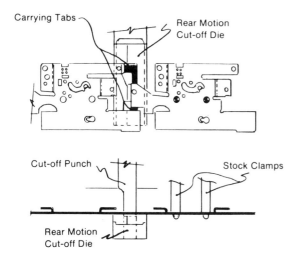

After the strip is fed into the forming area, it is held in place by the twin stock clamps, which also serve as pilots to locate the part. The rear motion cut-off die then advances to its forward position. The top tool, which contains the cut-off punch, descends under control of the first of its three cam rises to separate the part from the strip (Figure 10).

Forming Operations:

Figure 11

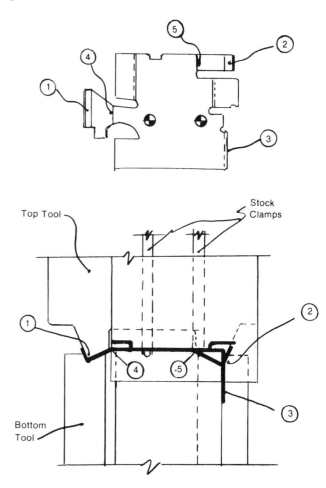

The top tool advances on its second cam rise, forming complete bends at points 1, 2 and 3, and partial bends at points 4 and 5 (Figure 11). The bottom tool, which is stationary in its up position, serves as a form die for the bends at points 1, 2 and 3. In addition, as the top tool advances, a knockout punch mounted on the adapter holding the top tool knocks the slug out of the rear motion cut-off die, which is now in its retracted position.

Figure 12

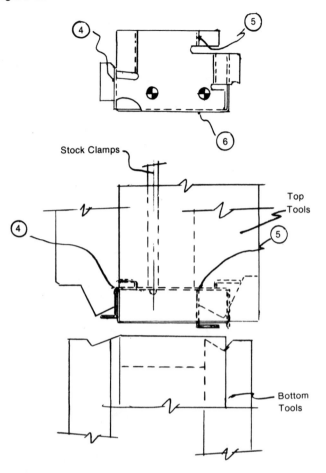

The bottom tool retracts down, and the top tool advances on its third rise to complete the bends at points 4, 5 and 6 (Figure 12).

Figure 13

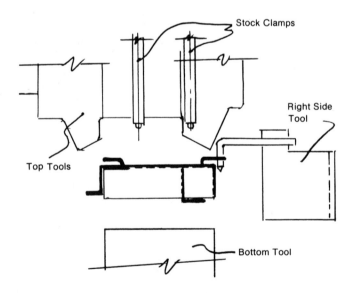

The top tool and twin stock clamps withdraw, and the right side tool advances, locating a stripper finger above hole #1. The bottom tool advances to its original up position, where the stripper finger is now inside hole #1. The finished part is stripped from the machine by the right side tool as it retracts (Figure 13).

Figure 14

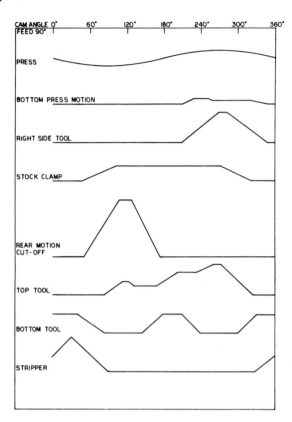

The timing of the tool motions involved in the forming operations is shown in the cam chart in Figure 14.

Results:

The control plate is produced on the V83 Verti-slide machine at a rate of 60-70 ppm. The rejection rate is much lower than previously experienced in making the part with secondary operations.

INDEX

Malfunction detection, 29
Mandrel, 239
Master die-set, 121
Metal stamping, **119-121**
Milling, 14
Multi-slide tooling, **260-262**
Motors, 130

N

NC, See: Numerical control
Non-ferrous metals, 136
Numerical control, 5

O

One side carrier, 71

P

Part ejection, 24, 97
Perforating, 57
Piercing, 34, 83, 103
Pilot
    breakage, 27
    spools, 82
Pinch trim, 87
Pitch
    notches, 78
    stop, 79
Positive stripper, 53
Press
    can making, 138
    crankshaft, 121
    double ended horizontal, 137
    speed, 121
    standun metal box, 138
    stoppage, 21
    tooling, 43
    turret punch, 15
    vertical, 139
Pressure, 123, 159, 197
Pressworking, **43-44, 66-67**
Primary stops, 24
Productivity, 18, **19-32**, 119, 123
Pulldown, 123
Punching, 44, 53, 126, 134
Push-back die, 25

Q

Quick change system, 189

R

Reactors, 130
Rear auxiliary slide, 257
Remote-control switches, 130
Rings
    impingement, 179
    spacing, 136

squeeze, 125
Rolls, 62
Rotary knock-out, 99
Rubber grippers, 112

S

SDT, See: Sliding die transfer
Safety, 121
Scrap
    chopper, 28
    ejection, 24
    skeleton, 151
Self-learning system, 16
Sharpening, 84
Shear line force, 198
Sheared-in process, 194
Shedder plunger, 109
Sheet
    metal, 60-61, 140-145
    steel, 130
Shell cams, 250
Shot pin location, 23
Side cam, 247
Side carriers, 71
Sliding
    key location, 22
    punch, 184
Sliding die transfer, 119-127
Slug
    pulling, 126
    retention, 27
Solid cams, 250
Solid carrier, 71
Spacing rings, 136
Spiral web, 96
Spring
    loaded fingers, 112
    pins, 82
Spring loaded pilot, 28
Squeeze rings, 125
Stainless steel, 63
Stamping, 52, **119-121**, 132
Steel
    bonded titanium carbide, 48
    carbon, 145
    cold-rolled, 133
    low-carbon, 132
    semiprocessed, 132
    sheet, **60-61, 140-145,** 160
    silicon, 131
    stainless, 63
Stock
    centralizers, 123
    clamp cam, 247
    grinding, 26
    lifters, 125
    removal, 49
    threading, 23
Strip
    layout, 76
    lifters, 82
    lubricator, 30
    width, 204
Stripper
    bolt, 42
    design, 52, 123
    mechanism, 123

plate, 46, 123
positive, 53
preloading, 123
Stripping pressure, 198

T

Tape preparation, 16
Tapping, **66-67**
Timing, 126
Titanium carbide, **48-61**
Tonnage, 195
Tool
    carbide, **130-133**
    construction, **193-196**
    design, **204-212**
    fineblanking, **182-188**
    kicker, 238
    material, 223
    standards, 222
    system, 202, 220
Tooling, **43-44, 130-133, 260-262**
Top
    cam, 247
    shoe, 126
Transfer
    cam, 247
    dies, 119

Transformers, 130
Trimming, 60, 83, 103
Tungsten, 162, 225
Turning, 14
Turret punch presses, 15
Two-piece can manufacturing, 148-159

U

U-slot clamping, 22
Ultrasonic checking, 64
Upper pressure pads, 88
Urethane draws, 62

V

Verti-slide, **263-266**
Vertical driveshaft, 121
V-ring, 198, 205, 225

W

Wire-cut electric discharge machines, 15